The Road to Capitalism

Economic Transformation
in Eastern Europe
and the Former Soviet Union

D0140494

The Road to Capitalism

Economic Transformation
in Eastern Europe
and the Former Soviet Union

Edited by

David Kennett and Marc Lieberman

The Dryden Press
Harcourt Brace Jovanovich College Publishers
Fort Worth   Philadelphia   San Diego   New York   Orlando   Austin   San Antonio
Toronto   Montreal   London   Sydney   Tokyo

Cover Design: Krista Moscarello

Address for Editorial Correspondence
The Dryden Press, 301 Commerce Street, Suitee 3700, Fort Worth, TX 76102

Address for Orders
The Dryden Press 6277 Sea Harbor Drive Orlando, FL 322887
1-800-782-4479, or 1-800-433-0001 (in Florida)

Library of Congress Catalog Card Number: 92-0811336

ISBN: 0-03-096374-5

Printed in the United States of America

2 3 4 5 6 7 8 9 0 1   067   9 8 7 6 5 4 3 2 1

The Dryden Press
Harcourt Brace Jovanovich

To Susan and Ella

THE DRYDEN PRESS SERIES IN ECONOMICS

Preface

In ordinary times, economic structures change at a glacial pace. An industry might be nationalized or privatized; the tax system made more or less progressive; the domain of market incentives slightly expanded or contracted However, in eastern Europe and in the new nations that are emerging from the former Soviet Union times are truly extraordinary. Political and economic systems are undergoing rapid and radical change. The entire structure of central planning is to be swept aside and replaced by market institutions. This economic, political and social transformation has been chronicled in our newspapers, and has been the subject of heated debate in many arenas, from network television studios to the local bar. Yet the reasons for the transformation, the dangers to be avoided, and the chances for success are often left unexamined.

Among economics students, both at Vassar and at Harvard, we found a high level of interest in these aspects of the changes, and a desire to learn more about them. Moreover, we found that this interest was not limited to economics students. The reforms are so sweeping, and the economic and political so closely linked, that east European politics cannot be understood without close study of the economic liberalization. International relations, so long focused on an ideological dispute over fundamental economic systems, have to be re-evaluated in the light of the economic transformation and the new trade and investment patterns that will emerge. Business now perceives eastern Europe as a prime opportunity for direct and portfolio investment as well as new forms of cooperation like joint ventures; students of international business need to understand these changes.

However, students who wanted to learn more about this fascinating topic – and professors who wanted to bring it into their curricula – have had difficulty finding a compact source of appropriate material. The available choices seemed to be either: (1) textbooks in comparative systems, concentrating on the operation of the now-defunct central planning system; (2) current news articles, which tell *what* is happening, but rarely *why*; and (3) a number of very insightful articles, both recent and "classic," that were unfortunately scattered among different academic and non-academic sources. Our goal was to collect these seminal articles and make them available in a single volume.

Preface

The book has been organized with flexibility in mind, and we anticipate its use in courses on Comparative Economic Systems, East European Economics, East European Politics, International Relations and International Business. The division into ten sections should facilitate selection of material to fit the instructor's needs and objectives.

We have chosen and edited the articles carefully, often quite heavily. We have not tried to catalogue what has happened on a week by week basis in, say, Poland or the Russian Republic. Rather, we want to give insight into the *process* of economic change, explaining *why* central planning failed, *why* the market may offer a way out, *what* a successful transformation must accomplish, and *how* a nation should go about it. We have tried to balance the -predomiant theme of reliance on markets with some authors who see the warts on the face of capitalism and counsel a continuing role for regulation and redistribution.

Our main goal in editing was to keep technical requirements to a minimum, so that students with limited exposure to formal economic theory would find the articles accessible. We also sought to eliminate as far as possible material whose relevance could be overtaken by events in the region. We believe the result is a very readable and useful collection of articles that will be relevant well into the nineties.

We would like to take this opportunity to thank all the authors whose work is included. Many have generously allowed us to edit their work to make it accessible to our readers and to fit within our space constraints. Professor Aryeh Blumberg, Coordinator of the Harvard University Summer Program in Economics, conceived the course at Harvard. Peter Breuer and Jennifer Cook assisted greatly in library research, while Krista Moscarello helped with various aspects of design and data input. Professor Anatoly Porokhovsky of the United States and Canada Institute, gave generously of his time and contacts in Moscow. Countless, and therefore nameless, friends and colleagues in the United States, Russia, Bulgaria and elsewhere gave us the benefit of their favorite articles, many of which we have included – but more of which we left out. Book space and students' time are finite.

David Kennett
Marc Lieberman
Vassar College
March 1992

CONTENTS

x

PART I

THE FAILURE OF CENTRAL PLANNING

The title of this section seems to render a rather subjective judgement. After all, the former Soviet Union used central planning to allocate resources for more than six decades, and Eastern Europe for almost as long. During most of this time, the socialist centrally-planned economies were able to feed, clothe and house their populations, provide regular increases in living standards, and support a military machine rivaling that of the NATO powers. Nevertheless, Soviet-type central planning *has* failed in a relative sense; it has been outperformed by the market.

This too seems heavily subjective. In theory, the plan and the market have different strengths and weaknesses as methods of resource allocation. The market has generally been judged more *allocatively efficient*, that is, better at exploiting opportunities for mutual gain, leading to higher standards of living. Centrally-planned socialism has, at least theoretically, the potential to be more *equitable*. Perhaps, then, we are imposing a market-based value judgement that allocative efficiency is more important than equity.

The reality of Soviet-type economies suggests that this is not the case. Central planning – while clearly failing to compete with market systems in the area of efficiency – also failed to deliver on its promise of equity. Officially, wage incomes appeared quite equitable in the Soviet Union and Eastern Europe, but the true distribution of purchasing power was far less so. Possessing rubles or zlotys did not necessarily mean "purchasing" power in Russia or Poland, because of incessant shortages of desired consumer goods. Besides cash, one also needed rights to shop in special stores, or connections with plant managers, or special permission to vacation in exclusive resorts. This non-monetary access to goods was *not* distributed equally among the population. Indeed, if market capitalism has a tendency to generate proletariat and capitalist classes, then centrally planned socialism developed its own class dichotomy: powerful party *apparatchiks*, and everyone else.

In any case, it is not "we" in the west who have rendered the ultimate

1

judgement on central planning; it is the people who lived under it themselves. In public elections and opinion polls, a majority of East Europeans and Russians have revealed a desire to change their primary method of resource allocation from the "plan" to the "market."

Anyone who wishes to understand this journey – the reasons for it, why it is so difficult, and the likelihood of its success – must understand not just the destination, but the point of origin as well. How was central planning actually accomplished in the Soviet Union and Eastern Europe? What was the problem with centrally-planned socialism, and why are the transforming economies so anxious to abandon it? The articles in this section help answer these questions.

We begin with "Soviet Central Planning" by Heinz Köhler, as a basic introduction to the central planning process and bureaucracy in the Soviet-type economies. Of course, the former East Bloc nations had idiosyncratic economic systems which differed – by varying degrees – from their Soviet parent. Nevertheless, if we are to choose one nation as "archetypal" of the region, it would be the U.S.S.R., largely because in the late 1940s, it simply imposed its own political and economic structure on several Eastern European nations. Thus, much of what we learn from Köhler can be applied to the entire region as well.

In "The Soft Budget Constraint," Janos Kornai introduces a characteristic of centrally planned economies referred to in many of the articles in this reader. A firm has a soft budget constraint when its managers or owners believe it likely that any losses will be covered from a source external to the firm (e.g., the state). Kornai describes various ways in which this "softening" can arise in different types of economies, but of more immediate relevance to central planning is the following key point: soft budget constraints are the causal link between microeconomic imbalance of the firm (the ability for costs to exceed revenues indefinitely) and macroeconomic imbalance overall (budget deficits, shortages of goods, increasing length of lines, and rising black-market prices). Kornai's article is largely theoretical, although his arguments are supported by his own research on the Hunarian economy. His most salient result is a strong negative correlation between original profit and final profit; the system of taxes and subsidies, largely on special and ad hoc bases, so profoundly affects final profitabilty as to make the financial results of most firms meaningless.

In "The Consequences of Central Planning in Eastern Europe" by Lipton and Sachs, we look at the current economic state of the region. To understand the difficulties faced by the transforming economies, we must first understand how four decades of centrally-planned socialism in Eastern Europe have shaped their current structure. Lipton and Sachs discuss the key problems faced by *all* of these nations: a severely underdeveloped private sector; distorted prices; a productive infrastructure out of touch with the pattern of consumer wants; chronic shortages of consumer goods and productive inputs, resulting in black markets and the need for firms to (inefficiently) produce their own inputs; unstable political systems; and bureaucracies opposed to market reforms.

Next we turn to an important theoretical issue. While market-capitalism offers clear advantages as a system of resource allocation (see the next section in this reader), it has severe defects as well. Two of the most glaring failures are (1) the lack of centralized coordination for pursuing important social goals and (2) extreme disparities in economic well-being among the population. Replacing the market with central planning held out the promise of redressing the first failure; replacing capitalism with socialism the second. A major lesson of this century has been that a combination of these two systems – as found in the centrally-planned socialism of Soviet-type economies – did not fulfill its promise.

But perhaps the failure was due to a reliance on *both* central planning and socialism. Perhaps there is a third way: a market system to ensure efficiency, combined in some way with *either* some limited central planning to meet broad social goals, or socialism to ensure equity. The next three articles explore this possibility, and conclude that a workable market system requires capitalism's private ownership, and, in addition, complete freedom from central planning.

In "Economic Calculation In Socialism," Ludwig von Mises begins by stating a key requirement for economic efficiency: consumers and producers must be able to measure and compare the values of the resources they use, and these values must reflect the scarcity of the resources. In a market system, such values are calculated automatically, as money prices, by the free choices of individuals interacting in markets. In a command economy with central planning, these values are lost.

Von Mises then asks a further question: might it not be possible to have a socialism (i.e., state ownership of resources) that somehow comes up with efficient prices and leaves individuals free to respond to them in making their own decentralized decisions – a "market socialism?"[1] He considers various ways in which this might be accomplished, and rejects all of them as unfeasible.

Like von Mises, Michael Keren concludes that market socialism is not a realistic possibility. But in "On the (Im)Possibility of Market Socialism," his approach is somewhat different. He combines economic reasoning with the sociology of large organizations and shows that market socialism, once in place, would soon degenerate into the kind of inflexible, command-socialism that is characteristic of Soviet-type economies in recent history.

His argument boils down to this: socialism, by definition, excludes private ownership and therefore excludes any capital market. Without a capital market, some other institution must be formed to allocate scarce capital among enterprises, and ultimately, this will be a large, state hierarchical organization which will inevitably bail out failing enterprises. In this way, firms develop a soft budget constraint, which changes their behavior and increases price volatility. Finally, price volatility creates pressure for the state bureaucracy to simply take over the entire process of production and distribution, and we end up with the inflexible, centrally-planned socialism we have observed in Soviet-type economies.

In "Why is the Plan Incompatible with the Market?" Larissa Popkova-Pijasheva asks whether the overall economy can be centrally planned, and still leave room for private ownership, individual economic decision-making, and the efficiency-creating discipline imposed by markets. Or, more simply, can a single capitalist economy combine the best aspects of the market and the plan to any significant degree? Her answer is no – the fundamental tenets of the two systems are in conflict. To Popkova-Pijasheva, this was the problem with Gorbachev's *perestroika* ("restructuring") of the Soviet economy – it tried to introduce aspects of the market system while maintaining the primacy of central planning. In her view, the only way to gain any of the benefits promised by the market is to abandon central planning completely.

---

[1] The debate over the feasibility of market-socialism has a long and complex history, and there may be disagreement over its outcome. In this reader, we are not concerned about the debate itself. Rather, we wish to explore some of the theoretical reasons why the newly emerging economies are rejecting market socialism in favor of market capitalism, and why attempts at market socialism – as in Hungary or Yugoslavia – had rather disappointing results. Those interested in a more extensive treatment of the debate should read Oskar Lange, *On the Economic Theory of Socialism* (Minneapolis: University of Minnesota reprint of the 1938 edition, 1964) and Peter Murrell, "Did the Theory of Market Socialism Answer the Challenge of Ludwig von Mises?" (*History of Political Economy*, 15, 1983, pp. 92-105).

1. Soviet Central Planning*

Heinz Köhler

The Planning Mechanism

Ignoring finer details, the planning procedure can be described as follows. During the first half of the year during which a plan is worked out (the planning year), the Central Planning Board (Gosplan) collects information on the state of the economy, showing accomplishments as well as any bottlenecks hindering further expansion. Subsequently, the Presidium of the Party's Central Committee and the Council of Ministers study this information and determine the major objectives that are to be sought during the following year (the plan year). These might be cast in very general terms, such as "increase the share of resources devoted to investment by 10%" or "cease expanding the coal industry, and rapidly enlarge chemicals production with emphasis on plastics." These *Party directives* are then used by Gosplan during the summer to work out a preliminary balance of the economy, specifying key output targets in physical terms as well as major inputs required for such outputs. Here we meet the core of the plan, the system of *material balances*, showing for thousands of specified commodities (18,000 in 1963) the intended sources of supply and places of delivery. A typical material balance, greatly abbreviated here, might look like Table 1.

Putting all material balances together and considering *all* goods produced would give us a table with innumerable gaps and inconsistencies. At this point in the planning process, all entries are tentative.

The data just derived are called *control figures* and are passed down the administrative hierarchy during the early fall, for instance, to the various production ministries or regional planning centers. The Ministry of Electric Power might be told to produce 544.44 billion kwh in 1966, the Foreign Trade Ministry to import 12.16, and the steel industry to expect delivery of 240, for example.

As a next step, each ministry or regional agency in turn will split up the aggregate into subtotals. The Ministry of Electric Power might, for instance, allocate the production of 544.44 billion kwh among the Soviet Republics or

* Excerpted from *Welfare and Planning: An Analysis of Capitalism versus Socialism,* John Wiley and Sons, copyright (c) 1966. Reprinted by permission of John Wiley and Sons.

other geographical units.

These in turn will add detail to the plan, passing it down to smaller geographic administrations and finally to the individual plants. Power plant X in the Ukraine will now have before it the control figures for 1966, telling it to produce 0.7 billion kwh, while expecting to receive x units of labor, y units of oil, z units of new equipment, etc.

Table 1. Material Balance, 1966, Electric Power (Billion kwh)

Sources		Uses	
Production	544.44	Industry	
Imports	12.16	(a) Electric Power	54.44
Inventory Decrease	---	(b) Steel	240.00
		(c) Milk	50.00
		Households	150.00
		Inventory Increase	---
		Government	50.00
		Export	12.16
Total sources	556.60		556.60

At this point the process is reversed. Plant officials will suggest changes in the control figures, arguing possibly that the inputs provided could not possibly produce the output required and requesting an increase in input allocations. The *draft plan* is now passed back up the hierarchy until it reaches Gosplan again. At each level, the planning agency has to reconcile conflicting demands between the higher authority insisting on producing so much with so little and the lower ones arguing for producing less with so much more. At each level, an attempt is made to "tighten" the plan by shifting allocations among firms or regions and insisting that they do the job. If absolutely impossible, the imbalance is passed back up onto the higher authority. Eventually, Gosplan will have to resolve all remaining conflict between sources and uses. Either targets have to be cut or more inputs must be made available.

The final balance being struck, the government approves the plan and turns it into *law*.

Now it is passed down the hierarchy of ministries, regional councils, etc. once more. At each step the plan law is again detailed until it reaches each individual firm. Firms are then required to enter with each other into legally binding contracts about the details of delivery to each other.

In addition to this physical core of the plan, concerned with high priority items, the production of goods and services considered less important is also planned, but in less detail and in *monetary* terms. Hence we have to consider prices. This is also necessary for another reason, namely, the fact that the execution of the physical plan itself is, among other ways, being supervised with the help of money flows, as observed by the State Bank.

The Role of Prices and Money

The Soviet government establishes essentially three types of prices and, once established, an attempt is made to keep them stable for as long a period as possible. The first type of prices is *wholesale prices for industry*. These are prices at which goods are sold from one firm to another. They are set to equal "planned, weighted-average, adjusted branch cost plus profit." It is here that for the first time we meet the real influence of Marxian ideology, for "cost" is interpreted in the Marxian sense, including only raw materials, depreciation, and labor, but excluding rent and interest.

Industrial Wholesale Prices

Taking raw material, depreciation, and wage costs for all firms in a particular branch of industry, say tractor production, price setters would exclude from consideration abnormally high average costs of some plants as not "socially necessary." The remaining "adjusted" cost data are then weighted by the output levels of the various plants to find the adjusted branch average. Finally, this is changed (probably downwards) to a planned figure, taking into account expected cost declines due to technical progress, while a small percentage of such figures is added as profit, giving the price sought. Such profit is set for accounting purposes and ideologically defended as the workers' production "for society at large." It is obvious from what we have said that such industrial wholesale prices do in no way, except by sheer accident, reflect relative scarcities. This is so for a variety of reasons: the exclusion of rent and interest, the use of average rather than marginal costs, and the use of planned rather than actual costs.

Agricultural Prices

The second major type of price is *agricultural procurement prices* at which the production of farms has to be sold. These prices are set with the major objective of fixing the terms of trade of the peasants so as to allow them to receive no more consumer goods than desired by the state. Given the prices of inputs collective farms have to buy (mostly at industrial wholesale prices) and the quantities they are supposed to buy according to plan (fertilizer, equipment, etc.), the price setters can estimate the revenue needed by the farms to cover their costs. If it were desired that collective farmers receive no money income whatsoever, since no industrial consumer goods are available for them, the projective cost figure would be divided by the planned output, establishing a delivery price per ton of product. If the output plan were fulfilled, the revenues would exactly cover costs, leaving no money income to the farmers. On the other hand, if it is desired that they have a negative (or positive) money income, because, let us say, farmers hold large idle money balances accumulated in the past (or there are industrial consumer goods available for them), the procurement price can accordingly be lower (or higher). Clearly, as in the case of industrial wholesale prices, prices so established would only by accident reflect relative scarcities of agricultural products. State farms, that is, those nationally owned, usually sell their products at the prices set for collectives, but workers in such farms have regular wage income, like those in industry.

Retail Prices and the Labor Market

A third major type of price is *retail prices* used by state retail stores (owned by the nation as a whole) and consumer cooperatives (owned, like the collective farms, by groups of individuals jointly). These prices differ in level and structure from industrial wholesale and agricultural procurement prices because of the imposition of a large and differentiated turnover tax on the latter two, providing a major source of revenue for the government. These prices are set with a view to clearing the aggregate market for each consumer good.

We have already seen how farmers may or may not have money income to demand goods offered in retail stores. Industrial workers are also paid in money for their work, though their income, as for laborers on state farms, is contractual and not residual like that of collective farmers. Workers have free occupational choice, and wages are differentiated by the state to get just the number of workers for each occupation that is required by the plan. This obviously minimizes the misery that would ensue if everyone were arbitrarily assigned to a job. If 200,000 miners are needed for the plan, that number will be procured, but, for example, by changing the wage up or down until that number is voluntarily forthcoming. Forced labor has shrunk to negligible proportions, but there are a few other qualifications to the above statement. The long-run supply of labor for various occupations is directed carefully by the state in controlling the number of people entering various types of training, and graduates are assigned to their first jobs. After a few years, however, they are free to do as they please, although the housing shortage seriously limits geographic mobility. Income earned by workers, as well as by farmers, can be freely spent; that is, there is free consumer *choice*. However, there is no consumer *sovereignty*. This means that the plan determines what kinds and quantities of consumer goods are produced, and each consumer decides which of these he wants. If any surplus or shortage for any one good should develop, production is *not* changed, as would happen if consumers were sovereign.

We can now return to the price-setting process. Planners make an estimate of consumer money income (wages, pensions, farm income) and deduct an estimate for other uses (taxes, saving). The result will be some figure such as 50 billion rubles. Planners also have (for instance, material-balance) data on planned availabilities of consumer goods (from production, imports, inventories minus exports, etc.). These will consist of items such as 5 million tons of ham, 100,000 TV sets, 15 billion pounds of bread, 5 million rubles worth of kitchen utensils, etc. From these two types of information a set of prices is then derived so that the *value* of ham, plus the *value* of TV sets, plus the *value* of bread, plus the *value* of kitchen utensils, etc. equals 50 billion rubles. Then it is at least *possible* that consumers spend exactly what they had intended, while buying exactly what had been provided. On the other hand, many things can and usually do go wrong. There are obviously an infinite number of price sets fulfilling the above condition. If quantity demanded was at the set price different from the estimate (and such estimate *is* a wild guess, since there is practically no demand research), shortages and surpluses will occur. If the price of ham was set at 1 ruble per pound, demand may well be for 1 or 15 million tons, causing a surplus or shortage (and in the Soviet system, *no* change in production or price). Furthermore, output plans may not be (and for consumer goods usually are not) fulfilled. Hence shortages may occur, even if by accident the "correct" price set was picked, leaving undesired money balances in the hands of consumers.

Again, such prices obviously have no connection with relative scarcities. Identical prices for two goods will typically not indicate the use of identical quantities of resources in their production.

As a "safety valve" for things that might go wrong under the above conditions, the Soviets also allow one pure remnant of private enterprise, the *kolkhoz market*. In thousands of different locations, peasants are designated trading areas and allowed to sell freely agricultural produce grown on their private (about 1 acre per household) plots. Households can thus dispose of any excess money they might have and are unable to spend in retail stores.

Prices in this market vary with supply and demand. The transactions, furthermore, serve the twofold purpose of providing extra, or even the only, money income to peasants and of allowing urban consumers to find an outlet for theirs. In both cases, this is an important element for incentives to work.

In summary, we can state that prices are essentially grafted onto the physical plan and manipulated to accomplish what has already been determined in that plan. That plan is usually expanded in monetary terms to include nonpriority goods, assigning to firms output and input targets in money, such as "produce 10,000 rubles worth of kitchen utensils, using 5,000 rubles worth of metal, 3,000 rubles worth of labor, etc."

State Bank Control

As a result of using money in the economy, it is possible to let the State Bank control the execution of the plan. Except for wage payments to households and their purchases of goods, the use of cash is severely restricted. Typically, an industrial or agricultural enterprise must deliver its output to other firms according to contractual obligations incurred as part of the detailed specification of the plan. Payment is not made by check, but by the acceptance method. The seller will send an order to pay to his State Bank office, which will deliver it to the buyer. Upon acceptance by the latter, the account of the buyer is reduced, and the seller's increased. In this way the State Bank can in theory check upon the purpose, timing, and size of every single transaction and prevent it unless it corresponds exactly to the predetermined plan. (Obviously, for the purpose of controlling real transactions via their counterpart money flows, any price set would do as well as any other. Hence the observed irrationality of prices is here irrelevant.) In fact, the State Bank has at its disposal stern sanctions, ranging from the expropriation of a firm's deposits to a full-scale Party investigation into enterprise affairs. Yet the burdens of surveying details of economic activity on the scale ideally required are enormous. Banks frequently only engage in "formalistic" controls, using sanctions sparingly and failing in their role of detailed overseer of the entire economy.

Incentives and Their Effects

Such detailed control missing, a number of things, having survived all administrative changes, go continuously wrong and have caused headaches for the central planners for many decades. The fact that a plan exists, no matter how feasible, internally consistent, and desirable it is, does not mean it will be carried out. Ultimately this depends on the *incentives* for work felt by millions of workers, peasants, and managers. We have already seen above that workers, whether in industry or on *state* farms, are essentially motivated by the same kind of rewards and punishments as in a capitalist economy. They receive wages and salaries with which they can buy goods in state stores or on the kolkhoz market. Their pay differs with the type of occupation they hold (training required, unpleasantness of work, importance attached to it by the planners) as well as the degree to which they exert themselves on the job (piece rates). Personal effort typically leads to promotion, lack of it to demotion or loss of job. In general, real incomes have risen steadily and substantially since the Second World War. All these things combined, there have been no particular problems with making people work. The case of peasants on collective farms is a different matter. [T]heir incentives have been typically wanting, though much less so for work on their private plots! This, as well as the low priority given to investment in agriculture, must undoubtedly have contributed to the continued undesirable performance of agriculture in the Soviet Union. Agricultural output has grown substantially, but less so than hoped for by the planners.

The case of managers of industrial firms deserves some further study. Fundamentally, they, too, are motivated to do their best by the same kind of incentives as the managers of a modern capitalistic corporation, namely, salary and promotion. Yet the environment they work in is in many ways incredibly different. As we have seen, the Soviet industrial enterprise is given by some higher planning authority a plan, covering its operations for a certain period. This plan specifies a minimum output to be produced in value terms (and for priority goods in physical terms as well). It specifies input targets for materials, equipment, and labor in value and possibly physical terms. And it specifies a host of other goals, ranging from profits, quality, and labor productivity to winning socialist competitions and keeping the plants clean. A manager, as a steward for the state, is to do all these things and, upon performing well, will be rewarded with high pay as well as certain other things money alone may not be able to buy, such as a home, a car, and vacations at the Black Sea. On the other hand, failure to perform may bring not only loss of his job, but also prosecution for criminal negligence and (under Stalin) possibly a bullet in the neck.

To be more specific, while the basic salary may influence people to choose one occupation rather than another, it is a *system of bonuses* that determines what kind of decisions are made in the day-to-day operations of any one job. These decisions, as we shall see, are frequently made contrary to the interests of the state, although the bonus system is set up to encourage decisions desired by the central planners. Bonuses are received by management for fulfilling or overfulfilling the plan targets. It is quite possible to receive up to 50% of the basic salary for plan fulfillment alone and up to 4% more for each percentage point of overfulfillment. Hence the difference between 99 and 100% plan fulfillment may mean up to 50% difference in the incomes of the managing group, and a manager overfulfilling the plan by 5% may receive up to 70% above his basic money income! No wonder the system elicits high managerial effort.

The planning authority, however, in order to make the system work and judge managers, will have to provide the key to what is meant by plan fulfillment. This is a tricky problem, for it is possible to overfulfill three and underfulfill nine out of twelve different targets! The traditional response has been to give priority to the fulfillment of the *output* target in physical or, if not available, in value terms. This should not surprise us, since we have seen how central is the concern with physical planning of inputs and outputs.

We have now at hand everything needed to explain the behavior of managers. More than anything else affecting their bonus, output plan fulfillment will receive their undivided attention. This will begin with the elaboration of the plan itself. The lower the plan target, the easier it can be fulfilled. Hence the urge is strong to *hide the true capabilities of the plant*. But as we know, nothing is more vital to the central planner than to be informed of the capability of the economy as accurately as possible. Soviet planners are aware of this and have introduced the practice of "flushing out reserves" by arbitrarily increasing all production targets annually, even if they know of no capacity increase having occurred. This will, indeed, flush out some hidden capacities, but it will also make it impossible for other firms to fulfill an unfeasible plan, eliminating bonuses and incentives alike and possibly bringing criminal prosecution upon the innocent.

While excessively ambitious plans may raise the efforts of some managers to increase output (and also may raise their ulcer rate), they will also tempt managers to *over-order and hoard raw materials or labor*. This is another way of stacking the deck beforehand. By claiming that more material and labor are needed than is in fact the case, possibly more will be received. They can be used to overfulfill or they may "just be kept around" for insurance against future needs when materials might not arrive in time in right quantity and quality. Frequently personal influence (blat) is used with the higher authorities to have input allocations raised. As a result, all kinds of inputs may be available in all kinds of places but be unused, which is clearly not in the interests of the state. Many firms, especially those liable to insufficient deliveries of inputs since they produce low priority output, employ special kinds of supply expediters or "pushers" (tolkachi) who push, legally or otherwise, for the interests of the firm at higher places and who arrange for informal exchange of hoarded materials among firms. Hence hoards may be lower than one may think at first. However, the fact that materials probably go into *low* priority channels still shows this activity to be against the state's interests. Again, the state tries to counteract this activity by frequently moving managers from one job to another. This is to disrupt the "family relation," the system of mutual support of the controllers and the controlled, at the bottom of the planning hierarchy.

The *over-ordering of capital equipment* follows similar lines of reasoning on the part of managers. This is reinforced by the fact that fixed capital is provided as a grant. No interest payment being necessary, and no depreciation being incurred, if the equipment is not used, managers try to get as much as they can by whatever means. Possibly output can be increased, possibly unwanted equipment can be traded. In any case, there is nothing to lose and everything to gain. Even a steel mill can use a cabbage-planting machine!

The high mobility of managers, which is to counteract the above, provides them with an extremely short-range view. Hence they are unanimously *opposed to technical innovations*. Replacing present equipment with new capital is entirely different from getting more of the old. It is risky business, and risk is not rewarded. It will upset the apple cart by interrupting continuous production, and production is rewarded. To make things worse, at the very moment when a technical innovation is introduced, causing the need to eliminate production bugs, to retrain the labor force, etc., the output target is typically raised to account for the superior productivity of the new equipment or production method. At best this will mean no bonus, hence no wonder that managers drag their feet before introducing novelties! Nothing short of a direct order will do. Managers prefer to repair old equipment no matter what the cost, since their bonus depends on uninterrupted output. As a result, the introduction of new technology is seriously hampered. Planners have been quite at a loss to do anything about this reticence. Giving a special bonus for innovating will have no effect if it is small, and if it is large, the output goal will be ignored entirely.

Another serious problem for Gosplan lies in managers' response to the way in which the output target is stated, leading to the *production of low quality output and incorrect assortments*. To maximize output, managers are tempted to reduce quality. If the task is to produce tons of metal, greater impurity may not be visible, just as fewer stitches on a garment or fewer screws or thinner parts on a machine would not affect the number of garments or machines counted as output, freeing some inputs to raise output. At the expense of quality, this is hardly desirable. Again, if the choice is between 500 machines with or 550 machines without spare parts, we do not have to guess about the manager's choice, if his income depends on the number of machines produced. As a result, the Soviet Union has been plagued by persistent shortages of spare parts and complaints about low-quality output.

A related problem is the disregard of industrial and private consumers' demand. If small nails are needed, but the output plan is stated in tons, only huge nails will get produced. If the output plan is stated in numbers, only the tiniest ones will be made, and no large ones at all. This is the same if output targets are more general and stated in value terms, such as 50 million rubles worth of kitchen utensils. Only knives may be made, if that can most easily fulfill the plan, no matter what the demand for pots, pans, and can openers. If one were to specify the physical quantity and quality of each item produced, we would be back at the impractical case of overcentralization of bureaucracy.

In summary, we may say that Soviet managers, while following the plan as far as possible, do engage in a variety of practices contrary to the interests of the state when it becomes apparent that they cannot otherwise fulfill the plan. Being subject to a multitude of controls (the superior planning agency, the State Bank, the Central Statistical Administration, the Ministry of Finance, the Party, the Ministry of State Security), managers react in these ways rather than risk open falsification of fulfillment reports. But even in this way they continually place themselves in a potentially dangerous situation, since they do violate the laws. As one scholar put it, operating under tremendous pressure to perform, they are like a neurotic whose problems express themselves in psychosomatic illness. If one of these is cured, another one just as surely springs up. Somewhere, the pressure has to escape.

2. The Soft Budget Constraint*

Janos Kornai

In many segments of contemporary economies a remarkable trend can be discerned: the budget constraints of economic units become "soft." The phenomenon appears in mixed economies and is conspicuously apparent in socialist systems. The "soft budget constraint syndrome" is usually associated with the paternalistic role of the state towards economic organizations and private firms, non-profit institutions and households.

I. Conceptual Clarifications

The term budget constraint is of course taken over from microtheory of the household. The assumption that the decision maker has a budget constraint is equivalent to the assumption that Say's[1] principle prevails. In agreement with Clower[2] the budget constraint is not a bookkeeping identity nor a technical relation, but a rational planning postulate. Two important properties must be underlined. First, the softening of the budget constraint occurs when the strict relationship between expenditure and earnings has been relaxed because excess of expenditure over earnings will be paid by some other institution typically by the State. A further condition of softening is that the decision maker expects such external financial assistance with high probability, and this probability is built firmly into his behavior. . . .

There are different ways and means to soften the budget constraint of the firm.

1. *Soft subsidies* granted by national or local governments. The subsidy is soft if it is negotiable, subject to bargaining, lobbying, etc. The subsidy is adjusted to past, present or future cost overruns.

2. *Soft Taxation*. The attribute soft does not refer to the rate of taxation.

---

* From "The Soft Budget Constraint," *Kyklos*, 1986,Vol. 39, fasc. 1, Kyklos-Verlag, Switzerland. Some footnotes omitted.

[1] [Editors' note: Say's principle is most simply expressed as "supply creates its own demand"; in this case the relevance is that a firm's long-run demand cannot be greater than its long-run supply of goods to market.]

[2] "The Keynesian Counter-Revolution: A Theoretical Appraisal," in F.H. Hahn and F. Brechling (eds.), *The Theory of Interest Rates*, London: Macmillan (1965).

Even with a low tax rate the taxation system can be hard, if rules are uniform, fixed for a long period and the payment of taxes rigorously enforced. In contrast taxation is soft, even with a high tax rate, if the rules are negotiable, subject to bargaining, political pressures. The tax rates are not uniform, but almost tailor-made according to the financial situation of different sectors or different regions or different forms of ownership. The fulfillment of tax obligations is not strict; there are leaks, ad hoc exemptions, postponements, etc.

3. *Soft Credit*. Again softness does not refer to the magnitude of the interest rate. The credit system can be hard even with a low interest rate (provided that the credit market generates a low rate), if the fulfillment of credit contracts is strictly enforced. The creditor lends money expecting discipline in debt service and not for the sake of assistance to an ailing firm which will not be able to service its debt. Enforcement of the credit contract continues to the bitter end; harsh sanctions in the case of insolvency, including receivership, bankruptcy, forced merger, sell-out or other similar legal means. In contrast, the credit system can be soft even with high interest rates, if the fulfillment of a credit contract is not enforced, unreliable debt service is tolerated and postponement and rescheduling are in order. Soft credit is used to assist firms in great and chronic financial trouble, without real hope of repayment of the debt.

4. *Soft administrative prices*. This can be applied in the case when the price is not set by a free contract seller and buyer, but by some bureaucratic institution. The administrative price is hard if, once set, it restricts expenditure and does not automatically adjust to cost increases. An administrative price is soft if it is set according to some permissive "cost plus" principle that automatically adjusts prices to costs.

These four means of softening the budget constraint are not mutually exclusive; they can be applied simultaneously or successively. The list is not exhaustive, there are other means as well. . . .

All four means of softening the budget constraint of the firm refer to dynamic processes; assistance fills up the gap between the flow of expenditures and the flow of sales-generated revenues of the firm. It is meaningless to talk of the hardness or the softness of the budget constraint of one individual firm, looking at the history of that firm. As mentioned in the general definitions, the subjective probability distribution of external assistance will depend on the collective experience. The decisive question in this respect is this: what was the regular experience of a large number of firms over a longer period in the past? And can it be expected that similar experiences will occur in the future?

"Hard" and "soft" are two extreme positions on a scale of stringency. In a deterministic maximizing model an upper constraint either holds or does not hold. But here we are facing a stochastic problem: subjective expectations concerning external assistance and the enforcement of financial discipline. Therefore, intermediate positions between a strictly binding and a totally redundant constraint may exist. Consider the speed limit on highways. Some people will observe it, some others not, exceeding the permitted limit more or less frequently, to a larger or smaller extent. The distribution of violations will depend on the enforcement of the limit. But even with soft enforcement, the mere fact that there is a limit may have some influence on speed. That is, the constraint is not completely redundant.

There is one more reason to think in terms of a stringency scale rather than in a "yes" or "no" framework, in which a completely binding or a completely ineffective constraint are mutually exclusive. External assistance is usually not granted automatically, as some effort is needed to obtain it. The firm's managers (and in the case of the private firm, also the owners) must resort to political pressure groups and lobbies, or to personal connections. Explicit bribery may be frequent or rare with experience varying from country to country. Some hidden corruption in [the] form of reciprocal favors is more wide-spread. In any case, rent seeking[3] and budget constraint-softening is not without costs. Therefore, even if it might be softened, the budget constraint has at least some influence on the behavior of the firm or of other microunits.

Hardness of the budget constraint is not a synonym for profit maximization. A profit maximizing firm, even if it is in the red will try to cut its losses. A hard budget constraint means that even if the firm tries hard to cut its losses, the environment will not tolerate a protracted deficit. The emphasis is on punishment. The budget constraint is hard if persistent loss is a matter of life and death; the more the loss maker is spared from tragic consequences, the softer is the constraint. What is really important is the psychological effect of the constraint; with a hard budget constraint, a deficit causes fear because it may lead to extremely serious consequences. Profit maximization refers to the internal goal-setting of the decision maker of the firm; the softness-

---

[3] [Editors' note: rent-seeking behavior is the effort to gain income by controlling the supply of a scarce resource or factor of production. The recent literature has been concerned with bureaucrats using their monopoly on official power to raise their own incomes through bribery or kickbacks. See Krueger, A.O., "The Political Economy of the Rent-Seeking Society," *American Economic Review*, (March 1974), *Vol. 64*, pp. 291-303.]

hardness of the budget constraint refers to the external tolerance-limits to losses.

It follows from this line of reasoning that the stringency of the budget constraint is not simply a financial matter. It reflects in financial form a deeper socio-economic phenomenon. Using a Marxian term: it reflects a certain social relationship between the state and the economic micro-organization. Clower and Due[4] wrote about Say's principle that it "constitutes an implicit definition of the transactor as distinguished from the concept of thief or a philanthropist." In the case of the soft budget constraint, the State and the firm are neither merely transactors nor is the firm a thief and the State a philanthropist. We are faced with a new kind of relationship. Different analogies come to mind: the State as a protective father and the firm as a child, the State as patron and the firm as client, the State as insurance company and the firm as the insured party. The soft budget constraint syndrome is the manifestation of the paternalistic role of the modern state.

The economic theory of the market concentrates on the horizontal relationship between seller and market. The sociological theory of bureaucracy, from its beginning with Max Weber up to now, studies the vertical relationship of superiors and subordinates within a hierarchy. The firm with a soft budget constraint is an issue at the intersection of these two disciplines. Our firm has a horizontal relationship with his customers and suppliers, and at the same time a very special relationship with the State. . . .

II. The Impact on the Firm's Conduct

The trend toward the softening of the budget constraints has many interrelated consequences. Here only three of them will be surveyed: the impact on price responsiveness, on efficiency and on the creation of excess demand. As in the second part of the previous section we still focus on the behavior of the firm.

The first issue is the effect of prices on the decision-making of the firm. The trivial case of a downward sloping demand curve by the firm for its inputs presupposes the existence of a hard budget constraint. The softer the budget constraint, the weaker the compulsion to adjust demand to relative prices. In the extreme position of a perfectly soft budget constraint, the own-price elasticity of demand is zero, the demand curve is vertical i.e. determined by other explanatory variables and not by the price. . . . [T]he exact slope of the original budget line does not matter too much if cost increases can be

---

[4] R.W. Clower and J.F. Due, *Microeconomics* (Homewood: Irwin, 1972.)

easily compensated by external assistance, so that the budget line is replaced by a fuzzy strip.

The softness of the budget constraint decreases the elasticity of demand of all alternative inputs, of all factors; diminishes the firm's sensitivity toward the interest rate, exchange rate and so on. Similarly, the multiproduct firm will be less sensitive to changes in relative output prices. Summing up: the general price responsiveness of the firm declines. . . .

A second issue worthy of attention is the impact on efficiency of the trend toward a softer budget constraint. Allocative efficiency cannot be achieved when input-output combinations do not adjust to price signals. Within the firm there is not a sufficiently strong stimulus to maximum effort; weaker performance is tolerated. The attention of the firm's leaders is distracted from the shop floor and from the market and to the offices of the bureaucracy where they may apply for help in the case of financial trouble.

The most important issue is dynamic adjustment. If the budget constraint is hard, the firm has no other option but to adjust to unfavorable circumstances by improving quality, cutting costs, introducing new products or processes, i.e. it must behave in an entrepreneurial manner. If, however, the budget constraint is soft such productive efforts are no longer imperative. Instead, the firm is likely to seek external assistance, asking for compensation for unfavorable external circumstances. The State is acting like an overall insurance company taking over all the moral hazards with the usual well-known consequences; the insured will be less careful in protecting his wealth. Schumpeter[5] emphasized the significance of "constructive destruction": the elimination of old products, technologies, organizations which were surpassed by the more efficient new ones. The soft budget constraint protects the old production line, the inefficient firm against constructive destruction and thus impedes innovation and development.

A third consequence of the soft budget constraint may show up in the formation of excess demand. Whatever goals the managers of firms have (maximizing short- or long-term profits, sales, growth of sales, size of firm, discretion and power) these objectives or any combination of them will be associated with expansion. And whatever specific input-output combination may serve expansion, the drive to achieve the goals listed above generates an ever-increasing demand for at least some inputs over time. If the budget constraint is hard, this demand is constrained. Expenditures on purchasing inputs is conditional on past, present, and future revenues generated by the

---

[5] *The Theory of Economic Development*, Cambridge: Harvard University Press, 1934.

sale of output, which again is constrained by the firm's demand for output. If, however, the budget constraint of many firms is soft, their demand for inputs becomes unconstrained (or at least unconstrained from the point of view of financing). Run-away demand will appear. These firms feel that when they cannot pay the bills, someone else will step in and bail them out. Therefore there is no compulsory limit on demand for inputs, and particularly on investment. If the share of economic units with a soft budget constraint and a tendency to run-away demand for inputs is large enough to have a strong effect on total demand, the system becomes a "shortage economy."

Here we arrive at some theoretical conclusions. As emphasized before, the existence of a (hard) budget constraint is equivalent to Say's principle being in force. If, however, the budget constraint is soft in sufficiently large segments of the economy, then Say's principle does not hold and, as a consequence, Walras' law[6] does not hold either. Say's principle assumes that the firm is ready to start the project only if it seriously believes that the flow of revenues from the sale of the output generated by the new project will cover the flow of expenditures needed to accomplish the project. True, in a world of uncertainty different decision-makers might exhibit different degrees of risk-aversion. But given the distribution of risk-aversion over all investment decision makers, total demand for investment resources (investment credits, investment goods, etc.) will be constrained, because of the genuine fear of financial failure, that is, because the budget constraint is hard. There will be self-restraint in the capital formation decision. This symmetric relationship between demand for investment resources and the supply generated by the same investment resources underlies the idea of Walras' law, i.e. the sum of the (positive and negative) values of excess demands will be zero.

This kind of symmetry gets lost in the case of a sufficiently large number of decision makers with soft budget constraints. The symmetry breaks down if financial support can appear like manna. The firm can start a project even though it may have the subconscious suspicion that the cost will be more than planned and the revenue less. In case of financial failure it will be bailed out. Under such circumstances there is no self-restraint in investment intentions; the demand is not counter-balanced by a "dead-serious" consideration of revenues and ultimately of supply.

There are identities in all economies: stock-flow balances of real inputs and

---

[6] [Editor's note: Walras' Law, simply stated, asserts that the value of excess demand in any market must equal the combined value of excess supplies in all other markets.]

outputs and of money. These identities self-evidently hold also in [an] economy with soft-budget constraints. But Walras' law is not an identity but a certain relationship between buying and selling intentions. Intentions can be inconsistent. In case of a soft budget constraint they are inconsistent. Subsidies, soft tax-exemptions, soft credits, etc., will be financed through the redistribution of income via taxation or inflation. Everyone takes into account the usual tax burden, inflation rate and so on when planning his finances. The expectation that the firm can spend more than its "earnings" because in case of failure it will be bailed-out, comes in on top of that. Here is the source of asymmetry: the possibility of run-away demand of the firm with soft budget constraints. The individual expectations can be incompatible with each other. The softening of the budget constraint is an inducement to such incompatibility: the softer the budget constraint and the larger the sphere of the economy where the syndrome prevails, the more incompatibility appears.

Another important aspect is the effectiveness of monetary policy. A monetary ceiling is a necessary condition of financial discipline, but is not sufficient to ensure it. The transmission between a tighter monetary policy and the micro-response becomes unreliable in the case of a soft budget constraint. The latter is like a cog-wheel in this transmission. The microunit will not react to monetary restraint by restricting its demands when it is not convinced of the dangers of financial failure. In the sphere of microunits with a soft budget constraint money is more or less passive[7]. . . .

III. The Experience of Socialist Hungary

We now turn to empirical observations. . . . The case of "classical socialism," i.e. the highly centralized pre-reform command economy, is rather straight forward. It is officially acknowledged that profitability must not play a decisive role: entry, exit, expansion and contraction of the firm does not depend on profitability, but is decided by higher authorities applying other criteria. A loss-making firm or a whole sector can survive indefinitely, provided that the higher organs of the State want it. . . .

In Hungary a research team is studying the financial situation of all State-owned enterprises (1,755 firms in 1982) which produce the bulk of total output. The balance sheets of all these firms have been processed and several special indicators have been computed for cross sectional and dynamic

---

[7]See Grossman, G. "Gold and the Sword: Money in the Soviet Command Economy," in Rosowsky (Ed), *Industrialization in Two Systems*, New York, Wiley, 1965 and Brus, W., *The Market in a Socialist Economy*, London, Routledge and Kegan Paul, 1972.

analysis. Here only a few examples of the numerical results can be presented.

Some explanation of terminology is needed. We distinguish four categories of profit.

1. *Original profit*. This is a hypothetical number: profit before receiving any kind of subsidies from the State and before paying any kind of taxes to the State. . . .

2. *Corrected original profit*. This is profit number 1 plus subsidies granted for the purpose of keeping certain consumer prices down minus turnover taxes levied for the sake of keeping certain consumer prices up. The rationale for this correction is as follows. We want to filter out the component of fiscal redistribution which aims at subsidizing or taxing the consumer households, not the firms.

3. *Reported profit*. This is the profit reported in the balance sheets and later on, in all sectoral and national statistics on profits. They reflect already a large degree of fiscal redistribution: most of the subsidies and most of the taxes are subtracted from original profit at this stage.

4. *Final profit*. After the reported profit is determined a few more subsidies are added and a few more taxes are subtracted.

The first observation is that the size of the fiscal redistribution is very large. . . . The State-owned sector as a whole is a net taxpayer. But the final net outcome is preceded by a far reaching reshuffling of profits crisscrossing among the original firms. The State takes away money from a firm with one hand – and then gives money to another firm (or perhaps to the same firm, but with another "entitlement") with its other hand. Or more precisely, the State has not only two hands but it is a Shiva with many more hands: there are a total of 276 types of taxes and subsidies used by different tax-levying or subsidy-granting authorities.

At this point a word of caution is in order. We do not suggest that profitability No. 1 is the indicator of genuine efficiency. With the given distorted relative price system that cannot be the case. Therefore it is not legitimate to draw the simple normative conclusion to stop differentiated financial distribution, and apply a kind of flat tax while maintaining the present price structure. We do not want to draw any normative conclusion here, only to point out the characteristic feature of the present situation. When fiscal redistributions are so widespread and so complex then "profitability" does not have and cannot have any reasonable meaning. Reported and final profitability depend at least as much on the generosity or tight-fistedness of different subsidy-granting authorities, as they depend on the success or failure in production and on the market.

The fiscal redistribution of profits shows a conspicuous tendency to give financial assistance to the losers. We computed the following indicator: the total subsidy given to a firm over total taxes paid by the same firm. We call it the "ratio of redistribution." The correlation coefficient between original profitability and the ratio of redistribution for the whole population of State-owned firms is -0.99 for 1980, -0.97 for 1981, and -0.92 for 1982. The very strong negative correlation demonstrates that the lower is original profitability, the higher is the probability of getting a larger subsidy and paying a smaller tax.

The redistribution pattern, therefore, is to redistribute profits from the winners to the losers. For the sake of demonstration, firms are classified in four categories: "loss-making" means profitability less than -2%; "low profitability" is between -2% and +65% "medium profitability" is between +6% and +20%; and "high profitability" is greater than +20%.

Firms with high original profitability have only an 11% chance to end up in the same category after redistribution; almost every second one will be downgraded to low profitability. In contrast 9 out of every 10 loss-making firms will be upgraded. This is a rather paradoxical form of "egalitarian" redistribution: profit incentives dampened by the leveling of profits.

Every year a few Hungarian State-owned firms go out of business. They are liquidated or merged into a larger firm. Our analysis as well as other studies, have shown that exit is not related to profitability. The relationship between profitability and the growth of the firm is also worthy of attention. For the sake of cross-sectional and dynamic comparison we defined an indicator of "investment activity": expenditure on real capital formation divided by the value of physical assets. . . . [We found] that investment activity is not correlated with profitability at all. . . .

IV. Experience in Mixed Economies

Socialist economies exhibit a rather extreme degree of budget constraint softness. To a lesser degree and in more restricted segments of the system, similar phenomena can be observed in mixed economies as well.

It is impossible to make general propositions about the degree of softness or hardness of the budget constraint in mixed economies. The variance is large; there are great differences between countries, and within a particular country the situation may change as parties and political currents in power change. [A] few words must be said about the forces which create the phenomenon. As a first approximation we consider the arguments of the organizations which are asking for and expecting external assistance. The variety of specific arguments is of course very large, but we can try to find out their most important common ingredients.

(a) The most frequently quoted reason for external help is the protection of jobs. In a system of perfectly hard budget constraints of firms and households, all adaptation – both cyclical macro-adjustments and structural micro-adjustments – would be associated with large lay-offs and with wages fluctuating in both directions according to the situation in the labor market. Exit of the firm hurts owners, managers and employees; they try to get State assistance to avoid shut-downs. During recessions, the demand for State intervention is supported by great masses. But also in upswings there are sectors or single firms which are still ailing. The employees feel that it is not fair that they are left out of the benefits of growth.

(b) Another rather frequent argument is the protection of domestic production against foreign competition. This frequently coincides with (a), i.e. with defending jobs. Not all protectionist measures imply the softening of the budget constraint, but quite a few have such implications. The most important measures in this respect are the subsidies to firms or whole sectors which – because of high domestic costs – have troubles in competition with foreign firms selling at lower prices.

(c) In many instances the softening of the budget constraint is related to redistributive policies in favor of the poor, the handicapped, the sick, the elderly. Redistributive objectives in the name of fairness, social justice and solidarity can motivate non-profit institutions, local governments or certain branches of the national governments in their demands for additional financial assistance.

(d) An important argument, closely related to (a) and (c), in favor of softening the budget constraint is the demand for security and stability: to protect the individual and ultimately society as a whole from fluctuations and uncertainties. We already used the analogy of the State as a general insurance company. This desire for security and stability is the motivation for impeding the "natural selection" executed by the market, for guaranteeing the survival of malfunctioning banks and producing firms.

(e) Each organization serves – almost by definition – a certain purpose: an important argument is to refer to the social importance of that particular purpose when arguing for external additional support. As mentioned before, the leaders of an organization "fight" for the survival and for the expansion of their unit, usually supported by their staff. In this fight, military leaders will refer to the importance of national defense, the top administrators of the police to the importance of public security, the top administrators of the heath-system to the importance of health care and so on. All these require-ments and claims are, of course, plausible and legitimate. Since they serve objectives which have no "market value," it is unavoidable that their relative value is determined by a political process.

Ultimately, the soft budget constraint phenomenon is a joint outcome of two closely related socio-political trends. First, the increasing, and often overloading demand of society on the State to become a "protector," responsible for the welfare, growth and the national economic interest, and second, the self-reinforcing tendency of bureaucratization. The softening of the budget constraint is an indicator of the fact that many basic allocative and selective processes are not left to the market, but are highly influenced or taken over by bureaucracies and by political forces. This trend proceeds with uneven speed in different countries; there are also reversals for some time. In any case, there is no contemporary mixed economy where the paternalistic role of the state and of political forces is not much stronger than, say, half a century ago.

A final remark on political and ethical implications. There will surely be readers who draw extreme conservative conclusions from the ideas outlined here. This is far from the intentions of the paper, which does not suggest that the hard budget constraint is "good" and the soft is "bad."

A system based on a perfectly hard budget constraint for every decision-making unit is a terribly cruel one. The symbols of such a system are the debtor's prison, the bailiff bringing under the hammer the home and the household goods of the insolvent family, mass lay-offs in bankrupt firms and so on. All changes departing from these brutal extremes contain some elements of a softer budget constraint. It can be hardly denied that the majority of the population in all countries wanted to move away from that extreme point.

Careful case-by-case considerations are needed if we turn to policy sugges-tions. Sometimes these are relatively easy. The budget constraint can be hardened for the sake of efficiency without (or with little) painful human consequences. In many other cases, however, the choice is much more difficult. There can be a trade-off between the two kinds of consequences of softening or hardening the budget constraints: the impact on efficiency and the impact on human well-being and suffering. The hardness of the budget constraint is based on fear of a financial catastrophe; the softness eliminates this fear. A hard budget constraint includes competition: the winner gains, the loser will be ruined. A soft budget constraint has mercy on the loser. It is not the purpose of this paper to "solve" the ethical dilemmas. There is no general solution; one has to search for acceptable compromises in each case. Here we want to emphasize only that there is a deep dilemma. Efficiency and security-stability are to a large extent conflicting goals.

3. The Consequences of Central Planning in Eastern Europe[*]

David Lipton and Jeffrey Sachs

Even with a consensus on the ultimate aims of reform, the tactical difficulties of creating a market economy are profound. Fundamental social, political, and economic changes must be carried out in the context of a deep and worsening economic crisis, inexperience in managing a market economy, fragile political institutions, the residual pressures of the communist power structure throughout society, the reemergence of historical enmities, and often very deep ethnic fissures. Moreover, the rapidly worsening economic crisis in the Soviet Union is producing an economic fallout in Council for Mutual Economic Assistance (CMEA) trade, and the risks of further instability in the Soviet Union hang like a pall over the region. Because the political and economic conditions in the various countries differ markedly, the prospects for success differ as well. The prospects appear to be brightest in the most westward countries: East Germany (where the process will occur as part of reunification), Poland, Czechoslovakia, Hungary, and Yugoslavia. In Bulgaria and Romania, the conditions are considerably less favorable, both economically and politically. And despite Gorbachev's strong orientation toward Western Europe, the Soviet Union remains a case by itself, where it is difficult to find a national consensus on almost any matter, including a return to Europe.

The Tyranny of Misleading Data

Western economists, accustomed to Western standards of analysis, sometimes take Eastern European data at face value. The data, however, can be misleading for several reasons.

First, under the communist regimes, data have simply been faked in some

---

[*] From "Creating a Market Economy in Eastern Europe: The Case of Poland," *Brookings Papers on Economic Activity*, Vol I, 1990. Reprinted by Permission of the Brookings Institution. Some footnotes omitted.

cases, and collected on a very inadequate conceptual base in other cases.[1] Real growth, for example, has been routinely overstated and inflation routinely understated in the data of Eastern Europe and the Soviet Union. Second, and most emphatically, in a shortage economy – in which goods are not available at official prices – measures of real living standards (such as the wage deflated by the price index) are likely to contain a serious upward bias. In a market economy, a fall in real wages usually means a drop in living standards. But in a shortage economy, a fall in real wages can simply mean the elimination of queues, and therefore a rise in living standards.

Third, almost all analysts of the socialist economies recognize the extreme bias toward heavy industry, much of which produces goods used by other heavy industry but without benefits – either current or in the future – for consumption. This output is given an important weight in the production and GNP accounts, but it is of little true economic value.

A Polish journalist recently put it well:

> For the entire period of real socialism, investments were poured into a close production circle that offered no profit: coal was necessary to produce electricîty; electricity was necessary to produce steel; and steel was necessary to mine coal. All that produced a statistical growth in national income, a growth which, as we now see, actually meant a decline in national wealth. Let us keep in mind that the prices for everything were taken out of thin air.[2]

It is bad enough that these data problems pose a serious barrier to analysis. What is worse is that the data can provoke unwarranted pressures on policy-makers. In the course of stabilization, for example, declines in measured real wages that will in fact vastly overstate the actual economic losses can nonetheless still generate strong political demands for government-mandated wage increases that could undermine the stabilization program itself.

With these data problems in mind, let us outline the main constraints on economic reform that face every government in the region.

---

[1] The following conceptual problems routinely lead to an overestimation of the rate of growth of net material product (a measure of the value added in production): double counting of inputs, inadequate depreciation allowances, inclusion of wasted materials, and, most important, an inadequate account of rising prices in the definition of nominal magnitudes. .

[2] Ernest Skalski, "The Idiot's Economy," *Gazeta International 90*, week 10, 1990.

The Stalinist Legacy

The countries in Eastern Europe have a socialist ownership structure. Industrial production is typically 90 percent or more state owned; the service sector is also heavily state owned, though an unknown level of activity takes place in the grey or black market. Agriculture is generally state owned and controlled, except in Poland, where farmers retained their private land after World War II, though under highly restrictive and repressive conditions.

The role of central planning as of 1990 differs considerably among countries. A summary statistic is the share of goods subject to central allocation by the central planning organs. By this measure, central planning remained in place until this year in Bulgaria, Czechoslovakia, East Germany, and Romania. Central allocation has been substantially phased out in Hungary and was progressively reduced in scope in Poland during the 1980s. In these latter economies, some portions of the economy, such as energy and trade with the Soviet Union, remained under central allocation until recently.

As Kornai has stressed, the shrinkage of the sphere of central planning in Hungary and Poland and the growing autonomy of enterprises did not mean the emergence of normal competitive market relations. Rather under the process of communist-led reform in Hungary and Poland, central planning was replaced in part by market-type controls but also by a burgeoning of ad hoc negotiations between the enterprise and the financial authorities. While in a nominal sense enterprises were guided by prices, interest rates, and tax rates, rather than material allocations, in practice the prices, interest rates, and taxes have all been the subject of continual negotiation.

State enterprises, whether in Eastern Europe or elsewhere, almost inevitably create financial problems in two main areas of decision making: wages (where they are prone to pay excessive wages out of the income stream that would otherwise accrue to the Treasury) and investment (where the manager has a craving for investment spending, because he stands to gain from control over a larger firm, but bears little or no cost if the investments fail). Even in Western Europe the state sector has run into repeated financial difficulties, and in Latin America the state sector has contributed significantly to the genesis of the debt crisis. But the situation in Eastern Europe is even more grave, since the state sector is not disciplined by being part of a larger market economy. To the extent that state enterprises have been decontrolled, but without introducing real market competition at the same time, the result has been a worsening of financial indiscipline of the firm and, eventually, of the macroeconomy. The state enterprise system does not rely on capital markets to allocate credit. Investment spending is typically negotiated between enterprises, the relevant government ministries, and the central planning commission. Once approved, investments are paid for by various reserve funds set aside by an enterprise, centrally allocated investment funds from the national budget, and loans from the central bank. None of these funding sources requires an adequate assessment of investment prospects.

The countries of Eastern Europe differ in the extent to which the private sector has been permitted to operate. It has been highly restricted in Bulgaria, Czechoslovakia, Romania, and Yugoslavia. A very small private service sector survived the socialization process in East Germany. A somewhat larger private sector has been allowed to operate under the reforms in Hungary and Poland. But even in these last cases, the private firms have been heavily restricted by administrative barriers, punitive tax laws, shortages of inputs, and unavailability of foreign exchange and credit, the allocation of which has been almost entirely directed to the state sector.

All the countries suffer from heavily distorted relative prices. Energy and household necessities (mainly food and rent) are heavily subsidized. The exchange rate is overvalued, in the sense that foreign exchange is rationed at the official price (both for current and capital transactions), so that the black market exchange rate is heavily depreciated relative to the official rate. Therefore, while import prices measured at the official exchange rate are cheap, most imported goods are severely rationed in supply (or simply not available), so that the effective price facing end users is extremely high.

On a sectoral level, the industrial structure in every country is strongly skewed toward heavy industry and capital goods and away from light industry, services, and consumer goods. This emphasis mainly reflects two factors: first, the obsessive growth orientation of the Stalinist model and, second, trade patterns instituted by the Soviet Union, which has induced the Eastern European countries to develop large industries to process Soviet raw materials and then re-export them to the Soviet Union in semifinished or finished form.

In Poland, for example, in 1987 the industrial and construction sectors produced 52 percent of GDP, compared with just 29 percent to 38 percent in Greece, Portugal, and Spain. By contrast, the growth of the service sector in Poland has been severely stunted by the focus on industry. In the same year the service sector in Poland employed 35 percent of the labor force, far less than in Greece, Spain, or Portugal (see Table I).

The organization of industry is designed to facilitate top-down planning, rather than market competition, with a heavy orientation toward large firms integrated both horizontally and vertically. There is a virtual absence of small

Table 1. Real GDP and Employment by Sector, Poland and Selected Market
Economies, 1980–87

Percent

Sector and country	Share in total GDP[a] 1980	1987	Average annual change in sector GDP, 1980–87	Share in total employment 1980	1987	Average annual change in sector employment, 1980–87
Industry[b]						
Poland	42.6	41.7	0.4	30.1	28.5	-0.9
Portugal	31.4	30.6	1.6	27.1	26.5	0.4
Spain	29.7	29.1	2.0	27.1	24.2	-1.8
Greece	26.1	25.1	2.3	20.7[c]	21.5	1.0
Agriculture						
Poland	10.7	12.1	2.5	30.4	29.1	-0.8
Portugal	7.0	7.8	3.7	27.3	21.9	-2.3
Spain	6.9	6.3	0.8	19.2	15.1	-3.6
Greece	14.5	12.9	-0.5	30.7[c]	27.0	-1.8
Construction						
Poland	12.6	10.5	-1.9	7.7	7.8	0.0
Portugal	6.1	5.5	0.5	9.5	9.3	0.4
Spain	8.3	8.2	2.0	9.0	8.2	-1.6
Greece	6.3	4.7	-3.3	8.3[c]	6.4	-4.0
Other sectors						
Poland	34.1	35.7	1.4	31.8	34.6	1.1
Portugal	55.6	56.1	2.1	36.1	42.3	3.1
Spain	55.1	56.4	2.6	44.7	52.5	2.2
Greece	53.1	57.3	2.4	40.4[c]	45.0	2.2

Sources: *Rocznik Statystyczny* (various years); OECD *National Accounts*, 1989; and OECD *Labor Force Statistics*,
1989. GDP calculations used GDP at factor price before adjusted to market price.
  a. Greece, billions of drachmae in 1970 prices; Spain, billions of pesetas in 1980 prices; Portugal, billions of
escudos in 1987 prices.
  b. Includes mining, manufacturing, electricity, gas, water.
  c. The employment figures for Greece are from 1981.

to medium-sized firms, with employment between 50 and 100, the kind of
firm that plays such a vital role in growth in the Western industrialized
economies. Part of this centralization results from large-scale production units,
and part from the tendency to group separate factories in a particular sector
together in a small number of enterprises. The anti-competitive nature of the
industrial structure is often exacerbated by the presence of enterprise
associations that tie together firms at the industry level and act as cartels.

Table 2. The Distribution of Employment in Industry by Size of Establishment, Poland, 1937 and 1986, and Selected Market Economies

Country	Average number of workers per establish- ment	Workers per establishment			
		100 or fewer	*101–500*	*501–1,000*	*Greater than 1,000*
		(percentage of all workers)			
Poland					
1937	54	33[a]	27	41[b]	n.a.
1986[c]	88	10	25	15	51[d]
State enterprises	378	6	21	16	58[e]
Cooperatives	30	42	54	4	1
Sample of					
Western economies[f]	80	35[g]	33	13	19
South Korea	n.a.	33[h]	67[i]		

Sources: Data on Poland from *Rocznik Statystyczny Przemysłu*; data on sample of Western economies in 1970 from Ehrlich (1985); data on South Korea in 1982 from World Bank (1989a).

n.a. Not available.

a. Includes employees in establishments of between 6 and 100 employees.

b. Includes all employees in establishments with more than 501 employees.

c. Socialized sector. Employees in the private sector work in establishments with an average employment of 2 workers.

d. Seventeen percent of all workers are in establishments with employment greater than 5,000.

e. Nineteen percent of all workers are in establishments with employment greater than 5,000.

f. Austria, Belgium, France, Italy, Japan, and Sweden. Percentage of workers employed in total manufacturing excluding mining.

g. Includes employees in establishments of between 10 and 100 employees.

h. Includes employees in establishments of between 4 and 99 workers.

i. Includes all employees in establishments with employment greater than 100. Twelve percent of employees are in establishments with employment of 101–200; 11 percent are in establishments with employment of 201–300; and 44 percent are in establishments with employment greater than 300.

Consider again the case of Poland. The average state enterprise in Polish industry (excluding the so-called cooperative sector, which represents 13 percent of employment in the state sector) has 1,132 employees, typically in multi-plant operations. The average number of employees per plant (again excluding the cooperative sector) is 378 (see Table 2), compared with about 80 workers per plant in a sample of Western economies. The 115 largest enterprises, each with more than 5,000 employees, account for more than one fifth of industrial employment and production. At the other end of the spectrum, only 982 enterprises in all of socialized industry in Poland have fewer than 100 employees. In Korea, where small and medium-sized enterprises have provided much of the impetus for growth and economic development, 33 percent of the labor force is employed in establishments with fewer than 100 workers. This contrasts with only 10 percent in the Polish state sector.

The socialist economies also lack adequate procedures for the entry and exit of enterprises. Enterprises are typically "founded" by ministries or local authorities, which at the same time arrange for the funding to begin operations. Absent such sponsorship, there is little chance that state enterprise activity can spring up to meet even the most obvious economic needs. On the side of exit, bankruptcy and liquidation of state enterprise activity has been virtually unknown. In fact, the absence of markets and meaningful relative prices in the economy means that it is difficult, if not impossible, to distinguish between enterprises that should and should not survive.

All countries of Eastern Europe suffer from chronic excess demand, though to varying degrees. The extent of shortages at official prices has been very high in Bulgaria, Poland, and Romania, and less severe in Czechoslovakia, Hungary, and Yugoslavia. In the former countries, the supply of basic consumer goods (such as food) has been erratic and often formally rationed. Active black markets exist in which goods are available at a multiple of the official price. In Czechoslovakia, Hungary, and Yugoslavia, markets for basic consumer goods have generally cleared (though quality is often low and variety is limited), while shortages remain acute for housing, telephones, automobiles, and other types of consumer durables.

At the enterprise level, excess demand is manifested in chronic shortages of basic inputs at official prices. There are informal supply networks through which state enterprises cope in part with the chronic supply shortages. In Hungary and Poland, where small-scale private firms have been allowed to operate, the private sector firms are generally cut out from these informal supply networks, and therefore face extreme shortages and the need to bribe individuals in state-owned enterprises to obtain even a haphazard supply of inputs.

Another coping mechanism of all enterprises has been an autarkic production strategy in which the firm eschews specialization, at great cost to efficiency, in order to produce all the necessary components for the production process. It is more or less the opposite of Japan's just-in-time (kanban) production organization, in which large firms rely on small, highly specialized firms to provide inputs on a carefully timed, highly reliable basis. In Eastern Europe, there are almost no small independent firms servicing large enterprises. All work is done in-house.[3]

The origins of excess demand lie deep within the system and include: the planners' drive toward rapid growth through heavy investment; the soft budget constraint of enterprises engaged in constant negotiation with the financial authorities; the planners' fear of unemployment; and the communist regime's lack of legitimacy to impose strong austerity measures with public support and its unwillingness or inability to do so by brute force.

Political Context

The collapse of communist one-party rule was the sine qua non for an effective transition to a market economy. If one proposition has been tested by history, it is that the communist parties of Eastern Europe would not lead a process of radical reform sufficiently deep to create a real market economy. There were too many barriers: the ideology of state ownership; the power structure of the party, based heavily on state enterprise managers and bureaucrats loath to allow real competition to the state enterprises; the communist leaderships' lack of legitimacy among the public, making it impossible to impose the short-run costs of deep economic restructuring; and the low regard in the West for the communist governments, making it impossible for them to mobilize the international financial support vital for the economic transition.

Thus, the emergence of noncommunist rule has been a fundamental watershed for real reform in Eastern Europe. But, at the same time, the emergence of noncommunist governments in the region not only does not erase all existing political difficulties, but actually introduces new ones. The economic strategy must take cognizance of the new political context, which, in our view, argues overwhelmingly for a very rapid, straightforward, and sharp program of economic reform.

The first point is the Latin American lesson of the 1980s, that a fragile democratic opening combined with a deep economic crisis is a fertile brew for populist politics. Only decisive actions by a reformist government can keep these populist pressures in check. In most countries, stabilization by

---

[3] The results are sometimes bizarre. During 1976 when food shortages were particularly severe, the industrial enterprises were instructed that they would be permitted to raise their own farm animals to feed their workforces. More generally, firms are integrated throughout the entire production process. A shoe company makes its own cardboard boxes for the shoes, an electronics firm makes its own metal castings, and so forth.

itself will require a sharp cutback in budget subsidies and a rise in unemployment. The restructuring of industry will also impose costs on particular groups. The urgent need to address the deteriorating infrastructure (including the environment) may also require a reduction in current consumption.[4]

These conditions will produce ample opportunities for politicians who promise illusory low-cost paths to reform. In the short-term, populist pressures will lead to opposition to cuts in subsidies and to calls for "reactivation" of the economy through wage increases and demand expansion. In the longer run populists politicians will find support among workers in declining industries who will press for protection, subsidies and other steps to halt the necessary industrial restructuring. The risks are compounded because both electorates and government officials will be highly inexperienced in the process of real economic reform.

Governments in the region may also be stymied by the likely reintroduction of prewar electoral rules based on proportional representation. Voting bases on proportional representation tends to produce weak multiparty coalition governments that have a particularly difficult time in reducing an inherited government deficit. The prewar history of the region amply demonstrates this proposition.

Another profound political difficulty relates to the bureaucracy. The new governments of Eastern Europe are inheriting bureaucracies created and appointed by the communist party. The structure and personnel in these bureaucracies will change only gradually over time. There are tens, if not hundreds, of thousands of officials whose professional experience lies in a lifetime of bureaucratic planning of economic life, whose links are to party-appointed managers of state enterprises.

The bureaucracy provides an extraordinarily important practical argument for radical free market policies, even in circumstances where "market failures" exists and pure theory might suggest more nuanced policies. It is naive to think of the existing bureaucracy as equipped, professionally or temperamentally, to implement sophisticated policies based on Western-style theories of the "second-best." The bureaucracy cannot be relied upon for efficiency in regulating monopoly prices, promoting infant industries, or implementing industrial policy.

---

[4] To some extent, cuts in military spending and investment in heavy industry, combined with new external financing from abroad, can reduce the need for large cuts in current consumption.

Other deep political fissures are likely to reopen, after decades of dormancy. The prewar rural-urban economic battles in the region are already revving up in Poland, and will likely do so soon in Hungary. The nationalist and ethnic battles, within countries and between countries, are also reawakening at an alarming rate. One can mention the recent nationalist violence in Yugoslavia, between Serbs and Albanians; in Romania, between ethnic Hungarians and Romanians in Transylvania; in Bulgaria, against the Turkish minority. Even many Slovak leaders are agitating for a break with the Czechs, or at least for national autonomy within a Czecho-Slovak federation with a weak central government.

4. Economic Calculation in Socialism[*]

Ludwig von Mises

Without calculation, economic activity is impossible. Since under socialism economic calculation is impossible, under socialism there can be no economic activity in our sense of the word. In small and insignificant things rational action might still persist. But, for the most part, it would no longer be possible to speak of rational production. In the absence of criteria of rationality, production could not be consciously economical.

For some time possibly the accumulated tradition of thousands of years of economic freedom would preserve the art of economic administration from complete disintegration. Men would preserve the old processes not because they were rational, but because they were sanctified by tradition. In the meantime, however, changing conditions would make them irrational. They would become uneconomical as the result not changes brought about by the general decline of economic thought. It is true that production would no longer be "anarchical." The command of a supreme authority would govern the business of supply. Instead of the economy of "anarchical" production the senseless order of an irrational machine would be supreme. The wheels would go round, but to no effect.

Let us try to imagine the position of a socialist community. There will be hundreds and thousands of establishments in which work is going on. A minority of these will produce goods ready for use. The majority will produce capital goods and semi-manufactures. All these establishments will be closely connected. Each commodity produced will pass through a whole series of such establishments before it is ready for consumption. Yet in the incessant press of all these processes the economic administration will have no real sense of direction. It will have no means of ascertaining whether a given piece of work is really necessary, whether labor and material are not being

---

[*] From *Socialism: An Economic and Sociological Analysis*, second edition, translated by J. Kahane, Yale University Press. First published by Jonathan Cape. Reprinted by permission of Random Century Group/London.

wasted in completing it. How would it discover which of two processes was the more satisfactory? At best, it could compare the quantity of ultimate products. But only rarely could it compare the expenditure incurred in their production. It would know exactly, or it would imagine it knew, what it wanted to produce. It ought, therefore, to set about obtaining the desired results with the smallest possible expenditure. But to do this it would have to be able to make calculations. And such calculations must be calculations of value. They could not be merely "technical"; they could not be calculations of the objective use-value of goods and services. This is so obvious that it needs no further demonstration.

Under a system based upon private ownership of the means of production, the scale of values is the outcome of the actions of every independent member of society. Everyone plays a two-fold part in its establishment, first as a consumer, second as a producer. As consumer, he establishes the valuation of goods ready for consumption. As producer, he guides production-goods into those uses in which they yield the highest product. In this way, all goods of higher orders also are graded in the way appropriate to them under the existing conditions of production and the demands of society. The interplay of these two processes ensures that the economic principle is observed in both consumption and production. And, in this way, arises the exactly graded system of prices which enables everyone to frame his demand on economic lines.

Under socialism, all this must necessarily be lacking. The economic administration may indeed know exactly what commodities are needed most urgently. But this is only half the problem. The other half, the valuation of the means of production, it cannot solve. It can ascertain the value of the totality of such instruments. That is obviously equal to the value of the satisfactions they afford. If it calculates the loss that would be incurred by withdrawing them, it can also ascertain the value of single instruments of production. But it cannot assimilate them to a common price denominator, as can be done under a system of economic freedom and money prices.

It is not necessary that socialism should dispense altogether with money. It is possible to conceive arrangements permitting the use of money for the exchange of consumer goods. But since the prices of the various factors of production (including labor) could not be expressed in money, money could play no part in economic calculations.

Suppose, for instance, that the socialist commonwealth was contemplating a new railway line. Would a new railway line be a good thing? If so, which of many possible routes should it cover? Under a system of private ownership we could use money calculations to decide these questions. The new line would cheapen the transportation of certain articles, and, on this basis, we could estimate whether the reduction in transport charges would be great enough to counterweigh the expenditure which the building and running of the line would involve. Such a calculation could be made only in money. We could not do it by comparing various classes of expenditure and savings in kind. If it is out of the question to reduce to a common unit the quantities of various kinds of skilled and unskilled labor, iron, coal, building materials of different kinds, machinery, and the other things which the building and upkeep of railways necessitate, then it is impossible to make them the subject of economic calculation. We can make systematic economic plans only when all the commodities which we have to take into account can be assimilated to money. True, money calculations are incomplete. True, they have profound deficiencies. But we have nothing better to put in their place. And, under sound monetary conditions, they suffice for practical purposes. If we abandon them, economic calculation becomes absolutely impossible.

This is not to say that the socialist community would be entirely at a loss. It would decide for or against the proposed undertaking and issue an edict. But, at best, such a decision would be based on vague valuations. It could not be based on exact calculations of value.

A stationary society could, indeed, dispense with these calculations. For there, economic operations merely repeat themselves. So that, if we assume that the socialist system of production were based upon the last state of the system of economic freedom which it superseded, and that no changes were to take place in the future, we could indeed conceive a rational and economic socialism. But only in theory. A stationary economic system can never exist. Things are continually changing, and the stationary state, although necessary as an aid to speculation, is a theoretical assumption to which there is no counterpart in reality. And, quite apart from this, the maintenance of such a connection with the last state of the exchange economy would be out of the question, since the transition to socialism with its equalization of incomes would necessarily transform the whole "set" of consumption and production. And then we have a socialist community which must cross the whole ocean of possible and imaginable economic permutations without the compass of economic calculation.

All economic change, therefore, would involve operations the value of which could neither be predicted beforehand nor ascertained after they had taken place. Everything would be a leap in the dark. Socialism is the renunciation of rational economy.

. . . Some of the younger socialists believe that the socialist community could solve the problem of economic calculation by the creation of an artificial market for the means of production. They admit that it was an error on the part of the older socialists to have sought to realize socialism through the suspension of the market and the abolition of pricing for goods of higher orders; they hold that it was an error to have seen in the suppression of the market and of the price system the essence of the socialist ideal. And they contend that if it is not to degenerate into a meaningless chaos in which the whole of our civilization would disappear, the socialist community, equally with the capitalist community, must create a market in which all goods and services may be priced. On the basis of such arrangements, they think, the socialist community will be able to make its calculations as easily as the capitalist entrepreneurs.

Unfortunately, the supporters of such proposals do not see (or perhaps will not see) that it is not possible to divorce the market and its functions in regard to the formulation of prices from the working of a society which is based on private property in the means of production and in which, subject to the rules of such a society, the landlords, capitalists, and entrepreneurs can dispose of their property as they think fit. For the motive force of the whole process which gives rise to market prices for the factors of production is the ceaseless search on the part of the capitalists and the entrepreneurs to maximize their profits by serving the consumers' wishes. Without the striving of the entrepreneurs (including the shareholders) for profit, of the landlords for rent, of the capitalists for interest, and of the laborers for wages, the successful functioning of the whole mechanism is not to be thought of. It is only the prospect of profit which directs production into those channels in which the demands of the consumer are best satisfied at least cost. If the prospect of profit disappears, the mechanism of the market loses its mainspring, for it is only this prospect which sets it in motion and maintains it in operation. The market is thus the focal point of the capitalist order of society; it is the essence of capitalism. Only under capitalism, therefore, is it possible; it cannot be "artificially" imitated under socialism.

The advocates of the artificial market, however, are of the opinion that an artificial market can be created by instructing the controllers of the different industrial units to act *as if* they were entrepreneurs in a capitalist state. They argue that even under capitalism the managers of joint stock companies work not for themselves but for the companies, that is to say, for the shareholders. Under socialism, therefore, it would be possible for them to act in exactly the same way as before, with the same circumspection and devotion to duty. The only difference would be that under socialism the product of the manager's labors would go to the community rather than to the shareholders. In such a way, in contrast to all societies who have written on the subject hitherto, especially the Marxians, they think it would be possible to construct a decentralized, as opposed to a centralized, socialism.

In order to judge properly these proposals, it is necessary in the first place to realize that these controllers of individual units would have to be appointed. Under capitalism the manager of the joint-stock companies are appointed either directly or indirectly by the shareholder. In so far as the shareholders give to the managers the power to produce by means of the company's (i.e., the shareholders') stock they are risking their own property or a part of their own property. The speculation (for it is necessarily speculation) may succeed and bring profit: it may misfire and bring about the loss of the whole or a part of the capital concerned. This committing of one's own capital to a business whose outcome is uncertain and to men whose future ability is still a matter of conjecture, whatever one may know of their past, is the essence of joint stock company enterprise.

Now it is a complete fallacy to suppose that the problem of economic calculation in a socialist community relates solely to the matters which fall into the sphere of the daily routine of the managers of joint stock companies. It is clear that such a belief can only arise from exclusive concentration on the idea of a stationary economic system – a conception which no doubt is useful for the solution of many theoretical problems but which has no counterpart in fact and which, if exclusively regarded, can even be positively misleading. It is clear that under stationary conditions the problem of economic calculation does not arise. When we think of the stationary society, we think of an economy in which all the factors of production are already used in such a way as, under the given conditions, to provide the maximum of things which are demanded by consumers. That is to say, under stationary conditions there no longer exists a problem for economic calculation to solve. The essential function of economic calculation has *by hypothesis already been performed*. There is no need for an apparatus of calculation. To use a popular but not altogether satisfactory terminology we can say that the problem of economic calculation is of economic dynamics; it is no problem of economic statics.

The problem of economic calculation is a problem which arises in an economy which is perpetually subject to change, an economy which every day is confronted with new problems which have to be solved. Now in order to solve such problems it is above all necessary that capital should be withdrawn from particular lines of production, from particular undertakings and concerns and should be applied in other lines of production, in other undertakings and concerns. This is not a matter for the for the managers of joint stock companies; it is essentially a matter for the capitalists – the capitalists who buy and sell stocks and shares, who make loans and recover them, who make deposits in the bank and draw them out of the banks again, who speculate in all kinds of commodities. It is these operations of speculative capitalists which create those conditions of the money market, the stock exchanges and the wholesale markets which have to be taken for granted by the manager of the joint stock company, who, according to the socialist writers we are considering, is to be conceived as nothing but the reliable and conscientious servant of the company. It is the speculative capitalists who create the data to which he has to adjust his business and which therefore give direction to his trading operations.

It follows, therefore, that it is a fundamental deficiency of all these socialist constructions which invoke the "artificial market" and artificial competition as a way out of the problem of economic calculation, that they rest on the belief that the market for factors of production is affected only by producers buying and selling commodities. It is not possible to eliminate from such markets the influence of the supply of capital from the capitalists and the demand for capital by the entrepreneurs, without destroying the mechanism itself.

Faced with this difficulty, the socialist is likely to propose that the socialist state as owner of all capital and all means of production should simply direct capital to those undertakings which promise the highest return. The available capital, he will contend, should go to those undertakings which offer the highest rate of profit. But such a state of affairs would simply mean that those managers who were less cautious and more optimistic would receive capital to enlarge their undertakings while more cautious and more skeptical managers would go away empty-handed. Under capitalism, the capitalist decides to whom he will entrust his own capital. The beliefs of the managers of joint stock companies regarding the future prospects of their undertakings and the hopes of project makers regarding the profitability of their plans are not in any way decisive. The mechanism of the money market and the capital market decides. This, indeed, is its main task: to serve the economic system as a whole, to judge the profitability of alternative openings, and not blindly to follow what the managers of particular concerns, limited by the narrow horizon of their own undertakings, are tempted to propose.

To understand this completely, it is essential to realize that the capitalist does not just invest his capital in those undertakings which offer high interest or high profit; he attempts rather to strike a balance between his desire for profit and his estimate of the risk of loss. He must exercise foresight. If he does not do so, than he suffers losses – losses that bring it about that his disposition over the factors of production is transferred to the hands of others who know better how to weigh the risks and the prospects of business speculation.

Now if it is to remain socialist, the socialist state cannot leave to other hands that disposition over capital which permits the enlargement of existing undertakings, the contraction of others, and the bringing into being of undertakings that are completely new. And it is scarcely to be assumed that socialists of whatever persuasion would seriously propose that this function should be made over to some group of people who would "simply" have the business of doing what capitalists and speculators do under capitalist conditions, the only difference being that the product of their foresight should not belong to them but to the community. Proposals of this sort may well be made concerning the managers of joint stock companies. They can never be extended to capitalists and speculators, for no socialist would dispute that the function which capitalists and speculators perform under capitalism, namely directing the use of capital goods into that direction in which they best serve the demands of the consumer, is only performed because they are under the incentive to preserve their property and to make profits which increase it or at least allow them to live without diminishing their capital.

It follows, therefore, that the socialist community can do nothing but place the disposition over capital in the hands of the state or to be exact in the hands of the men who, as the governing authority, carry out the business of the state. And that signifies elimination of the market, which, indeed, is the fundamental aim of socialism, for the guidance of economic activity by the market implies organization of production and a distribution of the product according to that disposition of the spending power of individual members of society which makes itself felt on the market; that is to say, it implies precisely that which it is the goal of socialism to eliminate.

If the socialists attempt to belittle the significance of the problem of economic calculation in the socialist community, on the ground that the forces of the market do not lead to ethically justifiable arrangements, they simply show that they do not understand the real nature of the problem. It is not a question of whether there shall be produced cannons or clothes, dwelling houses or churches, luxuries or subsistence. In any social order, even under socialism, it can very easily be decided which kind and what number of consumption goods should be produced. No one has ever denied that. But once this decision has been made, there still remains the problem of ascertaining how the existing means of production can be used most effectively to produce these goods in question. In order to solve this problem, it is necessary that there should be economic calculation. And economic calculation can only take place by means of money prices established in the market for production goods in a society resting on private property in the means of production. That is to say, there must exist money prices of land, raw materials, semi-manufactures; that is to say, there must be money wages and interest rates.

Thus the alternative is still *either* socialism *or* a market economy.

5. On the (Im)Possibility of Market Socialism[*]

Michael Keren

The mid 1980s witnessed the collapse of the Soviet economy, followed by that of the Soviet empire, and of the economies of most other CMEA countries. France's last fling with socialism was rapidly aborted, and, at roughly the same time, many institutions of the labor economy in Israel, a socialist island in a capitalist sea, also foundered. The events of the 1970s had something to do with the strains which inflexible institutions could not withstand, and at least some of these institutions were very inflexible. Not all these events are related, but there may be more than mere coincidence here. It is this fundamental nexus which this paper explores. In particular, are socialism and inflexibility inter-linked? Have socialist economies been led by bureaucracies because this is their "natural" way of coordination? Is "Market Socialism" at all feasible? The fondest hopes of many have been pinned on this solution, which seems to promise both social justice and efficiency, or at least the avoidance of gross waste, as well as freedom from bureaucracy and decentralized entrepreneurship. Even though there seems to be no organized attempt at present to implement this possibly utopian ideal, it is sure to return to the agenda some time in the future.

The term socialism, as used above and throughout this paper, refers to an economic system in which all means of production, all productive organizations, are state owned. Hence the discussion here is not germane to the Israeli, possibly not even to the Yugoslav labor-managed, economy. The question is really whether such a large organization can be freed from its bureaucratic shackles, can it be coordinated by a freely functioning price mechanism? The linchpin in this story is the capital market, coupled with what Kornai[1] has termed the "soft budget constraint" (SBC). The commitment to social

---

[*] Forthcoming in the *Eastern Economic Review*. Copyright (c) The Eastern Economic Association. Reprinted by permission of the Eastern Economic Association. Some footnotes omitted.

[1] See Article 2 in this book.

ownership of capital is, in effect, a commitment to an exclusion. It excludes the private sector from the ownership of productive resources and, in effect, removes productive firms from the jurisdiction of the capital market. It puts the firm under the control of a public hierarchy, and the key question is whether this hierarchy can simulate the capital market. Section 1 below argues why this cannot be done. Section 2 shows that this impossibility leads to the SBC. Once this is the case, the firm is freed from the need to fight for its continued existence through the unceasing search for profits. There is, therefore, no force which makes it change whatever non-profit-maximizing policy it may have strayed on, and, as a result, it becomes less sensitive to market signals, its supply response to price changes and to changes in demand is less elastic (section 3). As a result the hierarchy finds it necessary to help the markets clear (section 4). One of the most damaging effects is not on the current operation of the economy, but on its accumulation of stocks, on its investment activity. This is a direct outcome of the distorted incentives and the SBC (section 5). The concluding remarks in section 5, tie the deformed structure of capital to the paths of possible reforms.

1. Can Hierarchy Simulate the Capital Market?

The introduction has already defined "socialism" for the purposes of this paper as an exclusion: it is a regime in which productive assets cannot be transferred to private hands. This, in effect, excludes them from being traded on the capital market. It is assumed that these productive assets are subdivided and organized in so-called enterprises. Even if these enterprises were legal firms which issued their own shares, these shares cannot be traded on any stock exchange, since the ownership of these firms is not to be traded, and the capital market services can, therefore, not be enlisted to aid the running of these firms.

The basic service the capital market supplies is the evaluation of each traded firm's net worth. This signals to its management and its owners how the market judges its future prospects. If this value declines relative to that of similar firms, this may be taken as an indication that the market considers the firm's policies inferior to those of its competitors. In severe situations, this may convey a recommendation to change the top management team of the firm, possibly through a takeover by an alternative team. In extreme cases, when the market believes that the expected present value of the firm's cash flow is negative or significantly below the breakup value of the firm, the capital market may apply direct sanctions by bankrupting the firm. This indicates that the firm should be dissolved and its assets freed to alternative uses. The capital market, as well as providing for the birth of firms, also provides for their death and for changes in their course in mid-life. It plays a Darwinian role of selection. As in Darwinian evolution, here too the role of chance is great, and the dependence on time is paramount. What succeeds today may be what failed yesterday, because yesterday was not ripe for the idea or because it was not properly packaged. Without a capital market the present structure may atrophy. But the capital market does not fulfill these roles in a socialist economy. Who can take upon himself this role in socialism? If socialism does not allow an external capital market to operate, can it create an internal one, inside the state hierarchy.

The first question to settle is whether the role of the capital market can be fulfilled by independent boards, or whether it should, or would, devolve into the hands of the state hierarchy. It is the latter path that has not functioned well in the Soviet-type economies, and therefore it might seem that more individual supervision provided by separate boards may be preferable. Consider an arrangement in which a board of directors is appointed to oversee management and operations of each socialist firm, and to ensure that each firm maximizes profits. This may seem to be a good solution, but it only shifts the need for control one step higher; someone must oversee the performance of these boards. Even if the remuneration of the boards' members is linked to the profits of their enterprises, the problem remains the same. These boards are not traded in the market, and no independent evaluation of their work is automatically available. The hierarchy will therefore have to oversee the boards, instead of the enterprises. Even when they function properly serious questions arise about the boards' independence. Any profits which the enterprise makes would of course be paid into the treasury's accounts (except for that part used to pay the boards' members). But over the course of operation almost any firm's profit might become negative, in which case the national treasury would have to subsidize the firm. It is likely to use this opportunity to obtain some voice on the policy of the enterprise, at the least to have its own appointees on its board.

For permanently loss-making enterprises, it may even demand full control over the board. Clearly, the public boards cannot remain independent from those in control of the public purse, and eventually the whole public sector is likely to come under the control of some public hierarchy even if it did not start this way, either because the control of independent boards did not fulfill expectations, or because of usurpation by the treasury, finance ministry, or some other master of the purse. This public hierarchy is referred to below as the managing hierarchy or, in brief, as the planner.

Can the planner simulate the capital market? We might suppose that the superior in charge of an enterprise or its board of directors could be told to maximize enterprise profits, to change its management or CEO (chief executive officer) whenever he thought that the firm strayed from the profit maximizing path, and, under extreme conditions, to dissolve the firm when there was no hope for its profitable operation. The superior is likely to have one great advantage over the actors playing in the financial market: he should have much better inside information on the activities of his subordinates. This advantage is however outweighed by the disadvantages of opportunism.

Each bureaucrat has to consider his own and his colleagues' personal files: advancement in a hierarchy is based on past and expected services, on the way the bureaucrat has served the organization, (i.e. his superiors) in the past and is likely to serve in the future. Since his main task is to make decisions and see them through, i.e., coordinate their implementation with insiders and outsiders, his contribution to the organization is judged, at least partly, by the quality of the projects he has approved and guided throughout his career. Any reorganization decision affects these files. If he was also responsible for starting the firm and now decides the firm should be shut down, he raises a question mark about his wisdom in launching it in the first place. If his predecessor is the initiator, then an internal fight may erupt in the hierarchy, a fight that is likely to center around personalities rather than the economics of the situation.

Opportunistic behavior arises from the absence of competition. In a capital market, it is not one individual who decides the fate of firms but an interplay of many groups, each with its own assessment and its own resources, which it is ready to imperil so as to make a substantial gain (or avert a loss) if its gamble should succeed. The weighted opinion of the market determines the fate of the firm, where the weights are asset weights. In the hierarchy the bureaucrat is alone, without competing opinion. It is true that he can consult others, but neither he nor the others are putting their own money at risk.

Consequently a superior in a hierarchy has both motive and opportunity to act opportunistically [which] leads to rules, and the larger the organization, the weaker the supervision and the tighter the rules. It is this that turns large hierarchies into bureaucracies, and very large hierarchies into heavy bureaucracies. For particularly weighty decisions (and a reorganization – especially the dissolution – of an enterprise is such a decision) the procedures become very complex and usually require committees with quasi legal procedures. These procedures are costly in both time and organizational resources, and as in other judicial procedures, favor the "accused", i.e., those who stand to lose from the decision. And then the staff of the firm have their say as well. For them any forced change of firm policy, even more so a dissolution of the firm, involves some hardship, some learning of new skills, some investment in new specific human capital. The final decision of the hierarchy must therefore be perceived as fair, i.e., it cannot be made except under the due process. But this takes time and a lot of administrative energies. Hence, radical changes of policies and of leading personnel, and even more so bankruptcies, are likely to be very rare affairs at the best of times. More likely they will not take place at all. And if they do, the real cause may not be economics, but politics. In any case, a large hierarchy is incapable of carrying out the tasks of the capital market: it cannot bankrupt firms, except under very rare circumstances, and it will have difficulty changing the management on economic grounds. This leads directly to the soft budget constraint, as is argued in the next section.

2. The Soft Budget Constraint

Section 1 has argued that the planner in a socialist economy, lacking an external capital market, will find it very difficult to dissolve firms or even to effect radical changes of management, hence of policy. If in fact ailing enterprises cannot easily be weeded out, they must be allowed to continue their existence and must therefore be supported financially. This is the origin of the SBC. In a market economy composed of independently owned firms, special efforts are required to avoid insolvency when the cash flow is negative and liquid resources have been exhausted. An independent firm may be bankrupted by the very disinclination of credit suppliers to roll it over in times of financial need. When the same situation confronts a publicly owned firm, the decision to close down, to cease operations, requires a special effort. As long as this decision is not taken, the firm continues to exist and may continue operations without any change of course. In other words, the financial support of the firm continues to be provided by the parent institution in spite of the drain on its resources. The connection is not restricted to socialist economies: in the case of any larger organization, the winding up of operations of any of its parts, be it a plant or a division, is subject to an internal decision of the firm. Likewise in the case of the socialist enterprise, a positive decision on bankruptcy is required by its superiors, and this, as was argued in the previous section, is not likely to be forthcoming. Instead, an automatic supply of funds may come from the banking organizations: these have to supply all needed liquidity, because they have no right to bankrupt a firm by starving it of cash. The more complex forms of support (subsidies or price changes, cheap credits, stock purchases, etc.) require conscious organizational policy. In the Soviet case some of it is built-in: the rule that prices should equal average costs makes it possible for the pricing authorities to raise prices when costs exceed receipts.

The most important aspect of the SBC is the incentive effect; the enterprise itself, its management and its workers, are aware of the existence of the soft budget constraint, and it is this awareness that molds their behavior. An organization certain that it cannot fail just because it is not covering its costs behaves differently from one that has to concentrate first and foremost on keeping financially afloat. It is the incentive effect of the soft budget constraint, namely the reduction in elasticity, which is the subject of the next section.

3. The Soft Budget Constraint and the Firm's Response Elasticity

The effect of the SBC on a firm's incentives and behavior depends upon its perception of the likelihood that sanctions – which are ordinarily the task of the capital market – will be exercised against it.

Suppose first that the firm's management believes that its standing in the bureaucracy depends only on its profitability, or that its existence may be endangered if it slips into the red. In this case it would follow a rule of thumb that aimed at maximizing profits, provided that enough consumption on the job can be taken by the staff, i.e., that the level of effort exerted by the personnel not be excessive. The only capital market service that the firm is missing is the advice on policy and management provided by its valuation relative to that of competing firms. In other words, we have no outside opinion on the efficacy of the policy rules used by the firm. If, however, the firm's staff adopts the more natural belief that the firm is subject to a SBC and that it cannot founder, incentives are very strongly affected. The remuneration of the personnel now depends on those who soften the budget, i.e., on the whims of the hierarchical superiors: they will have to provide some other desiderata of the superior, which is not likely to be profits. The various groups of employees are now likely to collude together to divide among themselves some consumption on the job. The firm ceases to aim at profit as a maximand.

The colluding parties will have an unwritten agreement among them on conditions of work. Changes in hierarchical routines, in work assignments, or in their authority become substantial operations once the maintenance of bureaucratic peace becomes a paramount target of the firm. The adaptation of the mix of outputs, even more so of the mix of inputs, are more complex and difficult to engineer in the bureaucratic environment than in the economics textbooks. When the mix of outputs is changed, labor and machines have to be shifted around and implicit contracts have to be recontracted. When labor is moved, old habits are broken and friendships disrupted. All of this makes for disutility to veteran workers. In particular, a decrease in labor inputs causes frictions and exertion on the part of management; an increase in labor inputs requires new investments in specific human capital, in training the new recruits. These efforts will not easily be taken if their expected effect, some gain in profits, is only of secondary importance. In other words, the firm's price elasticity of both demand and supply declines. The price change required to bring supply and demand into balance increases. The use of prices to clear the market leads to very wide price volatility.

The effect of the lower price elasticity on the hierarchy are discussed in the next section.

4. Low Response Elasticity and Centralized Allocation

The replacement of the market by administrative allocation can be blamed directly on the lowered price elasticity of the enterprises. The higher price volatility, which is now required for market clearing, is unpopular for two reasons. The first one is political: price volatility or frequent price changes make the planning of purchases more complex and are, therefore, disliked by most consumers. Furthermore, price volatility also means that maintaining a balanced budget for all enterprises is more laborious and the work of the bureaucracy in its support of the SBC becomes more complex. Firms' profits become highly variable, but not in a manner which provides information on the relative efficiency of the various enterprises. When the profits of a firm turn negative, subsidies have to be provided if the firm is not to be bankrupted; when they become too positive, it may be thought necessary to siphon them off. The relative superiority of market allocation over administrative allocation declines, and the temptation to use quantitative targets and limits rather than prices as market clearing tools becomes irresistible.

Hungarian experience can be seen in this light: prices were allowed a fairly free rein after 1968. By 1972, some firms became very unprofitable, mainly large low-flexibility firms, whose continued existence was never in doubt. The hierarchy felt compelled to stop the "excessive" freedom of prices, and control market imbalances by direct – though informal – signals to the firms. These consisted of both informal messages to the firms, suggesting certain output levels for deficit products, and the general rule of "responsibility to supply", i.e., an informal understanding that firms who were customary suppliers of certain commodities were responsible for providing their customary clients with their reasonable needs. There was, in effect, renewed, though invisible, target fixing. Enterprises colluded with their superiors and obeyed these targets, which were not sanctioned by any written law.

5. Conclusion: What Remains of Market Socialism?

The aims of market socialism are many, but those that interest us here can be put in two groups, decentralization and equality. The former requires a debureaucratized economy, with enterprises free from central coercion, free to take their own initiatives. Equality requires the exclusion of private ownership of productive assets, which may lead to inequality in both assets and incomes, hence of consumption, and a difference in power – the aspect that interested Marx most. The message of this paper is that these two are in conflict: the exclusion of private property excludes the services of the capital market, and the hierarchy cannot function as its proxy. Instead, it softens the firm's budget constraint. The enterprises are aware that their budget constraint is soft, that they do not stand to gain much by higher profits nor lose much when profits slip. They become dependent on the hierarchy, reduce their sensitivity to price changes and make the control of costs a secondary objective. Their superiors are forced into using prices to balance budgets rather than markets, and use quantity targets as means of balancing the market.

This has an obvious and deleterious effect on current operations, on costs and on quality. Equally pernicious is the effect on the dynamics of the firm. Investments are channeled into projects that may help production target fulfillment, with little consideration for costs. There is no interest in new cost saving processes, and new products are introduced only if the superiors press the enterprise into producing them. Old physical capital is not discarded, because it can be maintained at high cost of maintenance workers at non-storming time and may be of use at storming time. Human capital is poorly invested: engineers have no cost consciousness, no quality consciousness, but are concerned with keeping the processes working at whatever the cost.

6. Why is the Plan Incompatible With the Market?*

Larissa Popkova-Pijasheva

I do not presume to deny the possibility of planning the activities of a private or a state firm. Any entrepreneur calculates both his expected expenditures and his profits, which enables him to make strategic decisions with regard to investments, updating, rationalization, or production cuts. Neither do I underestimate the part the state plays in regulating economic life, leveling cyclical fluctuations and mitigating the consequences of crises, providing for insurance against unemployment, and other steps it takes that indirectly influence the economic process through a mechanism of credit – monetary, tax, and social policy.

Neither do I claim that the state, under conditions of a market economy, is unable to plan its budget and distribute its revenue according to a plan approved and ratified by the Congress. Nor do I call into question the state's participation in private, mixed, or state-controlled long-term research projects of technological development. Neither do I rule out the possibility of indicative planning, of making up a plan-prognosis based on market analysis. All these forms of planning and state management coexist in the economic life of the market system and fulfill their stabilizing, regulating, or orienting function.

The present article deals with none of these forms of planning. It postulates that the idea of planning the entire economic process is incompatible either with the market institutions of property and power or with the market mechanism of regulating the economic processes.

The Incompatibility of Central Planning and the Market System

The main point is that the five-year plans of economic development either with monthly, quarterly, or yearly specification or without it, which are sent

* From "Why is the Plan Incompatible With the Market?," *Annals*, 507, January 1990. Copyright (c) Sage Publications, Inc. Reprinted by permission of Sage Publications Inc. Some footnotes omitted.

from the top to the bottom as binding directives, are incompatible with market-economy institutions.

It is either the State Planning Committee, the State Price-Control Committee, and the State Committee for Labor and Social Problems, or it is the stock exchange, the labor and capital markets, the joint-stock company, and so on. The two camps cannot actually coexist within the framework of a single mixed-management mechanism. Neither is it possible to solve specific socioeconomic problems under conditions of the existing centralization, which is treated as a rather abstract conception of society at large. And despite the fact that the planned character of the economy along with all-encompassing centralization have always been regarded as the primary virtues and advantages of socialism by our mainstream theorists, it is precisely the absence of a systematic character in activities, the disproportion in economic life, and the lack of centered effort in confronting such global issues as, for instance, ecology that can be thought of almost as inherent in the socialist system. Wherever environmental problems are put in care of society as a whole, whose noble aim is common well-being, the factory chimneys will emit more smoke and nuclear accidents will be more frequent than in a society of market "anarchy" and individual responsibility, in which there is a person responsible for any smoking chimney or any nuclear incident, a person who would pay for his or her carelessness both financially and juridically.

Reasons for Plan-Market Incompatibility

There are a number of reasons why the socialist planning system is incompatible with market institutions.

Valuation

The central principle of distribution in a planned system is "according to labor performed": "From each according to his ability, to each according to his work." But the very concept of socially useful labor in a socialist economy is different in principle from that accepted by economic theory in general. Socially useful labor is not that which has been acknowledged by the market and paid for by the consumer, but that which has been performed to fulfill the plan.

In a planned economy, any labor aimed at fulfilling the plan is regarded as socially useful and has to be paid for. The usefulness of a manufactured product is recognized in advance by the very fact of entering it in a plan. Is the mechanism of determining the social usefulness of output beforehand compatible with the market system, which does not acknowledge the result of production until it is sold and paid for by the consumer? It certainly is not. Usefulness can be determined either by the very fact of entering a product in the plan in advance or after the realization of the output, but never in combination.

Why not? Primarily because the planned economy presupposes full employment; it guarantees remuneration of any work performed by anyone employed irrespective of the result of his or her labor, that is, of its social usefulness. If one has fulfilled the plan task, one receives one's wages in certain cases, even bonuses. If one has not, one receives only wages, which are guaranteed by law.

As soon as the system is restructured and wages are paid after the realization of output, a certain number of workers are inevitably left out of the production process, since the planned economy presupposes a good deal of low-quality commodities without demand. As soon as the market mechanism of evolution and selection starts working, all excess labor will be automatically released; this mechanism is only too well known to the Western reader. But this will inevitably run counter to the proclaimed basic principle of full employment and that of every worker having his or her place of work and minimum wages guaranteed. Where labor is remunerated according to its final results, and thus unprofitable enterprises lose their position on the market through bankruptcy, ruin, merger, and so forth, we inevitably face the problem of some alternative that is, outside the state sector uses of labor and capital. That would be tantamount to the elimination of the state's monopoly of property, which has always been regarded as one of the gains of socialism. This would raise the question of transition to some other pattern of property and power, namely, the market, or capitalist, pattern.

Command versus economic freedom

The second reason why the market economy principle is incompatible with the planned-economy principle is that the directives in the form of plan tasks have to be executed and fulfilled no matter whether they come down in the old way, as plan tasks, or in the new form, as state orders. In both cases they are subject to fulfillment, for in the USSR a plan is a law approved by the Council of Ministers. Besides this, quotas for raw materials, equipment, and machinery are adjusted to and come down together with these plans. The latter practice accounts for the fact that enterprises find it profitable to receive a 100 percent state order. This is so because the absence of an open market of wholesale trade and the actual impossibility of purchasing the needed raw materials and matériel either on the internal or on the external market, deprive the enterprises of the possibility to make up a portfolio of orders that they find profitable.

No entrepreneur, no firm under the conditions of a market economy, would submit to state planning. No proprietor would obey the directives as regards production and sale or would tolerate being told what range of goods he should manufacture and what their quality should be. The most he would do would be to include the order in his portfolio and avail himself of the advantages the customer would thereby give him. But he would never let any such customer interfere with the firm's financial matters, its commercial strategy, or its relations with other suppliers and customers. The producer reserves the right to turn down any state order if he finds it wasteful or simply unprofitable. The market economy, with its principle of private property, is beyond nationwide state planning, no matter how much the ruling circles wish it were under their control.

This is not the case with the planned economy where there is no private property in the means of production and where enterprises have the right neither to develop a commercial strategy of their own nor to have any commercial secrets, not even to appropriate their own profits. In the socialist economy, it is the state that plans the economic process for every five-year period with annual, quarterly, and monthly quotas and sends down the binding plan directives to all branches and ministries, which then distribute these directives among individual enterprises. The ministry reserves the right to correct the plan tasks: to raise plan norms for one enterprise and to lower the norms of another, that is, to make some transfers, so to speak, depending on the specific economic and financial situation. But no enterprise is allowed either to conclude a contract unless it is sanctioned by the ministry – or to turn down a plan task. The forthcoming reform envisages a certain compromise in this respect. Not until the problem of a wholesale trade market is solved, however, can the problem be really solved.

In the absence of economic freedom – of the right to dispose of one's own earnings, to determine one's own commercial strategy, to make up one's own portfolio of orders, to have a free choice of suppliers and customers, to purchase all that is needed on the domestic or foreign market, and to fix prices according to the state of the market – there can only be such a form of self-supporting management – self-financing – that may be defined in terms of "it would be desirable . . ." or "we should . . ."

As long as an enterprise that does not have these freedoms – which are inherent in the market economy – is given binding state orders, or plans; as long as all normative indices – the fixing of the wages fund, the rationing of employment and specification of rates of productivity growth, and even regulation of profitability level – are centrally planned; and as long as the domestic wholesale commerce market is not open – which means that enterprises are not allowed to buy raw materials, matériel, equipment, machinery, and all kinds of technological know-how on the foreign market – a switch from plan-based administrative management to economic methods that could replace the former is impossible.

It is either the plan or the market. Just as a plan cannot be a little bit a market plan, a market cannot be a little bit planned or an enterprise a little bit free. Either prices call the tune – that is, credits, taxes and monetary privileges, or sanctions are used by the state as levers of regulation – or the State Planning Committee shapes our economic life according to its science-based conceptions, planning our needs and demands as well as bringing them into correlation with actual possibilities. There is no third way.

The plan is incompatible with the market system because there is no actual possibility of calculating the right prices and of correlating them with a science-based plan.

. . . There is a popular belief in our official circles – including those of experts – that, without any violation of socialist principles – state property, controlled prices, full employment, and so on – we can inject into our economy some elements of market relations as just a working tool that would in no way affect or change the institutional forms of the social system. The market cannot be a working tool, however, unless the economy is demonopolized. Wherever there is monopoly, there can be no market since there is neither competition nor "struggle" for the consumer. The principle is valid for any economic system.

The socialist economy, which has done away with private property and private enterprises or companies, freed all its enterprises from any competition. Certainly, if we give the situation a strictly scientific analysis, we have to admit that the planned socialist economy may be regarded as a particular case of market economy with underdeveloped institutions of commodity-money exchange, an entirely monopolized structure, a specific – monopolized – market with fixed prices, and a very peculiar fierce socialist competition for state limits, funds, state subsidies, and a characteristic socialist competitiveness of enterprises for diplomas, badges, and titles of shock workers.

This somehow blurs the distinction – a very fundamental one – between the two systems: one that is market liberal – that is, capitalist, in Weber's view of capitalism as a society with free competition and private entrepreneurship – and the other, totally monopolistic – that is, socialist, in Marx's conception of socialism as a society with nationalized ownership, confining more and more the sphere of commodity-money relations, which are supposed to die out in the long run. I do not see any justification for such an identification.

The socialist market may be represented as a mirror image of the capitalist market. In the latter, goods are in search of consumers. In the former, the buyer seeks the goods. On the capitalist market, supply, as a rule, exceeds demand by far. On the socialist market, the very opposite is true demand nearly always exceeds supply, which accounts for shortages, deficits, long lines, and the black market.

In my opinion, free price formation is a *sine qua non* of any market system. The self-financing system will not be viable if the state reserves the right to fix prices, to dictate them to both producer and consumer, and if it goes out of its way to neutralize the black marketeers who play the part of regulator of what has always been spontaneously regulated on the market. Free pricing is the primary and most fundamental precondition for a switch to a new economy; prices must be determined on the market as a result of the interaction of demand and supply, which reflects any marketing and structural fluctuations in production and responds to any changes in consumer demand. But, clearly, all this runs counter to the interests of the State Planning Committee, which sees its function as the planning of production on the basis of calculated, stable prices. In other words, it is either the market or the State Planning Committee. We cannot get away from this dilemma.

State versus private capital

Another reason why the plan is incompatible with the market is that state capital can in no way successfully compete with private capital. The practice of both capitalist and socialist economies witnesses to the fact that private capital is more profitable and more efficient than state capital. Private capital has these qualities for the simple reason that it is more flexible and more mobile and because it admits of all kinds of risks as regards its investment. State capital and private capital can hardly coexist because the deployment of private entrepreneurship would inevitably exclude any state production from economic life, and a number of people would have not only to forgo their ideological principles but also to leave their cushy jobs in the hierarchical system of administrative power. Under conditions of fair competition – that is, where the state and private investors are on an equal footing – it is private capital that will inevitably call the tune. If we opt for this solution, all our socialist gains will fall into oblivion. Instead we shall have gains of other kinds: shop windows will be crammed with goods, all sorts of services will flourish, and food shortages will be a thing of the past, while our mode of life will become easier and more comfortable. The public health system will be much more adequate, young people will be interested in getting good training because many new channels and ways of social advancement will have been opened for them. But this general progress will have nothing to do with nationalized ownership, or with the socialist law of planned and proportional development, or with free public consumption funds, or even with other so-called achievements proclaimed by the socialist ideologists.

What makes our ideologists, who have always failed to plan the country's economic life, try so hard to develop a model of a mixed economy and thereby solve an extremely complicated economic problem? . . . The answer is simple. The plan – the law – is an expression of the omnipotence of our party, which exercises unlimited control over all economic life. Giving up centralized management and the planning system would be tantamount to giving up political power. That is why perestroika ideologists go out of their way to try and make the incompatible compatible: to leave intact the plan-based centralized principle and at the same time to open the market; to introduce freedom of trade, thereby attaining acceleration of rates of development, but not allow the private traders to enrich themselves. They are ready to grant the right of private enterprise and initiative to all, but not to permit any social differentiation or inequality in the distribution of earnings.

What is the main function performed by the market? It is that of distribution. By reflecting in prices supply-demand relations, the market constantly aims at a balance in which all output would meet its consumer and would thus be recognized by society. Under conditions of the planned economy this market function – performed in the market system quite by itself and quite efficiently is performed by an inflated apparatus whose sole *raison d'etre* is to determine consumption norms and allocation quotas. A transition to the market system would entail the liquidation of this bureaucratic administrative apparatus, which distributes both material and spiritual goods according to standards that it considers to be the correct ones.

The plan is backed up by the party *apparat*, which has at its disposal the "common stock"; the market, for its part, plays into the hands of private traders: individuals, cooperators, craftsmen, traders, and entrepreneurs. Peaceful emulation or fair competition between the two is out of the question because the state holds full monopoly and state business has all priority rights, while individual traders and cooperators are in no way protected by any law ensured by the state and are, moreover, deprived of any organization-al or political power. A peaceful coexistence of the two is unbelievable: like that of a wolf and a lamb. As the wolf grows hungry it will devour the lamb without a second's hesitation. Thus, once the private trader or cooperator has realized he is an owner, he will claim his right to power, a right that is, anyway, more justified and legal than that usurped by the party elite. The wolf will eat up the lamb. The horns and legs of the poor victim will be displayed as a reminder of the abortive second New Economic Policy – abortive because the plan is incompatible with the market.

Either our society develops along some hypothetical lines devised by the mainstream socialist theorists as planned laws sanctified by socialist ideals even if it means being chronically hungry, cold, and badly organized, or it gives up all plan-oriented ideology and state-minded psychology and makes way for the power of the market, that is, the producer – both economic and political power. For a system in which those who construct are different from the ones who enrich themselves and profit by running the economy is not viable. If the market, which entails economic liberalism and classical bourgeois pluralism as a basis of a democratic social structure, comes to power, there will be no question of calculating another five-year plan and of sending it down to the bottom. No proprietor-entrepreneur would put up with such an infringement of his economic freedom and his commercial initiative, which always presupposes certain individual risks and personal responsibility but which, however, promises profits in the long run.

Viewed in this light, the plan seems to be incompatible with the market. Economic liberalism and planned centralism would never form an intermin-gling homogeneous whole. Wherever the State Planning Committee is the manager and wherever the Council of Ministers approves the plan, which *ipso facto* becomes a law, market relations – economic liberalism and freedom of enterprise – simply cannot take root. For more than seventy years, we witnessed planned prices bringing unceasing anarchy into the economic process, thereby disturbing all economic proportions, making for a permanent imbalance in practically every link of the economic system, and resulting in an everlasting contradiction between the economic interests of both large and small enterprises in agriculture, industry, and services. Just as Diocletian's edict on prices or the decree on limited prices issued by the French revolu-tionaries resulted in severe punishment, confinement, and the death penalty, so the Soviet decrees on agricultural prices have cost us several million human lives.

That was the case wherever and whenever the state interfered in pricing, thereby forcing some people to sell and coercing other people to consume. For wherever price formation is done by centralization methods, commodity shortages, on the one hand, and overstocking, on the other, are closely associated.

Private Property, Initiative and Command

Surplus of goods coupled with acute shortage: such a state of affairs never resulted in anything positive. Due to the fact that the "correlation of social forces" in this country has made it possible to go on with what we started in 1917, it is only natural that we have come to a "purely collective ownership," which has been characterized by General Secretary M. Gorbachev as a property that "seems to have become no one's." Steps have been taken to restore to life private ownership and individual handicrafts, to broaden the sphere of small services and build a network of cooperatives that are based on both private ownership and private capital. Emancipation of prices – that is, a switch to market pricing – will be the *sine qua non* in implementing this program. If not, private commercial activities will be rather short-lived owing to several objective factors:

- lack of freedom to sell raw materials, materials, equipment, and machinery as one thinks best;
- lack of a right to free trade; and
- lack of necessary stimuli and incentives for efficient and productive work owing to the chronic contradiction between prices and economic interests.

How is it possible to inject market competition into the planned economy? How does one make planned price formation compatible with market pricing? How does one realize the social-democratic principle "competition – as far as possible; planning – as far as necessary," which was designed for the market economy based on principles of budget planning introduced into it, an indicative form of planning that is in no way binding for any entrepreneur whatsoever? If, and only if, we give up state planning through directives, denationalize property, organize private enterprises – as cooperatives or joint-stock companies, or firms, or any other form – provided they enjoy complete autonomy and may stake their own real capital. If, and only if, we do away with centralized distribution of funds, the state monopoly over appropriation and distribution of earnings, the system of centralized public investments, and so forth. Until we come to realize that, as F. Hayek has said, "anarchic, separate, uncoordinated efforts of individuals are able to bring about a complicated ramified economic structure in the long run," any reforming steps will take us nowhere. Unless individual energy and initiative cast off the fetters of administrative management, we shall see no raising of economic well-being. We have no other way to ensure growth and solve the food problem.

Are we ripe for action? Private cooperative property, individual labor activity, family contracts, privately owned farms, joint-stock property, and some other items of the *perestroika* program are arguments in favor of the market model. Time will show whether the switch will be radical and consistent enough.

Environmental Protection and Economic Systems

In conclusion, there is one more question of paramount importance. Was it absolutely necessary for humankind to proceed along a path on which smoking chimneys and accident-prone nuclear power stations more and more disturb the ecological balance and damage the environment? I do not presume the liberty to judge, but it seems that humanity has had no other way of feeding itself. There is no alternative. We either limit the birthrate by the conditions of natural sustenance or introduce some new, ecologically harmful, self-reproducing technologies. The more complicated and the more ramified the economic process is, the higher are the expenses of reproduction. The planned system is both less efficient and less profitable than the market economy, and thus neither is it so well equipped for environmental protection. The ecological calamities for which our country is responsible cannot but corroborate my central thesis.

PART II

THE LURE OF THE MARKET

In both Eastern Europe and the former Soviet Union, intellectuals and reformers often view market capitalism with a kind of awe. Here is a system in which individuals act primarily to benefit themselves, yet they generate a level of national wealth that the "rational" centrally-planned economies have been unable to match. In this section, we take a closer look at market capitalism. How, exactly, does a market system work? What are its essential features? Why has it performed so well in some areas – growth, allocative efficiency, technological innovation – and so poorly in others – most notably, equity?

It is surprising that so much of what we know today about the free-market system was understood by Adam Smith in 1776. In this short selection from *The Wealth of Nations*, Smith argues that self-interest is the engine that drives the economy toward the social good. He begins by noting that within the animal kingdom, only human beings have a "propensity" to exchange commodities with one another. But this exchange takes place in a particular way: by appealing to each other's self-interest. And it is through self-interest – through the desire to better our standard of living – that we are led to specialize in one particular activity, and to learn to do it well. Hence, a "division of labor" arises naturally in market societies, which, in turn, generates the highest possible level of production for the nation as a whole. In this way, we are guided as if "led by an invisible hand" to promote the public good, even though this is not our intention. Indeed, a conscious effort to promote the public interest – as is frequently attempted by governments – will often result in waste and inefficiency, and thus work against the public good. Therefore, government should restrict itself to three functions: national defense, enactment and enforcement of laws, and provision of certain public goods and services, largely social infrastructure.

In "What Markets Do," Lipsey, et al., provide a more modern, operative description of market capitalism. Like Smith, they show how self-interested individuals can help bring about the public good, in this case, unintentionally creating allocative efficiency. Their exposition stresses the role of profits and losses in shifting resources from place to place, in order to best serve consumer desires. They conclude with a list of advantages of using markets rather than central planning to allocate resources: the enormous simplification of information requirements, the rapid development of new technologies, the prevention of waste and inefficiency, the constant adjustment of production to the desires of consumers, and the decentralization of power into the hands of millions of individual producers and consumers.

It is precisely this last issue − the decentralization of power − that concerns Milton Friedman. In "Economic Freedom and Political Freedom," he argues that the free-market system itself is an indispensable requirement for individual freedom more broadly defined. This is for two primary reasons: (1) the economic freedoms found only in a free-market system − the freedom to decide where and how much to work, what to buy, what to produce, etc. − are themselves an important component of individual freedom; and (2) these same economic freedoms help sustain other, more political, components of individual freedom.

Focussing on the latter contention, Friedman argues that historically, market capitalism appears to be a necessary component of political democracy. Free markets also enable diverse preferences to coexist and take some power away from government which, by its nature, already concentrates too much power into too few hands. In Friedman's view, the key to preserving freedom is to limit the role of government to those social necessities that the private market cannot provide efficiently. But even here, he urges caution. We must always remember that one of the "costs" of government action is the restriction of individual freedom that accompanies it.

In the last two articles of this section, we turn to the goals of the economic transformation currently taking place in the newly-emerging economies. To what extent are former "central planners" prepared to embrace the market? The article "Man, Freedom, and Market" comes from the introduction to the well-publicized *500-day Plan for Transforming the Soviet Economy*. The plan was formulated by a working group commissioned by President Mikhail Gorbachev, although he rejected the final document in late 1990 in favor of a more gradual approach. Nevertheless, the plan remains a highly influential document. President Boris Yeltsin very early accepted it in principal as the guiding plan for the Russian Republic, and it reflects the thinking of a number of prominent Soviet economists. In "Man, Freedom, and Market", the working group clearly rejects the principals of central planning and fully embraces the essential features of market capitalism.

Finally, John Kenneth Galbraith offers a sober warning: that in their "Rush to Capitalism," the nations of Eastern Europe may be moving too far and too fast. Eastern European reformers rely too heavily on the advice of Western free-marketeers, who themselves have a distorted view of their own economies. These Western advisors downplay the role of the public sector in the success of their own free-market systems. Without severe restraints, market capitalism would be not only inhumane, but unsustainable. While Galbraith agrees that central planning has failed to deliver the goods and services people want and that a move toward the market is long overdue, he warns us of the dangers of moving too rapidly toward a market that is too free.

7. The Wealth of Nations

Adam Smith

Man's Disposition to Barter

[T]he propensity to truck, barter, and exchange one thing for another. . . is common to all men, and is to be found in no other race of animals, which seem to know neither this nor any other species of contracts. Nobody ever saw a dog make a fair and deliberate exchange of one bone for another with another dog. Nobody ever saw one animal by its gestures and natural cries signify to another, this is mine, that yours; I am willing to give this for that. When an animal wants to obtain something, either of a man or another animal, it has no other means of persuasion but to gain the favour of those whose service it requires. A puppy fawns upon its dam, and a spaniel endeavors by a thousand attractions to engage the attention of its master who is at dinner, when it wants to be fed by him. Man sometimes uses the same arts with its brethren, and when he has no other means of engaging them to act according to his inclinations, endeavors by every servile and fawning attention to obtain their good will. He has not time, however, to do this upon every occasion. In civilized society, he stands all the time in need of the cooperation and assistance of great multitudes, while his whole life is scarce sufficient to gain the friendship of a few persons.

Pursuit of Self-Interest Leads to the Social Good

In almost every other race of animals each individual, when it is grown up to maturity, is entirely independent, and in its natural state has occasion for the assistance of no other living creature. But man has almost constant occasion for the help of his brethren, and it is in vain for him to expect it from their benevolence only. He will be more likely to prevail if he can interest their self-love in his favour, and show them that it is for their own advantage to do for him what he requires of them. Whoever offers to another a bargain of any kind, proposes to do this. Give me that which I want, and you shall have this which you want, is the meaning of every such offer; and it is in this manner that we obtain from one another the far greater part of those good offices which we stand in need of. It is not from the benevolence of the butcher, the brewer, or the baker, that we expect our dinner, but from their regard to their own interest. We address ourselves, not to their humanity but to their self-love, and never talk to them of our own necessities but of their advantages.

Nobody but a beggar chooses to depend chiefly upon the benevolence of his fellow citizens. Even a beggar does not depend upon it entirely. The charity of well-disposed people, indeed, supplies him with the whole fund of his subsistence. But though this principle ultimately provides him with all the necessities of life which he has occasion for, it neither does nor can provide him with them as he has occasion for them. The greater part of his wants are supplied in the same manner as those of other people, by treaty, by barter, and by purchase. With the money which one man gives him he purchases food. The old clothes which another bestows upon him he exchanges for other old clothes which suit him better, or for lodging, or for food, or for money, with which he can buy either food, clothes, or lodging, as he has occasion.

As it is by treaty, by barter, and by purchase, that we obtain from one another the greater part of those mutual good offices which we stand in need of, so it is this same trucking disposition which originally gives occasion to the division of labour. In a tribe of hunters or shepherds a particular person makes bows and arrows, for example, with more readiness and dexterity than any other. He frequently exchanges them for cattle or for venison with his companions; and he finds at last that he can in this manner get more cattle and venison than if he himself went to the field to catch them. From a regard to his own interest, therefore, the making of bows and arrows grows to be his chief business, and he becomes a sort of armourer. Another excels in making the frames and covers of their little huts or moveable houses. He is accustomed to be of use in this way to his neighbours, who reward him in the same manner with cattle and with venison, till at last he finds it his interest to dedicate himself entirely to this employment, and to become a sort of house carpenter. In the same manner, a third becomes a smith or a brazier; a fourth a tanner or dresser of hides or skins, the principal part of the clothing of savages. And, thus, the certainty of being able to exchange all that surplus part of the produce of his own labour, which is over and above his own consumption, for such parts of the produce of other men's labour as he may have occasion for, encourages every man to apply himself to a particular occupation, and to cultivate and bring to perfection whatever talent or genius he may possess for that particular species of business.

Exchange as a Necessary Prerequisite of Efficient Division of Labor

The difference of natural talents in different men is, in reality, much less than we are aware of; and the very different genius which appears to distinguish men of different professions, when grown up to maturity, is not upon many occasions so much the cause, as the effect of the division of labour. . . . [D]ifferent tribes of animals, however, though all of the same species, are of scarce any use to one another. The strength of the mastiff is not in the least supported either by the swiftness of the greyhound, or by the sagacity of the spaniel, or by the docility of the shepherd's dog. The effects of those different geniuses and talents, for want of the power or disposition to barter and exchange, cannot be brought into a common stock, and do not in the least contribute to the better accommodation and convenience of the species. Each animal is still obliged to support and defend itself, separately and independently, and derives no sort of advantage from that variety of talents with which nature has distinguished its fellows. Among men, on the contrary, the most dissimilar geniuses are of use to one another; the different produces of their respective talents, by the general disposition to truck, barter and exchange, being brought, as it were, into a common stock, where every man may purchase whatever part of the produce of other men's talents he has occasion for.

The Invisible Hand

In that rude state of society in which there is no division of labor, in which exchanges are seldom made, and in which every man provides everything for himself, it is not necessary that any stock should be accumulated or stored up beforehand, in order to carry on the business of the society. Every man endeavors to supply by his own industry his own occasional wants as they occur. When he is hungry, he goes to the forest to hunt; when his coat is worn out, he clothes himself with the skin of the first large animal he kills; and when his hut begins to go to ruin, he repairs it, as well as he can, with the trees and the turf that are nearest it.

But when the division of labor has once been thoroughly introduced, the produce of one man's own labor can supply but a small part of his occasional wants. The far greater part of them are supplied by the produce of other men's labor, which he purchases with the produce, or what is the same thing, with the price of the produce of his own.

Every individual is continually exerting himself to find out the most advantageous employment for whatever capital he can command. It is his own advantage, indeed, and not that of society, which he has in view. But the study of his own advantage naturally, or rather, necessarily leads him to prefer that employment which is most advantageous to the society.

He generally, indeed, neither intends to promote the public interest nor knows how much he is promoting it. By preferring the support of domestic to that of foreign industry, he intends only his own security; and by directing that industry in such a manner as its produce may be of the greatest value, he intends only his own gain, and he is in this, as in many other cases, led by an invisible hand to promote an end which was no part of his intention. Nor is it always the worse for the society that it was no part of it. By pursuing his own interest, he frequently promotes that of the society more effectually that when he really intends to promote it. I have never known much good done by those who affected to trade for the public good. It is an affectation, indeed, not very common among merchants, and very few words need be employed in dissuading them from it.

The Functioning of Markets

The market price of every particular commodity is regulated by the proportion between the quantity which is actually brought to the market and the demand of those who are willing to pay the natural price of the commodity.

. . . [W]hen the quantity of any commodity which is brought to market falls short of the effectual demand, all those who are willing to pay the whole value of the rent, wages, and profit which must be paid in order to bring it thither cannot be supplied with the quantity which they want. Rather that want it altogether, some of them will be willing to give more. A competition will immediately begin among them, and the market price will rise more or less above the natural price, according as either the greatness of the deficiency or the wealth and wanton luxury of the competitors happen to animate more or less the eagerness of the competition.

. . . [W]hen the quantity brought to market exceeds the effectual demand, it cannot be all sold to those who are willing to pay the whole value of the rent, wages, and profit which must be paid in order to bring it thither. Some part must be sold to those who pay less, and the low price which they give for it must reduce the price of the whole.

On the Role of Government

Great nations are never impoverished by private, though they sometimes are by public, prodigality and misconduct. The whole, or almost the whole, public revenue is in most countries employed in maintaining unproductive hands. Such are the people who compose a numerous and splendid court, a great ecclesiastical establishment, great fleets and armies, who in time of peace produce nothing, and in time of war acquire nothing which can compensate the expense of maintaining them, even while the war lasts. Such people, as they themselves produce nothing, are all maintained by the produce of other men's labour.

When all systems either of preference or of restraint are taken away, the obvious and simple system of natural liberty establishes itself of its own accord. Every man, as long as he does not violate the laws of justice, is left perfectly free to pursue his own interest his own way and to bring both his industry and capital into competition with those of any other man or order of men. The sovereign is completely discharged from a duty, in the attempting to perform which he must always be exposed to innumerable delusions and for the proper performance of which no human wisdom or knowledge could ever be sufficient - the duty of superintending the industry of private people and of directing it toward the employments most suitable to the interest of the society. According to the system of natural liberty, the sovereign has only three duties to attend to; three duties of great importance, indeed, but plain and intelligible to common understandings: first, the duty of protecting the society from the violence and invasion of other independent societies; secondly, the duty of protecting, as far as possible, every member of the society from the injustice or oppression of every other member of it, or the duty of establishing an exact administration of justice; and thirdly, the duty of erecting and maintaining certain public works and certain public institutions.

8. What Markets Do[*]

Richard G. Lipsey, Peter O. Steiner, Douglas D. Purvis and Paul N. Courant

How Markets Coordinate

Any economy consists of thousands upon thousands of individual markets. There are markets for agricultural goods, for manufactured goods, and for consumers' services; there are markets for intermediate goods such as steel and pig iron, which are outputs of some industries and inputs of others; there are markets for raw materials such as iron ore, trees, bauxite, and copper; there are markets for land and for thousands of different types of labor; there are markets in which money is borrowed and in which securities are sold. An economy is not a series of markets functioning in isolation but an interlocking system in which an occurrence in one market affects many others.

Any change, such as an increase in demand for a product, requires many further changes and adjustments. Should the quantity produced change? If it should, by how much and by what means? Any change in the output of one product will generally require changes in other markets and will start a chain of adjustments. Someone or something must decide what is to be produced, how, and by whom, and what is to be consumed and by whom.

The essential characteristic of the market system is that its coordination occurs in an unplanned, decentralized way. Millions of people make millions of independent decisions concerning production and consumption every day. Most of these decisions are not motivated by a desire to contribute to the social good or to make the whole economy work well but by fairly immediate considerations of self-interest. The price system coordinates these decentralized decisions, making the whole system fit together and respond to the wishes of individual consumers and producers.

The basic insight into how a market system works is that decentralized, private decision makers, acting in their own interests, respond to such signals as the prices of what they buy and sell. Economists have long emphasized price as a signaling device. When a commodity becomes scarce, its free-

---

[*] Excerpted from *Economics*, 9th. Edition. Copyright (c) 1990 by Harper and Row, Publishers, Inc. Reprinted by Permission of HarperCollins Publishers.

market price rises. Firms and households that use the commodity are led to economize on it and to look for alternatives. Firms that produce it are led to produce more of it. When a shortage occurs in a market, price rises and profits develop; when a glut occurs, price falls and losses develop. These are *signals*, for all to see, that arise from the overall conditions of market supply and demand.

The Role of Profits and Losses

Although the free-market economy often is described as the *price system*, the basic engine that drives the economy is economic profits. Except when there is monopoly, economic profits and losses are symptoms of *disequilibrium*, and they are the driving force in the adaptation of the economy to change.

A rise in demand or a fall in production costs creates profits for that commodity's producers. Profits make an industry attractive to new investment. They signal that there are too few resources devoted to that industry. In search of these profits, more resources enter the industry, increasing output and driving down price, until profits are driven to zero. A fall in demand or a rise in production costs creates losses. Losses signal the reverse and an excess of resources devoted to the industry. Resources will leave the industry until those left behind are no longer suffering losses.

The importance of profits and losses is that they set in motion forces that tend to move the economy toward a new equilibrium.

Individual households and firms respond to common signals according to their own best interests. There is nothing planned or intentionally coordinated about their actions, yet when, say, a shortage causes price to rise, individual buyers begin to reduce the quantities that they demand and individual firms begin to increase the quantities that they supply. As a result, the shortage begins to lessen. As it does, price begins to come back down, and profits are reduced. These signals in turn are seen and responded to by firms and households. Eventually, when the shortage has been eliminated, there are no profits to attract further increases in supply. The chain of adjustments to the original shortage is completed.

Notice that in the sequence of signal-response-signal-response no one has to foresee at the outset the final price and quantity, nor does any government agency have to specify who will increase production and who will decrease consumption. Some firms respond to the signals for "more output" by increasing production, and they keep on increasing production until the signals get weaker and weaker and finally disappear. Some buyers withdraw from the market when they think that prices are too high, and perhaps they reenter gradually, as prices become "more reasonable." Households and firms, responding to market signals, not to the orders of government bureaucrats, "decide" who will increase production and who will limit consumption. No one is forced to do something against his or her best judgment. Voluntary responses collectively produce the end result.

Because the economy is adjusting to shocks continuously, a snapshot of the economy at any given moment reveals substantial positive profits in some industries and substantial losses in others. A snapshot at another moment also will reveal windfall profits and losses, but their locations will be different.

The price system, like an invisible hand (Adam Smith's famous phrase), coordinates the responses of individual decision makers who seek only their own self-interests. Because they respond to signals that reflect market conditions, their responses are coordinated without any conscious planning.

Coordination in the Absence of Perfect Competition

To say that the price system coordinates is not to imply that it always leads to the results that perfect competition would produce. The price system coordinates responses even to prices that are "rigged" by monopolistic producers or that are altered by government controls. The signal-response process occurs in a price system even when the prices have not been determined in freely competitive markets.

When an international cartel of uranium producers decided to reduce production and raise the price of uranium, they created a shortage (and a fear of worse future shortages) among those electric utilities that depend on uranium to fuel nuclear power plants. The price of uranium shot up from under $10 per pound to over $40 in less than a year. This enormous price rise greatly increased efforts among producers outside the cartel to find more uranium and to increase their existing production by mining poorer grade ores previously considered too costly to mine.

The increases in production from these actions slowly began to ease the shortage. On the demand side, high prices and short supplies led some utilities to cancel the construction of planned nuclear power plants and to delay the construction of others. Such actions implied a long-run substitution of oil or coal for uranium. Only the fact that the OPEC cartel had also sharply raised the price of oil prevented an even more rapid reversal of the previous trend from oil to nuclear powered generators. With the prices of both uranium and oil quadrupling, the demand for coal increased sharply, and its price and production rose. Thus, the market mechanism generated adjustments to the relative prices of different fuels, even though some prices were set by cartels rather than by the free-market forces of supply and demand. It also set in motion reactions that placed limits on the power of the cartel.

The Case for the Market System

In presenting the case for free-market economies, economists have used two different approaches. One of these may be characterized as the formal defense. It is based upon showing that a free-market economy consisting of nothing but perfectly competitive industries would lead to an optimal allocation of resources.

The other approach is at least as old as Adam Smith and is meant to apply to market economies whether they are perfectly competitive or not. It is based on variations and implications of the theme that the market system is an effective coordinator of decentralized decision making. The case is intuitive in that it is not laid out in equations representing a complete formal model of an economy, but it does follow from some hard reasoning, and it has been subjected to much intellectual probing. What is the nature of this defense of the free market?

Flexible and Automatic Coordination

Defenders of the market economy argue that, compared with the alternatives, the decentralized market system is more flexible and leaves more scope for adaptation to change at any moment in time and for quicker adjustment over time.

Suppose, for example, that the price of oil rises. One household might prefer to respond by maintaining a high temperature in its house and economizing on its driving, while another might do the reverse. A third household might give up air conditioning instead. This flexibility can be contrasted with centralized control, which would force the same pattern on everyone, say by rationing heating oil and gasoline, by regulating permitted temperatures, and by limiting air conditioning to days when the temperature exceeded 80 degrees fahrenheit.

Furthermore, as conditions change over time, prices will change and decentralized decision makers can react continually. In contrast, government quotas, allocations, and rationing schemes are much more difficult to adjust. As a result, there are likely to be shortages and surpluses before adjustments are made. The great value of the market is that it provides automatic signals *as* a situation develops, so that all of the consequences of some major economic change do not have to be anticipated and allowed for by a body of central planners. Millions of adaptations to millions of changes in tens of thousands of markets are required every year, and it would be a Herculean task to anticipate and plan for them all.

A market system allows for coordination without *anyone* needing to understand how the whole system works. As Professor Thomas Schelling put it:

> The dairy farmer doesn't need to know how many people eat butter and how far away they are, how many other people raise cows, how many babies drink milk, or whether more money is spent on beer or milk. What he needs to know is the prices of different feeds, the characteristics of different cows, the different prices [for milk], the relative cost of hired labor and electrical machinery, and what his net earnings might be if he sold his cows and raised pigs instead.

It is, of course, an enormous advantage that all the producers and consumers of a country collectively can make the system operate without any one of them, much less all of them, having to understand how it works. Such a lack of knowledge becomes a disadvantage, however, when people have to vote on schemes for interfering with market allocation. This contrast lies at the heart of the intuitive argument in favor of market systems.

Stimulus to Innovation and Growth

Technology, tastes, and resource availability are changing all the time, in all economies. Twenty years ago there was no such thing as a personal computer or a digital watch. Front-wheel drive was a curiosity. Students carried their books in briefcases or in canvas bags that were anything but waterproof. Manuscripts only existed as hard copy, not as computer records. In order to change one word in a manuscript, one often had to retype every word on a page. Video cassettes did not exist. The next 20 years will surely also see changes great and small. New products and techniques will be devised to adapt to shortages, gluts, and changes in consumer demands.

In a market economy individuals risk their time and money in the hope of earning profits. While many fail, some succeed. New products and processes appear and disappear. Some are passing fads or have little impact; others become items of major significance. The market system works by trial and error to sort them out and allocates resources to what prove to be successful innovations.

In contrast, planners in more centralized systems have to guess which are going to be productive innovations or products that will be in demand. Planned growth may achieve wonders by permitting a massive effort in a chosen direction, but central planners also may guess wrong about the direction and put far too many eggs in the wrong basket or reject as unpromising something that will turn out to be vital. It is striking that the last decade has seen the two largest centrally planned economies in the world, the Soviet Union and mainland China, make increasing use of markets.

Relative Prices Reflect Relative Costs

A market system tends to drive prices toward the average total costs of production. When markets are close to perfectly competitive, this movement occurs quickly and completely; but even where there is substantial market power, new products and new producers respond to the lure of profits, and their output drives prices down toward the costs of production. . . . [M]arket choices are then made in the light of opportunity costs. Firms will choose methods that minimize their own cost of producing output, and in so doing automatically will minimize the opportunity cost of the resources that they use. Similarly, when households choose commodity A over commodity B, even though A uses resources of twice the total value of the resources used to produce B, they will have to pay the (difference in) price. They will only do so when they value A correspondingly more than B at the margin.

When relative prices reflect relative costs, producers and consumers use the nation's resources in a manner that is consistent with allocative efficiency.

Self-Correction of Disequilibrium

Equilibrium of the economic system is continually disrupted by change. If the economy does not "pursue" equilibrium, there would be little comfort in saying things would be bright indeed if only it reached equilibrium. (We all know someone who would have been a great surgeon if only he or she had gone to medical school.)

An important characteristic of the price system is its ability to set in motion forces that tend to correct disequilibrium.

To review the advantages of the price system in this respect, imagine operating without a market mechanism. Suppose that planning boards make all market decisions. The Board in Control of Men's Clothing hears that pleated shirts are all the rage in neighboring countries. It orders a certain proportion of clothing factories to make pleated shirts instead of the traditional men's dress shirt. Conceivably, the quantities of pleated shirts and traditional shirts produced could be just right, given shoppers' preferences. But what if the board guesses wrong and orders too many traditional shirts and not enough pleated shirts to be produced? Long lines would appear at pleated-shirt counters, while mountains of traditional shirts would pile up. Once the board sees the lines for pleated shirts, it could order a change in quantities produced. Meanwhile, it could store the extra traditional shirts for another season or ship them to a country with different tastes.

Such a system can correct an initial mistake, but it may prove inefficient in doing so. It may use a lot of resources in planning and administration that could instead be used to produce commodities. Further, many consumers may be greatly inconvenienced if the board is slow to correct its error. In such a system the members of the board may have no incentive to admit and correct a mistake quickly. Indeed, if the authorities do not like pleated shirts, the board may get credit for having stopped the craze before it went too far!

In contrast, suppose that in a market system a similar misestimation of the demand for pleated shirts and traditional shirts is made by the men's clothing industry. Lines develop at pleated-shirt counters, and inventories of traditional shirts accumulate. Stores raise the prices of pleated shirts and at the same time lower them for traditional shirts. Consumers who care more about price than fashion could get bargains by buying traditional shirts. Pleated-shirt manufacturers could earn profits by raising prices and running extra shifts to increase production. Some traditional-shirt producers would be motivated to shift production quickly to pleated shirts and to make traditional shirts more attractive to buyers by cutting prices. Unlike the planning board, the producers in a market system would be motivated to correct their initial mistakes as quickly as possible. Those who would be slowest to adjust would lose the most money and might even be forced out of business.

Decentralization of Power

Another important part of the case for a market economy is that it tends to decentralize power and thus requires less coercion of individuals than does any other type of economy. Of course, even though markets tend to diffuse power, they do not do so completely; large firms and large unions clearly do have and do exercise substantial economic power.

While the market power of large corporations and unions is not negligible, it tends to be constrained both by the competition of other large entities and by the emergence of new products and firms. This is the process of creative destruction that was described by Joseph Schumpeter. In any case, say defenders of the free market, even such aggregations of private power are far less substantial than government power.

Governments must coerce if markets are not allowed to allocate people to jobs and commodities to consumers. Not only will such coercion be regarded as arbitrary (especially by those who do not like the results), but the power surely creates major opportunities for bribery, corruption, and allocation according to the tastes of the central administrators. If at the going prices and wages there are not enough apartments or coveted jobs to go around, the bureaucrats can allocate some to those who pay the largest bribe, some to those with religious beliefs, hair styles, or political views that they like, and only the rest to those whose names come up on the waiting list. This line of reasoning has been articulated forcefully by the conservative economist and Nobel Prize winner Milton Friedman, who argues that economic freedom – the ability to allocate resources through private markets – is essential to the maintenance of political freedom.

9. Economic Freedom and Political Freedom*

Milton Friedman

It is widely believed that politics and economics are separate and largely unconnected; that individual freedom is a political problem and material welfare an economic problem; and that any kind of political arrangements can be combined with any kind of economic arrangements. The chief contemporary manifestation of this idea is the advocacy of "democratic socialism" by many who condemn out of hand the restrictions on individual freedom imposed by "totalitarian socialism" in Russia, and who are persuaded that it is possible for a country to adopt the essential features of Russian economic arrangements and yet to ensure individual freedom through political arrangements. The thesis of this chapter is that such a view is a delusion, that there is an intimate connection between economics and politics, that only certain combinations of political and economic arrangements are possible, and that in particular, a society which is socialist cannot also be democratic, in the sense of guaranteeing individual freedom.

Economic arrangements play a dual role in the promotion of a free society. On the one hand, freedom in economic arrangements is itself a component of freedom broadly understood, so economic freedom is an end in itself. In the second place, economic freedom is also an indispensable means toward the achievement of political freedom.

The first of these roles of economic freedom needs special emphasis because intellectuals in particular have a strong bias against regarding this aspect of freedom as important. They tend to express contempt for what they regard as material aspects of life, and to regard their own pursuit of allegedly higher values as on a different plane of significance and as deserving of special attention. For most citizens of the country, however, if not for the intellectual, the direct importance of economic freedom is at least comparable in significance to the indirect importance of economic freedom as a means to

---

political freedom.

Historical evidence speaks with a single voice on the relation between political freedom and a free market. I know of no example in time or place of a society that has been marked by a large measure of political freedom, and that has not also used something comparable to a free market to organize the bulk of economic activity.

Because we live in a largely free society, we tend to forget how limited is the span of time and the part of the globe for which there has ever been anything like political freedom: the typical state of mankind is tyranny, servitude, and misery. The nineteenth century and early twentieth century in the Western world stand out as striking exceptions to the general trend of historical development. Political freedom in this instance clearly came along with the free market and the development of capitalist institutions. So also did political freedom in the golden age of Greece and in the early days of the Roman era.

History suggests only that capitalism is a necessary condition for political freedom. Clearly it is not a sufficient condition. Fascist Italy and Fascist Spain, Germany at various times in the last seventy years, Japan before World War I and II, tzarist Russia in the decades before World War I are all societies that cannot conceivably be described as politically free. Yet, in each, private enterprise was the dominant form of economic organization. It is therefore clearly possible to have economic arrangements that are fundamentally capitalist and political arrangements that are not free.

Even in those societies, the citizenry had a good deal more freedom than citizens of a modern totalitarian state like Russia or Nazi Germany, in which economic totalitarianism is combined with political totalitarianism. Even in Russia under the Tzars, it was possible for some citizens, under some circumstances, to change their jobs without getting permission from political authority because capitalism and the existence of private property provided some check to the centralized power of the state.

The relation between political and economic freedom is complex and by no means unilateral. In the early nineteenth century, Bentham and the Philosophical Radicals were inclined to regard political freedom as a means to economic freedom. They believed that the masses were being hampered by the restrictions that were being imposed upon them, and that if political reform gave the bulk of the people the vote, they would do what was good for them, which was to vote for laissez faire. In retrospect, one cannot say that they were wrong. There was a large measure of political reform that was accompanied by economic reform in the direction of a great deal of laissez faire. An enormous increase in the well-being of the masses followed this change in economic arrangements.

. . . Historical evidence by itself can never be convincing. Perhaps it was sheer coincidence that the expansion of freedom occurred at the same time as the development of capitalist and market institutions. Why should there be a connection? What are the logical links between economic and political freedom?

. . . The basic problem of social organization is how to co-ordinate the economic activities of large numbers of people. Even in the relatively backward societies, extensive division of labor and specialization of function is required to make effective use of available resources. In advanced societies, the scale on which co-ordination is needed, to take full advantage of the opportunities offered by modern science and technology, is enormously greater. Literally millions of people are involved in providing one another with their daily bread, let alone with their yearly automobiles. The challenge to the believer in liberty is to reconcile this widespread interdependence with individual freedom.

Fundamentally, there are only two ways of co-ordinating the economic activities of millions. One is central direction involving the use of coercion – the technique of the army and of the modern totalitarian state. The other is voluntary co-operation of individuals – the technique of the market place. The possibility of co-ordination through voluntary co-operation rests on the elementary – yet frequently denied – proposition that both parties to an economic transaction benefit from it, provided the transaction is bi-laterally voluntary and informed.

Exchange can therefore bring about co-ordination without coercion. A working model of a society organized through voluntary exchange is a free private enterprise economy – what we have been calling competitive capitalism.

In its simplest form, such a society consists of a number of independent households – a collection of Robinson Crusoes, as it were. Each household uses the resources it controls to produce goods and services that it exchanges for goods and services produced by other households, on terms mutually acceptable to the two parties to the bargain. It is thereby enabled to satisfy its wants indirectly by producing goods and services for others, rather than directly by producing goods for its own intermediate use. The incentive for adopting this indirect route is, of course, the increased product made possible by division of labor and specialization of function. Since the household always has the alternative of producing directly for itself, it need not enter into any exchange unless it benefits from it. Hence, no exchange will take place unless both parties do benefit from it. Co-operation is thereby achieved without coercion.

Specialization of function and division of labor would not go far if the ultimate productive unit were the household. In a modern society, we have gone much farther. We have introduced enterprises which are intermediaries between individuals in their capacities as suppliers and as purchasers of goods. And similarly, specialization of function and division of labor could not go very far if we had to continue to rely on the barter of product for product. In consequence money has been introduced as a means of facilitating exchange, and of enabling the acts of purchase and of sale to be separated into two parts.

Despite the important role of enterprises and of money in our actual economy, and despite the numerous and complex problems they raise, the central characteristic of the market technique of achieving co-ordination is fully displayed in the simple exchange economy that contains neither enterprises nor money. As in that simple model, so in the complex enterprise and money-exchange economy, co-operation is strictly individual and voluntary provided: (a) that enterprises are private, so that the ultimate contracting parties are individuals, and (b) that individuals are effectively free to enter or not enter into any particular exchange, so that every transaction is strictly voluntary.

It is far easier to state these provisos in general terms than to spell them out in detail, or to specify precisely the institutional arrangements most conducive to their maintenance. Indeed, much of technical economic literature is concerned with precisely these questions. The basic requisite is the maintenance of law and order to prevent physical coercion of one individual by another and to enforce contracts voluntarily entered into, thus giving substance to "private." Aside from this, perhaps the most difficult problems arise from monopoly - which inhibits effective freedom by denying individuals alternatives to the particular third parties for which it is not feasible to charge or recompense them.

So long as effective freedom of exchange is maintained, the central feature of the market organization of economic activity is that it prevents one person from interfering with another in respect of most of his activities. The consumer is protected from coercion by the seller because of the presence of other sellers with whom he can deal. The seller is protected from coercion by the consumer because of other consumers to whom he can sell. The employee is protected from coercion by the employer because of other employers for whom he can work, and so on. And the market does this impersonally and without centralized authority.

Indeed, a major source of objection to a free economy is precisely that it does this task so well. It gives people what they want instead of what a particular group thinks they ought to want. Underlying most arguments against the free market is a lack of belief in freedom itself.

The existence of a free market does not of course eliminate the need for government. On the contrary, government is essential both as a forum for determining the "rules of the game" and as an umpire to interpret and enforce the rules decided on. What the market does is to reduce greatly the range of issues that must be decided through political means, and thereby to minimize the extent to which the government need participate directly in the game. The characteristic is that it tends to require or enforce substantial conformity. The great advantage of the market, on the other hand, is that it permits wide diversity. It is, in political terms, a system of proportional representation. Each man can vote, as it were, for the color of tie he wants and get it; he does not have to see what color the majority wants and then, if he was in the minority, submit.

It is this feature of the market that we refer to when we say that the market provides economic freedom. But this characteristic also has implications that go far beyond the narrowly economic. Political freedom means the absence of coercion of a man by his fellow men. The fundamental threat to freedom is power to coerce, be it in the hands of a monarch, a dictator, an oligarchy, or a momentary majority. The preservation of freedom requires the elimination of such concentration of power to the fullest possible extent and the dispersal and distribution of whatever power cannot be eliminated – a system of checks and balances. By removing the organization of economic activity from the control of political authority, the market eliminates this source of coercive power. It enables economic strength to be a check to political power rather than a reinforcement.

Economic power can be widely dispersed. There is no law of conservation which forces the growth of new centers of economic strength to be at the expense of existing centers. Political power, on the other hand, is more difficult to decentralize. There can be numerous small independent governments. But it is far more difficult to maintain numerous equipotent small centers of political power in a single large government than it is to have numerous centers of economic strength in a single large economy. There can be many millionaires in one large economy. But can there be more than one really outstanding leader, one person whom the energies and enthusiasms of his countrymen are centered? If the central government gains power, it is likely to be at the expense of local governments. There seems to be something like a fixed total of political power to be distributed. Consequently, if economic power is joined to political power, concentration seems almost inevitable. On the other hand, if economic power is kept in separate hands from political power, it can serve as a check and a counter to political power.

The Role of Government in a Free Society

The need for government . . . arises because absolute freedom is impossible. However attractive anarchy may be as a philosophy, it is not feasible in a world of imperfect men. Men's freedoms can conflict, and when they do, one man's freedom must be limited to preserve another's – as a Supreme Court Justice once put it, "My freedom to move my fist must be limited by the proximity of your chin."

The major problem in deciding the appropriate activities of government is how to resolve such conflicts among the freedoms of different individuals. In some cases, the answer is easy. There is little difficulty in attaining near unanimity to the proposition that one man's freedom to murder his neighbor must be sacrificed to preserve the freedom of the other man to live. In other cases, the answer is difficult. In the economic area, a major problem arises in respect of the conflict between freedom to combine and freedom to compete. What meaning is to be attributed to "free" as modifying "enterprise"? In the United States, "free" has been understood to mean that anyone is free to set up an enterprise, which means that existing enterprises are not free to keep out competitors except by selling a better product at the same price or the same product at a lower price. In the continental tradition, on the other hand, the meaning has generally been that enterprises are free to do what they want, including the fixing of prices, division of markets, and the adoption of other techniques to keep out potential competitors. Perhaps the most difficult specific problem in this area arises with respect to combinations among laborers, where the problem of freedom to combine and freedom to compete is particularly acute.

A still more basic economic area in which the answer is both difficult and important is the definition of property rights. The notion of property, as it has developed over the centuries and as it is embodied in our legal codes, has become so much a part of us that we tend to take it for granted, and fail to recognize the extent to which just what constitutes property and what rights the ownership of property confers are complex social creations rather than self-evident propositions. Does my having title to land, for example, and my freedom to use my property as I wish, permit me to deny to someone else the right to fly over my land in his airplane? Or does his right to use his airplane take precedence? Or does this depend on how high he flies? Or how much noise he makes? Does voluntary exchange require that he pay me for the privilege of flying over my land? Or that I must pay him to refrain from flying over? The mere mention of royalties, copyrights, patents; shares of stock in corporations; riparian rights, and the like, may perhaps emphasize the role of generally accepted social rules in the very definition of property. It may suggest also that, in many cases, the existence of a well specified and generally accepted definition of property is far more important than just what the definition is.

Another economic area that raises particularly difficult problems is the monetary system. Government responsibility for the monetary system has long been recognized. It is explicitly provided for in the constitutional provision which gives Congress the power "to coin money, regulate the value thereof, and of foreign coin." There is probably no other area of economic activity with respect to which government action has been so uniformly accepted. This habitual, and by now almost unthinking, acceptance of governmental responsibility makes thorough understanding of the grounds for such responsibility all the more necessary, since it enhances the danger that the scope of governments will spread from activities that are, to those that are not, appropriate in a free society, from providing a monetary framework to determining the allocation of resources among individuals.

In summary, the organization of economic activity through voluntary exchange presumes that we have provided, through government, for the maintenance of law and order to prevent coercion of one individual by another, the enforcement of contracts voluntarily entered into, the definition of the meaning of property rights, the interpretation and enforcement of such rights, and the provision of a monetary framework.

Action Through Government On Grounds of Technical Monopoly and Neighborhood Effects

The role of government just considered is to do something that the market cannot do for itself, namely, to determine, arbitrate, and enforce the rules of the game. We may also want to do through government some things that might conceivably be done through the market but that technical or similar conditions render it difficult to do in that way. These reduce to cases in which strictly voluntary exchange is either exceedingly costly or practically impossible. There are two general classes of such cases: monopolies and similar market imperfections, and neighborhood effects.

Exchange is truly voluntary only when nearly equivalent alternatives exist. Monopoly implies the absence of alternatives and thereby inhibits effective freedom of exchange. In practice, monopoly frequently, if not generally, arises from government support or from collusive agreements among individuals. With respect to these, the problem is either to avoid governmental fostering of monopoly or to stimulate the effective enforcement of rules such as those embodied in our anti-trust laws. However, monopoly may also arise because it is technically efficient to have a single producer or enterprise. I venture to suggest that such cases are more limited than is supposed but they unquestionably do arise. A simple example is perhaps the provision of telephone service within a community. I shall refer to such cases as "technical" monopoly.

When technical conditions make a monopoly the natural outcome of competitive market forces, there are only three alternatives that seem available: private monopoly, public monopoly, or public regulation. All three are bad so we must choose among evils.

. . . A second general class of cases in which strictly voluntary exchange is impossible arises when actions of individuals have effects on other individuals for which it is not feasible to charge or recompense them. This is the problem of "neighborhood effects." An obvious example is the pollution of a stream. The man who pollutes a stream is in effect forcing others to exchange good water for bad. These others might be willing to make the exchange at a price. But it is not feasible for them, acting individually, to avoid the exchange or to enforce appropriate compensation.

. . . Neighborhood effects impede voluntary exchange because it is difficult to identify the effects on third parties and to measure their magnitude; but this difficulty is present in governmental activity as well. It is hard to know when neighborhood effects are sufficiently large to justify particular costs in overcoming them and even harder to distribute the costs in an appropriate fashion. Consequently, when government engages in activities to overcome neighborhood effects, it will in part introduce an additional set of neighborhood effects by failing to charge to compensate individuals properly. Whether the original or the new neighborhood effects are more serious can only be judged by the facts of the individual case, and even then, only very approximately. Furthermore, the use of government to overcome neighborhood effects itself has an extremely important neighborhood effect which is unrelated to the particular occasion for government actions. Every act of government intervention limits the area of individual freedom directly and threatens the preservation of freedom indirectly, for reasons elaborated [earlier].

Our principles offer no hard and fast line how far it is appropriate to use government to accomplish jointly what it is difficult or impossible for us to accomplish separately through strictly voluntary exchange. In any particular case of proposed intervention, we must make up a balance sheet, listing separately the advantages and disadvantages. Our principles tell us what items to put on one side and what items on the other and they give us some basis for attaching importance to different items. In particular, we shall always want to enter on the liability side of any proposed government intervention, its neighborhood effect in threatening freedom, and give this effect considerable weight. Just how much weight to give to it, as to other items, depends upon the circumstance. If, for example, existing government intervention is minor, we shall attach a smaller weight to the negative effects of additional government intervention.

10. Man, Freedom and Market*

G. Yavlinsky et alia

This program could happen only in the era of perestroika, which began in 1985. It is a natural outgrowth of that policy. M.S. Gorbachev and B.N. Yeltsin initiated the program and it can be realized only if they unite their efforts in its support.

The long rule of the totalitarian socio-political system dragged our society into a profound crisis. Indecisiveness of the government and the mistakes it made in economic policy brought the country to the brink of collapse. Life is getting more and more difficult, and people are becoming desperate. Only well-calculated and energetic actions, supported by the people and relying upon their unity and patriotism, can achieve a breakthrough.

Our society has developed an extreme experience of economic reforms, which people have come to associate only with changes for the worse in their lives. Life, unfortunately, has taught them to believe more easily in bad than in good things. The realization of the suggested program is expected to combat this sentiment.

Its basic difference from all previous attempts lies in the fact that it relies upon a fundamentally new economic concept. It plans to move towards a market-oriented economy at the expense of the state, but not at the expense of the people.

For a long time, economic policy did not consider the people's interests. The state was wealthy while the people were poor. The state accumulated under its control almost all the resources for production. Such resources were thoughtlessly squandered on giant and ineffective projects, for increasing military power, and for certain ideologically flavored practices overseas, even though the times have long passed since we could afford this.

This program sets forth the task of taking everything possible from the state and giving it over to the people. There are good reasons to believe that giving back to the people a considerable part of property and resources on

---

* Excerpted from "On the Program Developed by Academician S.S. Shatalin, from *500 Days: Transition to Market*. St. Martin's Press: New York, 1991. Reprinted by permission of the publisher.

various terms will ensure more effective use of these resources and forestall many negative side effects in the transition to a market economy. It is necessary to slash dramatically all state expenditures, including those kept secret from society.

Only when the people see that all the possibilities and resources currently devoured by the giant state machine have been channelled to serve the people will the leadership of the country be in a position to appeal to the people to be patient, to take up another heavy load in the name of the Motherland and of their own future and the future of their children.

We must also turn to other countries for assistance. They will support us if they consider our program decisive and efficient, and if they are convinced that the assistance they grant will find a reasonable and effective use for the good of the people.

Each person, each enterprise, each area or sovereign republic is sure to find in the suggested program a response to its own individual interests and a chance to start immediately realizing those interests.

Another basic feature of the program is that people should not wait for permission or orders, but should act in their own best interests. The program shows how to do it in the best and most effective way. Anybody who carefully reads this program can decide what is good for him and make a preliminary estimate of what he should do and what terms he should demand for the realization of his economic rights and interests.

Nobody seeks to impose anything on anybody. Everybody has a right to choose, guided by his own wishes and capabilities, whether to become an entrepreneur, an employee of the state apparatus or a manager at a stock company, to engage in individual labor, or to become a member of a co-op. The reform grants citizens the right to economic self-determination, setting the rules which will prevent certain people, groups, enterprises and regions from infringing upon the economic rights of others while pursuing their own interests. It is freedom of choice which is the basis for personal freedom and for the realization of individual creative potential. These are not yet rules for the future market economy, which will emerge only in the course of the formation and development of a market-oriented society. The economic thrust of the suggested program is the transition to the market, laying the groundwork for a society based upon new economic principles.

It is the system of economic relations and management of the economic complex created in this country that is to blame for the fact that a most hardworking people in a most rich country live at a standard which in no way matches the resources of the territory or the people's talents and effort. People live much worse than they work, because either they make things they do not need or what they make is being lost or misused.

The suggested program develops ways of transition to an economic system which could transform this situation and grant to every citizen a real opportunity to make his or her life better. Thus the program can be considered as a guide to realizing the right of citizens to a better, more decent life.

The Right of Citizens for the Freedom of the Consumer Market and for Fair Prices

Among the rights and freedoms of the new economic system, the right of the consumer to choose is not the least. The domestic consumer market today is almost totally destroyed, and, accordingly, our consumers − all of us − have no rights. Citizens of a great power have become hostages of empty shops and enslaved by production and distribution monopolies.

Among the many causes that have brought about this state of things, one of the most important is inflated money, which has no goods behind it. The bulk of this money has been paid to the population over the past several years. Recurrent talk about an overhang of extra money, which should in some way be taken away from the population, is immoral. Is it really possible to call "extra" savings, which are not much more than a thousand and a half per capita? If we take into consideration the mostly scanty personal belongings of people, we realize that most people who have this extra money are not very far from the poverty threshold. Even the total sum of money the consumer is ready to pay now is extremely small. But even this weak monetary opposition is deadly for our consumer market.

We must normalize the consumer market through liberalizing pricing policy. During the transition period we will create commodities reserves, including import supplies, to encourage the coming gradual transition to free prices for many commodities. The exchange market will operate with a freely fluctuating rate of exchange. A number of major banks will get the right to sell currency at market prices and Soviet citizens will be given the right to keep currency freely in banks.

Some argue that transition to the market is impossible without administrative price hikes. Our program, however, allows this transition without any centralized increase in prices. The market regulates price fluctuations. In the administrative system, especially over the past years, prices only rise. Our still non-market economy shows how fast life is getting more and more expensive, and this is a faster process than the official statistics would recognize.

Why should people trust Goskomtsen[1] to come up with fair prices if it has never done so in the past? Certainly, there can be no guarantee that free market prices will immediately become fair, but with the market it will happen sooner or later. It never happens with the administrative system. Administrative control and centralized management of prices can never set adequate prices. Even when the government through administrative measures manages to keep prices low for this or that commodity (especially if the commodity is in shortage), the consumer's only consolation, as a rule, is the knowledge that these low prices exist somewhere. These commodities are not available in stores or they go to privileged strata of the population. Most consumers buy them at the market or on the black market at much higher than official prices. Transition to free prices will be gradual and will start with goods which are not prime necessities and which mostly high-income people buy. Thus rising prices will mostly affect this upper strata of the population.

The Right of Society

Our society has an indisputable right to live better right now, not in the far-off future, and the suggested program of transition to a market-oriented economy is aimed at the fullest possible realization of this right.

S. Shatalin, N. Petrakov, G. Yavlinski, S. Aleksashenko, A. Vavilov, L. Grigoriev, M. Zadornov, V. Martynova, V. Machits, A. Mikhailov, B. Fyodorov, T. Yarygina, E. Yasin.

---

[1] [Editor's note: *Goskomtsen* was the State Committee for Prices in the former Soviet Union.]

11. The Rush to Capitalism*

John Kenneth Galbraith

That the past months have been marked by the greatest changes of our times is a matter on which I need not dwell. What has been only moderately less evident is the flow of economic advice which has crossed national frontiers in these months. In the common reference communism having failed, capitalism is triumphant. And from this the conclusion: from the high priesthood of capitalism must now come the guidance, indeed the writ, on what the previously afflicted countries should do and have. Who could be qualified better to offer advice and guidance than the most relentless exponents of the successful system?

Much of this advice has flowed from our own country. We, not surprisingly, harbor and give voice to a considerable number of the archexponents of free enterprise. It has helped that this advice emanating from our shores is wonderfully inexpensive as compared with the more substantive help that many of us have urged as a way of easing this great transition.

In my view, some, and perhaps much, of the advice now being offered the Central and Eastern European states proceeds from a view of the so-called capitalist or free-enterprise economies that bears no relation to their reality. Nor would these economies have survived if it had. What is offered is an ideological construct that exists all but entirely in the minds and notably in the hopes of the donor. It bears no relation to reality; it is what I have elsewhere called the primitive ideology.

This advice has two features. Some comes from people who have long regretted the concessions that Western economies have accorded to social action − to the welfare state and public support to the impoverished; to the essential and growing role of the public services; to trade unions; to measures designed to achieve greater equality in income distribution; and to the larger post-Keynesian responsibility for the effective performance of the economic system as a whole. They don't like what they see at home, so it naturally forms no part of their recommendations for countries now emerging from

* From "The Rush to Capitalism," *The New York Review of Books*, October 25, 1990. Reprinted by Permission of the author.

communism. And, it is clear, they are not without audience there: in economics and politics, as in religion, the new convert is often the most ardent in belief.

The second and related feature of the flow of advice currently reaching the countries that are now in transition is its casual acceptance of – even commitment to – human deprivation, to unemployment, inflation, and disastrously reduced living standards. This is even seen as essential therapy: out of the experience of unemployment and hunger will come a new and revitalized work ethic, a working force eager for the discipline of free enterprise. To each according to his ability, from each according to his need. In one ardently expressed view, which I heard just a few days ago from a business adviser recently returned from Poland, such deprivation – unemployment, low wages – will cause foreign investors and entrepreneurs in years ahead to come in for the rescue. Only a few years of suffering and all will then be well. This, I choose my words carefully, is insanity. Nothing over the centuries has more often been urged than the social reward of hardship by those who will not have to suffer it. The biblical poor were told that unlike the rich they would have easy access to heaven. In the simplest form much of this counsel consists in urging the replacement of a poorly functioning economic system with none at all.

The economic system which Central and Eastern European countries see in the West and in Japan is not capitalism in its pristine and primitive form. It is a system deeply modified by ameliorating social services, by supported incomes, and by public controls. It is by these that the system has survived. In Britain, Mrs. Thatcher, and until lately in the United States, Mr. Reagan and his acolytes, have indeed pictured themselves as archexponents of unfettered capitalism. In fact they owe, or have owed, their eminence to earlier generations of socially minded leaders who made their citizens economically and socially more comfortable and secure – and now, in their voting, conservative. Mr. Reagan and Mrs. Thatcher were, or are, preserved in office because, in practice, their free-enterprise rhetoric was mostly unmodified by action. Had Mr. Reagan during his first term mounted a major assault on the welfare system – pensions for the old, compensation for the unemployed, health care for the unfortunate, income support for farmers – his presidency would have come abruptly to an end in January of 1985.

Nor, indeed, are the social tasks of capitalism yet complete. Many of our people still live outside the system: they hear much of democracy but do not find it worth their while to vote. It is a grim but wholly unshakable fact, as I've elsewhere said, that no one in search of a better life would wisely move from East Berlin to the South Bronx. Not even in search of liberty, for nothing so represses freedom as an effective absence of money, food, and a place to live. The administration of Mr. Bush, according to recent reports, is considering sending experts to the Soviet Union to advise on creating the various institutions of capitalism, and included would-be experts on the construction of "private housing." Presumably they will tell of how this industry has failed in virtually all capitalist countries to create adequate shelter for the poor, and has left millions homeless in the United States. With all else the politics of our time has its own grim humor.

I return to my main point: what is being seen in the West from east of the one-time Wall is not traditional capitalism. It is a still imperfect social democracy. In a very real sense, both East and West, our task is the same: it is to seek and find the system that combines the best in market-motivated and socially motivated actions.

There are in this search no overarching rules by which to be guided. In the nations now in transition I would, of course, urge the return of less essential consumer goods and services to the market. Here, it is all too evident, the planning and command system of past experience did not work. Consumer demand is diverse, unstable, and only the market conveys its message from producer to consumers. Action here need not be abrupt; it should occur when plausible entrepreneurs and managers become available and public financial institutions are created to finance the transfer of ownership or the creation of new firms. Like all change it should come from thought, not formula. . . .

For food and housing I would see a longer continuing role for the state. Any large and sudden movement in the price of essential nutrients and in housing rents is certain to create distress and stir resentment, as has already been made evident in the case of food in Poland and the USSR. Public subsidy here is not an unusual thing. It is normal. The United States, all the EEC countries, and Japan subsidize their food supply at large public cost and, as I've noted, capitalism nowhere provides adequate and affordable shelter for lower-income citizens.

I would also urge any practical steps to return agriculture and notably the marketing of most farm products to the price system. It is a matter of worldwide observation and experience that agriculture works best when under the self-motivated and often self-exploitative command of the individual farmer. I do not doubt the difficulty in moving from the more comfortable world of the collectives and state farms. I would not doubt, however, that this is necessary. But moderation, not ideology, must again be the rule. More than civilized caution is involved here. Farmers work well and invest well only when they have assurance about eventual price and income. Agriculture in the United States over the last half century has had huge gains in productivity, far exceeding those in industry. This has been so partly because farmers have been able to invest for a publicly assured return.

As to the large industrial or commercial enterprise that is the centerpiece of the modern capitalist or socialist economy, the question of ultimate ownership is not so important. In the Western countries and Japan there are well-functioning firms under both private and public ownership. In Switzerland where I live some part of my life we travel on a publicly owned railroad, talk over a publicly owned telephone. Our apartment is insured by the commune. Our neighboring farmers are accorded income in keeping with their needs. A good house is a human right. The exceptionally fine store that supplies our food and much else is a cooperative. Our bank account is with a publicly owned bank. We cannot, in fact, cut down a tree, possibly even plant one, without public permission. The lovely Alpine meadows are preserved by farmers who are subsidized by the state to pasture them. The Swiss, nonetheless, are celebrated for their diligent adherence to free enterprise.

In the United States our railroads failed under private operation and have been partly redeemed under public management. Private failure in our financial institutions is now being redeemed at a cost of hundreds of billions of dollars by the state. The phrase "taken over by government" appears daily on our financial pages. Apart from the exceptional and much criticized case of the corporate raider, stockholders – owners in the great firms of modern capitalism – are dispersed and mostly unknown. They have no power over the professional management that appoints the directors who are presumed to control their operations. This, in the phrase of the late James Burnham, a notable conservative, was the Managerial Revolution. In modern capitalism managers, not capitalists, are the decisive power. And in the modern mature capitalist economy. I note with emphasis, it is not about power that we should worry, it is about incompetence.

What is important – my urging at this point goes back to early observation and experience in India – is to give the enterprise authority over, and the rewards of, its own performance. It must not be united with or controlled by a ministry of the state; there must not be what in India I called "post-office socialism." No normal person performs well when another has the full authority for his actions. So equally the corporate or business enterprise. If larger enterprises are given freedom from the disaster of ministerial, i.e. bureaucratic, control and they are thus accorded the right to set their own prices, produce their own materials, and make their own subcontracts, the location of actual ownership is not a matter of prime importance. I would urge that ownership be widely distributed, and I am attracted by the proposed action in Poland, which is strongly supported by my colleague Professor Jeffrey Sachs, to distribute the shares widely to the citizenry, with a special advantage for employees of the particular enterprise. The equity of such an arrangement has an obvious appeal, as also the resulting sense of participation.

It is assuredly acceptable as compared with one alternative now being comprehensively discussed. That is for foreigners to come in large numbers to invest and manage. I am not opposed to joint enterprises; they can in a marginal way, like McDonald's and Pepsi-Cola, be useful. But any large-scale alienation of ownership and management to foreigners would surely ensure an adverse response. As Americans would not (and do not) look forward to working for the Japanese, efficient as they may be, Poles, Czechs, and Hungarians can hardly look forward to working for Americans, Germans – or Japanese.

It should not be a criticism of this transition that it is done gradually and with thought. The return to normal productive activity in Western Europe after World War II, a task less complex than that faced by Eastern Europe and the USSR, took the better part of a decade. In Britain it took some seven years before sterling was fully convertible, and food rationing and associated price controls were similarly continued. Sudden action, once again, is for those who do not themselves suffer, do not think before acting, who proceed by formula, not fact. Only if time is allowed can there be time for thought – the thought that is attuned to pragmatic result and not to primitive ideology.

PART III

THE LEGAL SYSTEM

Legal reform is of vital importance if the Eastern European economies are to make a successful transition into modern free-market systems. In "The Role of Law in Market Economy," David Kennett discusses some of the ways that the law interacts with the economy. The basic logic is that the law has evolved along with the market system and its chief utility lies in the minimization of information costs and transactions costs. Thus, appropriate legal structure and economic efficiency go hand in hand.

Some aspects of reform will prove easier than others. There is no shortage of foreign technical expertise to draft new laws, and a statute book, though massive in proportions, could be assembled in quite short order. Indeed, the pace with which the Supreme Soviet, first of the Union and now of Russia, has passed decrees is astounding. However, a law book is not everything; a trained and competent judiciary will take time to develop, and an important element of all law is precedent, which can only accrue over time.

However the most difficult problem is the one that John Litwack addresses in his paper "Legality and Market Reform in Soviet-Type Economies." Legality is defined as (1) a mutually consistent set of laws; and (2) a belief by the population in the stability and enforcement of these laws. In the Soviet Union in its last days, and by implication in the successor states, he asserts, there is no legality because the population believes that the government can and will change the law at any time, even after the fact, and hence there is no stability.

Litwack illustrates this by reference to the policy of *uravnilovka*, which is best translated as "levelling": enterprise taxes and subsidies to firms are not consistently applied but are changed in order to serve the goals of bureaucrats. Profits are transferred out of enterprises and given as subsidies to others in a time-inconsistent and firm-inconsistent way. He quotes one bureaucrat as saying, "We first undress enterprises and then think about how to dress them up at least a little." This is, of course, the same as the "soft-budget constraint" that we have already met in the work of Kornai and Keren.

In the absence of legality to define economic relationships, there is a great reliance on personal contact, with gifts, favors and other near-corrupt practices prevalent. This does little to advance economic growth. The establishment of market arrangements within the state structure have made matters worse; the biggest fortunes being made are from arbitrage between a state-subsidized official sector and an excess-demand private consumer sector. (See also Grossman, Article 23).

While Litwack considers the establishment of legality to be necessary for a successful transformation, he sees many formidable barriers. Three are legacies of the past. First is the reputation of the past leadership, including those committed to reform, for changing their policies and worse, the rules that govern those policies. This may have undercut future confidence in the consistency of all leadership. Second, there will be an ideological hangover from the previous regime; laws that legitimate people who are sometimes reviled as "speculators" may have problems gaining support. Third, the network of personal ties will not evaporate overnight, and favors around the laws will still be expected and granted.

The fourth and potentially most serious problem may be the time-inconsistency of a successful transition program and the instability of the transition period. The transition will necessarily involve change and institutions and laws will have little opportunity to evolve. Changes will be required that will have to redistribute rights throughout the transition. Such changes, although necessary, may well encourage further cynicism and a decline in legality. The final problem is the centrifugal tendency in the former Soviet Union. Regional autonomy is on the rise and a new division of authority is being established; this raises the possibility of laws being inconsistent across geographic space.

His somewhat depressing conclusion is that, in the Soviet Union at least, the moves towards transition may well have hindered rather than assisted in the establishment of legality. In other East European states where the political transition has been less tortuous and economic policy more consistently applied, especially Poland, the Czech and Slovak Republic, and Hungary, the prospects are by no means as bleak.

12. The Role of Law in a Market Economy

David Kennett

One of the most serious, although frequently neglected, problems of the transforming economies is the lack of a viable legal framework within which market institutions can develop. In turn, the development of such a framework is one of the most difficult and complex tasks in the whole of the transformation process.

This absence of infrastructure is, of course, no accident. The theory of the centrally planned economy (CPE) relied on the absolute power of the government and the assumption at the center of total control over all aspects of the economic system. In that sense the government lay above the law. Only when individuals are convinced that their property and rights are above infringement by the government will enterprise prosper. The growth of all Western free market economies has been accompanied by the extension of an ever-more complex system of civil and business law. Modern scholarship tends to see this legal structure as contributing to economic efficiency through the reduction of transaction costs. It can be convincingly argued that no free market system can prosper where manipulation of the law is the unchecked preserve of the government of the day.

If the formerly centrally planned economies are to grow into the complex economic systems of the West they must develop legal institutions that are in turn like those found in the West.

Ownership as a Fundamental of a Market System

The first and most fundamental right to enable the operation of a free market is the right to own property.

Ownership seems at first glance a simple concept, but in fact it comprises three separate rights. The first of these is the right to *use* property as the owner sees fit; the second is the right of the owner to enjoy *income* from that property; and the third is the right of the owner *to exchange or sell* that property at a price accepted as fair by the seller.

In the classic centrally planned economy (CPE), the citizens have had only minimal rights in any of these dimensions of ownership. In the Soviet Union, for example, Article 10 of the old constitution was clear. "The foundation of the economic system of the USSR is socialist ownership of the means of production in the form of state property." Thus, the institution of private property ownership is, in and of itself, a revolutionary step forward; it was the first of the necessary rights defined in the Shatalin/Yavlinsky 500 Day Plan.[1]

We should note that as a practical matter, it is not necessary for a workable market system that an individual, or private economic enterprise, should have universal rights to own any and all kinds of property. Most mixed market economies grant to the individual less than full freedom in the acquisition, use, and disposal of property. Society may wish to collectively own certain classes of property or prevent individuals from exercising all of the three aspects of ownership, implicitly justifying such action by the presence of market imperfections and externalities. Even casual consideration reveals that in Western economies rights of ownership are often constrained: some types of property cannot be owned, let alone produced, by private citizens (firearms, drugs, nuclear power stations); planning restrictions prevent individuals from using some property as they see fit – factories cannot be located in residential areas, or landfills in resort areas; the State will frequently intervene to prevent sellers from charging whatever the "market will bear"; the tax systems in all economies intervene to prevent the individual from enjoying the full income stream from practically any economic activity.

An important feature of the right to ownership is that to play a role in the economy it must be effective, not merely nominal, and be *perceived* as having permanence. The legal system must, therefore, have both the intent, and the power to prevent property from being stolen by others or appropriated by the State for a foreseeable time horizon, and this must be accepted by the populace. Again, Litwack addresses this and defines as part of legality a "belief by the population in the stability and enforcement" of a legal system. Without this condition any, would-be entrepreneur or trader will have one eye always looking for a capricious intervention by the State and that will adversely affect his or her behavior and hence the rational structure of prices.

The Role of the Law in Promoting Economic Efficiency

While even the limited right of ownership will ensure the development of some form of market, alone it will only go a limited way in stimulating efficiency. It will, in the words of Evgenii Yasin, the Russian reform

---

[1] See Article 10 in this volume.

economist, be a "bazaar" rather than a "market." A market *system* requires much more. The legal system that has grown up in western nations can be viewed as a complex series of rules one of the tasks of which is to promote efficiency and economize on scarce resources. Of course, this is not the sole function of the law in western nations. It must also protect individual and group rights against a variety of incursions, and the emergent legal codes in the Eastern European nations must fulfill the same tasks too. Also, it must be admitted that a good deal of legislation has been passed in developed nations, at the behest of narrow interest groups, that does little either for economic efficiency or human rights. However, a great deal of legislation has evolved to contribute to the efficient operation of a market economy. These too must at least be matched, and if possible improved upon, in Eastern Europe if the economies there are to thrive and to be as efficient as those in the West.

Freedom to Engage in Economic Activity

In order for prices of goods to approximate resource costs,[2] markets must be relatively competitive, and this involves the right of individuals, and groups of individuals or firms, to engage in whatever economic activity they perceive as having the greatest return. In simple terms, individuals must have the right to choose their own professions, among them being a self-employed entrepreneur, and choose the physical locations of where they pursue these professions. This is much the same as giving individuals the right to enter any business or industry that they choose and to live wherever they choose.

In most of Eastern Europe and the Soviet Union these rights were not guaranteed; most trades, especially those of buying and selling or wholesaling, could not be pursued by individuals under threat of punishment. Such activity, which depended on buying cheap and selling dear, was frequently labelled as simply "speculation."[3] Many of the social benefits of a market system depend on legal codes allowing individuals to respond to incentives. Indeed, one of the most fundamental recommendations of the joint report of the multilateral agencies, produced pursuant to the Houston Summit, was the

---

[2] See Article 8 by Lipsey et al. in this volume.

[3] In actual fact most of this activity was arbitrage, rather than speculation, since it involved moving goods from one market to another, hence lessening price differentials between the markets. However, the distinction is not crucial since most economists recognize that both speculation, which involves buying now and storing in the belief that prices will rise later, and arbitrage contribute to market stability and efficiency.

decriminalization of activity that was "both rational and socially beneficial."[4]

Without a guarantee of free entry, private monopolies, with their attendant inefficiencies, replace state monopoly. Prices will not reflect the resource costs of production and monopoly rents[5] are earned, yielding inefficiency. A major target of Smith's *Wealth of Nations* was the system of royal licensing and monopoly that restricted the action of the individual. If the state can prevent the entry of individuals into a trade or profession, then the consumer, and society as a whole, is the loser while the monopolist, or the official that grants him monopoly powers, the winner.

This freedom must also embrace the ability to move and to relocate in pursuit of economic goals. In the Soviet Union, especially, freedom of movement was restrained by the government and movement into certain areas required a pass, or *propiska*. In any case, under central planning wage rates were determined by the planners; labor did not automatically flow to where demand was highest.

Once again, however, we must recognize that free entry into all economic activities in Western systems is not guaranteed. Many professions and trades require licenses or permits; these are usually defended as being efficient in that customers cannot always gather all the information they need, and certifying lawyers, stockbrokers, or auto-mechanics provides cheap information and protects the customer. Although market radicals, like Milton Friedman, denounce them in many cases as monopolistic and therefore inefficient restrictions, such barriers are an integral part of economic life in most market systems.

The Enforcement of Contracts, and Compensation

While ownership and entry will create an infrastructure in which a rudimentary market can exist, such a market would by necessity operate with a very short time horizon. Longer term views of economic relationships can be made viable by the use of contracts that bind parties to specific performance standards. Contracts are an integral part of moving from the "bazaar,"

---

[4] See *The Economy of the USSR: Summary and Recommendations*, authored and published jointly by the International Monetary Fund, the World Bank, the Organization for Economic Co-operation and Development and the European Bank for Reconstruction and Development, 1990, p. 35. A summary of the chief findings of this group is included as Article 31 in this book.

[5] Monopoly rent is the margin above normal profit that results from the exercise of monopoly power.

where already-produced goods are exchanged, into a longer term system of stable inter-relations enabling planning and foresight. A contract binds both parties to specific performance standards, whatever the change in external circumstance, and provides for enforcement or compensation for non-performance.

The ability of individuals to make contracts, either verbally or in written form, and to have those contracts enforced by the law, is an important part of even the simplest economies and this provides some evidence of its social value. Some forms of long-term relationships can take place even in the absence of enforceable contracts, since the market can produce its own remedies. A supplier, for example, who persistently failed to deliver would have a great deal of difficulty in finding future customers, as knowledge of his persistent failure to perform became widespread. However, contract law removes part of the costs of gathering information from the contracting parties by providing general remedies and compensation for failure to perform and to deliver. This obviates the need for a socially expensive search.

The current situation in much of Eastern Europe, and especially in the Soviet Union, is that the making of contracts is running ahead of the law. Western lawyers are attempting to establish joint ventures with Soviet entities in ways that are not at all covered by Soviet law. A form of contract did exist under Central planning, but such agreements were not freely entered into by the firms, the key element in Western contract theory. Rather they were a way of conveying to lower levels the decisions made by the center in the planning process.

The contracts being signed now in Eastern Europe are less than optimal for several reasons. First, because there is no body of contract law and no precedent, the contracts must be unusually detailed in establishing performance criteria, and must anticipate and provide for all eventualities; this is time consuming and costly in legal resources. Secondly, there is no real enforcement behind them; many contracts in fact stipulate recourse to a Swedish arbitration agency in the event of problems, but this has no real legal force behind it. Because of this the contracting parties will probably only maintain their relationship as long as the business is *mutually* beneficial; the contracts are unlikely to provide any protection for one party if the other finds the arrangement no longer to his liking.[6]

---

[6] This means in effect that both parties must make money from the beginning of the project. "Without solid contract law it is a rare executive, Russian or western, who will risk $100 million on a project that will not generate revenue for a year," "The Art of a Russian

To promote economic efficiency, contract enforcement need not always require strict performance to the letter of the contract, but it may instead give the injured party compensation for the losses incurred as a result of non-performance. Strict enforcement would be burdensome and inefficient in some cases where expected circumstances have changed and fulfilling the contract in its literal terms is impossible. However, the law must provide both the means for the injured party to be compensated and an appropriate system of adjudicating damages resulting from non-performance.

A Fully Defined System of Property Rights

In the introduction to this section, we explicitly limited the discussion to one of *physical* property. Now we must broaden the definition to include *rights* as a form of property; economic efficiency may be best served if, in some cases, rights can be exchanged in much the same way as physical property. Economic analysis of the law has developed very quickly in recent years and one widely accepted result has been that a clear definition of property rights is necessary for the efficient use of resources, although the extreme position that full definition of property rights would eliminate all market failure due to externalities (known as the Coase theorem) is in dispute.

The range covered by the term property rights is broad; included in it are rights as varied as the right to clean air, the right to quiet, the right to access to sunlight, the right to earn income from an invention, the right to broadcast over the air waves. In the West, property rights have developed incrementally, and they have been adapted and extended to take account of new complexities, both by legislation and by precedent in law. New technologies and new external circumstances have required new rights to be defined. Environmental property rights, software property rights, and the right of access to radio frequencies are three areas that have recently leapt to prominence.

In centrally planned economies, the State not only owned the physical means of production but also almost all property rights. As a result, such rights were not well defined. Since the State owned everything, there was no need to enforce, exchange, or dispute over rights using either the market or the courts. In the Soviet Union, the institution of *arbitrazh* developed in part to resolve property rights disputes between state enterprises, but its scope was limited and its functions confused since it made rules, interpreted them, and enforced them.

Deal," *New York Times*, January 17, p.1.

In theory the State represented everyone; the old saying, "that which belongs to all belongs to none," was confirmed in the CPEs. Since no-one could patent an invention, and hence secure in pecuniary terms the economic rent, there was a lower incentive to invent, or even for foreign entities to disclose any modern technology, process, or software innovation. Environmental degradation reached extremes in Eastern Europe because the citizenry had no means to establish or defend property rights to air, ground, or water. Moreover, the bureaucracy was able to appropriate for personal gain the property rights of the state, providing a barrier to reform.[7]

The extent of required legislation is very large. Western societies have been codifying and amending rights for centuries, and still changes in technology reveal glaring gaps. For half a century, few property rights have existed in the centrally planned economies. As always, being a latecomer has its advantages; rights can, in theory, be assigned in equitable and socially efficient ways. But the magnitude of the sheer task of definition and the political struggle over the acquisition of property rights means that a lot of confusion will occur in the short run.

The Corporate Form

One of the most important innovations of Western economies is the ability to create corporations. A corporation is a legal entity that can, through the sale of shares, raise capital from a large number of individuals, each of whom shares in the profits of the firm. It has a second important feature; each investor is liable only for the amount of money that each has invested. Thus, the overall liabilities of the firm are limited to the net worth of the firm, rather than the total debts and obligations. Thus, the downside in a corporate form is less than that in an equivalent partnership or proprietorship, where the owners would be liable for the full value of the obligations.

The development of the corporate form in Western economies was crucial in providing a means to raise large sums of capital and limiting the risk of each investor, particularly important when the number of investors is large and no one investor can be responsible for the oversight of the operation of the firm. Without the corporate form it is difficult to gather together the finance to undertake large scale operations.

Corporations may be either privately held, where the shares are not traded on stock markets, or public corporations where ownership is liquid and traded on stock markets. The transforming economies must ultimately develop stock

---

[7] See Winiecki, Article 29 in this book.

markets though there are considerable barriers to their rapid development, discussed by van Agtmael.[8]

It should be noted that although the corporation is efficient in encouraging large and risky ventures, its very presence does limit the effectiveness of contract law. A corporation's liability is limited to the extent of its assets, and situations may result where its liability under a contract exceed those assets.

Bankruptcy Law

Frequently overlooked in the discussions of infrastructure is the role of bankruptcy legislation. Capitalism is, in Schumpeter's words, a "gale of creative destruction." Company failure and the dissolution of corporations must be regarded as a normal aspect of the system.

The efficient operation of that system, however, is highly dependent on an orderly disposition of the assets of the firm in the event of failure. A necessary condition for orderly capital markets is a full and enforceable set of defined property rights; bankruptcy law is one component of these rights.[9] The risks that lenders and materials suppliers assume in supplying a firm can only be assessed when there is full knowledge of the "pecking order" in which debtors will be arrayed should the firm go into bankruptcy.

Accounting and Financial Disclosure

The law plays a vital role by requiring that firms must report their financial results in a specified standard accounting system and that this information is made publicly available. The efficiency aspects of this are made obvious by considering the alternative: without required and standardized disclosure the costs of information to an individual or other firms, whether potential shareholders, suppliers, or customers, would be very high. This, required disclosure has clear social efficiency in reducing information costs. This is obviously of the greatest importance in the operation of stock markets, where buying shares without access to company information would be undesirably risky, and share prices would not reflect underlying values. It is also of great relevance to those who supply the company with raw materials and inputs and those who provide credit to firms in more direct ways.

---

[8] See Article 16 in this volume.

[9] See J. Mitchell, "Managerial Discipline, Productivity and Bankruptcy in Capitalist and Socialist Economies," *Comparative Economic Studies*, vol 22, no. 3 (Fall, 1990).

Tax Law

Taxes are, like death, inevitable; governments, even those highly limited in scope, must gather their resources from somewhere. One of the most important features of an overall legal system must be the creation of a tax regime that is visible, consistent, and, to some extent, regarded as fair. The particular form of the tax system is not absolutely important. Different, successful Western and western-style economies have widely different tax regimes, some reliant on indirect taxation (sale taxes and value added taxes) and others rest upon direct taxation (income and profits taxes). Some systems place more burden on the individual and less on business than others.

What is important is that the tax laws should be considered and consistent, and that they should be subject to adjudication by some authority external to the taxing authority. Businessmen, like sportsmen, can operate under widely different conditions as long as the rules of the game are clear and are not subject to capricious change. One of the greatest deterrents to investment is uncertainty with respect to the tax treatment. This is especially important for the foreign investor, whether setting up a wholly owned subsidiary or entering into the joint-ventures that are the most frequent of capital inflow into the former CPEs at the present time.

That said, it is desirable that tax systems should be as neutral as possible and not result in undesirable implicit subsidies for particular kinds of industrial organization, firm organization or ownership. Taxes that favor or disfavor (say) vertically integrated structures, individual proprietorship, or domestic ownership, lead to economically inefficient distortions.

A Clear Definition of Governmental Responsibility

Just as the lack of clarity and stability in tax matters is a major disincentive to investment, so is the lack of clarity as to the appropriate role of government, and where relevant, which level of government has what responsibilities. Under classical central planning, the State was all powerful. In an important sense, it was both the owner of everything, from land to air quality, and responsible for everything, from housing to providing food. What is required now is that there should be a scaling down of governmental responsibility and a definition of where the public sector ends and the private sector begins. Under central planning, because the State was both a producer and a provider of social services, firms quite frequently assumed a social role inappropriate in a free market economy. What may be required for an efficient labor market is a complete overhaul and redefinition of what is known in the West as the social safety net. Without a well-defined social safety net, the strains on society of growing unemployment may prove too great for fragile democratic movements to survive.

Similarly because all power was, in theory at least, held in the center, the responsibilities of various governmental levels was not appropriately defined. Again, as in much of what we have discussed, the "developed" economies have many of the same flaws. Disputes between the competencies of federal, state, and local governments in the United States are frequent, and when they occur are socially costly in terms of delay and wasted resources. This set of problems is particularly pressing in the natural resource area where, in the pre-Commonwealth USSR, there was dispute between three levels of government over the ownership of natural resources located in the "entrails" of the earth. Now, of course, the "center" has ceased to be a contender, but strain still exists between the Republics and the localities.

This, again, is not dissimilar from the United States; however, in the United States there is a both a body of legislation and a body of legal precedent to resort to. An individual can – with foresight – take legal opinion, and either narrow his liability or at least know better the distribution of risk. Uncertainty is always and everywhere the enemy of stable economic activity and part of the law's function is to narrow that uncertainty.

A System of Civil Compensation

The law of liability, as it existed in centrally planned economies, has been likened to military law. Blame, when it could be assigned, was a criminal matter and would be redressed by the punishment of the offender rather than by the compensation of the victim. Tort law, which deals with the redressing of private or civil wrongs through suit, did not exist in the centrally planned economies. The United States may suffer from what its vice-president refers to as a plague of lawyers, many of whom make their business through civil suit, and the prospect of a tort-free society might seem attractive. However, it is clear that the threat of suit does have positive consequences; a firm found guilty of injury will ameliorate its behavior in the future, the more so if it is forced to pay punitive damages.

It might be argued that a chief executive officer will be even more careful about the behavior of his corporation and underlings if he were liable to a jail-term rather than merely dipping into the shareholders' profits to settle a suit. However, this system of criminal redress would have two consequences. First, it would affect the behavior of potential victims by encouraging untoward caution since they know no monetary compensation will be available. Second, it will discourage quite legitimate business activity, because of fear of criminal punishment.

Consider a Western business engaged in (say) an extractive industry, wishing to start operations in (say) Russia. The technique, like most, is not without risk either to his own workers or other nearby individuals. In the West, the businessman would know that he is subject to civil suit in the case of accidents, but to criminal liability only in the case of gross negligence. In Eastern Europe and the former USSR, it is quite possible that the redress would occur only through criminal proceedings. What is true for the Western investor is also true for the domestic Russian businessman. Removing the greatest problems to investment while retaining some censure over dangerous behavior, and ensuring the ability of the victim to be compensated, requires the development of a civil liability code.

Conclusion

In a short piece it is only possible to give some idea of the role of law in market economies, and the extent of required legal reforms in the transforming ones. The problems faced are large but on the whole well-known. Access to foreign experts in each of these fields of law has opened and already large amounts of legislation have been passed. Moreover, the situation is not wholly without precedent: the commercial and tax codes of Japan were entirely rewritten on an American model by the occupying forces in the aftermath of World War II. For Eastern Europe, the more appropriate models may be French or German codes, especially since the ultimate objective of much of Eastern Europe is to join the European Community.

While the codes may be reformed in a relatively short space of time, the legal infrastructure will take several years to adapt and become efficient. Well trained lawyers and judges will be in short supply for many years and this will hamper the speed and, therefore, the efficiency of the courts. Also, law in Eastern Europe will have to build its own history of precedence. Thus, reform cannot be achieved overnight, though it is necessary for the efficient operation of a modern economy.

13. Legality and Market Reform in Soviet-Type Economies[*]

John M. Litwack

> *"Who's the Boss: we or the law? We are masters over the law, not the law over us − so we have to change the law; we have to see to it that it is possible to execute these speculators!"*

Nikita Khruschev (1961)[1]

The classical Soviet-type system operates in the virtual absence of economic legality, which is a prerequisite to a successful transition to a market economy in the Soviet Union and the nations of Eastern Europe. In the absence of economic legality, the leadership of these countries will not be able to implement a credible commitment to private property rights or any other effective market incentive mechanism. In addition, they will be unable to promote the growth of multilateral impersonal trade. Without legality, a shift away from central planning toward market allocation may very likely lead to economic decline, inflationary pressures, and a polarization in income distribution, which, in turn, could unleash political reaction against the reform process in general.

This paper begins by introducing a working definition of economic legality, and then contrasting such legality with the systems of coordination, incentives, and distribution in the classical Soviet-type economy. The paper then argues the vital necessity of establishing economic legality in the transition period, and outlines some important difficulties. Finally, the experience of the Soviet economy is briefly examined, where it is suggested

---

[*] From the *Journal of Economic Perspectives*, Col 5, Number 4, Fall 1991. Reprinted by permission of the author and The American Economic Association. Some footnotes omitted.

[1] As quoted in K. Simis, *USSR: The Corrupt Society* (New York: Simon and Schuster, 1982).

that the failures of recent years derive, in large part, from these same difficulties.

A Definition of Economic Legality

"Legality" is associated with rule by law as opposed to the discretion of leaders. Recent research in economic history has emphasized the importance of the replacement of legal for discretionary rule in explaining the rapid economic development of the western world, as well as the disparities in wealth between the advanced capitalist and underdeveloped countries.

This paper will employ the following two-point working definition of legality: (1) a mutually consistent set of laws; and (2) a belief by the population in the stability and enforcement of these laws.

Notice that the presence or absence of legality in any given country is a matter of degree in this definition. In addition, according to the second condition, legality is a social phenomenon depending on the beliefs of the population. Instability or the lack of enforcement of laws does not necessarily imply an absence of legality, and the presence of consistency, stability, and enforcement is not sufficient to imply legality, unless the population believes that these respective legal climates exist and will continue.

"Economic legality" refers to laws in the economic sphere, particularly contract, tax, and bankruptcy laws. Although reforming socialist countries, especially the Soviet Union, have been writing and rewriting such laws at a mind-boggling pace in recent years, these countries have not yet succeeded in building genuine legality.

The Classical Soviet-type Economy and Legality

It is impossible to comprehend the difficulties in the current transformations in Eastern Europe without an understanding of the functioning of the classical Soviet-type economic system. This system contains particular mechanisms of coordination, incentives, and distribution that function in the virtual absence of economic legality. The fundamental features that explain how the system actually works are the discretionary power of bureaucrats over subordinates, enforced by the political dictatorship of the Communist Party, and the reputation effects from personal, often informal, long-run ties.

In a modern capitalist economy, hierarchical organizations interact in the context of a market. In a Soviet-type economic system, any existing market activity functions in the context of a large administrative hierarchy. This hierarchy largely replaced the market in coordinating economic activity between individuals and organizations.

The fundamental document for implementing an administrative allocation of resources is the yearly material-balance plan, which emerges through extensive bargaining between various levels in the hierarchy. Superiors in the hierarchy, who have the last word in this bargaining, typically press for greater output and less inputs while individuals at the lower levels, in possession of local information, lobby for the converse. The plan primarily specifies yearly flows of inputs and outputs, as well as an allocation of government investment. The basic method of plan construction is marginal adjustments based on what was achieved in the proceeding year. Once this plan has been drafted, it is given the status of law, and underfulfillment of the plan is technically a violation of law. Thus, the Soviet-type coordination mechanism on paper appears to rely on legality, with the yearly plan as the fundamental legal document.

In reality, a forceful argument can be made that little legality in material-balance planning exists in the Soviet-type system. The plan is important in specifying an initial division of resources. But after it is drafted, a process of continual adjustment begins in which bureaucrats continually employ their discretion in changing production orders and redistributing resources. As stressed by many specialists, these continual discretionary adjustments and reallocations are a prerequisite to the very feasibility of Soviet-type planning. The hierarchical structure of power in the Soviet system also implies that these adjustments can be made unilaterally. The fact that the plan is so unstable has led some scholars to prefer the term "centrally managed" or "administered" in describing the Soviet-type economy, rather than "centrally planned." In addition, plan underfulfillment is a common occurrence and not treated as a violation of the law in practice, although, as discussed below, there often exist significant incentives to fulfill the final version of the plan. Thus, the plan is generally not stable or mutually consistent, and although it does affect behavior, it does not satisfy the criterion of legality.

Given the plan, an intricate web of personal horizontal contacts comes into play in coordinating economic activity, which contrasts sharply with the multilateral impersonal trade that is commonly associated with a developed market. This is not to argue the unimportance of personal relationships in a market economy. But the protection of trade by legality significantly decreases the need to depend on these relationships. Virtually every Soviet-type enterprise has an employee that works as an expeditor (*tolkach*), whose primary responsibility is to establish long-run personal relationships with other organizations for the purpose of procuring needed supplies, particularly in emergency circumstances. The presence of these informal relationships is critical to the coordination mechanism of the economy itself. It is well-accepted that it is impossible to be a successful manager in a Soviet-type economy without continually breaking the law and relying on these personal contacts. In the consumer sector, citizens commonly rely on "pull" (*blat*) through "acquaintances" (*znakomstvo*) to obtain goods and services. Again, this features mostly long-run mutually-beneficial relationships between individuals. In these relationships, trust can be maintained, even in the absence of legality, through reputation and a mutual advantage to continuing transactions.

Of course, market transactions between individuals without well-established personal ties can also occur in the Soviet-type system. The most common example are the small number of legal markets, such as farmers' markets and flea markets (*barakholki*). Street vendors sometimes engage in semi-legal or illegal indiscriminate sales of goods. But given the fact that market transactions in the Soviet-type system are, by and large, illegal and contract violations cannot be prosecuted, the transaction costs associated with impersonal trade can be prohibitively high, which favors long-run personal ties as a primary means of horizontal transaction. A major dilemma of the reform period has been the inability of the leadership, by legalizing this trade, to significantly reduce these transaction costs and also make market transactions subject to taxation.

Vertical relationships between superiors and subordinates in the Soviet-type system also tend to be highly personal. Subordinates commonly give large gifts (*prinoshenie*) to superiors in the ministerial and party apparatus. These gifts are generally not bribes in the sense of being a direct exchange for specific goods and services at one moment in time. They are an investment in a long-term personal relationship. In addition, special orders are continually fulfilled for superiors or other important personal contacts at the expense of all other work.

Incentives in the Soviet-type economy include pecuniary rewards, communist party discipline, and the system of promotion and demotion (*nomenklatura*) in the Communist Party hierarchy. A claim of this paper is that nonpecuniary incentives are actually more important than pecuniary ones in the Soviet-type system. Virtually all management positions in economic organizations belong to the *nomenklatura* network of appointments, promotion and demotion in the party hierarchy. In addition, virtually every economic organization in the classical Soviet-type system possesses its own internal party committee that engages in monitoring and the enforcement of labor discipline. In the past, mobilizations and massive propaganda campaigns, as well as terror and coercion, have been used in the context of this nonpecuniary incentive system. The incentives provided through this system, however, have become less effective in the Soviet Union since the 1950s, as well as in the countries of Eastern Europe. Regardless of the degree of effectiveness, the incentives provided through the party hierarchy are devoid of legality. They are oriented toward the obedience of orders that are given at the continual discretion of superiors.

In discussing compensation for workers and managers, it is important to distinguish between official and underground channels. Neither operates on a basis of legality, the first because of instability and continual violations of rules and regulations, and the second because of explicit illegality.

On paper, the official pecuniary reward system involves elaborate bonus and tax schedules. Bonus funds as well as salaries can be withdrawn from the government bank as cash by organizations as opposed to the earmarked blocked funds. Over half of the pay of managerial personnel can depend on bonuses that are functions of performance that are typically tied to the plan but also can depend on profits, productivity, cost reduction, technical progress and other variables. In the postwar period, organizations have also been given the right to carry out limited decentralized investment as a function of profits and other measures of performance.

In reality, salaries, bonuses, and other decentralized funds are regulated on a discretionary basis, with the purpose of expropriating excess profits from organizations that reveal themselves to be more productive and guaranteeing "normal" salaries and bonuses. Often in explicit violation of regulations governing stability, norms and tax rates are continually adjusted for this purpose. The adjustment in tax rates is often realized implicitly through numerous policy variables such as fines (*sankstii*), the distribution of various types of funding, and differentiation in prices that different enterprises receive for the same commodities. Prices are also subject to comprehensive periodic adjustments. The essence of this system is captured by a Russian word that found its way into the vocabulary of all the Eastern European countries: *uravnilovka*, which translates as "equalization" or "levelization." *Uravnilovka* is qualitatively quite different from an explicit dynamic tax scheme, which would imply the presence of economic legality. Under *uravnilovka*, actual tax rates and norms are continually set and adjusted only after superiors in the hierarchy observe existing conditions. Inequalities are observed and subsequently leveled off.

This important after-the-fact connotation of *uravnilovka* is also captured in another commonly used description of the distribution system: "The principle of one big till (*kasa*)." Everything is first centralized and then divided up or, as Soviet bureaucrats often remark: "We first undress enterprises and then think about how to dress them up at least a little." The distribution system is therefore also devoid of legality as defined in this paper. It is unstable and often in direct violation of written regulations that are meant to govern the stability of norms and taxes. The absence of an independent judiciary in the Soviet-type system also implies that economic organizations have very limited means for seeking redress for violations of written regulations. Such an action could also jeopardize the vitally important personal relationships that subordinates must forge with their superiors.

Market Reform and Legality

It is sometimes suggested that the complex network of horizontal personal ties that exists in the socialist economies may already provide a foundation for the creation of a market economy. In a sense, markets already exist. They simply need to be legalized, expanded, and improved; the high transaction costs imposed by the classical Soviet-type system need to be reduced. But at least two fundamental problems must be confronted here. First, institutions to support legality are needed to facilitate flexible, often impersonal trade that could replace, to some degree, the reputation effects from personal relationships in promoting cooperation. Second, the former system of *uravnilovka* must be replaced by genuine profit incentives, which will substitute for *nomenklatura* and party discipline in motivating economic activity. The remainder of the paper will focus on the second problem.

The preceding discussion of the classical system immediately suggests difficulties in creating profit incentives. If managers in Soviet-type economies could be characterized as bonus maximizers, as is suggested in some studies, creating profit incentives would be a straightforward exercise, involving a shift in emphasis in bonus schemes from the fulfillment of central directives to profits. But this is simply not true. Effective legal pecuniary incentives of any type do not exist, and therefore must be built from scratch. The primary task facing central authorities is the credible commitment to stable sharing rules for profits and losses between the government and individual organizations. This, in turn, implies the creation of economic legality. At least five major interrelated obstacles must be overcome:

The Reputation of the Past Leadership and Adaptive Expectations. The history of reform in the USSR has featured continual broken promises by the government to establish commitment to stable pecuniary incentives. Other

Eastern European countries have had similar experiences. The population has already become accustomed to an environment of *uravnilovka*, devoid of legality, where written commitments are not honored. It should be noted that genuine private property rights, now a goal in many of the socialist countries, cannot exist in an operational sense without legality in taxation. The current changes of political leadership in many of the socialist countries may help in altering the expectations of the population. But given the reputation of past leadership and the orientation of the population to a society without legality, beliefs may not change rapidly. As discussed above, legality depends on the beliefs of the population. Those countries with political leaderships that have most clearly signalled a break for the past have a natural advantage in affecting these beliefs. But it is crucial that new leaders do not begin by tarnishing their own reputations for upholding commitments.

Ideology. In the socialist countries there is a general orientation, supported by Marxist-Leninist ideology, against private entrepreneurs and "speculators." ...[B]ut even in the absence of communist power, the social atmosphere may remain anti-entrepreneur. In the USSR, for example, potential entrepreneurs are not only afraid of the political leadership, but their own neighbors who may decide to carry out their own notion of social justice.

Personal Ties and Tax Evasion. The presence of the large network of underground horizontal ties in the socialist economies poses a potential threat of institutionalized tax evasion. This is further complicated by the lack of an internal revenue service, reflecting the fact that the classical Soviet-type system conducted taxation in the legal economy automatically through the central bank. Only income net of taxes could be withdrawn.

The Time-Inconsistency of a Successful Transition Program and the Instability of the Transition Period. Given the complex nature of the transition from administrative to market resource allocation, it is natural to expect discretionary behavior on the part of the leadership that must continually adapt to new information and conditions. But complete discretionary behavior contradicts legality and stable sharing rules for profits, losses, and risks between the government and other organizations. After the fact, the government has an incentive to absorb surpluses from organizations that reveal themselves to be very productive and profitable. If organizations expect future profits to be taxed away, they may simply choose not to become profitable in the legal economy.

Regional Autonomy and the Division of Authority. Many of the reforming socialist economies have struggled with the emergence of defiant regional authorities that often set their own laws and regulations in conflict with central legislation. This threatens the necessity of a mutually consistent set of laws for the establishment of legality.

The Soviet Experience

These [five] trends have caused the rapid deterioration of the incentive mechanism of the classical Soviet-type system. Although the institution of yearly central plan has remained, there has been a general breakdown in coordination and plans have commonly gone underfulfilled. Many economic organizations have been encouraged to plan their own production, sell directly to consumers, and retain a portion of the profits. A series of decrees in 1987 first proposed a comprehensive transformation to a market economy that features decentralized trade, pricing, and profit incentives. These decrees centered around a new "Law on the State Enterprise." For the criterion of strong incentives, this law prescribed stable taxes for a five-year period.

Soviet reform efforts have also sought to expand the legal private sector. This began with the expansion of opportunities for small cooperative businesses in 1986 and a "Law on Cooperation" in 1988 that declared cooperative property rights to have the same legal status as government property. As with the state sector, profit incentives were to be protected by a clause in the law that guarantees stable tax rates for at least a five-year period (sec. 21, art. 6). More recently, the Soviets have expanded opportunities for nongovernment property rights, promoting first long-term leasing and now joint stock companies and small private businesses.

Despite these and other measures, the Soviet economic situation has deteriorated at an alarming rate in the last few years. Budget deficits have spiralled out of control since 1985, leading to an increase in government debt from about 15 percent of GDP to 50 percent in 1990. Crime has increased sharply. Moreover, there has been a significant polarization of the income distribution, which makes inflationary pressures quite threatening for the poorer segments of the population. The current decline and crisis in the Soviet economy can be explained primarily by the fact that, despite the plethora of recent laws, the Soviet leadership has made no progress in establishing economic legality, and no effective incentive mechanism has replaced the declining authority of the party and ministerial apparatus.

The history of legislation in the Gorbachev period has been entirely inconsistent with legality. Virtually every law, for example, that has promised

stable taxation to eliminate *uravnilovka* and make profit incentives operable
has been overtly violated or revoked to the preservation of the discretionary
expropriations. This includes the 1987 package of laws and subsequent
legislation, including all promises of stability in taxation discussed above. The
absence of legality and corresponding beliefs by the population that profits
will be expropriated and losses compensated has led many Soviet enterprises
to respond to less central planning and party discipline by reducing activity
in the legal state sector of the economy. This decline in the state sector and
tax evasion in the nonstate sector decreases government tax revenue, which
feeds into the deficit crisis. The Soviet leadership has responded to this
revenue crisis by making discretionary changes in tax laws, including the
introduction of very harsh "emergency measures" since 1989 to absorb
surpluses from profitable organizations. While ratios of government
expenditures to GNP have actually been declining in the USSR since 1987,
the widening deficit can be explained by greater declines on the revenue side.

The legal private sector has been the hardest hit by the continual policy
reversals and emergency measures. Measures by various authorities to
expropriate rents from this sector have been reinforced by a general witch-
hunt atmosphere for "speculators." The remnants of communist ideology
have no doubt contributed to this orientation, but it is also true that the
distorted environment of the transition period has served to justify suspicions
of private entrepreneurs. The most profitable ventures have typically involved,
to one degree or another, arbitrage profits from the diversion of state
resources at low or negligible prices to the private sector. Perhaps the most
profitable and popular activity of Soviet cooperatives is to pump (*perkachat*)
money illegally from earmarked blocked investment funds into cash through
the cover of a contract between a cooperative and a state enterprise. A state
enterprise pays the cooperative out of its own blocked investment funds or
earmarked bank credit, which the latter organization can withdraw as cash. A
serious argument can be made that activity in the private sector has generally
contributed to the current economic crisis. Efforts have been diverted away
from value-adding activities to arbitrage and tax evasion, which has polarized
income distribution. As market activity has expanded in the USSR, it has
tended to take the form that market activity took in the past: personal ties and
income hidden from the government.

Mutual consistency has also been a problem. When a comprehensive
reform package of 1987 was passed, a major investment was made in
establishing consistency. After these laws were drafted, over 1,200 previous
all-union decrees were declared defunct, along with about 7,500 republican-

level decrees, and over 33,000 all-union and 800,000 republican ministerial rules and regulations. Subsequent laws and reform programs have appeared on at least a yearly basis, however, and have not been accompanied by such attention to the consistency of rules, regulations, and local laws. Now, as the regional disintegration of the Soviet economy has reached serious proportions, contradictory laws and regulations have become the rule rather than the exception. The rejection of central law has become a deliberate act of defiance in some of the republics, including Russia. All of this has led to a situation where, in the recent words of a Soviet journalist, "Today the people have become absolutely convinced that new Soviet laws do not operate."

All in all, the Soviet leadership has made essentially no progress in establishing economic legality, which is a prerequisite for creating incentive that could support a healthy market. On the contrary, as the continual policy reversals and economic decline of recent years have undermined the credibility of the leadership, it may be that the reform movement in the USSR has actually moved farther away from the institutional prerequisites necessary to support a market economy.

PART IV

THE FINANCIAL SYSTEM

In the transforming economies, years of consumer frustration, combined with sudden political freedom, mean that no regime can survive without rapid economic growth. But growth, in turn, requires these nations to generate savings and make them available for the purchase of capital equipment by the most efficient and dynamic firms. Hence, it is crucial that banks, bond markets, and equity markets be established and that the public develop confidence in these institutions.

Conversely, *without* an efficient financial system in place, virtually all other aspects of market reform will encounter bottlenecks. For example, privatization cannot proceed very far without the contribution of a sound financial system, since would-be entrepreneurs will need long-term credit to buy state assets, and newly privatized firms will need access to short-term credit for day-to-day operations. Similarly, price reform will be hyperinflationary without a strong central bank capable of resisting pressure to print money.

In "The Role of Central Banks in the Emerging Market Economies," Gerald Corrigan begins with the two tasks every banking system must perform: mobilizing savings and facilitating the payments process. In Corrigan's view, the best system to accomplish these tasks is the one found in most market economies: a "two-tiered" banking system consisting of a *government* central bank and a *privately-owned* commercial banking sector. Private ownership ensures that bank owners have their *own* capital at risk, so they will ensure that loans are granted only to the most efficient enterprises. This, in turn, leads not only to allocative efficiency, but also to the highest possible economic growth and the highest return for household savings.

But an entirely private banking system would generate frequent, systematic bank failures. This not only disrupts the payments process, but also harms the public's trust in financial intermediaries, which would decrease the level of household financial savings and the rate of economic growth. Thus, there is also a need for a central bank designed to serve the wider public interest.

These are just two examples of how a healthy, two-tiered banking system contributes to economic growth and stability in a market economy. Corrigan's article is multifaceted and complex; it is worth reading more than once.

While Corrigan suggests where banking in the formerly planned economies ought to go, Marc Lieberman's "Banking in the Former Soviet Union," suggests how long the journey will be. Banking systems in planned and market economies differ radically because they arise to further such radically different purposes. Banking under central planning is designed to facilitate the process of control from above; banking in a market system arises when someone decides there is profit to be made by operating a bank. Lieberman's article first explores the general differences between the two types of banking systems and then turns to the specific case of the former Soviet Union. He concludes with some of the obstacles to financial reform that the new Commnwealth of Independent States must overcome.

Antoine van Agtmael's article, "Requirements for a Successful Equity Market," is both a "how-to" guide for emerging economies trying to establish stock markets, and a review of what they can expect as their markets develop. Stock markets, like all financial intermediaries, must provide households with a high degree of liquidity in order to mobilize household savings. But liquidity, in turn, requires wide participation in the market – a large number of suppliers of equity shares, and a large number of demanders. Van Agtmael introduces us to all of the major players on both sides of the market, and reviews the policies, institutions, laws, and skills that will encourage their participation. As you go through the article, note how often government enters the picture: where the right kind of government action is needed, and the wrong kind of government action will harm the market's progress.

14. The Role of Central Banks in Emerging Market Economies[*]

E. Gerald Corrigan

I am pleased to appear before you today to discuss the role of central banks and the financial system in the specific context of the recent efforts on the part of a number of Eastern European countries and the Soviet Union to shift their economies toward more market-oriented and competitive systems. I am especially pleased to have the opportunity to discuss these issues in the presence of the distinguished group of central bank governors from those nations who are gathered with us today.

For the sake of emphasis, let me begin my remarks by citing several propositions that, in my judgment, are central to the discussion as a whole. These propositions are:

First, the stability of the banking and financial system is an absolute prerequisite for the growth and stability of the economy at large.

Second, of all the elements of structural reform that are necessary in the transition from a centrally planned and controlled economy to a market economy, none is of greater importance than the reform of the banking and financial system.

Third, while the development of capital markets – especially an efficient market and secondary market for national government securities – is clearly important, the highest priority should be placed on the reform and adaptation of the commercial banking system.

Fourth, successful reform of the commercial banking system presupposes parallel reform in the central banking system. At a minimum, this reform should take central banks out of the business of directly financing government deficits and provide mechanisms through which central banks can increase or decrease liquidity in the economy without allocating credit for specific purposes or functions.

Finally, and most importantly, at the end of the day, commercial banks and

---

[*] From *The Federal Reserve Bank of New York Quarterly Review*, Summer,1990, vol. 15, no. 2.

central banks have only one asset that really matters, and that asset is public confidence. Accordingly, the task of reform in all its detail must be approached with enormous weight given to this overriding consideration. Indeed, the confidence factor will become all the more important over time as the ownership of banking and financial institutions shifts to private hands. The crucial question is not whether particular reforms will work as a matter of theory or abstraction, nor even whether a particular approach has worked in other countries. Rather, the bottom line is the issue of whether specific reforms are likely to work and to build confidence in the specific context in which they are applied.

Before discussing these issues in greater detail, I should make two important qualifications. First, my thinking about these very difficult issues is naturally conditioned by my own experience and environment. Thus, much of what I have to say reflects how things have – and have not – worked here in the United States and in other western industrial countries. I say this because I am acutely mindful – in part from my association with reform efforts in developing countries in Latin America and elsewhere – that successful elements of structural economic reform cannot be insensitive to traditions, customs, cultures, and histories in the reforming countries. On the other hand, there are certain basics – even when considered in the light of national histories and cultures – that are essential in virtually any setting.

The second qualification follows from the first: namely, I do not consider myself an expert on the details of the commercial or central banking systems in any of the countries whose officials are gathered here today. But I do know enough about each and enough about reforms already under way to know that much of what I have to say will not apply equally in all cases and in some may apply in only limited ways. However, even where the latter is the case, I am quite convinced that there is value and discipline to be gained in going back to basics.

Against that background, I believe it is fair to say that it is universally recognized that a particularly important function of a banking and financial system in a market economy is to help mobilize a society's savings and to channel those savings rigorously and impartially into the most efficient and effective uses or investments. That process is, of course, the very lifeblood of economic development and rising standards of living. As a corollary, it is also universally recognized that the banking and financial system must provide the vehicles through which payments for goods and services can be made quickly, efficiently, and safely in a context in which both the seller and the buyer of such goods and services have confidence that instruments used to make such payments will be honored and accepted by all parties to that transaction and to subsequent transactions. Without that confidence, the system simply cannot work. Stated differently, these crucial economic functions of mobilizing savings and making payments are often taken for granted. In reality, however, it is very difficult to forge a set of legal and institutional arrangements within which these functions are performed that would be consistent with the often conflicting goals of free choice, economic efficiency, and safety and stability.

Indeed, economic history tells us in wholly unmistakable terms that no society has found it easy to forge its financial institutions in a way that these goals are appropriately balanced. Even today, within and among the most successful industrialized countries of the world, there is great debate as to how best to go about that task. Certainly, that is true here in the United States. The reasons for the inherent difficulties in this area are an almost classic blend of political and economic considerations that have their roots in the crucial functions the banking system must perform in a market economy.

As an illustration, take the example of the typical household. Clearly a society's long-term economic prospects are best served when such households make the decision to freely save some of their current income. But that is not enough, since there must also be a way in which those savings can be mobilized and put to work in productive investments. That, of course, means that the household must see not only an inducement to save freely but also an inducement to entrust those savings to someone or something else that can directly or indirectly put those savings to work in sound and productive investments. Under any circumstances, the household will see some risk in parting with its savings and it will expect to be compensated accordingly. But, and this is a very large but, under any circumstances, any household in any society will also want to maintain some fraction of its savings in the form of highly liquid assets, including assets which can easily be used to finance day-to-day and week-to-week transactions needs.

For that reason a household's willingness to entrust its savings – especially its highly liquid savings – to some institution presupposes that it has confidence in the financial integrity of that institution. If that confidence is not there in the first instance, the society's ability to mobilize its savings will be compromised and its ability to reap the benefits of economic specialization in the production and distribution of goods and services will be undercut. Similarly, if that confidence is lost, households will simply rush to redeploy their savings, raising the specter of a flight to cash and/or to hard goods with all its implications for inflation and destabilizing runs on banks.

This, of course, is why confidence in banks is so crucial, and this single factor goes a very long way in explaining why banking institutions and banking instruments have evolved in the way that they have over centuries. What this says, of course, is that no matter what the precise legal and institutional financial framework in a particular country, there are certain preconditions that must exist if the financial system is to be able to perform its essential tasks of mobilizing and allocating savings and facilitating day-to-day transactions. Thus, there must be a class of financial institutions and financial instruments that the public views as safe and convenient outlets for their savings, where at least some fraction of those savings are highly liquid and can be used to make payments. The problem, of course, is that any institution that provides the public with access to financial instruments having those characteristics must be one that invests the public's savings carefully and prudently, but also invests those savings in a way that promotes economic efficiency and growth.

In virtually all countries, the single dominant class of institution that has emerged to play this crucial role as both the repository of a large fraction of the society's liquid savings and the entity through which payments are made is the commercial bank. Indeed, even in mature industrial countries with highly developed capital markets – such as the United States – the commercial banking system is still the most important single element of the financial system, especially when it is kept in mind that the capital markets rely very heavily on the banking system for day-to-day and standby financing facilities.

But from the earliest days of commercial banking, experience has repeatedly shown that the combination of functions typically provided by such institutions carries with it the unique risk that a loss of confidence in individual institutions can spread to the system as a whole. This, of course, is the so-called systemic risk phenomenon. And as the broad sweep of history tells us, there are many instances in which the loss of confidence in financial institutions has caused major damage to the real economy. In other words, systemic risk is not an abstraction; it can be quite real.

It has long been recognized by all governments that banking and financial institutions must be subject to at least some form of regulation or official oversight because the functions they provide are indispensable to economic success, even though these same functions by their very nature introduce potential risks that are capable of undermining the prospects for such economic success. I am fond of pointing out – and I will do it again in this context – that Adam Smith forcefully took this position in *The Wealth of Nations*.

In most countries there is either an explicit or a tacit recognition that one of the crucial functions of the central bank is to help preserve and enhance the stability of the banking and financial system. Indeed, while the primary task of most contemporary central banks is viewed as the conduct of monetary policy, many central banks – certainly including the Federal Reserve – were established largely with a view toward preventing or at least containing financial shocks and disruptions.

My own vision of the role of the contemporary central bank – framed by a sense of history, by my experience in the United States, and by my utter conviction as to the importance of the efficiency and stability of the financial system – is one in which the central bank houses a trilogy of functions. At the center of the trilogy is, of course, monetary policy. But there are two other crucial functions of the contemporary central bank that are closely related to monetary policy and constitute a single theme. These other two functions are the broad oversight of the financial system and the oversight of and/or direct participation in selective aspects of the operation of payment systems. These are the functions, but the single theme is stability – stability in the purchasing power of the currency of the country and stability in the workings of the financial system, including the payments system. This single theme of stability is a package deal in that each of the parts is dependent on the other parts.

But if it is appropriate to think of the role of the central bank in the context of this trilogy of functions, and if it is fair to suggest that financial stability is a necessary – but not sufficient – condition for economic growth and stability, then it must follow that the structure and workings of the banking system are of great importance to this process as a whole. Looked at in this broad light, the challenge of reforming the banking system is formidable indeed, especially since the paths chosen to effect such reform cannot be viewed in isolation from reforms of the central bank. Neither can they be viewed independently of emerging developments in capital markets, in particular the need to develop mechanisms whereby central governments can more effectively finance budget deficits in a manner that does not constrain the monetary policy process. None of this is easy, but the greatest challenge may lie in forging the individual pieces of the reform effort in such a way that they fit together into a cohesive whole that will serve the dictates of stability, growth, and confidence. From this perspective, it seems clear to me that the first priority is the mobilization of private savings.

This, in turn, brings one's attention immediately to the liability side of the balance sheet of the major financial intermediaries – the commercial banks.

Indeed, in the short run, I would argue that the design of the transactions-like and savings-like liability instruments of the banks is more important than the design of the overall structure of the system. And it is not simply the design of the instruments that is important but also the design and workings of the broad infrastructure that goes with such instruments. For example, for transactions-type accounts and especially for interbank movements of funds, efficient, safe, and speedy collection and payments systems are a must if confidence is to be built and maintained. Indeed, banking instruments and institutions are only as good as the infrastructure that supports them. The ability of the banking system to mobilize savings by attracting deposits is one thing. But its ability to retain such deposits and to put them to good use is quite another, which of course brings me to the asset side of the balance sheet. The bank's choice of its assets is crucial for two reasons:

First, if the bank is careless in the credit it extends, it will incur losses and will not be able to honor its obligations to its depositors. If its ability to honor its deposit obligations is in question, the bank will always be subject to the risk of deposit runs. This is the subtle genius of the banking system, for it is a key feature of the banking system that creates the incentive for the bank to extend credit wisely, judiciously, and impartially.

Second, even where capital markets are well developed, the credit decisions of the banking system remain the single most important element determining how the society's savings are deployed. Those credit decisions therefore determine which firms, which farms, and which entrepreneurs will receive the credit and which will not. If the system is working correctly, those who receive credit will be the most efficient, the most competitive, and the most profitable. Therefore, they will be the most capable of producing the stream of goods and services that will permit the economy to grow and standards of living to rise.

It should be clear that the objectivity and impartiality of the credit decision-making process are absolutely indispensable features of an efficient and market-oriented banking system. Partly because of the obvious problems of political pressures, but for other reasons as well, the government or the state is not well equipped to make these decisions. To be sure, the state can establish tax or other incentives for certain activities – something we see in all societies – but the decision as to who gets credit and who does not must be left to private initiative in a context in which those making the decisions have a major stake – their own economic livelihood – in the credit decisions they make.

This is also one of the more fundamental reasons that the development of sound and internationally acceptable accounting systems in emerging market economies is so vitally important. Accounting systems serve a variety of purposes, but none is more important than their role in helping creditors make the rigorous decisions as to which enterprises can meet the market test of efficiency, competitiveness, and profitability that will permit those enterprises to meet their obligations and, in turn, permit their creditors to meet their obligations.

Another subject of importance in regard to the structure of banking institutions is the size and composition of the bank's capital account. The capital account, representing the ownership interests in the bank, serves two obvious purposes: first, it is a source of permanent funding, and second, it provides a cushion for absorbing losses. But the capital base also serves another, more subtle function: namely, it creates a constituent group of individuals or institutions that has a direct interest in the profitability of the bank, which in turn should strongly reinforce the impartiality of the credit decision-making process.

For these reasons, it should be obvious that private ownership of banks is the preferred arrangement. Having said that, I would add that it is also true that government ownership of commercial banks is quite common in developing nations and, in fact, is also to be found in some major industrial countries. Also, in virtually all countries – the United States included – special purpose banking organizations entailing government ownership, guarantees, or sponsorship are not uncommon. I mention this only because the drive for private ownership of banks may – particularly in the short to intermediate run – have to be tempered with some realism as to what kinds of arrangements are workable. Thus, some or all of the initial capital stock of commercial banks may have to come from the government – an outcome that can be acceptable if three conditions are also met. Those conditions are:

First, the management of the bank is independent of the government such that the government does not direct credit decisions and allocation. In other words, government ownership must not preclude competition.

Second, having provided the initial capital, the government is not responsible for the overall funding of the bank.

Third, the government's ownership interests are structured such that at some later date they can be easily sold to private interests.

While individual countries have considerable latitude with regard to the precise legal and organizational structure of their commercial banking system, the basic functions are common to all countries. And by their very nature, those functions entail risk taking on the part of individual institutions and the system as a whole. In the face of that risk taking and the need to maintain public confidence in the banking system, banking in all countries is subject to a higher degree of official oversight and regulation than is the case for most other forms of private enterprise. As an extension of that, all countries have put in place some form of a so-called safety net that is associated with the operation of the banking and financial system.

In practice, the specific form of the safety net − in both de jure and de facto terms − can differ appreciably from one country to the next. In generic terms, however, the safety net is usually designed to provide the following functions: first, the regulation of the affairs of banking institutions, usually including the inspection and examination of such institutions; second, some form of protection against loss on the part of at least small depositors and investors; third, some form of emergency liquidity facility; and finally, some form of official regulation of or participation in the workings of the payments system.

In virtually all countries. the central bank plays a direct or indirect role in the operation of one or more of these central features of the safety net. For example, the emergency liquidity facility is almost always the discount window of the central bank. In many countries − including the United States − the central bank also plays an important role in both the supervision of banking institutions and in either or both the regulation and the operation of the payments system. Given the concept mentioned earlier of the trilogy of central bank functions, it will come as no surprise when I say that I strongly believe that central banks should play an important role in both of these areas. In this regard, I would place a particularly high priority on the need to develop a strong program of bank supervision, especially in the early phases of the changing role of the commercial banks. Similarly, the central bank can also play a highly valuable role in the early development of critical aspects of the payments system such as the interbank deposit market and the emerging markets for government securities.

Regardless of how broadly or narrowly, how explicitly or implicitly the legal mandate of the central bank is drawn, it seems to me inevitable that the central bank will always have an important role in helping to build and maintain confidence in the underlying stability of the banking and financial system. In turn, that necessarily implies that there must be a high degree of public confidence in the central bank itself. Achieving and maintaining that public confidence is, in the first instance, squarely related to the success the central bank has in the discharge of its monetary policy responsibilities. That is why monetary policy stands at the center of the trilogy of central bank functions. It is also the reason that central banks must have special status within the governments they serve. At the very least, that special status implies that central banks should not be expected to finance the budgetary deficits of governments directly. It also implies that the central bank normally should not be responsible for the direct financing of other types of enterprise. Indeed, such arrangements run the clear risk that the central bank's balance sheet can become weighed down with low-quality assets. In such circumstances, confidence in the financial integrity of the central bank can only suffer.

Having said that central banks should not be responsible for the direct financing of government deficits, I should add that it is also true that central banks typically are major holders of government debt. But in the ideal order, a central bank's holdings of such government debt should arise in connection with its orderly efforts to supply liquidity to the economy as a whole through open market operations or other suitable vehicles. This is one of the many reasons that the development of a market for government securities – including a viable secondary market for such securities – is such a high priority. Indeed, a well-functioning government securities market will serve three vital purposes: first, it will provide a more market-oriented way to finance budget deficits; second, it will facilitate a more effective approach to monetary policy and the strengthening of the balance sheet of the central bank; third, it will provide the foundation upon which other elements of capital markets can be developed. But as with all markets, the development of a smoothly functioning government securities market presupposes that there is a complete infrastructure that will support an emerging secondary market for such securities that, at the least, provides the liquidity whereby such securities can be readily bought and sold by the central bank and other market participants. Without that infrastructure and liquidity, it will be very difficult to design government debt instruments that institutions and individuals will find attractive as investments and it will be equally difficult to free the monetary policy process from the need either to directly finance government deficits or to engage in various forms of credit allocation, or both.

I said at the outset that the task of reforming the banking and financial system was one of the most important tasks facing the countries of Eastern Europe and the Soviet Union. It is also one of the most difficult. In part those difficulties are technical, in part they are economic, and in part they are political. But most fundamentally, these difficulties arise from the fact that the reform of the banking system must come to grips with that great intangible – public confidence. It is in this area in particular that the role of the central bank is vitally important not only in the context of its monetary policy responsibilities but also with regard to the inherent responsibility of the central bank to help ensure the essential stability and viability of financial institutions and markets.

15. Banking in the Former Soviet Union

Marc Lieberman

As this book goes to press, the former Soviet Republics are attempting to reform their banking systems along market-oriented principles. To understand why this is such a difficult and all-encompassing task, we must first understand what Soviet banking was. We begin with a general comparison of banking in market-type and centrally-planned economies, then outlines the structure and operating principles of Soviet banking in particular. The article concludes with a few thoughts on future reforms.

Market-Type Banking versus Soviet-Type Banking

Every nation has its own unique banking system, and any simple division into two categories – "market-type" and "Soviet-type" – of necessity blurs the differences within a category. But we lose very little and gain quite a bit by doing so. To compare, for example, the old Soviet and Polish banking systems is like comparing two different species of plants; to compare Soviet banking with, say, American or French banking is like comparing plants with animals.

The most striking differences between the two systems are as follows:

(1) Basic structure: In *market-type economies* (MTEs), the banking system is almost always "two-tiered". The top tier is a government-run *central bank*, while the bottom tier consists of numerous *private banks* and other lending institutions. The functions of the two tiers are usually non-overlapping: the central bank regulates private banking behavior and controls the national money supply, while private banks take deposits and make loans to the private sector.

In *Soviet-type economies* (STEs), all banking functions were performed by the State bank, which Western observers aptly called a "monobank." Private banks were not permitted to exist.

(2) Credit Allocation: In MTE's, the allocation of credit is *decentralized*, since it is performed by thousands of independent lending institutions, all attempting to maximize the profits of their owners. In addition, individuals

132

and enterprises can extend credit to each other, bypassing the banking system entirely. For this reason, one expects credit allocation in a MTE to be *efficient*; credit flows to those firms that can pay the highest rates of return, i.e., to those that respond best to consumer desires.

In a STE, credit allocation was entirely *centralized* – a by-product of the centralized production plan. The monobank played an essentially passive role, providing credit wherever the plan directed. If the plan called for capital expansion in a particular enterprise, the monobank would grant long-term credit to purchase the new equipment. When the plan required an enterprise to purchase inputs before it received revenue from outputs, the monobank granted short-term credit. Thus, the allocation of credit in a STE was no more efficient than the plan itself. There was no profit motive, no competition among lenders or borrowers, no threat of bankruptcy, nothing at all to force credit allocation to respond to consumer desires.[1]

(3) Monetary Policy: In MTEs, the central bank possesses a monopoly on the creation of currency reserves which it exploits to influence the money supply. In this way, it can affect key important macroeconomic variables – interest rates, output, employment, and prices.

In STEs, this kind of monetary policy did not exist, for two reasons. First, as explained below, the monobank had no discretion over the quantity of money. Its money-creation activity – like its credit activity – was entirely passive, arising as a byproduct of the production plan. Second, changes in the quantity of money or credit would not have affected important macroeconomic variables anyway, because these were all fixed by the planners. An increase in money or credit might lead to additional household spending, but this, in turn, would only lengthen lines at state-controlled stores, or increase prices in the black market. It would have no effect on officially set prices and interest rates, or centrally planned output and employment levels.

We can see that "banking" in the traditional STE was very different from what we call banking in a market economy.[2] In the rest of this article, we

---

[1] The centralization of credit allocation was reinforced by another characteristic of Soviet-type banking systems: no alternatives to bank credit were allowed. Stock and bond markets did not exist, and interfirm lending was forbidden by law (and enforced by the monobank's ability to exert "control by the ruble" – see below).

[2] Even at this level of generalization, we should note some important exceptions to the above dichotomies. Yugoslavia departed from a typical STE banking system in 1954 and Hungary in 1968. Poland, which on the whole followed traditional STE banking until the late 1980s, nevertheless permitted widespread use of interfirm credit. On the Western side, it should be noted that in France, the functions of the two tiers have often overlapped. The

focus on banking in the former Soviet Union. Nevertheless, much of the discussion pertains to other STEs, whose banking systems, to a greater or lesser extent, all sprang from Soviet parentage.

The Banking System of the Former Soviet Union

The Structure of the Soviet Banking System

Gosbank (literally, "State Bank") has traditionally been the core of the Soviet banking system. Shortly before the dissolution of the Soviet Union at the end of 1991, Gosbank had over 150,000 employees working in over 6,000 branch and collection offices nationwide. Over 250,000 enterprises, 40,000 collective farms, and nearly half a million government organizations held accounts with Gosbank.

In addition to Gosbank, three other financial institutions comprised the Soviet monobank. Sperbank ("Savings Bank"), with over 70,000 branch offices, was the sole bank for household savings deposits, which earned a positive but very low rate of interest.[3] Stroibank ("Investment Bank"), was responsible for disbursing funds to enterprises for long-term investment, according to the dictates of the central plan. Finally, Vneshtorgbank ("Foreign Trade Bank") handled all transactions involving imports and exports.

Even though the Soviet system (like that of other STEs) was divided into more than one "bank," it was still a "monobank" in the sense described above. The additional "banks" merely administered funds or accepted deposits from households. They did not compete with Gosbank, and were ultimately under the orders of the same central authorities as Gosbank. Indeed, Sperbank became an official department within Gosbank in 1963.

Money in the Soviet Union

In developed market economies, the fundamental types of money are cash (coin and currency) and the private checks of households and businesses. In the Soviet Union (as in most other STEs), there were few private checking accounts. Nevertheless, there was something *like* a checking account in the

---

Banque de France, for example, was at one time a major competitor for private sector deposits and has often played an important role in allocating credit.

[3] Until 1963, Sperbank was controlled by the Finance Ministry as a separate institution from Gosbank, even though Sperbank deposits were themselves automatically deposited with Gosbank, where they were considered part of the government's general revenue. After 1963, the two banks merged, and Sperbank became an official department within Gosbank.

enterprise sector, and that was "bookkeeping money" on account with Gosbank.

Indeed, these bookkeeping accounts were the only type of money used between one enterprise and another. Whenever one enterprise shipped its output to another enterprise which used it as input, the Gosbank account of the "output-enterprise" would be credited, while that of the "input-enterprise" would be debited. In this way, goods made their way through the production process without occasioning any exchange of cash.

Besides this "bookkeeping money," there was cash, which was used for only two purposes. First, enterprises paid their workers with cash provided by Gosbank (the account of the enterprise would be debited). Second, households purchased goods with cash, which was then turned over to Gosbank (the account of the store would be credited).

The participation of Gosbank in virtually every financial transaction not only provided the financial clearing operations for these transactions to take place, but also enabled Gosbank to closely monitor adherence to the production plan. This monitoring function of Gosbank was known as *control by the ruble*.

Control by the Ruble

Let us take a simple example of consumer goods production in the Soviet Union: a milk farm produces milk and ships it to a cheese factory, which turns it into cheese and ships it to a State store. Finally, the State store sells the cheese to a household. How would Gosbank be involved in each of these transactions?

When farm delivered its milk output, it would obtain a document from the cheese factory verifying that the latter had received its milk input. The document was then turned over to Gosbank, which credited the farm's account according to the value of the milk delivered, and debited the cheese factory's account by the same value.

Likewise, after the cheese was produced and shipped to the State food store, the cheese factory obtained a document verifying its delivery of cheese. Again, the document was turned over to Gosbank, which this time credited the cheese factory's account and debited the store's account. Finally, when households purchased the cheese with cash, the State store deposited its cash receipts with Gosbank and was given a credit of equal value.

With this simple example, we can see how every transfer of *physical* output from one location to another, and every bit of value added in production, was mirrored by an associated *financial* transfer through Gosbank. If less than the planned amount was delivered on any given day, Gosbank would know. If delivery were late, Gosbank would know. If inputs or outputs were stolen and diverted to the black market, Gosbank would know. Of course, this did not mean that everything went according to plan. Shortages, time delays, and diversion to the black market were notorious problems of Soviet central planning. But control by the ruble did mean that glitches were discovered, investigated, and dealt with in some manner.

Control by the ruble was strengthened by severe restrictions on the use of money and credit in the Soviet Union. As for bookkeeping money, inter-enterprise credit was simply not allowed; one enterprise could not "lend" bookkeeping money to another by permitting late payment for goods received. Also, enterprise accounts with Gosbank were "blocked," that is, they could only be used to pay for the type and quantities of inputs that were specified in the plan. Otherwise, Gosbank would refuse to release them.

As for cash, enterprises were virtually forbidden to hold it for any purpose other than payment of wages. Even the cash receipts of State stores had to be deposited with Gosbank, and then withdrawn again to pay the wages of the store workers.

Finally, control by the ruble extended to imports and exports as well. All goods produced for export were "sold" to Vneshtorgbank, which credited the producer's account with bookkeeping rubles. Vneshtorgbank would then sell the goods abroad for foreign currency. In turn, the foreign currency was used to pay for imports into the Soviet Union, which were then sold to a Soviet enterprise whose bookkeeping rubles would be debited. In this way, the authorities could carefully monitor foreign currency exchange, and ensure that scarce "hard currency" (i.e., freely convertible currency like U.S. dollars or German marks) was used only for "desired purposes."

In general, control by the ruble was designed to prevent deviations from the central production plan. But since the plan itself was often inconsistent, providing an enterprise with too little of one input and too much of another, managers – in order to meet their output requirements – were forced to develop sources of supply that could bypass Gosbank's clearing operations, i.e., sources that required neither bookkeeping money nor cash. Hence, the immense amount of interfirm bartering that took place in the Soviet Union. An enterprise with excess coal might be lucky enough to trade it for some desperately needed steel. More likely, it would trade its excess coal for some rubber that it didn't need, and would then go about finding an enterprise that had excess steel but needed rubber. Or, worse still: it would trade coal for rubber, then trade rubber for steel knives, and finally melt down the knives to obtain raw steel.

Of course, barter requires human resources that could otherwise be used productively. In this way, control by the ruble was *another* cause of economic inefficiency in the Soviet Union, above and beyond that caused by inconsistencies in the plan itself.

Banking and Macroeconomic Balance

The most unpredictable component of Soviet central planning was the purchase of household consumer goods. Microeconomically, it was impossible to predict how a given amount of spending would be allocated among different goods and services. Macroeconomically, planners had difficulty predicting even the *total* value of goods and services consumers wished to buy in state stores. Consumer goods were purchased exclusively with cash, so to understand the source of macroeconomic imbalance in the Soviet Union, we need to understand how the supply of cash was determined.

Diagram 1: Cash Flows in the Former U.S.S.R.

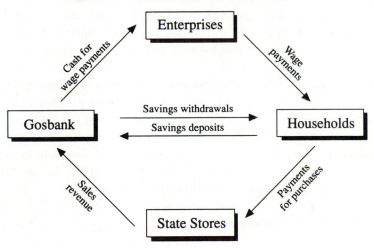

Ignoring some minor details, cash followed a very simple route in the system: from Gosbank to enterprises to households (for wage payments); and then from households back to Gosbank again, either directly (as savings deposits) or indirectly (as cash revenue of stores which was then re-deposited into Gosbank). The process is outlined in diagram 1[4].

If, for simplicity, we assume that movements of cash into and out of savings accounts were about equal, then – for Gosbank – equality between inflows and outflows of cash would require that wage payments equal purchases of consumption goods. We can call this situation "macroeconomic balance," and it is essentially what the planning authorities strived for each year. Macroeconomic balance meant that Gosbank would be able to pay all wages from its cash inflows, so the supply of cash rubles could remain constant.

But macroeconomic balance was rarely achieved. Most commonly, especially in the late 1970s and 1980s, cash outflows for wages consistently exceeded cash inflows from goods purchased, primarily because consumer goods (at least those desired by consumers) were in short supply. As long as unemployment could not be tolerated and wages had to be paid, Gosbank had no choice but to print up additional cash for wages. The result was an ever-increasing supply of rubles, without a matching increase in supply of goods.

The consequences were: (1) ever lengthening lines at State stores with fixed prices; (2) continuing inflation in the unregulated kolkhoz and black markets; and (3) a continual flow of "forced savings" into Sperbank or into cash hoards, since there weren't enough goods and services to absorb all the rubles households might wish to spend.

The later result is of particular importance for reform efforts in the former Soviet Union, for after years of forced saving, there exists a considerable stock of liquid wealth in the household sector, both in the form of deposits with Sperbank, and also cash hoards stuffed into jars and flower pots and dresser drawers. In early 1991, estimates of this *ruble overhang* in the USSR ranged from 50 billion rubles to over 200 billion rubles, a huge source of potential spending with dangerous inflationary potential.

The Reform of Soviet Banking

The Gorbachev Reforms
Before the dissolution of the Soviet Union in late 1991, several important

---

[4] Note that the diagram excludes final goods (e.g., defense goods) purchased by the government, since these were paid for with bookkeeping money and required no cash to change hands. But government *services* (e.g., legislators' services) were purchased with cash. In this case, the government could be thought of as an "enterprise," those providing services were the enterprises's "workers," and payments for these services were wage payments.

changes were made in the Soviet banking system. While these reforms moved the system closer to Western-style banking, they did not move it very far. The most important elements of the banking reforms, which began in earnest in 1987, were as follows:

(1) Private banking was legalized as part of the 1988 "Law on Coopera-tives." Banks could be organized as joint-stock companies (with stock owned by enterprises, local governments, or social organizations) or as cooperatives. Enterprises were now permitted to maintain surplus cash, and the new banks were free to compete for household and enterprise deposits and to make long- and short-term loans. At the time of the dissolution of the USSR, there were several hundred of these banks in existence.

(2) Commercial bank operations (allocating credit, accepting deposits) were stripped from Gosbank and transferred to three new specialized banks (Agroprombank, Promstroibank, and Zhilsotsbank) each handling deposits, lending, and payments services in a different sector of the economy. The intention was to convert each of these banks into a joint stock company, although by late 1991, this had only been accomplished for Agroprombank, the agricultural-sector bank. Sperbank (Savings Bank) continued to accept household deposits, although now it had to compete with private sector banks and was forced to raise interest rates. And enterprises were given more freedom to deal in foreign currency, reducing the power of the foreign trade bank (which had been given the new name, "Vneshekonombank").

(3) Gosbank began its transformation into a Western-style central bank, establishing reserve requirements, capitalization requirements, and lending regulations for the nascent private banking sector.

These steps fell far short of what the most radical reformers thought necessary. In particular, the Gosbank monopoly on enterprise loans and deposits was simply replaced with three new monopoly banks, each responsi-ble for its own sector of the economy. None of the three new banks were permitted to compete for customers or clients with the others, and Sperbank, with its 70,000 branch offices, retained a virtual monopoly on household savings deposits, since its only competitor was the tiny commercial banking sector. Finally, monetary policy remained essentially passive, since Gosbank was still forced to print up cash to finance wage payments in State enterpris-es.

The gradual dissolution of the Soviet Union led to a virtual collapse of Gosbank by the end of 1991. Increasingly, individual republics (most importantly, the RFSR) ordered enterprises within their borders to turn over cash revenue to them, then used it to expand the role and size of their *own* governments. Since the central Soviet government refused to shrink itself out of existence, Gosbank was forced to accelerate cash-printing to pay the wages of workers in enterprises and agencies still controlled by the center. In the first 11 months of 1991, the quantity of rubles in circulation increased from 132 billion to 234 billion. By late 1991, the only constraints on cash growth were physical: the printing presses – which were capable of printing notes of specific denominations only (the largest being a 200-ruble note) – were running 24-hours a day.[5] Shortages of consumer goods intensified, lines at State stores grew even longer, and the inflation rate reached roughly 3 percent per week by late 1991.

The Future of Banking in the Former Soviet Republics

As this article is being written, the banking system in the former Soviet republics remains very much undefined and unstable. The Russian Central Bank has taken over most of the functions of Gosbank, and the Russian government has indicated a desire to move rapidly toward a Western, perhaps American model, but it remains unclear how quickly it will move, and to what extent the Russian financial umbrella will extend over the other republics. There remain several troubling obstacles to successful banking reform in the former Soviet republics.

First, the pace of banking reform is inextricably tied to the pace of reform in other areas. Three examples of this are as follows:

(1) A decentralized banking system can allocate credit only if private banks have a way of ascertaining the credit risks of potential borrowers. This, in turn, requires the development and application of market-type accounting procedures, as well as the establishment and strict enforcement of truthful disclosure laws. Progress on both of these fronts, in turn, requires transformation of human capital in the legal and accounting professions. A glitch in any one of these processes can sidetrack the development of the banking system.

(2) If credit-allocation is to be even roughly efficient, then the ability to

---

[5] One of President Yeltsin's first announcements in January 1992, after the Russian Republic took over the printing presses, was that production of 500 ruble notes had already begun, and 1,000-ruble notes would be produced by the end of the month. A few weeks later, bank officials hinted they would soon produce 5,000 ruble notes as well.

repay loans – as assessed by banks – must correspond in some way with the pattern of consumer desires. Thus, soft-budget constraints and State price controls (see Kornai, Article 2), which enable firms to escape the harsh rule of consumer sovereignty, hinder the development of efficient banking.

(3) Without a social safety net that enables the body-politic to tolerate temporary unemployment, the central bank will face tremendous pressure to print money in order to keep troubled firms afloat. In the troubled economies of the former Soviet republics, this would certainly lead to hyperinflation, loss of faith in the currency, and ultimately, to a barter system in which financial services would have no value.

Thus, political developments that inhibit price reform, budgetary reform, or technical assistance from the West will surely delay progress in the development of the banking sector.

Second, efficient banking will require a significant transformation of public attitudes about banks and bankers. Western observers are often amazed at public statements by the Soviet "man on the street" who, before the CNN television cameras, makes speeches about the market system that sound as if scripted by Milton Friedman. We need to remind ourselves that these educated, English-speaking, gregarious Muscovites are a random sample of a very special subset of the Russian population; we simply do not see the others.

More scientific public opinion polls show a lingering skepticism and resentment about capitalist institutions and values.[6] Even in the non-communist world, banking has been the capitalist institution least understood and most readily attacked by those who do not fully understand it; among those steeped in Marxist culture, this tendency is even more extreme. A people may be willing, even anxious, to get on with needed market reforms, but their negative views of banking and bankers will not disappear overnight. An efficient, decentralized banking system will require thousands of competing banks with hundreds of thousands of professional employees; in a hostile social atmosphere, potential bankers may shy away.

Finally, a stable banking system requires a (semi)-permanent decision on the degree of financial integration among the former Soviet Republics, and this must be decided in the context of economic integration more generally. At present, the desired extent of unity is unclear. Individual visions of the new Commonwealth of Independent States vary from little more than a free-

---

[6] See, for example, Shiller, Boycko and Korobov, Article 31 in this book.

trade area to full economic integration with a common currency.

The advantages of a single currency controlled by a unified central bank are clear, as the twelve nations of the EEC have recently recognized. It has been estimated that, in the EEC, firms spend $13 billion each year in commission charges for currency conversion. Billions more are spent on accounting staff to track costs and revenues in twelve currencies, and financial staff to assess and manage exchange-rate risks whenever inputs or outputs cross international frontiers. These factors so reduced the gains from comparative advantage in production, and hiked the cost of capital investment throughout the EEC, that monetary sovereignty seemed insignificant in comparison; in December 1991, the EEC reached a decision (with the possible, wavering exception of Britain) to adopt a unified currency by 1996.

The argument for monetary union in the former Soviet republics may be even stronger, since years of Stalinist specialization have left the productive infrastructures of the republics even more interdependent than those of the EEC nations. Since the republics will need to trade so intensively anyway, why not take away the obstacles and inefficiencies of different currencies?

On the other hand, the *cost* of giving up monetary sovereignty may be larger in the former Soviet republics than in the EEC. The Soviet republics, unlike the EEC, face an unprecedented transformation of their economic systems, but they differ widely in standard of living, level of education, and political culture. They also differ as to the desired pace and ultimate goals of market reforms. A common currency would tend to constrain different republics to move in tandem, which could harm (and perhaps even halt) the reform process in many of them.

An example of this constraint on the pace of reform occurred on January 2, when the Russian Republic hiked prices on a wide variety of goods and services. In order for the price hikes to help reduce shortages, it was decided that Russian wage earners would not be fully compensated, and purchasing power went down dramatically. The Ukraine and Belarus did not want to move quite so fast in cutting standards of living, but if they refused to raise prices in tandem with Russia, they would have to choose between: (a) permitting a flood of Russians crossing into their republics to buy up cheap goods, exacerbating their own shortages; or (b) refusing to sell to non-residents and thus beginning a trade war in the new Commonwealth of Independent States; or (c) establishing their own money supply, and thus introduce new risks and inefficiencies into inter-republic trading. In the end, a compromise solution was chosen: prices were hiked as in Russia, but the two republics distributed coupons to supplement their residents' ruble incomes and keep standards of living temporarily unchanged. Thus, the fiction of a common currency was, for the moment, maintained, even though in reality the two republics had effectively established independent money supplies.

As the example shows, banking reform and the degree of economic integration are closely linked, and deciding on the precise form of economic integration in the former Soviet republics will not be easy, nor will any solution necessarily be stable. This may well be the most serious obstacle to banking reform in the former Soviet republics.

16. Requirements for a Successful Equity Market[*]

Antoine van Agtmael

The basic prerequisites for the establishment and continued success of an equity market include:

* a reasonably stable political environment;
* conducive macro-economic policies, to ensure an attractive long-term yield for equities in comparison with other domestic and foreign investment alternatives;
* a growing economy;
* a favorable government attitude and an economic structure in which private enterprise is allowed to play a significant role;
* a sufficient demand for and supply of stocks;
* reasonably well-developed accounting and auditing standards:
* non-discriminatory tax treatment of investment in shares in comparison with other investment alternatives, or even special temporary tax and other incentives;
* the existence of at least a small group of intermediaries (underwriters, dealers, and brokers); and
* an adequate legal framework, including protection of outside investors through securities legislation and its enforcement.

Without these elements, a viable equity market cannot develop; it will either remain dormant or be subject to excessive speculation. It is obvious that several of these factors are closely related to the level of economic development which a country has achieved and the type of development path it has chosen.

---

[*]From *Emerging Securities Markets*, 1982. Material first published by Euromoney Publications, London. Reprinted by permission of Euromoney Ltd.

1. Political and economic environment

Investors are very sensitive to political uncertainty. In countries which are in domestic turmoil, engaged in major border conflicts, or involved in a war, there is little interest in establishing a stock market and investing in shares. If a market exists, trading activity and prices are usually in decline. Political disruption nearly always affects economic activity because companies postpone investments and scale down their growth projections. In contrast, rapid economic growth leads to a sense of confidence among investors and entrepreneurs and opens up new markets, providing companies with a strong inducement to expand their operations. Their need for finance, including share capital, grows.

Economies dominated by government enterprises (as in many socialist and African countries) or with scarce entrepreneurial experience are not likely candidates for the establishment of a stock market. An exception is countries where the government has made a conscious decision to change course and sell its stake in government corporations to allow them to be run on a private enterprise basis.

Unfavorable or unstable macroeconomic policies (for example, high inflation, negative real interest rates, frequent devaluations, discriminatory tax treatment of shares) are a major reason for the lack of activity of securities markets in many developing countries. Erratic monetary policies create a suspicion of all kinds of financial paper; frequent devaluations and negative real interest rates at home tempt investors to invest abroad. Inflation has eroded return on equity in many countries for long periods. Inevitably investors turn away from equity when the expected yield on shares is likely to be lower than that on other less risky investment alternatives. Indeed, it is surprising how well many emerging securities markets have developed despite the enormous handicaps under which they have operated.

2. The demand for stocks

The demand for stocks depends on a variety of factors.

2.1 Individual demand

The first important factor is the number of financially sophisticated individuals with enough money to purchase shares. In a country without a stock market, this number is difficult to estimate, although the size of the population, in particular the urban population, and the level of per capita income give rough indications. A better approximation can be derived from estimating the numbers of businessmen, professionals (doctors, engineers, accountants, lawyers, and higher level employees in companies), and senior civil servants. If such data are not available, the number of car owners, bank depositors, or holders of government bonds can be useful. In their early stages, stock markets cater to as few as 10,000 shareholders, of whom only several hundred may be active traders. Remittances from workers abroad can play a significant role in the demand for shares, as happens in Jordan and Turkey.

2.2 Institutional demand

In many emerging markets, demand from insurance companies, pension or provident funds, and mutual funds is negligible; in some, like Brazil, Chile, Korea, Pakistan, and Indonesia, their presence plays an important role. This is an area of extensive discrimination against equity markets in many developing countries. Regulations governing the obligatory reserves of insurance companies have a major impact on their investment activities. Government controlled pension funds are usually not fully funded or can invest only in government securities. Private pension or provident funds can only be active buyers if they are allowed to do so by rules channelling their investments into various categories or pertaining to their fiduciary responsibility. Private parties and government authorities interested in the development of a stock market are often not sufficiently aware of the potential importance of institutional investment; without them there is a great risk of a market dominated by individual speculators.

2.3 Foreign portfolio investment

Only in a few emerging markets (Hong Kong, Singapore, Malaysia and Mexico) do foreigners play a significant role. In many other markets, foreign portfolio investment has been discouraged. This situation appears to be changing, however. Mexico, Brazil, Korea, and Taiwan have recently changed their legislation to allow foreign investment through mutual funds. Korea is planning to internationalize its market further and permit foreign institutions and individuals to participate more directly in the future.

2.4 Investment alternatives

The attractiveness of shares in comparison with other investment alternatives is crucial to individual as well as institutional investors. Rational investors look at overall return, risk, liquidity, and tax treatment in determining where and how to invest their money. In theory, they should calculate future expectations regarding these factors, but in reality most investors, especially the less sophisticated speculators, look primarily at recent performance. For example, hopes for capital gains play a major role in buying decisions when prices have begun to soar, but are easily ignored when a stock exchange does not yet exist or trading is dormant. In inactive markets, dividend yield tends to be more important than capital gains expectations. The overall return (or yield) on shares (including both dividends and capital gains) must be higher than the interest yield which the investor would receive on bank deposits or bonds because most investors view shares as more risky.

Since policies influence after-tax yield to the investor, government measures to improve the tax treatment of shares can have a major impact. Liquidity, or investors' ability to sell shares quickly without affecting the market price, is also important when investors compare the after-tax yields of shares and bonds or deposits. A comparison of potential capital gains, including their tax treatment, is especially relevant when land or real estate is appreciating rapidly.

2.5 Information

Public awareness of the stock market and of shares as an investment medium is essential. Promotional campaigns on television and radio and regular newspaper coverage of stock market activities are helpful in educating the public. At a later stage, it is essential to have adequate disclosure of information on traded stocks.

3. The supply of stocks

Not having enough stock issues to trade adequately is often a greater constraint on the development of an active equity market than the number of investors. Too few stocks may at first deter investors from entering the market at all; later, when trading is active, too many people may be chasing too few stocks, thus adding to price volatility.

Another potential problem frequently encountered in developing stock markets is the lack of float, the percentage of a company's capital available for stock market trading to outside investors rather than being held by the major existing owners.

Before a stock market can start at least 20 companies, each with a float of about 25 percent of their capital, should be available for trading. Stock markets such as Korea, Thailand, and Jordan started with such relatively small numbers. Active emerging markets now have 300 or more listed stocks, of which at least 25-50 are actively traded on a daily basis.

3.1 Factors influencing supply of securities

Size. The size of the economy, its level of development and growth rate, and its free enterprise orientation largely determine the number of sizeable corporations which are likely to be available for listing their shares on the stock exchange.

Attitude. Equally important is the attitude of existing owners to allowing outsiders into the company and opening up their books. This attitude usually depends on whether the companies are still managed by the original owners or whether professional managers have been brought in. In the latter case, existing shareholders are more likely to be willing to list their companies on a stock exchange and sell some of their shares, especially if they can make an attractive profit.

Need. A major factor inducing companies to go public may be the need for a sizeable amount of additional capital. Such a need exists when the company is growing so rapidly that internally generated cash flow or the owner's resources are outstripped by the capital requirements of major expansion. This happens frequently in rapidly growing economies. In such an environment, the availability of other investment opportunities may provide new horizons for the original owners, while bank credits may be in short supply and companies already over-leveraged.

Interest rate policies. When interest rates are generally held below inflation levels for sustained periods or loans with a large subsidy element are easily available, entrepreneurs find it advantageous to borrow rather than to issue shares to the general public. Such interest rate policies have been widespread in many developing countries.

Tax policies and other inducements. These may provide an additional or even a key reason for existing owners to sell their shares to the public, rather than transferring ownership to their heirs.

Legislation. No incentives can overcome the obstacle of unrealistically low or artificially determined prices. In many countries, under outdated company laws, the prices at which shares can be sold to the public are determined by government authorities on the basis of par or book value and rights issues must be offered first to existing shareholders. It would be more advantageous for underwriters to evaluate the earnings potential of the company and the expected demand for an issue in current market conditions.

Government participation. In some countries, governments dominate the ownership of major enterprises. This means that they may be in a position to increase substantially the supply of stocks available for trading, by divesting their interest in public sector corporations which are profitable and professionally managed.

4. Tax policies and other inducements

A flexible and positive government attitude to the establishment and development of an equity market is essential. Many countries discriminate against equity by a less than favorable tax treatment of dividends and capital gains. In contrast, interest on bank deposits, government bonds, and bank-sponsored bonds may be tax-exempt, giving these investment alternatives, which offer a high level of safety, an additional advantage. Share transactions may be registered (and thus be accessible to tax authorities), while bonds may be in bearer form and transactions in real estate may be difficult to trace.

Companies may not want to go public because they fear that tax authorities could catch them more easily at tax evasion, a widespread practice among privately-held companies in many countries. Tax incentives are designed to counter such fears and to provide a positive inducement for companies to go public or for owners to sell (supply incentives) and for investors to buy shares (demand incentives).

4.1 Demand incentives

Examples of demand incentives are:
*   Tax exemption or reduction for capital gains on shares of listed companies.
*   Tax exemption or partial exemption up to a certain amount for dividends. Corporate income is usually already taxed and a withholding tax on dividends or their inclusion in taxable income would amount to double taxation. This may have the effect of deterring owners of private companies from letting their companies go public; it may also result in unequal tax treatment in comparison with bank deposits or bonds which are often officially or *de facto* tax-exempt.
*   Special tax credits or deductions for individuals and possibly companies investing in shares of publicly held companies. Sweden,

France, Brazil, Mexico, and Egypt have various forms of such incentives. Sometimes they are for investment in new issues or mutual funds only, in other cases for all investment in shares of listed companies. Usually there is a requirement that such shares must be held for a minimum period, perhaps two years. These tax advantages can take the form of a deduction from taxable income or a straight tax credit, and are usually limited to a specific amount or a percentage of taxable income.

* Tax-deferred retirement plans to stimulate long-term savings and investment. Special tax deductions or benefits may be given to long-term investments, which are committed until retirement age, in shares, bonds, and possibly other financial instruments. Dividends, interest, and capital gains on such investments may be exempt from taxation until paid out after retirement.

* Freedom from tax on the transfer of shares for shareholders of a listed company, while transfer of shares in privately held companies is taxed.

4.2 Supply incentives

The most widely used supply incentive is a lower corporate income tax for public companies than for privately held companies. The differential should be at least 10-20 per cent, sufficient to negate the customary tax evasion of privately held companies. An insufficient differential, or none at all, would be a deterrent rather than an incentive. An exemption from or reduction of tax paid on the profits of such sales is a strong inducement to the existing owners of privately held companies to sell shares to the general public.

4.3 Other inducements

Other measures to induce companies to go public include special investigations by the tax authorities of companies identified as potential public companies but which have chosen not to go public (as done in Korea) and limitations on the amount of, or conditions for, bank credit applying to private companies but not to public companies. These approaches have proved successful in several countries, inducing a large number of corporations to go public within a short time.

5. Financial intermediaries

An equity market cannot function without brokers, dealers, and underwriters. Brokers handle the mechanics of completing trades on the floor of the exchange (or in an over-the-counter market), the transfer of shares from the old to the new owner, and the payments involved. Brokerage houses may also have research departments which analyse the quality, prospects, and relative attractiveness of shares in comparison with other investment alternatives.

Dealers make a continuous market in shares, step in when price gaps develop and smooth out price fluctuations. Such dealers may be specialized companies (such as jobbers in the UK and specialists in the US) or may also act as brokers. In the latter case, regulation is necessary to ensure that broker/dealers give their clients equal access to the trading floor and do not give preference to transactions for their own account.

Underwriters assist companies in going public and increasing their capital by taking the risk of buying whatever portion of an issue is not sold to final investors. They also help to structure the deal, write the prospectus, find investors, and handle the mechanics of the distribution process.

A well-organized securities industry typically includes a number of brokerage houses. Some of these may provide the full range of investment banking services from trading in shares, bonds, and money market instruments to underwriting investment management and financial advisory services.

6. The Legal Environment

6.1 Company law

Changes are typically required in a country's company law (or civil and commercial code) to enable securities underwriting and trading to take place. Items which need to be covered include the easy transfer of shares; ownership registration in the name of intermediaries such as brokers, underwriters, and central custodial facilities; regulations on take-overs, etc.

6.2 Securities legislation

Outside investors need to be protected against stock manipulation by insiders (major shareholders, directors, and management) and the risk that insiders will skim off profits before they ever reach outside investors. Other aspects of investor protection, are the need to establish standards for professional conduct by brokers and underwriters and to avoid excessive speculation caused by market rumors and too easy availability of margin loans.

Without some form of investor protection, stock scandals, swindles, or the bursting of speculative bubbles are too likely to occur. Such protection can be exercised by a securities commission or other government watchdog, or through self-regulation by the stock exchange and an association of stock brokers and underwriters. Usually both types of protection are found, with major responsibility allocated to one sector. In securities markets based on the US model, such as Korea and most of Latin America, the securities commission plays the major role through extensive securities legislation. In securities markets based on the UK model, such as Hong Kong or Singapore, self-regulation is the dominant factor. A third model – with a combined securities exchange and commission – has been chosen in several new, small markets such as Thailand and Jordan.

Typically, measures to protect outside investors include requirements relating to disclosure and financial reporting, accounting and audit standards, listing insider trading, margin loans, trading floor procedures, and professional standards.

It is politically impossible, and in practice unfeasible, to introduce too many rules or legislation at the same time. "Overkill" can easily strangle a stock market during its early growth, so legislation is usually introduced in distinct stages. On the other hand, a too gradual approach should be avoided because it leads to uncertainty and confusion.

Disclosure and financial reporting requirements. Outside investors must be able to make an informed judgment regarding the operations of a company, its profitability, financial health, growth, and prospects. Even if the investors themselves do not study the financial information carefully, their brokers or investment advisors will be able to do so. Unless they are required to open their books, companies are usually reluctant to do so.

Ideally, disclosure requirements for public companies should also be applicable to private companies which have reached a certain size. In most cases, this requires changes in local company laws.

Disclosure should cover not only the need for a prospectus at the time of a new issue, but also regular publication of financial information afterwards through audited annual reports, quarterly reports, immediate release of material information to the stock market, etc.

Accounting and auditing standards. Financial information may not be accurate or comparable from company to company without the adoption and enforcement of generally accepted accounting standards. Such standards go along with the need for a strong and independent auditing profession.

Listing requirements. Independent of the disclosure requirements of a securities commission, a stock exchange may set specific requirements before a company can be listed and thus traded.

Insider trading. Manipulation by directors or management, who are in a better position to know the prospects of the company than outsiders, is not uncommon without regulation. Insiders may be asked to disclose their sales and purchases of the company's stock on a periodic basis or may be otherwise restricted. Legislation and regulations in the area are usually very controversial and difficult to police. It may be necessary or desirable to control insider trading on an informal basis during the early days of an exchange and only formalize regulations later.

Margin loans. Without some general guidance brokers have a tendency to over-extend margin loans to customers, endangering not only their own financial health but also fuelling speculation. Examples of limitations include:

*   a list of shares which are eligible as collateral for margin finance;
*   rules requiring brokers to know their customers through detailed account information;
*   specific margin limits and margin calls;
*   standard formats for margin loan contracts between brokers and clients; and
*   limits on the amount of credit extended to any single customer or for any particular stock.

Trading floor procedures. A fair, open, and competitive market should give investors confidence. Rules and regulations of the stock exchange, approved by the securities commission if it exists, are aimed at this objective. Collusion between brokers, fraud by trading floor personnel, handling of large blocks of shares by prearrangement at a price which is different from the current market price, and transactions by brokers for their own account before purchases/sales are made for clients are common problems in the absence of regulation. To control speculation in the short run, some stock exchanges set daily limits on price changes, but such measures are usually not effective.

Professional standards of brokers and underwriters. Such standards can be established by legislation or through self-regulation by brokers and underwriters associations. Incorporation of brokerage houses with minimum capital is often desirable. Brokers and securities analysts may be asked to undergo examinations before they are qualified to deal with the public or analyse corporate statements for prospectuses.

7. Stages in the development of a stock market

No two stock markets develop in exactly the same way. Nevertheless, five stages can usually bc observed: the dormant stage, manipulation, speculation, consolidation or crash and maturity.

7.1 The Dormant Stage

During the first, dormant stage, only a few people are aware of the existence of the stock market, trading is low, few companies are listed and prices remain close to par. As time goes by, shares become undervalued, especially in a dynamic economic environment. Inevitably, brokers or individuals may discover that dividend yield – even excluding potential capital gains – exceeds the yield on other investment alternatives. Then they may begin to buy shares, cautiously at first and actively later.

7.2 Manipulation

Manipulation begins when some market participants discover that the small supply of stocks, and thus limited liquidity, makes it possible to drive up the price of one or more stocks with even minor purchases. As soon as prices soar others are encouraged to buy, enabling the manipulators to get out of the market with quick profits.

The start of more active trading may also be induced by government measures making investment in stocks more attractive. In other cases, a sudden dramatic upturn in the fortunes of a country or company starts the buying fever.

7.3 Speculation

As soon as some people begin to make substantial capital gains and boast of their profits, a wider group of speculators is attracted. A speculative stage begins during which prices are driven up well beyond their fundamental values and trading volume soars. New issues are so heavily oversubscribed that many companies go public and the supply of available stocks is broadened because the original owners see attractive opportunities to sell out. Responsible government action, such as an increase in margin requirements, higher brokerage commissions, selling by institutional investors, increases in board lots, divestiture of government owned shares, or activation of new underwriting of major companies, may dampen speculation, but it is probably not possible to avoid it altogether.

7.4 Consolidation or crash

At some point the amount of new money available for investment dries up. New issues become less oversubscribed and investors begin to realize that prices have been driven so high that they no longer bear any relation to their underlying value. Quite suddenly, stock prices begin to waver and prices drop. Depending on the extent of the earlier boom during the speculative stage, prices either decline gradually or tumble deeply. The consolidation stage or crash has set in.

It may take investors months or even years to regain confidence in the stock market after such a price decline. Much depends on the extent of the price drop as well as on interest rates, economic growth, corporate profitability, inflation yields on other investment alternatives, new incentives to restimulate buying, and the behavior of institutional investors. During this consolidation stage, many speculators become, out of necessity, investors. Unwilling to sell their shares at a loss, they hold on to them for long-term investment in the hope that prices will improve in the future.

7.5 Maturity

A new stage of maturity can begin when the initial investors regain confidence and are joined by new groups of investors who were not hurt during the first price decline. An enlarged presence of institutional investors could also play an important role in making a market more mature. Trading volume is likely to be more consistent, investors more sophisticated, the supply of shares broader, and, thus, liquidity greater. Prices will continue to fluctuate but the swings may become less violent.

If large price volatility continues, it is often caused by problems other than market factors themselves. These include:

* major political problems (e.g., Hong Kong in 1982)
* monetary and exchange rate policies (Argentina, Mexico in 1981-82)
* economic crisis (Brazil, Chile in 1982)
* changes in government-dictated dividend policies (Korea, Turkey in 1982)
* changes in tax policies (Thailand, Pakistan).

PART V

MARKET FAILURE

A major goal of reform in the emerging market economies – and the subject of most of the other articles in this book – is to get the government *out* of activities which are better served by the market. These are activities where, as Adam Smith has told us, individuals acting in their own self-interest will unwittingly serve the public good.

But another aspect of reform is the reverse of this: getting the State *into* certain activities that it *should* undertake, activities that the market will not perform well. There are numerous situations where individuals, acting collectively through their governments, can generate mutually beneficial improvements over the free-market result. We call these situations "market failures," because the market "fails" to generate the best possible outcome. The most commonly-cited cases of market failure are (1) monopoly power; (2) externalities; and (3) public goods. In this section, we consider examples of each of these market failures in the transforming economies and explore the problems they pose for economic reform.

Monopoly power is a clear-cut case of market failure. When a firm is the single supplier (or one of a few suppliers) of a good or service for which there are no close substitutes, then the owners of the firm – acting in their own self-interests – will tend to charge "too high" a price and produce "too little" of the good, compared to what would best serve the public at large. It is then necessary for the government to tamper with the market, so that the good or service will be provided at a lower price and higher quantity.

As Heidi Kroll shows in "Monopoly and Transition to Market," the problem of monopoly power is particularly severe in the Soviet Union, where, to facilitate central planning, the guiding principle for industry was the smallest possible number of the largest possible enterprises. If these large State firms are merely privatized and prices decontrolled, the result would be a degree of monopoly power unprecedented among market economies.

The standard remedies for monopoly power are three: (1) government *regulation* of the monopoly; (2) anti-trust efforts to break up the monopoly; and (3) policies to encourage competition and the free entry of new firms.

Kroll considennrs each of these standard remedies in turn. Regulation, which keeps prices low, will actually help to *perpetuate* monopolies, since it is precisely high prices and high profits that will attract new entrants into the industry.

Antitrust efforts, while effective in eliminating small pockets of monopoly power, will probably not work in the over-monopolized environment of the Soviet Union. Only the final option – encouraging competition and free entry – has any hope of success in the near term. Specifically, her anti-monopoly policy would combine three elements: (1) the relaxation of restrictions on the private sector to encourage the development of small and medium-sized competitors to monopolies; (2) a convertible ruble to encourage foreign competition from imports; and (3) tight fiscal and monetary policies to restrain resource-use by the government, so as to free up scarce inputs for the budding private sector. These recommendations pit Kroll against many other reformers, who have argued that privatization and price decontrol are dangerous unless the economy is de-monopolized *first*. Kroll argues that, on the contrary, de-monopolization is a long-term process, and making it a prerequisite for other reforms provides pseudo-reformers with yet another excuse to stall.

In Part II of this reader, we learned that the allocative efficiency of free markets rests on one central pillar: commodity prices reflect relative scarcities. In practice, however, this condition is not always fulfilled under free markets. An *externality* occurs when a resource used up in producing some commodity is not reflected in that commodity's price. Clean air, clean water, other people's time -- these are just a few examples of "scarce resources" that individuals often use in a free-market without paying for them at all, or paying very little.

The result of an externality is overuse of the resources involved. The solution: collective action to make sure that individuals pay higher-than-market prices for these resources. The classic example of an externality is pollution, which is the "using up" of clean environmental resources (air, water) without paying for them, and it is the example we explore in this section.

Ironically, socialist, centrally-planned economies have been among the worst environmental polluters, as shown in Stanley Kabala's article, "The Environmental Morass in Eastern Europe." Kabala points out three major reasons for this. First, the overall economic inefficiency in these countries results in greater energy usage – and therefore more energy-related pollution – per unit of output. Second, the obsession with industrial growth caused a severe bias toward heavy industry, which tends to be the most polluting. Finally, since governments in these countries maintained strict control over information and political expression, they were free of the pro-environment political pressure faced by the more democratic market-economies.

Kabala argues that, in Eastern Europe, as elsewhere, pollution control will require an active government environmental policy. But he also argues that the key to environmental reform in the region is reversing the historical process that created the damage. Specifically, increasing economic efficiency, expanding services and light industry at the expense of heavy industry, and encouraging political freedom may pay higher dividends in restoring and preserving the environment than any direct environmental policy.

The third and final case of market failure we explore here is that of *public goods*, i.e., goods which the private market will not produce because there is no efficient way to charge people for their use. The classic examples of public goods are national defense, police protection, and environmental protection. In all three cases, everyone in the community benefits, whether they have individually paid for the goods or not, and so everyone will try to be a "free rider" on a train that is moving anyway. Since no entrepreneur can easily overcome the "free rider problem," the market simply does not provide the good, or provides too little of it.

Another example of a public good – and the one we explore in this section – is public information, in particular, national information on economic performance. Once this information is gathered, it is difficult to limit its use to those who pay. The market, if left to itself, would therefore fail to generate this information, to the detriment of us all. The task, as in the other examples of public goods, must be performed collectively, i.e., by the State. The governments of the centrally planned economies did attempt to gather information on economic performance, but it is widely acknowledged that they did a very poor job. The article entitled "Statistical Issues," prepared collectively by several international organizations, treats the case of the Soviet Union.

Although the article refers to the government agencies and data-gathering processes of the former central government, most of these agencies, together with their methods, were simply taken over intact by the Russian Republic. The problems discussed in the article – the tendency to "count" rather than sample; the over-reliance on labor and under-reliance on technology in data processing; the incentives to distort information – are now the problems of the Russian Republic and, ultimately, the other republics as well.

17. Monopoly and Transition to the Market*

Heidi Kroll

In the past, Soviet planners viewed monopoly as a purely capitalist affliction. They now contend that the monopolistic structure of Soviet industry is a key reason for the failure of Mikhail Gorbachev's initial enterprise reforms and the deterioration of the economy since 1988. The reforms aimed to induce enterprises to produce what buyers wanted by allowing them greater freedom to set their own production targets and by linking bonuses and wages to income from sales. Instead, enterprises have used their increased autonomy to cut production targets, to shift their output mix in favor of higher-priced products, to avoid concluding disadvantageous delivery contracts, and to impose conditions on buyers such as requirements for barter exchange, payment in hard currency, or delivery of unwanted goods. By many Soviet accounts, producers owe their power to dictate the terms of contracts to a complete or virtual monopoly on the supply of their products. According to the director of Goskomstat, the output of key industries declined or fell short of plan targets in 1989 largely because of shortfalls in the delivery of critical parts by monopolists and near-monopolists.

The recognition of the virtues of competition marked a significant step forward in Soviet reform debates. The new Soviet thinking on monopoly, however, is not without pitfalls. For example, the structural problem of high industrial concentration is often conflated with the macroeconomic problem of excess demand. The behavior ascribed to monopoly is attributable in large part to the disequilibrium created by large budget deficits and an accommodating expansion of money and credit, coupled with the retention of administrative control over prices. More disturbing is the impact of the new thinking on economic policy. Instead of pushing the reform process in the direction of marketization, the growing awareness of monopoly quickly

---

* From *Soviet Economy*, 1991, vol. 7, no. 2, published by V.H. Winston and Sons, Inc. Reprinted by permission of the publisher.

became an impediment to market reforms by furnishing the government with yet another excuse to defer the lifting of price controls.[1]

Industrial Concentration: Evidence, Causes and Significance

Data released since the advent of *glasnost* reveal an exceptionally high degree of horizontal concentration. What is distinctive about the implied industrial structure is the prevalence of monopolies in the strict sense of a single producer in the country of a particular good. According to Goskomstat SSR,[2] more than one-third of the most important types of machine-building products are produced by a single enterprise and approximately the same share is produced by only two enterprises. A 1988 survey by Goskomstat counted 166 enterprises that were absolute monopolists and 180 monopoly plants.[3] According to Gossnab,[4] 80 percent of the volume of output in machine-building enterprises is manufactured by monopolists and 77 percent of machine-building enterprises are monopolists. The Gossnab data show a higher level of concentration because they are less aggregated than Goskomstat data. Another statistic from Gossnab is that about 2,000 enterprises are the sole producers of a specific type of product.

Concentration tends to be relatively low in consumer-oriented industries.[5] Branches with a non-monopolized structure include building material, light industry, food, woodworking and certain consumer oriented branches of machine building. Nationwide concentration levels, however, may be misleading. Regional decentralization of control over enterprises manufacturing consumer goods has created an artificial geographical division of the market that negates the effect of low concentration levels nationwide. As shortages of consumer goods have intensified and local authorities have responded by restricting the sale of locally produced goods to other localities, the impact of geographical divisions in raising effective concentration levels for consumer products may have increased.

---

[1] [Editor's note: By early 1992, prices had been liberalized in Russia, Belarus, and Ukraine, although ahead of a program of privatization and demonopolization, leading many commentators to worry about the abuse of monopoly power.]

[2] [Editor's Note: Goskomstat was the central statistical agency of the former union.]

[3] See the Economist (August 11, 1990, p. 67) for a table of more disaggregated data on industrial concentration.

[4] [Editor's note: Gossnab was the Soviet state agency responsible for distributing industrial inputs to enterprises.]

[5] The watch industry is reported to have a competitive structure and there are more than 500 enterprises in the shoe industry.

Both enterprises and ministries are highly integrated vertically as well as horizontally. Machine-building plants typically satisfy most of their own requirements for prefabricates,[6] and branch ministries generally produce a large share of products outside their main line of specialization.[7] Ironically, Soviet economists used to complain that vertical integration leads to excessive duplication among enterprises in different ministries and insufficient specialization and concentration, especially for intermediate products. A related problem is the low level of standardization of machinery and component parts.

In capitalist economies, data on industrial concentration overstate monopoly power because they ignore foreign competition. That problem does not yet arise with the Soviet economy. The monopolization of industry is compounded by a foreign trade system that, despite recent decentralizing reforms, serves to protect domestic producers from foreign competition.

Two explanations dominate Soviet discussions of the causes of industrial concentration. One stresses that enterprise production profiles are narrowly specialized for final products. According to this explanation, the belief that economies of scale could be realized through increased specialization led to a policy that concentrated the production of a particular product in one or two enterprises in an effort to eliminate "wasteful duplication and parallelism" of production facilities. Concentrating the production of each type of product in a single place also facilitates central control of the economy.

The alternative explanation focuses on the large average size of state enterprises. Soviet enterprises are much larger on average than enterprises in industrialized capitalist economies. In a pioneering study, Pryor compared measures of enterprise size in socialist economies to those predicted by regression equations derived from data for ten capitalist economies.[8] For the

---

[6] A frequently cited survey by the Central Statistical Administration (now Goskomstat) found that out of every 100 machine-building enterprises 71 produced their own iron castings, 27 their own steel castings, 84 their own forgings, 76 their own stampings, and 65 their own hardware. As of 1980, less than 5 percent of the total output of billets and castings was produced in specialized plants, and there were no specialized plants for forgings and stampings.

[7] A 1983 study estimated that one-fifth of the output produced by the ministries was outside their main line of specialization, and for certain ministries the share was much higher. For seven particular industries, the same study found that the share of total output produced under the specialized ministry nominally in charge of the product ranged from a high of 67 percent of forge and press equipment to a low of 32 percent of plastic products.

[8] Frederic L. Pryor, *Property and Industrial Organization in Capitalist Nations.* Bloomington: Indiana U.P.,1973, pp. 192-193.

Soviet Union, he estimated that the average number of workers employed by state enterprises in 1964 was 610, as compared with a predicted value of 178, and that 59.6 percent of the labor force worked in enterprises employing more than 1,000 workers, as compared with a predicted value of 40.8 percent. Since the 1960s, the size of Soviet enterprises has grown even larger. The average number of employees per enterprise rose to 813 in 1987-88, and 73.4 percent of the labor force now work in enterprises employing more than 1,000 workers; indeed, enterprises with 10,000 workers or more employ 21.6 percent of the labor force, while those with 500 workers or fewer employ only 14.9 percent of the labor force.

From an economic standpoint, large enterprise size is justified in industries where technology allows large producers to manufacture products at lower unit costs than smaller producers. The availability of technological economies of scale, however, does not fully explain the size structure of Soviet enterprises. Enterprise size in the Soviet economy has been artificially inflated by several factors. One was the nationalization of industry and oppression, for ideological and political reasons, of small-scale private and cooperative production. Prior to Gorbachev, private enterprise was permitted, usually subject to licensing, in a narrowly restricted range of fields, and employment of hired labor was prohibited apart from collective farms, which are nominally producer cooperatives, the cooperative survived chiefly in rural areas as a nominally independent, but de facto state-controlled, branch of retail trade. A second factor was the Stalinist penchant for large enterprises, often termed "gigantomania," which equated large size with efficiency.

Finally, the complexity and cost of coordinating the economy from the center create a systemic bias toward large enterprises. To put it simply, it is easier for central planners to control a small number of large enterprises than a large number of small ones. Likewise, vertical integration of successive stages of production saves on the cost of centralized management by reducing the number of inter-firm transactions coordinated by the center.

The increase in the average size of enterprises in the 1970s is largely the result of the merger movement ordered by Brezhnev in 1973. Thousands of formerly separate enterprises were absorbed into large industrial conglomerates (*ob"yedineninya*, usually translated as associations) of two types: production associations (POs) and scientific-production associations (NPOs), which included branch R&D establishments. The associations were predominantly horizontal mergers combining producers of similar products. The formation of associations was expected to raise efficiency through increased specialization and concentration, and to lower administrative costs by reducing the number of production units and streamlining the bureaucracy. The NPOs also were supposed to promote technical progress by placing R&D facilities and enterprises under a common management, thus facilitating coordination of R&D with production. By many accounts, however, the ministries implemented the mergers in a formalistic manner, and the expected benefits of the associations in promoting efficiency or technical progress never materialized. As discussed below, these results have implications for merger policy under *perestroika*.

Another structural condition required for competition is the absence of barriers to entry of new firms. The theory of contestable markets posits that free entry can constrain incumbent firms to behave efficiently, even in markets dominated by a small number of producers. In the Soviet economy, however, monopolization of production is compounded by artificial impediments to entry. The traditional restrictions on entry into the private and cooperative sectors already have been described; as discussed below, Gorbachev's reforms have progressively eased these restrictions, but stopped far short of removing them altogether. Within the state sector, competition among enterprises is precluded by barriers to entry that are fully institutionalized by the planning mechanism used to control their activities. Under the traditional system of output planning and its counterpart, the centralized distribution of inputs, producers are restricted to a narrow range of final products by mandatory production targets set from above, and buyers are assigned to specific suppliers by supply planning agencies.

As a result, enterprises have virtually no freedom to enter or exit any industry or to choose from which suppliers to purchase inputs. Soviet sources often stress the centralized distribution of supplies and its corollary, the centralized attachment of buyers to suppliers, as a cause of what they call the *diktat* of the producer.

Problems of industrial structure, while severe, are not primarily responsible for the deterioration of industrial conduct and performance since 1988. Even before the reforms, the sellers' market allowed producers to ignore the demands of buyers, while forcing buyers to accept what is offered or go without. Under *perestroika*, the expansion in the flow of money and credit available to enterprises, combined with declines in production, has greatly exacerbated the disequilibrium in the producer sector. As the purchasing power of the ruble has become more uncertain, enterprises increasingly have tried to protect themselves by demanding payment in real goods or hard currency. Repressed inflationary pressure and the consequent loss of confidence in the ruble, not the monopolistic structure of production, are the driving forces behind the rise of barter trade among enterprises and the flight to dollars. Yet demands for payment in kind or hard currency are among the "monopolistic practices" prohibited by new Soviet antimonopoly legislation described below.

Soviet economists and officials frequently express concern about the power of monopolists to raise the price of their output. The resulting fear that lifting price controls would trigger a burst of uncontrolled inflation appears to have influenced the decision to defer price liberalization. Western economic theory teaches, however, that the power of a monopolist to set the price of its output is constrained by a downward sloping demand curve. Continuous inflation from the supply side is possible only with an accommodating policy of monetary expansion. To the extent that market power arises from excess demand rather than the fewness of firms, a tightening of monetary and fiscal policy, combined with the decontrol of prices, could prevent much of the dysfunctional enterprise behavior that Soviet sources often attribute to monopoly.

The Role of Antitrust Policy in the Transition

Drawbacks of antimonopoly regulation

Economic theories of regulation suggest that regulation of pricing and other aspects of market conduct has inherent drawbacks as a means of inducing firms to behave efficiently. Asymmetric information is the root of the problem. The firm's managers are better informed than the regulator about cost conditions, and the regulator can monitor the firm's behavior only imperfectly. Price regulation under asymmetric information leads to imperfect incentives and consequently to inefficient outcomes.

Despite the drawbacks, regulation to prevent "abusive conduct" by dominant firms is a standard antitrust remedy in Western Europe. This prompts the question: if capitalist countries use regulation to control monopoly conduct, what is wrong if the Soviet Union emulates this policy?

The West European approach is inappropriate for the Soviet economy for several reasons. First, the standard economic justification for West European antitrust policy generally does not apply to the Soviet Union. The regulatory solution may have some justification in smaller capitalist economies as a means of exploiting technological economies of scale. Most other capitalist countries have smaller domestic markets than the United States, and higher concentration levels may be required fully to exploit technological economies of scale. Historically, plant sizes abroad have tended to be much smaller on average, and the incidence of suboptimal scale plants higher, than in the United States. In contrast, Soviet enterprises are already much larger on average than firms in the United States or other advanced capitalist economies. As emphasized earlier, enterprise size in the Soviet economy has been artificially inflated by gigantomania, the suppression of private enterprise, and by the systemic bias toward large enterprises arising from the high cost of coordinating the economy from the center. To the extent that Soviet enterprises owe their large size to such artificial forces, rather than to technological economies of scale and market size, the efficiency justification for regulating dominant firms does not apply to the Soviet economy.

Second, the Soviet economy is far more concentrated than the capitalist economies of Western Europe; and Soviet enterprises, unlike firms in Western Europe, are not only completely sheltered from foreign competition, but they also operate in a sellers' market. As a result, the domain of price controls and other anti-monopoly restrictions, and consequently their attendant drawbacks, would be much greater in the Soviet economy than in the West European economies.[9] Further, the inherent drawbacks of antimonopoly regulation are likely to be compounded by the incompetence of the existing Soviet bureaucracy.

Finally, whereas the West European countries already have functioning market economies, the Soviet Union has yet to make the transition from central planning to a market economy. Extensive price controls will impede the development of markets and competition. In this regard, the most compelling argument against price controls comes from Lipton and Sachs,[10] who point out that a transitory period of monopoly prices can promote competition by attracting entry into the private sector. If monopolies are subject to price controls, the proper price signals will be absent. Use of regulation to prevent monopolies from charging excessive prices not only fails to create competition, but may actually prevent competition from developing and thus perpetuate the structural conditions that give rise to monopoly power.

---

[9] This may partly explain Leonid Abalkin's puzzling assertion, in April 1990, that even more bureaucrats would be needed to oversee a regulated market economy than were used to run the old system of central planning (*The New York Times*, April 10, 1990, p. 1)

[10] David Lipton and Jeffrey Sachs, "Creating a Market Economy in Eastern Europe: The Case of Poland," *Brookings Papers on Economic Activity*, I:75-133, 1990.

Trustbusting and Demonopolization of the State Sector

In theory, the structural remedy is more effective than regulation in promoting competition because it eliminates the incentive for anticompetitive behavior, barring collusion among the units. The breakup of large state enterprises into smaller units is widely viewed as a promising method of introducing competition into socialist economies of the Soviet type. According to one common variant of this view, large state enterprises should be broken up, and then privatized, before prices are decontrolled in order to create a "critical mass" of competition that will induce enterprises to exercise their decision-making freedom efficiently. Nikolay Petrakov has advocated a similar strategy.[11]

Introducing competition prior to the freeing of prices is without question a desirable strategy. Whether the strategy is practicable, however, is dubious. Implicit in the proposed strategy is the premise that breaking up state enterprises can introduce competition into the Soviet economy without difficulty.

The antitrust experience of capitalist economies does not support that premise. As the earlier comparison of U.S. and West European policy toward dominant firms suggests, the structural remedy of breaking up incumbent firms is rarely used in capitalism. That in itself may be an indication that breaking up firms is not easy to do. The little experience there is with the structural remedy is not encouraging. In Japan, large industrial conglomerates (*zaibatsu*) were broken up by occupying forces after World War II, but they were restored in the form of the modern *keiretsu*, which now play a key role in protecting Japan's domestic market from foreign competition. Even in the United States, the one capitalist economy with a tradition of breaking up dominant firms, the impact of structural remedies in reducing concentration has been modest.

Analogies with capitalist experience can be misleading. Consider the British privatization program. After an initial wave of privatization in competitive industries, the program was extended to industries long regarded as natural

---

[11] Petrakov asserted that "...the first thing to do before unrestricting prices is to create the right conditions for competition, without which there can be no price freedom. One of the first measures to be taken is therefore to demonopolize our economy, which is the most highly monopolized in the world because, in addition to technological monopolies, there are organizational monopolies – the ministries and very big enterprises, such as Intourist and Aeroflot which are well known abroad. However, to split Aeroflot into several companies, for instance, all we need is the political will. It is very easy to break organizational monopolies." (*Le Monde*, March 25, 1990, pp. 1, 41).

monopolies, in which introducing competition by breaking up incumbent firms is impractical. That is not the problem in the Soviet economy, since the domain of monopolies and near-monopolies encompasses industries capable of operating under competitive conditions. More generally, the previous section suggested that the possible loss of scale economies made the structural remedy difficult to apply in many capitalist countries, whereas the artificially inflated size structure of Soviet enterprises does not present the same difficulty.

Nevertheless, introducing competition into the Soviet economy by breaking up state enterprises is bound to be difficult. In part, this is because industrial concentration is so high to begin with. The sheer number of enterprises that would have to be broken up in order to create a competitive industrial structure is a formidable obstacle to success.

Compounding the immensity of the task is the indivisibility of many industrial monopolies. Multiplant enterprises or production associations formed from geographically dispersed enterprises are easily divided into separate parts. As Petrakov has pointed out, however, heavy industry is densely populated with what he calls "technological monopolies," that is, giant producers that are physically impossible to break up because they comprise a single giant plant or an enterprise situated on a single site.[12]

Further, the existing system of bureaucratic coordination is likely to reject efforts to break up enterprises before the lifting of price controls. As noted earlier, the high cost of coordinating the economy from the center creates a systemic bias toward high concentration. As long as central controls on production and supply remain in place, the systemic bias toward high concentration will persist, and will tend to frustrate efforts to reduce concentration. The continuation of mergers in the initial stage of perestroika is a manifestation of the link between central planning and high industrial concentration.

Finally, there are formidable political obstacles to the breakup of monopo-

---

[12] Petrakov further observed that "the second type of monopolism is technological. This is our notorious gigantomania. We always thought that a large plant is bound to be better than a medium or small one. We artificially propagated monopolists. An industrial gant that has already been built is impossible to break up into parts. This means that it will long remain a technological monopoly....Fortunately, there are not so many of them in the light and food industries. Here it is easier to organize competition. But if you are talking about heavy industry, it is chock-full of such monsters – monopoly producers. And to speak about some kind of competition here is impossible. We will have to introduce price controls and antimonopoly legislation." (*Rabochaya tribuna*, April 24, 1990, p. 2).

lies. The British experience with privatization is instructive on this point. British Telecom (BT) was not broken up before it was privatized, even though long-distance service is no longer regarded as a natural monopoly because of changing technology. One explanation is that selling BT with its monopoly intact raised its sales value and allowed the government to accomplish its major objectives of rapid privatization (which requires that shares be underpriced) and maximizing the proceeds from the sale. Thus, privatization benefitted shareholders and taxpayers at the expense of consumers. In addition, the contrast between the treatment of BT and the breakup of AT&T by U.S. antitrust authorities suggests that the lack of a national precedent or tradition for breaking up monopolies also weighed into the decision.

If politics and national tradition are important in shaping antitrust policy, that does not bode well for Soviet policy on trustbusting. Traditional Soviet attitudes and views on firm size and concentration are much closer to the West European antitrust tradition than to the procompetitive stance of U.S. antitrust policy. Notwithstanding the new rhetoric on the advantages of small firms, the view that large size promotes efficiency is still dominant and influential.

The sobering reality is that there is no historical precedent for the kind of far-reaching demonopolization that would be required to make the structure of the state sector competitive. Trustbusting has made an important difference in certain sectors and industries of the U.S. economy, but the United States is an outlier in its structural policy even among other advanced capitalist economies. Although the breakup of large enterprises into smaller units may be able to produce some reduction in industrial concentration and could make an important difference in certain economic sectors, it is hard to believe that this policy could create a "critical mass" of competition in the Soviet economy, especially prior to the creation of a market. Indeed, in light of the obstacles to demonopolization noted above, postponing the liberalization of prices until after the state sector is demonopolized is likely to delay the creation of a market indefinitely.

Entry and the Expansion of the Private Sector

Given that no capitalist country except for the United States relies on the breakup of dominant firms to promote competition, and indeed that industrial policy outside the United States historically has tended to tolerate, and even actively support, monopolies, mergers, and cartels, what accounts for the development and survival of competition in capitalism? The answer lies in systemic features that advanced capitalist countries share in common. Primary among these is a sizeable private sector with large numbers of small- and medium-sized firms, in which entry and exit of firms is relatively free of state interference. As noted above, monopoly profits act as a signal to attract entry of new firms into the private sector, thereby promoting demonopolization. The lesson from capitalist experience is that the expansion of the private sector as a result of the entry of new firms may ultimately prove more effective than the restructuring of state enterprises as a method of promoting competition in the Soviet economy.

Support for this view comes from the strategy for the transition to a market economy proposed by Janos Kornai[13] based on the example of Hungary. Kornai focuses his analysis more on ownership than competition, and argues that the grass-roots development of independently founded private businesses is more important in creating a private sector than the privatization of state enterprises. As evidence of the vitality of the private sector, Kornai points to the way the Hungarian private sector, unlike the state sector, spreads spontaneously, without directives issued from above, and in spite of a multitude of arbitrary government restrictions, the hostility of the surrounding climate, and a historical legacy of suppression. Kornai stresses that people do not have to be coerced to enter the private sector. The mere removal and relaxation of state restrictions on private activity is sufficient to encourage its development.

Conventional wisdom holds that the Russian cultural tradition is hostile to private enterprise, or that seven decades of socialism have extinguished the entrepreneurial drive. Nevertheless, just like the private sector in Hungary and Poland, the Soviet cooperative movement has mushroomed, despite restrictive government policies and a hostile social climate. With all their shortcomings, the cooperatives remain the only bright spot in Gorbachev's economic reforms to date.

The revival of the cooperatives had little if any influence in promoting competition, despite rapid growth in their numbers. That failure is attributable to the halfway nature of reforms in the rest of the economy, which loosened control over financial flows without creating markets. The resulting excess demand extinguished competitive pressure and made it difficult for cooperatives to obtain inputs. To promote competition, the lifting of restrictions on the private sector must be combined with effective macroeconomic stabiliza-

---

[13] *The Road to a Free Economy, Shifting from a Socialist System: The Example of Hungary.* New York: W.W.Norton & Company, 1990, p. 36.

tion measures and the decontrol of prices. The stabilization package should include the elimination of most subsidies and the tightening of credit to state enterprises, so that state enterprises face a real threat of financial failure if private firms enter and take away their business.

Additional measures may be necessary to ensure that small private businesses have access to the credit they need to get started. In Poland, rapid stabilization and liberalization were successfully carried out, but the amount of credit given to the private sector by the banking system is disturbingly low. Western aid could play a useful role in encouraging the private sector by providing entrepreneurs with start-up capital.

The above considerations further undermine the proposition that demonopolization of the state sector is a prerequisite for the liberalization of prices. Postponing the transition to the market until after the breakup of state enterprises would actually inhibit competition by impeding the development of the private sector. Encouraging the expansion of the private sector is by no means an easy way of introducing competition into the Soviet economy, but it seems to me a far more promising approach than trying to restructure and deconcentrate the state sector.

Implications for the Role of Import Competition

Some analysts have suggested that import competition is not an essential method of promoting competition in the Soviet economy in particular, or in reforming socialist economies in general. Two versions of this argument will be considered here. One rests on the difference in size between the Soviet economy and the economies of Eastern Europe. According to this view, whereas import competition is essential to the success of reforms in the East European countries because of their small size, the Soviet economy is sufficiently large and diverse to reform successfully without first opening up to foreign trade.

The alternative version is based on the infant-industry argument for protecting domestic industries from foreign competition, particularly as exemplified by the postwar experience of Japan. According to this view, since all sectors of both the Soviet economy and the East European economies have an absolute disadvantage relative to world standards, the entire economy should initially be protected from foreign competition with a deliberately undervalued exchange rate to make imports artificially expensive and a ban on almost all direct foreign investment. A necessary complement to this protectionist trade policy is a strong antitrust policy to promote competition in the domestic economy.

This author is sympathetic to the concern that a sizeable share of the state sector would not long survive competition from foreign producers. It may be unrealistic to suppose, however, that competition can be stimulated rapidly without opening up the economy to imports. Even though the Soviet economy is much larger than the individual East European economies (and will remain so even if most of the non-Russian republics secede), at present it is just as concentrated and monopolized as the smaller East European economies, if not more so. In that sense, it is hard to see why it will be any less difficult to promote domestic competition in the Soviet Union than is the case in Poland, Hungary, or Czechoslovakia.

As for the infant-industry argument, postwar Japan may be a misleading role model for the Soviet Union. Japan's industrial structure was far more conducive to domestic competition to begin with. Japanese industry has a "dual structure," comprising a highly oligopolized sector of large firms and a much larger sector of smaller firms. An international comparison of the size structure of firms concluded that the size structure in Japan is much smaller even than that in capitalist countries with a small type size structure. Even within the oligopolized sector, despite a high propensity toward cartelization that has been encouraged by industrial policy, large firms are prone to intense rivalry and competition for market share. As a result, Japan did not have to supplement its protectionist trade policy with a strong antitrust policy to promote domestic competition.

The complement to Japan's protectionism was not a strong antitrust policy, but rather an export-promotion strategy that pressured domestic producers to compete on foreign markets. Critics justifiably charge that the combination of protectionism and oligopolistic collusion gave Japanese producers an unfair advantage over foreign rivals by allowing them to charge high prices on the domestic market while offering low prices on competitive foreign markets. Apart from protectionism, however, Japan's competitive edge derives from innovative manufacturing techniques, such as just-in-time inventory control, which permit Japanese producers to produce high-quality products at a low cost. Even allowing for the fact that Japanese manufacturing once had a reputation for producing shoddy products, it may be optimistic to suppose that the Japanese strategy is transferable to the Soviet Union.

Both versions of the argument share the common premise that antitrust policy can promote domestic competition in reforming economies in a rapid and effective manner. Contrary to this assumption, the considerations outlined in the two previous sections suggest that domestic competition may well develop at a relatively slow pace in the early phase of the transition to a market economy. In part, this follows from the contention that breaking up incumbent state enterprise is not likely to prove very effective in promoting competition. In addition, although it was argued that the expansion of small- and medium-sized firms in the private sector will ultimately prove very effective in promoting competition, this process could take a long time. The implication is that import competition, along with competition from joint ventures and wholly foreign-owned companies, may be necessary to constrain the market power of domestic enterprises in the interim.

Also implicit in both versions is the premise that antitrust policy is a good substitute for import competition. The historical experience of capitalist countries casts doubt on the validity of this assumption. Consider, for example, the U.S. auto industry. U.S. automakers operate under the most procompetitive antitrust policy in the world, but casual observation suggests that competition from Japanese automakers has been far more effective than antitrust policy in pressuring U.S. automakers to cut costs and improve quality. Many other examples could be cited. In capitalism, as in socialism, real market competition cannot be simulated by artificial regulations.

If there is a role for antitrust policy in the transition from central planning to a market economy, it is one of secondary importance. Macroeconomic stabilization, the liberalization of prices and private enterprise, and the creation of a convertible ruble are far more promising methods of promoting competition than either regulatory or structural antitrust remedies. The Soviet government's current reform strategy calls for demonopolization to precede the transition to the market. That sequence looks good on paper, but in reality it is putting the cart before the horse. In a recent critique of the notion that Western antitrust law is transferable to the Soviet economy, the Soviet jurist R. Khalfina[14] warned that an attempt to graft antitrust law onto the present system, without solving the real organizational and legal problems of creating a functioning market economy, can only divert attention from those problems and create an illusion of progress toward the market. It can only be hoped that Khalfina's criticism foreshadows a reevaluation of the new Soviet thinking on monopoly and the painfully slow transition strategy the new thinking has been used to justify.

---

[14] "Ob antimonopol'nom zakonodatel'stve (On Antimonopoly Legislation)," *Ekonomika i zhizn'*, 9:14, February, 1991.

Afterword

As this study goes to press, the Supreme Soviet has just approved a program for bringing the economy out of the crisis. The draft of the program issued by TASS includes a mix of regulatory and structural antitrust remedies. After expressing the intention of completing the staged transition to primarily free price formation by October 1,1992,[15] the draft calls for the introduction of a special mechanism for regulating and limiting price for output from monopoly producers. On the structural side, the draft calls for multiplying the number of producers both by breaking up the monopolies "where expedient" into smaller units, and by measures aimed at promoting the expansion of cooperatives, family businesses and other non-state economic entities, and also small enterprises. Support for the development of competing firms is supposed to come, in part, from the confiscation of "unlawfully" obtained profits from monopoly producers. In common with earlier measures, the program is based on the premise that a competitive industrial structure can be produced by bureaucratic fiat, rather than as a consequence of market forces.

---

[15] [Editor's Note: This was largely achieved in Russia, Ukraine, and Belarus with the January 1992 price reforms.]

18. The Environmental Morass in Eastern Europe*

Stanley J. Kabala

Forty years of economic expansion have resulted in acute environmental problems throughout Eastern Europe. One-third of the forests in the region are damaged by air pollution. The Baltic and Black seas are polluted by industrial wastes, sewage, and oil. Large tracts of scarce farmland are contaminated by carcinogenic heavy metals generated by industry. The water in 95 percent of Poland's rivers is unsuitable for municipal use; in 42 percent of the country's rivers the water is unfit even for industrial uses. In parts of industrial Upper Silesia, Poland's most polluted region, the concentration of smoke – perhaps the most harmful common air pollutant – regularly exceeds European Community (EC) standards by as much as 600 percent.

The situation is similar in industrial areas across the region. In northern Bohemia, Czechoslovakia's industrial core, 70 percent of the rivers are heavily polluted. Seventy percent of wastewater goes untreated and half the forests are dying or damaged. What was formerly East Germany is home to what may be the most polluted town in the world – Bitterfeld. In these and other industrial areas throughout Eastern Europe, rates of pollution-related birth defects and illnesses including leukemia, tuberculosis, respiratory ailments, and heart disease far exceed national norms.

Fouled Air and Water

Poland's Upper Silesia, Czechoslovakia's northern Bohemia, the southern provinces of eastern Germany, and the Ukraine's Donetsk Basin are today's equivalents of industrial areas such as the Ruhr or Pittsburgh half a century ago. These four regions receive average monthly deposits of sulfuric compounds that exceed 1,000 micrograms per square meter – the highest in Europe. A larger zone that covers most of Czechoslovakia, half of Poland, eastern Germany, and part of western Germany records monthly deposits of more than 500 micrograms per square meter. (Most of Eastern Europe's damaged forests, including those experiencing *waldsterben*, or forest death, are in areas in which sulfur dioxide pollution hovers at around this level.)

The intensity of pollution in the region can be gauged by comparing sulfur dioxide levels in countries on opposite sides of the old East-West divide in Europe. While deposits in West Germany had reached roughly 10 tons per square kilometer annually by the middle of the 1980s, figures for Czechoslovakia and East Germany were 22.6 and 35 tons respectively. Poland had average annual deposits of 14 tons per square kilometer, with a much smaller gross national product (GNP) to show for its pains than West Germany.

[Table I] shows sulfur dioxide emissions for several industrialized countries in terms of population and land area. Poland's emissions of the pollutant per person are nearly five times those of comparably sized West Germany and a third higher than those of the United States.

Water quality in Eastern Europe parallels the region's poor air quality. Austria, Czechoslovakia, Hungary, Yugoslavia, Bulgaria, and Romania join in an assault on the Danube River as it makes its way to the Black Sea. Pollution that begins near Vienna increases so steadily that by the time the river reaches Budapest, swimming in its water is not recommended. Germany's Elbe river carries effluents to the Baltic,

Sulfur Dioxide Emissions for Selected Countries

	Emissions (thousand tons)	Emissions per capita (kilograms)	Emissions per $ of GNP (grams)
East Germany	5,258	317	31
Czechoslovakia	2,800	179	24
Bulgaria	1,030	114	21
Poland	4,180	110	20
Romania[1]	1,800	78	19
Hungary	1,218	115	17
Soviet Union[2]	10,124	35	5
United Kingdom	3,664	64	5
United States[3]	20,700	84	4
Sweden	214	25	1
France	1,226	22	1
West Germany	1,300	21	1

Unless otherwise noted, data are preliminary figures for 1988.
[1]Emissions data from 1980.
[2]European part of the Soviet Union.
[3]Emissions data are for sulfur oxides.

Source: Hilary French, "Green Revolutions: Environmental Reconstruction in Eastern Europe and the Soviet Union," Worldwatch Paper no. 99 (Washington, D.C.: Worldwatch Institute, 1990).

Table I

where they contribute to the deterioration of that sea.

Water pollution in Eastern Europe is largely the result of decades of deferred investment in wastewater treatment by municipal as well as industrial polluters. In many countries seepage from improper solid waste disposal sites contaminates not only soil but also groundwater, posing a threat to city water supplies. Most cities, towns, and industrial plants discharge their waste-water untreated into nearby rivers.

Energy Intensity: A European Comparison

	GDP (in millions of dollars)	Gross Energy Consumption (in MtCE)*	Energy Intensity	Pollution Intensity**
Belgium	79,080	60.82	0.77	7,656
West Germany	624,970	381.28	0.61	6,299
Spain	164,250	105.53	0.64	30,660
Hungary	20,560	42.42	2.06	33,800
Poland	70,439	180.67	2.56	28,757
Yugoslavia	44,730	62.62	1.41	28,571

*MtCE = million tons of coal equivalent
**Tons per year of sulfur dioxide per million tons of coal equivalent

Sources: World Bank, *Poland-Energy Investment: The Transition from Central Planning to Regulate* Markets (Washington, D.C.: 1988), and United Nations Economic Commission for Europe, *National Strategies and Policies for Air Polution Abatement* (New York: United Nations, 1987).

Table II

The Developmental Bind

The environmental crisis in Eastern Europe has its structural roots in factors common to all centrally planned systems. Such systems have a bias toward heavy and extractive industries and production processes with low efficiency levels in the use of energy and materials. [Table II] compares energy use, economic output, and pollution intensity in several European countries. As the table shows, the formerly centrally planned economies have energy intensity levels far higher than those in comparably developed economies in Eastern Europe. When the energy is derived principally from coal, usually burned without benefit of pollution control devices, high levels of energy intensity mean high levels of pollution will be found as well.

The emphasis on resource intensive activities such as coal-mining, steel-making, and chemical and heavy manufacturing is a legacy of the postwar development of modern industrial economies in the region. This effort was guided by the Stalinist model, which drove national economic growth by channeling labor, capital, and natural resources into heavy industry. In demographic terms, this meant draining the pool of rural labor for employment in industry and bringing women into the workforce. In financial terms, it meant forcing direct investment in industrial capacity at the expense of consumption, social goods, and, later, the environment. However impressive the Stalinist model may have been in transforming the Soviet Union from backwardness to modernity, adopting it in Eastern Europe meant following a pattern designed for a country with different cultural, economic, and political characteristics, and unmatched natural resources.

While the pursuit of industrial modernity seemed reasonable in Poland, with its underused agricultural population, relatively large size, and substantial reserves of black coal, it made considerably less sense elsewhere in the region. Hungary pushed the development of steel and other metallurgical industries despite a virtual absence of indigenous ores and hard coal. Czechoslovakia directed its efforts away from diversified manufacturing and invested in coal, steel, and similar industries; by the end of the 1970s, it ended up with a redundant, obsolescent heavy-industrial economy. East Germany, essentially an agricultural region in highly industrialized pre-war Germany, created an industrial economy of its own fueled by indigenous, low-quality brown coal. Romania, the only country in the region with significant domestic reserves of oil, steadily resisted Soviet urging to become the breadbasket of the Council for Mutual Economic Assistance (CMEA) and embarked on its own program of national industrial development.

The result today is twofold. These countries are under strain from the weight of bloated industrial sectors and suffer from a lack of services and social goods – goods produced in what the Stalinist system designated as the "nonproductive" sectors. At the same time, the so-called "productive" sectors are so inefficient that they use three times as much energy per unit of economic output as the same sectors in the economies of Western Europe and North America. This means three times as much coal burned for each kilowatt generated or ton of steel or cement produced. It also means that because pollution controls are lacking, three times the air pollution than one should expect is produced. And three times more energy, materials, and pollution than necessary are used to pay for the foreign technology, goods, or petroleum they need to run modern societies.

This developmental bind has had domestic political implications. One source of social dissatisfaction in Eastern Europe has been the region's Western European tastes and Eastern European means. Freed from Communist economics, the region's governments will strive to fulfill pent-up consumer demand and to continue industrial and economic growth in order to meet it. But because the Eastern European economies use energy and natural resources so intensively, increased production to meet consumer demand will place increased pressure on the environment. Concern for environmental quality will not stand in the way of rising expectations. The question for Eastern Europe is how to change paths of economic redevelopment that both supply the people's needs and respect the environment.

An Environmental Movement for Eastern Europe

The linking of economic and political power was almost inevitable in political systems in which the regime's principal claim to legitimacy was its guarantee of economic stability. As a result, government gave ministries considerable freedom, including the freedom to pollute, so long as they delivered the goods. In any political system, information on pollution is the chief weapon of the environmental activist. Communist regimes severely restricted access to such information, because of their well-known preference for secrecy. This limited the pressure that environmentalists and an aroused public could bring to bear on the Communist governments of Eastern Europe for action on pollution control.

Events in Hungary in 1989 and 1990 showed how crucial the control of information was to the Communist system in Eastern Europe. The Hungarian environmental movement was the vanguard of the organized opposition that toppled the country's Communist regime. The movement's principal tactic was to confront the government with information that it did not want disclosed for public discussion. According to representatives of the Danube Circle, Hungary's leading environmental organization, the group simply attacked the foundation and key survival technique of the Communist regime: the control over information by one political force. It did this by disseminating information on the environment that was outside the government's control. In Hungary and throughout Eastern Europe the crumbling of the government's monopoly on information extended from the environmental arena into all areas of life.

The environmental movement in Eastern Europe has been characterized as a training ground for democracy, a focus of anti-regime sentiment, and a foil for nationalism. Environmental activism played an important role in redefining the field of public political activity in Eastern Europe, making possible the open political action that eventually destroyed the Communist's stem in the region. In both Eastern Europe, where insistence on national ecological prerogatives meant defiance of Soviet-inspired policies, and the Soviet Union's "breakaway" republics, where insistence on republic ecological prerogatives meant defiance of Moscow's programs, environmentalism was the vehicle for nationalism's rise to prominence.

Until the mid-1980s, the environmental problems of Eastern Europe (except for Poland) and the Soviet Union were unknown to all but a few professionals in the region and an even smaller group of observers in the West. Data on it were treated as confidential information. But beginning in Poland during the Solidarity era of 1980-81 and then in Hungary at mid-decade, the environment emerged as one of the main issues in opposition politics in the region.

Throughout the 1980s, environmental deterioration acted as a delegitimizing agent in societies moving at various speeds away from the Communist pattern of monolithic organization. Growing political participation by an environmentally concerned public spearheaded the development of general political participation. At the same time, "pluralist" behavior in society strengthened the position of advocates of environmental protection.

The Environment, Economics and Politics

If central planning brought the countries of Eastern Europe to their present ecological impasse, market-oriented economics will not necessarily lead them to improved environmental quality. The West's experience ought to make clear that while market pressure may be a necessary condition for the efficient use of resources, it is not sufficient to induce economic actors to attend to ecological concerns. If anything, the Western experience shows that regulation and management of the environment, along with adequate public participation in decision making, are necessary to compensate for "market failure."

Moreover, most of the countries of Eastern Europe remain in the condition summarized by a Polish environmental economist as "no longer centrally planned but without a market as well." Shaping effective and efficient environmental protection programs in such an uncertain situation is a daunting task.

A market framework of real prices and ownership structures that allowed firms to reap the benefits of increased efficiency in resource use could have a strong effect on environmental quality. In the 15 years after the oil embargo by the Organization of Petroleum Exporting Countries (OPEC), the United States economy grew some 40 percent while per capita energy consumption remained virtually constant. This significant achievement, which was in direct response to a steady increase in the price of energy, allowed the United States to avoid having to choose between economic growth and energy efficiency that would preserve the environment.

The countries of Eastern Europe were insulated from the impact of rising energy prices by their right to buy oil and natural gas from the Soviet Union at low "fraternal" rates that substantially trailed world prices. This turned out to be a mixed blessing, because the low prices removed Eastern Europe's motivation to engage in the conservation that has made it possible for the United States, Western Europe and Japan to increase energy efficiency while decreasing environmental impact.

While the link between price and environmental quality is fairly clear in the case of energy, it is not so with all economic inputs. History shows that the one cost firms seek to avoid in the interest of profitability is that of pollution control. Market theorists argue that this results from the absence of effective prices for air, water, and land that firms would have to pay for the privilege of destroying these natural elements by pollution. If prices for these resources were set high enough, the theory goes, firms would find it in their financial interest to reduce or eliminate pollution. Over the last 25 years, however, regulation rather than price has been the tool of choice in market economies. The government has set and enforced environmental standards in response to public demands for protection of the environment and health.

Cleaning Up Eastern Europe

As they proceed to integrate environmental protection into their policies, the countries of Eastern Europe must gradually and progressively allocate resources to cleaning up lingering problems such as stored waste, toxic dump sites, and contaminated soil, and to controlling ongoing problems such as sewage treatment and air pollution. At the same time, they must adopt an approach that prevents pollution and preserves existing natural assets. This has already begun to happen in the West, where attention is shifting from "the end of the pipe" to the source – where, in many instances, prospective pollutants can be tackled quite effectively. Eastern Europe must take advantage of the opportunity to leapfrog the West's experience, and tap available expertise on reducing waste and pollution at their source. If they do so, they may find that controlling pollution can save, rather than cost, money.

The countries of Eastern Europe also need to recognize the possibilities for environmental protection at this unique moment in their history. The suddenness with which they cast off their old political system has created opportunities not available to other countries. Before the process of privatization of resources is too advanced, governments should consider aggressive action to shield tracts of land from development or exploitation, perhaps by designating them as national parks or protected lands. In a pleasant irony, one category of undeveloped land now under consideration for protection is the old Iron Curtain – formerly barbed-wire-covered border zones hundreds of miles long, untouched by development for nearly 50 years. The Hungarian government has already proposed that its former border security strips become protected greenbelt.

Continuing a policy conceived under the Communist regime, the Polish government is in the process of deciding how to protect the largely pristine northeastern fifth of the country under a program called "the Green Lungs of Poland." (The motto of the program is "protection = development.") In a move hailed by conservationists around the world, Romania has abandoned plans for development of the Danube delta; the program, designed at the behest of fallen dictator Nicolae Ceausescu, would have transformed one of Europe's largest remaining natural wetlands into a massive industrial zone.

Foreign Aid

Some areas of Eastern Europe are so badly polluted that they pose distinct risks to human health and require immediate action, including international aid. In the worst regions – northern Bohemia, Upper Silesia, parts of Romania, and the Donetsk Basin in the Ukraine – many large, inefficient, and highly polluting facilities will have to be closed. Beyond this, however, additional reductions in pollution will require financial assistance for air and water pollution control equipment and capital for the updating of outmoded industrial processes. Updating could increase efficiency and productivity immediately, but the payback period for investment in pollution control devices will be lengthy; thus the benefits must be measured in terms of long-term improvement of the environment and human health.

With limited resources, Eastern European countries will want to get the most "bang" for their pollution control "buck." Removing a pollutant becomes more costly and difficult with each attempt. It may be the case, for example, that the first 50 percent of a pollutant coming out of the smokestack can be eliminated for the same price as the next 25 percent; thus, getting rid of a unit of pollution in the second batch is twice as expensive as getting rid of one in the first. The governments of Eastern Europe may have to choose a combination of actions that partially reduces pollution in several locations without eliminating most of it in any one location, thereby doing away with more currently generated pollution for the money. The economics of pollution control may also dictate purchasing less expensive equipment that does a less thorough job rather than highly effective state-of-the-art technology.

How can the countries and institutions of the developed West aid Eastern Europe in this context? By providing great sums of money is the obvious answer, but one circumscribed by political and economic realities. However helpful financial assistance from the West may be, it will come in amounts that are smaller than needed.

The enormity of the task can he grasped from an assessment prepared by the Polish Ministry of Environmental Protection and Natural Resources, which adopts a 30-year time frame. Beginning in 1991 and continuing for five years, efforts would focus on addressing immediate environmental threats to human health in hard-hit areas such as Upper Silesia. By the year 2000, according to the assessment, Poland would attain national compliance with EC environmental standards. Finally, by 2020 the country will have been put on a course of "sustainable economic development" that integrates ecological concerns. The Polish government estimates that $260 billion will be needed to accomplish the program's goals. Comparable estimates exist for each country in the region.

While price tags for cleanup are in the hundreds of billions, as in Poland's grand scheme, foreign assistance is tallied in the hundreds of millions. The World Bank, for example, is lending Poland $150 million for an energy conservation project that targets district heating systems, and $100 million to upgrade highly polluting processes in chemical plants and at power generating stations. The bank is also lending Hungary nearly $300 million for projects to improve energy efficiency and produce clean fuels. United States environmental assistance began with embarrassingly modest allocations of a few million dollars and has only now reached tens of millions of dollars.

This disparity between the amount needed and the amount that has been provided indicates that East European countries will have to pull themselves out of their environmental morass largely by their own bootstraps. The countries of Eastern Europe with their high levels of education and technical ability, do not need access to knowledge as much as they need access to experience. Education and technical ability need to be catalyzed and redirected in effective channels, with advice from countries that have been there before, in a decades-long process of reconstruction.

In Western experience, shaping responses to environmental protection has been a three-sided process. Current activity on the part of industry in the United States and Europe to comply with environmental regulations stems in part from fear of fines and future legal liability and in part from the recent recognition that preventing pollution can be cheaper than controlling it. To a great extent the burgeoning $200 billion-a-year American market in goods and services geared toward environmental protection is driven by the regulatory force of the federal and state governments.

Yet to say that all Eastern Europe needs to clean itself up are improved techniques in industry and tighter government regulation is to leave out the force that initiated the process in the West and still drives it: public pressure on government for action on environmental quality. Public participation is the third element in the process, the one element missing from environmental affairs in Eastern Europe under its Communist regimes. The efforts of Western governments and environmental groups to expand the capabilities of non-governmental environmental groups in Eastern Europe is very much on target, as a means of simultaneously pursuing environmental quality and building democratic experience there.

Western cooperation can greatly help this process, even if some in Eastern Europe think the actual amounts of aid are too small. The thrust of grants, loans, and debt-for-nature swaps from the United States and the EC is to help increase energy efficiency, mitigate hazards to health in the most polluted areas, and build institutional capacity in government, industry, and civic organizations. If mitigation assistance amounts to giving a hungry man some fish, then the latter effort of capacity-building corresponds to teaching him how to fish.

The advice and assistance that Eastern Europe receives from the United States will be guided by a concern to address economic and political as well as ecological objectives. The United States will support the design of sustainable sectoral policies based on the recognition that policies for industry, energy production, agriculture, and transportation often have a greater impact on environmental quality than "environmental" policies as such. It will encourage the simultaneous development of credible, enforceable environmental regulations to replace the fanciful system of stringent standards and virtually nonexistent enforcement that characterized environmental regulation under the former Communist regimes. In supporting specific investments, United States aid will target pollution prevention rather than traditional "end-of-pipe" pollution control. At the same time, assistance will be offered to support public participation in decision-making processes.

Finally, the countries of Eastern Europe will be encouraged to frame regional approaches to shared environmental problems. This last element carries a full measure of the irony that characterizes international relations in the new Eastern Europe. Now that they have regained full national sovereignty, the countries of the region are more inclined to cooperate with each other than they were as "fraternal allies" in the Soviet sphere. That the countries of Eastern Europe are no longer unwilling members of the Soviet camp may very well turn out to be the most significant fact in their cleanup of the environment and their future development. For decades social innovation in the more advanced societies of Eastern Europe was hobbled by the need to wait for progress in the Soviet Union; the tension generated by this led more than once to confrontation between government and people. Now that they are free to chart their own course unhindered by an ill-suited ideology, the countries of Eastern Europe have the chance to join their industrialized counterparts in Europe and North America and engage in economic redevelopment that respects the basic needs of both people and nature.

19. Statistical Issues[*]

IMF/IBRD/OECD/EBRD

Introduction

As a country's economy evolves, it typically finds that it must adapt its statistical system to meet changing circumstances. Nowhere is this phenomenon more apparent than in the USSR. Reform initiatives in the 1980s have underscored problems with the existing statistical system, and created a demand for new indicators and methods of gathering data. These initiatives have prompted major changes in Soviet statistical work that can be expected to continue as the USSR undergoes further reform. ......

[I]t is clear that changes to both the accounting systems in enterprises and in government statistics would help accelerate the transition to a market economy. Efficient decentralization of decision-making will take place only if managers and investors have a full and fair view of an enterprise's financial performance. Achieving this will require the implementation of uniform accounting standards, training in these new concepts, auditing of accounts to ensure that the standards are being met, and the dissemination of audited accounts for use by shareholders, creditors, and supervisory authorities. Just as improved accounting systems are a prerequisite for efficient microeconomic decision-making, so are improved macroeconomic statistics necessary for improved policy formation. Converting the balance of payments from a settlements basis – which includes transactions related barter trade, gold exports and trade credits – to a transactions basis would provide a more comprehensive picture of the USSR's external position. Adapting the national accounts to the SNA framework and revising the methodology used to calculate implicit price deflators for these accounts would permit a more accurate measurement of real growth. Introducing comprehensive measures of unemployment and modifying the methods used to calculate retail and wholesale price indices would provide a clearer picture of the social impact of policy changes. Soviet authorities have already sought outside advice in some of these areas; further technical assistance could play an important role

[*] From *A Study of the Soviet Economy*, published by the International Monetary Fund/World Bank. Reprinted by permission of the IMF and the World Bank. Some footnotes omitted.

185

in promoting the transition to a market economy.

Overview of the Soviet Statistical System

Organization of the statistical system

Although the Soviet statistical system is relatively centralized, there are no fewer than five organizations involved in statistical work. The chief coordinator is the State Committee on Statistics (Goskomstat USSR), but as shown in Chart 1, it shares the responsibility for statistical collection with several other agencies. Banking, monetary, and budgetary statistics are compiled by the Ministry of Finance, although the source of most financial and balance of payments statistics is Gosbank. Statistics on crime, corruption, alcoholism, and other social problems are the domain of the Ministry of Internal Security. Until 1989, foreign trade statistics were the exclusive responsibility of the Ministry for Foreign Economic Relations (MVES). Although many of these data are now compiled directly by Goskomstat, this ministry continues to gather a number of important external sector statistics, as does Vneshekonombank. Finally, the Ministry of Defense maintains all statistics on military production and other defense-related activities.

The sources of data for statistics on the domestic economy, external sector, fiscal accounts, and money and credit are summarized in Chart 2. Given that it requires specialized expertise to compile many of these series, it is not surprising that a few institutions are the sole providers of certain statistics. The degree to which access to a given organization's statistics is restricted, however, is surprising. For example, Goskomstat has a legitimate interest in acquiring data on net factor income from abroad to compile GNP statistics for the USSR, but has yet to obtain these data from the other agencies. As a result, its GNP statistics exclude net factor income from abroad and therefore are actually GDP figures, though no statistical compendia mention this. Similarly, one cannot go to a single ministry for a composite picture of external settlements, although this would seem to be of interest to a variety of Soviet organizations in carrying out their official activities.

Glavlit, the state censorship office, is not formally part of the national statistical network, but has nonetheless played an important role. By forbidding publication of articles containing statistics not authorized by the central statistical authorities, it traditionally controlled the dissemination of information on the Soviet economy. Glavlit's degree of control, however, has been reduced. For example, since 1987 Soviet scholars have been able to publish growth rates that differ from official statistics. Legislation has been introduced that would restrict the scope of state censorship.

The role of statistical agencies
   Soviet statistical agencies provide indicators of macroeconomic performance, as do their western counterparts. They are also expected, however, to serve as a mechanism for monitoring plan fulfillment by individual enterprises. This latter role has given rise to several notable characteristics of the Soviet statistical system, which include the following:

(1) Complete enumeration preferred to sample surveys.
The success of enterprises in meeting plan targets cannot be assessed unless data are gathered for all relevant establishments. The practice of compiling statistics based on comprehensive reports filled out by each firm is at considerable variance with western methods of data collection, which are based primarily on sample surveys.

(2) Large statistical workforce.
Monitoring individual enterprise performance is labor intensive. For example, to process the forms it receives, Goskomstat currently employs 27,000 persons – down from 41,000 employed as recently as 1987. By contrast, approximately 13,000 full-time employees are involved in federal statistical work in the United States (where sample surveys predominate). The relatively high employment figures reflect not only the practice of gathering data via complete enumeration, but also the poor quality of much of the available data processing equipment. This frequently necessitates hand tabulation of many indicators.

(3) Emphasis on data processing over data analysis.
Given finite resources and the plethora of reports submitted by individual enterprises, the attentions of Goskomstat and other Soviet statistical organizations have traditionally been focused on data processing rather than data analysis. Statistics thus tend to be gathered in a manner that facilitates easy compilation, though not necessarily easy interpretation or use.

(4) Incentives to distort.
Because bonuses have generally been paid upon proof of plan fulfillment, enterprises have had a strong incentive to exaggerate their performance. Goskomstat maintains a large force of investigators to audit reports, but falsification is still widespread. Soviet analysts estimate that exaggerated

reporting inflated output by three percent on average during the late 1980s, but was as high as 25 percent for some raw material sectors. It is not possible to judge whether the incidence of inflated reporting has risen over time. To the extent that reforms have substituted state orders and autonomous direct contracts among enterprises for planning norms, there are now fewer output targets and thereby fewer incentives to falsify production levels.

Reform and the statistical system
     The glasnost and perestroika campaigns had a delayed impact on the Soviet statistical system. The campaign for change began in earnest in 1987, following the publication of an unprecedented series of challenges by Soviet scholars regarding the accuracy of official statistics. Soviet authorities responded to these criticisms in 1987 by mandating a restructuring of the country's statistical system. In the following months, the former Central Statistical Administration (TsSU) was renamed Goskomstat, and elevated to state committee status. Indicators that had been omitted from existing yearbooks for decades were restored, the Information and Publishing Center was created, and many new, sector-specific statistical handbooks were published. Concerted efforts were made to increase Soviet participation in international statistical conferences, and a new director for Goskomstat was appointed in 1989 to oversee the continuation of reform initiatives.
     While these measures represent a substantial change from past practices, many problems remain. Goskomstat still monitors fulfillment of plan targets, and the systemic problems that role engenders (noted above) continue to be in evidence. The statistical agency's work force has been reduced by a third at a time when increasing demands are being made of its services. Finally, there is still widespread uncertainty regarding various methodological approaches and the quality of many macroeconomic indicators.

National accounts
     Most of the criticism of Soviet economic statistics has been directed at its national accounts. The problem most frequently noted is that real growth rates for these accounts are upwardly biased by the failure to account fully for inflation but there are also problems of coverage, undocumented changes in methodology, and distortions imposed by the economic system, all of which complicate comparisons of Soviet national accounts statistics with those from other countries as well. Each of these issues is discussed below.

Problems of coverage

Traditional Soviet national accounts are prepared in accordance with the system of Balances of the National Economy (MPS). This means that unlike the national accounts of most countries (which are prepared according to the U.N. System of National Accounts (SNA)), Soviet accounts exclude depreciation and the output of most so-called nonmaterial services.[1] Levels of output implied by traditional Soviet indicators, such as national income produced (hereafter referred as net material product, or NMP), therefore understate the true level of economic activity.

Goskomstat has moved in recent years to address these coverage problems by also compiling national accounts estimates on an SNA basis. As shown in Table 1, gross national product (GNP) statistics produced on this basis to date have been built up from NMP data using translation keys, although corresponding GNP estimates have been developed from the expenditure side that are fully consistent with these figures. While broader in scope than traditional NMP statistics, these GNP estimates are not without problems. On the one hand, Goskomstat has been unable to obtain statistics on net factor income from abroad. This means that their GNP estimates are effectively gross domestic product (GDP) figures, and would generally be different if net overseas income were taken into account. On the other hand, the difference between NMP and GDP – 40 percent in 1989 – is much larger than for Eastern European economies, suggesting that GDP estimates may be overstated.

...... [I]t is important to note that neither the NMP nor GDP statistics compiled by Goskomstat take into account levels of activity in the "second," or shadow economy. Estimates of gross output in the shadow economy vary considerably, with Goskomstat estimating a figure of rub 70 billion, and the Chairman of the Soviet KGB maintaining that it is closer to rub 150 billion. Even if only half of these estimates represent undocumented value-added, they would imply that official GDP statistics are understated by 4 to 8 percent. While figures such as these are quite rough, they are consistent with other estimates of the output of the shadow economy, and highlight continuing problems of coverage in Soviet national accounts – a problem also noted in the national accounts of Western countries.

---

[1] Nonmaterial services include personal transport, banking and insurance, medical care, education, scientific research, housing, and government services. Services that facilitate material production – such as construction, freight transport, communications, and trade – are by contrast included in the national accounts.

Methodological uncertainties

Methodological changes to Soviet national accounts are not always well documented. At worst, this can allow unflattering economic results to be concealed. A recent example of this was the revelation that the statistical authorities had originally excluded declining alcohol sales from the national accounts for 1985 and 1986 to boost artificially rates of aggregate growth. At best, incomplete documentation still has the potential to mislead users of data, even if that is not the intention. For example, one methodological problem not publicly documented concerns the valuation of inventories in calculating stockbuilding. Soviet statisticians apparently make no adjustments for inflation in inventories when calculating changes in stocks. During periods of low inflation this has little effect on national income utilized, but as prices increase, the consequent rise in inventory values imparts an upward bias to national income accounts. This problem could seriously distort measurement of economic activity in the USSR if controls on prices were lifted as part of economic reforms.

Distortions imposed by the economic system

The fact that the USSR is a planned economy has traditionally made interpretation of its national accounts problematic. Foremost of the difficulties imposed by the economic system are problems of valuation. As resources have traditionally been allocated by plan rather than market, most prices in the USSR are set administratively. This means that national accounts are valued at prices that do not necessarily reflect consumer preferences, and increases in NMP or GDP may thus not indicate an improvement in consumer welfare. In addition, the sectoral composition of value-added is distorted by the presence of large turnover taxes and subsidies. Finally, comparisons of output per capita with other countries are complicated by vast differences in relative prices, as well as the absence of a market-clearing exchange rate to convert Soviet national accounts into dollars.These problems of valuation have been the driving force behind Western estimates of Soviet GNP, most notably the "adjusted factor cost approach." They are, however, not the only distortions introduced by the economic system. For instance, as already noted, considerable rewards have accrued to enterprises reporting fulfillment of their economic plans, providing an incentive for these firms to exaggerate their output.

Biased rates of growth

Few indicators have been singled out for greater criticism than the official real growth rates for NMP. Soviet critics maintain that official growth rates are overstated because of inadequate accounting for inflation.

How large is this bias? Official NMP growth rates for 1966-85 averaged 5.3 percent, compared to much lower alternative estimates by Soviet analysts ranging from 2.2 to 2.9 percent. Researchers at the USSR Institute of World Economy and International Relations have recently estimated that real growth in NMP between 1913 and 1987 was approximately one-third the official rate. Soviet scholars have gone as far as to use CIA estimates of real growth in Soviet GNP to suggest that official growth rates are twice as high as actual growth. In an even more unusual turn, Goskomstat has used CIA estimates of real growth to call into question the reliability of even lower growth rates set forth by Soviet critics.

While these alterative estimates of real growth should be regarded with caution, the message they send is unmistakable. Official growth rates are upwardly biased because inflation has not been accounted for fully. The only point of contention is the magnitude by which growth has been overestimated, Goskomstat has sought to address these problems by introducing an improved method for calculating real growth rates in 1990 (for 1989 data). This involves the calculation of actual NMP deflators, which are reportedly developed according to international standards on the basis of changes in prices of a representative sample of commodities.

Price indices

Official price indices that are used simply to monitor price developments in the economy have also come under fire. Problems with Soviet price indices are threefold. First, there are problems of availability. While a retail price index has been compiled for decades, an agricultural procurement price index has been calculated only since 1984, compilation of a wholesale price index was resumed only in 1988 after a 10 year hiatus, and a price index for services did not exist until 1990. Significantly, the USSR still has no true consumer price index (with weights drawn from household budget surveys rather than retail trade statistics), although income-indexing called for in some reform plans would require such an index.

Second, there are problems of measurement. Prior to 1989, the retail price index was not particularly good in picking up so-called hidden inflation, that is, the inflation associated with the introduction of new models or quality improvements. If a product in the sample was upgraded or a new model introduced, standard practice was simply to ignore price increases that were accompanied by the supposed increase in product quality. It is widely believed, however, that in many cases these price increases could not be fully justified by quality changes. The official price index thus failed to account for a fairly pervasive form of inflation in the USSR. Goskomstat introduced changes in 1989 aimed at capturing this so-called hidden inflation. The improved price index for that year shows a rate of inflation of 2.0 percent – a full 1.5 percentage points higher than would have resulted from simply assuming all so-called quality improvements were non-inflationary.

Finally, there are problems of sample design, and more generally of measuring so-called repressed inflation. For its retail price index, Goskomstat attempts to gather prices for a remarkably large sample of 3,000 commodities. Not every commodity is in stock when the survey is conducted, however, meaning that the effective sample used for the retail price index is smaller than stated, and changing every month. Goskomstat's apparent solution to this problem is to use official list prices when shortages preclude obtaining prices in the field. The problem with this approach is that shortages indicate excess demand, strongly suggesting that the true transaction prices of these goods in parallel markets are above the state list prices. Of course, to the extent that the retail price index also includes cooperative prices, some of the effective price increases manifested by shortages in state run stores are captured, but directly addressing this problem is not an easy task. The U.S. Bureau of Labor Statistics has been working with Poland to devise methodologies for imputing prices of scarce goods in the context of measuring inflation – research that is obviously relevant to the USSR as well.

Goskomstat has recently attempted to quantify the extent of repressed inflation in the state retail sector, and estimates that in 1989 it amounted to approximately 5.5 percent. Although the methodology used to arrive at this estimate is quite rough, it would suggest that the true rate of inflation for the USSR in 1989 was in the neighborhood of 7.5 percent (the official rate of 2.0 percent, together with repressed inflation of 5.5 percent). It should be kept in mind, however, that little research has been conducted in the USSR on direct measurement of inflation in parallel markets, providing no real benchmark against which Goskomstat's estimates of repressed inflation can be assessed.

Employment and living standards

The availability of standard labor indicators has traditionally been a problem in the USSR.... Goskomstat does not compile labor force statistics as they are understood in the West (i.e., the employed population, plus those who are unemployed but who desire work), and thus has no official measures of unemployment that are comparable to western statistics. It instead prepares estimates of total "labor resources," which divide the working age population into those who work, and those who for various reasons do not (housewives, students, prisoners, the handicapped, and individuals who are involuntarily unemployed). Experimental unemployment rates that have been computed to date are generally the ratio of a subset of nonworkers to total labor resources, despite the fact that not all of these individuals desire work or are even capable of it. The crux of the problem is that official accounting of unemployment cannot formally proceed until the government adopts the Law on Unemployment, which provides a definition of the status of unemployed individuals. Pending approval of this law, Goskomstat expects to begin compiling official unemployment statistics in 1991. Accelerating work on these statistics is particularly important in the context of the economic reform initiatives now under discussion, for most reform programs assume that unemployment will rise at least temporarily as inefficient firms are closed.

Soviet authorities have expressed increasing interest in data on standards of living. Goskomstat has acted to meet the growing demand for this type of data by increasing the sample size in its family budget surveys by 45 percent, thereby increasing the representativeness of household income and expenditure statistics. The record of reporting on other aspects of living standards is less commendable. For example, grain output per capita is an important measure of the USSR's ability to meet its food needs, yet until 1989 grain output statistics were reported in "bunker weight" which includes dirt and other foreign matter that clearly cannot be consumed. Similarly, official statistics on meat consumption are inflated by the inclusion of substandard cuts, lard and bones. Statistics on the sales of passenger cars were also artificially boosted in the early 1970s by the undocumented inclusion of used cars. While a careful reader of Soviet statistics on living standards may be able to allow for these peculiarities, they may well prove misleading to others.

Chart 1. USSR: INSTITUTIONAL RESPONSIBILITIES IN STATISTICS

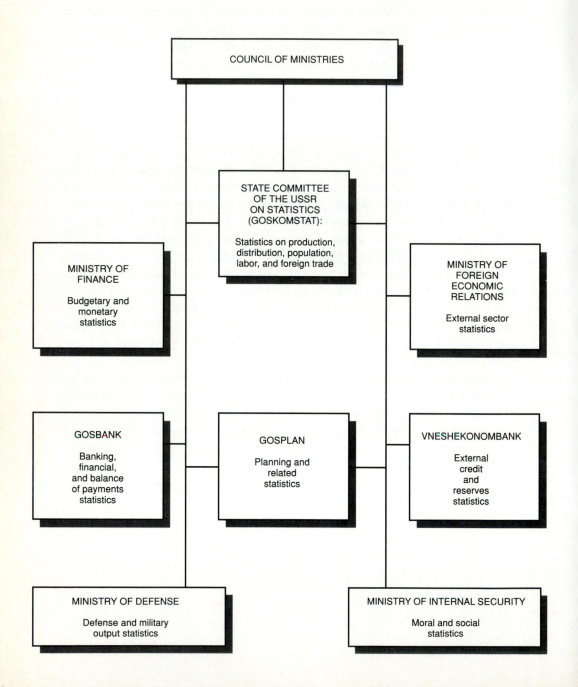

Chart 2. USSR: SOURCES OF DATA BY SECTOR

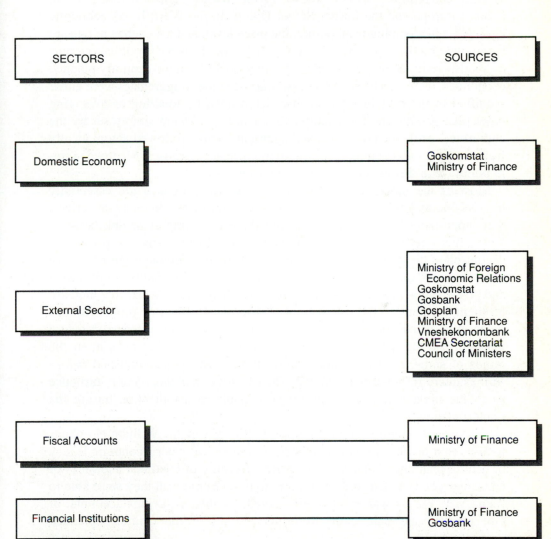

PART VI

THE MACROECONOMY

Macroeconomics – as it is known in the West – is a new discipline in Eastern Europe and the former Soviet Union. In the West, broad economic aggregates like employment, output, the price level, and the exchange rate are determined by fiscal policy, monetary policy, and the behavior of participants in goods, credit, labor, and foreign currency markets. In the centrally planned economies, there was no such process. Macroeconomic aggregates were either specified in the plan directly, or else determined by totalling or averaging other plan parameters. For example, exchange rates were simply set by the authorities, while the price level and aggregate output followed automatically from the prices and output quotas set in individual enterprises. Macroeconomic policy, as a distinct entity, was nonexistent.

Most of the individual components of reform programs are essentially microeconomic reforms: privatization of enterprises, freeing up prices, demonopolizing key industries, etc. But there is an important link between these micro reforms and macro phenomena. Most clearly, as prices are decontrolled on the micro side, inflation is a likely – although not necessary – result on the macro side. Similarly, as soft budget constraints are hardened and privatization proceeds on the micro front, there will be a sizeable increase in unemployment on the macro front. These macroeconomic problems need to be anticipated and dealt with. In the minds of many reformers, macro instability is the most serious political threat to successful reform; in the minds of some, macroeconomic stabilization must be accomplished *before* serious micro reforms are attempted. The two articles in this section introduce us to the main issues and controversies in macro stabilization during the transformation.

In "Macroeconomic Stabilization in the Soviet Union," William Nordhaus focuses first on an especially troubling and universal macroeconomic legacy of central planning: "monetary overhang." Because of continual shortages of consumer goods, households had more money income than they were able to spend. The excess was involuntarily saved – either in savings accounts, or else hoarded as spare cash. Reformers in all of the centrally planned economies have had to face the real danger that this store of cash could erupt into hyperinflation in the midst of the reform process. Poland had its "zloty overhang" to contend with; Czechoslovakia its "crown overhang," and now the former Soviet republics have to face their enormous "ruble overhang." Nordhaus discusses how this ruble overhang arose, explains the dimensions of the problem, and discusses some alternative methods of dealing with it.

Ordinarily, we think of micro problems in Soviet-type economies causing macro problems. For instance, micro problems like soft budget constraints and price setting have caused the macro problem of suppressed inflation. But Nordhaus points out how a *macro* problem in the Soviet Union has led to a serious *micro* problem. Because the economy suffered from chronic excess demand, individual enterprises would count on selling their goods, regardless of quality, service, or variety. This has created a noncompetitive "culture" within the enterprise. Nordhaus implies that, during the transformation, stimulative macro policies designed to prevent unemployment may also retard the development of market-based attitudes and habits.

In "Reform, Inflation and Adjustment in Planned Economies," Thomas Wolf observes that the transition from plan to market has been almost invariably accompanied by inflation. This is a cause for concern, because inflation threatens the overall reform process in two ways. First, inflation can destroy social tolerance for reform. Second, inflation invariably leads to balance of payments deficits, which increases indebtedness and brings the emerging economy precariously close to the lending limits of the West. This, in turn, threatens imports that are desperately needed during the transition. In these two ways, inflation may cause reforms to be aborted.

Wolf asks: is there something about the reform process that invariably generates inflation? To Wolf, the link is a political one: given the traditional concern for equity in the planned economies, price decontrol always leads to pressure for compensating wage increases by enterprises. Since, during the transition, wages are still paid by the State, wage hikes mean budget deficits and, given the structure of the banking system (see Lieberman, Article 15 in this book), deficits are automatically and fully monetized. Thus, price decontrol – which is always an early step in the reform process – invariably has led to expansionary monetary policies. Once this process begins, and inflationary expectations take hold, the economy becomes addicted to new money creation, needing more and more money just to stay in the same place.

Since the reform-inflation link arises from psychological and institutional factors, the elimination of the link requires psychological and institutional changes. More specifically, workers and managers must adopt attitudes that prevent any decline in real wages during the reform process. At the same time, the economy needs an independent central bank, capable of restricting money supply growth regardless of the unpleasant consequences faced by workers and their managers. These changes are crucial for the success of reform and should be initiated as early in the process as possible.

20. Macroeconomic Stabilization in the Soviet Union*

William D. Nordhaus

A central task of managing economic reform will be to maintain macroeconomic stability during the transition. On the whole, this is a new topic for socialist reformers. Until recently, socialist macroeconomics referred to economic planning and ensuring plan fulfillment. Unemployment was nonexistent in principle and, for the most part, in fact. Inflation of official prices was contained by leaving official prices fixed for long periods. When aggregate demand became excessive, these economies suffered "repressed inflation," a syndrome in which too-low prices result in high black market prices, long lines for goods, and forced saving. What Western economists call "macroeconomics," in the sense of the determinants of national income and output in the short run, is not yet a discipline among Soviet economists.

As socialist economies begin to liberalize their prices and allow enterprises to fire workers, the familiar symptoms of a market economy emerge. People lose their jobs, liberalized prices (in both the state and private sectors) begin to rise, and the populace complains about unemployment and inflation. At this point the Soviet Union will come up against the need for stabilization policy as the nation makes the transition to the market.

The task of short-run macroeconomic policy is to ensure that the economy is in overall or aggregate balance. Using fiscal and monetary policies, policy makers aim for internal balance, which signifies that nominal aggregate demand is close to the potential output of the economy at the existing price level.[1] Internal balance involves both a level (or stock) and a growth (or flow) requirement. The level requirement is that desired spending in the economy (by households, enterprises, and the government) be close to the

---

* From *Brookings Papers on Economic Activity*, vol. 1, 1990. Reprinted by permission of the Brookings Institution.

[1] Macroeconomic balance also entails external balance, in which the current account and capital flows are in balance. I concentrate on issues of internal balance as these seem more pressing for the Soviet Union in the near term.

current-price value of output; the growth requirement is that total incomes and total spending grow at about the same rate as potential output. If desired spending in the economy greatly exceeds the current-price value of potential output, then the economy will tend toward repressed or open inflation.

By these criteria, the Soviet economy currently has many serious macroeconomic problems. To begin with, the government budget is seriously out of equilibrium, resulting in flow imbalance. The budget deficit has grown from 2 percent of GNP in the early 1980s to around 11 percent of GNP in 1989. There is also stock imbalance, with the government debt at around 44 percent of GNP and growing. In a market economy, such a large deficit and debt could be mopped up by borrowing; in the Soviet economy, however, the absence of marketable securities means that the deficit is effectively monetized. The large quasi-monetary imbalance is sometimes referred to as a "ruble overhang," which denotes a large accumulation of undesired holdings of money and other liquid assets by households and enterprises.

The easiest way to determine the size of the ruble overhang is to calculate the ratio of household liquid assets to household income. Based on fragmentary data, this ratio is estimated to have risen from around 0.6 in the 1970s (when there was little ruble overhang) to around 0.95 in 1989.

Applying the crude quantity theory suggests that prices would have to rise more than 50 percent to extinguish the overhang.[2] Unless neutralized, the ruble overhang will produce a sharp, one-time rise in prices when prices are decontrolled.An understandable response to the peril of a large and growing ruble overhang – indeed a policy followed by the Soviet government since late 1989 – is to clamp down tighter on prices. But that strategy works no better than tightening the lid on an overheated pot. It is not possible for centrally planned economies to avoid difficulties from excessive demand by controlling prices. In an economy with price controls – whether the Soviet Union in 1990 or the United States in 1944 – the result of excess demand is shortages, long lines, and an increasingly inefficient distribution system. One result of the German decontrol of 1948 or of the Polish decontrol of 1990 is

---

[2] The reasoning based on the quantity theory runs as follows. Assume that household liquid assets (which are primarily currency and savings accounts) are the only "outside money." That is, they are the only nominally denominated exogenous variable in the economy. Further suppose that the economy was in macroeconomic equilibrium with an asset-income ratio of 0.60 and that the asset-income ratio rose to 0.95 today. Then, if the only factor out of equilibrium were the ruble overhang, prices would have to rise by a factor of 0.95/0.60, or slightly over 50 percent, to reestablish the earlier desired asset/income ratio.

that goods magically appear in the shops. (The problem is that they are too expensive to buy.) The inefficiencies of repressed inflation are yet another reason why it is imperative for East European economies to get and retain control of their fiscal and monetary policies.

Figure 1. Impact of Ruble Overhang: Increase of Demand from Deficit

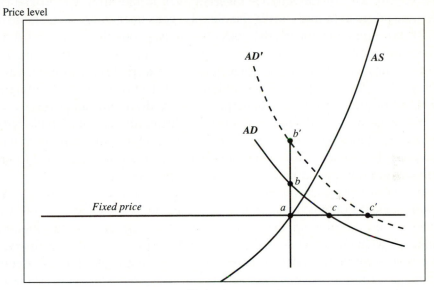

Price level

National output

Figure 1 illustrates the impact of a growing ruble overhang. At an initial equilibrium, with aggregate demand of AD and aggregate supply of AS, prices are fixed below market-clearing levels. State firms are producing at point a, and the excess of desired spending over output is given by the segment ac. The actual outcome depends upon the rationing mechanism, but we can simplify by assuming that goods are rationed by queuing, that the length of the queue adjusts to balance supply and demand, and that the goods obtained by queuing are then resold at black market prices. Under these assumptions, point b in figure 1 is the "true" price as measured either by the black market prices or by the shadow prices of output including costs of waiting, bribing, and using influence.

As the budget deficit increases the ruble overhang, aggregate demand rises to AD′. Because prices are fixed, there is of course no official inflation. But the excess demand gets worse as the amount people wish to buy at the official price level increases while the supply is unchanged. The ex ante shortage – which is the difference between aggregate demand and supply at official prices – grows to ac'. The black market prices or shadow prices rise to b'.

What is the result? The shelves get barer and barer; lines get longer and longer; the stores have nothing to offer but rusty tins and rotten cauliflower; the street price of hard currency diverges even further from the official rate; the free prices in farmers' stalls rise sharply; consumers must spend more and more time foraging for goods; consumers buy goods they don't need as a desperate form of saving; people from high shortage regions take long trips to the cities and other low-shortage regions, exacerbating regional tensions; those who have or sell goods at the high social shadow prices are vilified and accused of profiteering; economic planners are driven to ration basic goods – like soap, meat, and sugar – in effect replacing the devalued ruble with a multitude of local and commodity-specific currencies in the form of rationing coupons. In essence, by an extension of Gresham's law[3], overvalued things (rubles) are driving out undervalued things (goods).

It is clear that, whatever the pace of reforms, the Soviet government must restore macroeconomic balance. One approach often discussed is to attack the problem by soaking up the ruble overhang. Some call for a "monetary reform," which in effect confiscates some of the ruble overhang by introducing a new currency at unfavorable rates to existing ruble holders. Another approach is to introduce a "parallel currency," perhaps one convertible into hard currencies. Yet a third approach, similar to that taken in Poland at the beginning of 1990, would be to let prices rise sharply so that the real value of ruble holdings declines to the level desired by ruble owners.

In fact, these ideas will at best solve the stock, or level, problem and leave the flow, or growth, problem of a large budget deficit untouched. If the budget deficit continues at high levels, aggregate demand will grow rapidly, and the "inflationary gap" between desired spending at existing prices and real output will continue to widen, producing continued repressed or open inflation. A durable solution to the macroeconomic problem of excess demand will require a reduction in the budget deficit. This point leads to an important linkage between macroeconomic and structural policies. Almost all observers of the Soviet economy believe that the structure of the budget is inefficient

---

[3] [Editor's note: Gresham's law, simply stated, is that "bad money drives out good," i.e., if there are two currencies in circulation, people will hoard the more valuable one, leaving only the less valuable one in circulation.]

and undesirable. There are substantial subsidies to food and agriculture (amounting to 24 percent of the Soviet budget, or 12 percent of GNP) and to unprofitable enterprises (about 10 percent of the budget, or 5 percent of GNP). Defense probably absorbs 20 percent to 30 percent of the budget, although the exact size of the Soviet defense establishment at realistic prices is probably known by no one. A promising approach to reform, therefore, is to restructure the budget to ensure macroeconomic stability, to align relative prices with social priorities, and to make room for growth in private consumption.

Some Soviet economists have recommended creating a two-level banking system to help limit money growth as a means of controlling inflation. Without doubt, creating a market-oriented banking system will be a vital part of a reformed Soviet economy. But it seems certain that there is today no way that monetary policy can operate to control spending independently of fiscal policy. There are virtually no retail banks, no credit market instruments, and no variable-price or variable yield assets. The total value of equity-like "stocks" is around 0.02 percent of national income. Mortgages are unheard of. The chief household nonmonetary financial assets are savings accounts and lottery bonds, both of which are virtually perfect substitutes for money.

Because of the structure of financial markets, most of the government deficit is effectively monetized.[4] Even with a broader menu of assets, it is difficult to identify components of spending that are interest sensitive. For example, without hard budget constraints, why would firms tighten their belts in response to interest or credit signals? For all these reasons, monetary policy is not an independent macroeconomic policy instrument at this time. In the near term, therefore, the task of controlling excessive aggregate demand will fall largely on fiscal policy.

In studying the performance of socialist economies, a Western macro-economist cannot fail to notice the disastrous side effects of producers operating in a sellers' market. Until now, socialist enterprises have had no fear of depressions or idled capacity. The symptoms of high-pressure economies have been queues for any reasonably high-quality good, sellers' rationing, deterioration of product quality and variety, poor service, lack of labor discipline, and low rates of innovation.

The experience of Eastern Europe leads one to wonder whether Arthur Okun overestimated the advantages of a high-pressure economy in promoting

---

[4] [Editor's note: A deficit is *monetized* when the government's shortfall of revenue is financed through money creation by the central bank.]

many economic objectives when he wrote in 1973, "The greater diffusion of opportunity and of upward mobility in a full utilization economy is a vital social benefit; and that benefit helps to explain why the pursuit of full employment is an integral part of a liberal's creed.

The conventional worry about Okun's emphasis on a high-pressure economy has been the dangers of high inflation. There may in addition be subtler macroeconomic costs involving lowered overall market discipline. The unhappy lesson of Eastern Europe is that super-full employment and chronic full utilization of capacity seem less effective than unemployment and excess capacity in promoting attention to quality and variety of product, product and process innovation, adjustments to structural change, and a general sense of market discipline among workers and managers.

In sum, there will be no substitute for governmental budget discipline – reducing the budget deficit and perhaps mopping up the ruble overhang – in reducing the pandemic and growing shortages and excess demand in the Soviet economy today. Although fiscal austerity may have unpopular elements, it can be sweetened if the fiscal reforms involve reducing defense spending and uneconomic subsidies. However, the primary attraction of a tight fiscal policy will be to restore value to the currency and to reduce inefficient nonmonetary rationing devices like queues, coupon rationing, and bribery.

21. Reform, Inflation and Adjustment in Planned Economies[*]

Thomas A. Wolf

Faced with continuing structural problems, mounting imbalances, and declining growth rates, many centrally planned economies (CPEs) have been impelled in recent years to experiment with reforms of their economic system. Several CPEs – China, Hungary, and Poland – have launched relatively ambitious programs of market-oriented reform, while other CPEs have watched with interest and, in some instances, have begun to initiate reforms of their own. Although market-oriented programs have occasionally been accompanied by improved economic performance, the hoped-for stimulation to structural change and growth has often not materialized. Moreover, reform has tended to be accompanied by an acceleration of "open" (or measured) inflation, combined, in some periods, with large external imbalances. This has prompted concerns in some quarters about how best to create the necessary conditions to ensure the sustainability of market-oriented reform.

Macroeconomic developments have differed widely among these countries, reflecting influences unique to the economy at hand. But a quick look at two critical indicators – inflation and the current account – shows a disturbing pattern. In Hungary, the first of the three to undertake significant market-oriented reform, beginning with the adoption of the New Economic Mechanism in 1968, the measured rate of inflation gradually accelerated from an annual average rate of 1 to 3 percent in the early 1970s to over 15 percent in 1988-89. Moreover, throughout most of this period, Hungary incurred current account deficits in its trade in convertible currencies. In China, cycles of deterioration and improvement in the external balance since reforms were launched in 1978 have been accompanied by generally increasing open inflation, rising from annual rates of 2 to 3 percent in most of the early years

---

[*] From *Finance and Development*, March 1990, a quarterly of the International Monetary Fund and the World Bank. Reprinted by permission of the IMF and the World Bank.

of reform to almost 30 percent in 1988, before being brought down to less than 10 percent by October 1989.

The acceleration of inflation, in particular, has been much more dramatic in other countries undergoing reform. In Poland, the 1981-82 reform program began with a doubling of the price level in 1982, aimed at eliminating an accumulated liquidity overhang. After falling to an annual rate of 22 percent in 1983 and 15 percent in 1984-85, inflation began to accelerate in 1986, soaring to 60 percent in 1988 and over 200 percent in 1989. This most recent inflationary surge has also been accompanied by a deterioration in Poland's current account balance in convertible currencies.

Even in Yugoslavia, which had already moved away from traditional central planning by the early 1950s, the problem of inflation has intensified in recent years. From an average annual rate of a little less than 20 percent in the 1970s, inflation rose to well over 100 percent in 1986-88, and sharply accelerated in 1989 to over 1,000 percent. Yugoslavia's reform experience differs in some important respects from that of the three countries under review here, but in the end, its inflation has also been shaped by some of the same forces that tend to characterize inflation in those that have only relatively recently decided to depart from the classical Soviet-type economic mode.

At this stage, it is thus well worth asking whether the process of market-oriented reform may bring with it a new set of pressures and institutional arrangements that effectively result in a loosening of macroeconomic policies and thus increased inflation. This is critical because if reform is indeed accompanied by a serious worsening of inflationary pressures, and these pressures exceed the population's tolerance for open inflation and the borrowing capacity of the economy, the authorities may be forced to react with a tightening, rather than a further relaxation, of controls over prices and imports.

These controls in turn must almost inevitably lead to an increase in price distortions, and they will certainly trigger greater *de facto* restrictions on the autonomy of enterprises, as scarce inputs and capital goods are both formally and informally rationed. Tightened price controls – effectively "repressing" all or most of the underlying inflation – and increased quantitative rationing would also mean an expanded scope for bureaucratic bargaining, which will further weaken financial discipline and incentives for boosting efficiency. With internal, and possibly external, imbalances activated, the reform process could easily degenerate into a series of stop-and-go measures, and the momentum of the reform away from the system of central planning could be lost or even reversed.

Whether countries embarking on market-oriented reform can avoid a loosening of demand management may depend on the sequencing of the reform measures themselves. In particular, it may turn on whether enterprise financial discipline can effectively be imposed either before, or simultaneously with, the liberalization of prices and wages.

The Traditional CPE

Between the end of World War II and the early 1950s, a number of countries, including China and most of those in Eastern Europe, embraced the basic features of the economic system, as well as most of the major policy objectives, that had been developed in the Soviet Union of the 1920s and the 1930s. In this system, usually characterized as the traditional CPE, virtually all the means of production were turned over to state ownership. The central authorities, comprising the state planning commission and other agencies, worked out detailed plans for the inputs and outputs of state-owned enterprises, with inputs generally being centrally allocated. The flow of information connected with the planning process and the evaluation of firms, typically on the basis of their degree of plan fulfillment, took place largely within a vertical, bureaucratic setting, rather than through the market. While the traditional system was frequently referred to as a "command economy," in reality there was a great deal of bargaining within the system among the central planners, the branch ministries, and the enterprises – over the plan figures and the allocation of physical resources.

Although in most CPEs workers had some freedom to change jobs, the wage structure and wage bills of enterprises were closely regulated from the center. The state banking system was effectively a monolith, in which commercial bank branches belonging to the central bank passively accommodated the credit demands of state enterprises, as these firms attempted to fulfill plans that were largely expressed in physical terms. Foreign trade was conducted by state-owned foreign trade organizations (FTOs), essentially noncompetitive entities that enjoyed a monopoly over foreign trade in particular groups of products. And price differences faced by FTOs between domestic prices – fixed by the authorities for long periods – and border prices were offset by variable taxes and subsidies. This separation of domestic from foreign prices, together with the state foreign trade monopoly, essentially insulated the domestic economy from outside influences and competition.

These systemic features were combined with an economic strategy of accelerated industrialization centered on the rapid mobilization of capital, labor, and material inputs, with far less emphasis on productivity improvements and the production of consumer goods. The appeal to the populace of the CPE was intended to lie in retail price stability, low prices for staples such as food and housing, an egalitarian wage structure, full employment, and an exceptionally high degree of job security.

Macroeconomic demand management was essentially reflected in the aggregate of the innumerable microeconomic decisions in which the central authorities involved themselves. These ranged from quantitative plan targets and wage bills of individual firms to the determination of product- and enterprise-specific subsidies. Although the planners were interested in minimizing inflationary pressures, in the final analysis these economies frequently experienced substantial repressed inflation, as prices were held steady despite a growth in demand that outstripped supply. The fiscal and monetary authorities, faced with above-plan subsidy and credit demands from enterprises, would frequently subordinate their own financial plans to the higher priorities of meeting quantitative targets in the national economic plan and holding prices stable, regardless of the underlying price pressures that were building up. Under central planning, the exchange rate had only an accounting function, and interest rates – to the degree they existed – were set at negligible levels, thus having little allocative impact or influence on the desired level of saving of households.

With virtually all prices fixed and playing little role in resource allocation, and with much of economic activity subject to direct controls, indirect instruments of macroeconomic policy commonly used in market economies, such as credit ceilings, even if used, could not necessarily be relied upon to achieve a specific internal or external objective. Moreover, even when a specific objective was attained by means of direct instruments, it might well not involve genuine adjustment, in the sense of moving the economy toward equilibrium in all markets – external and internal – and within the latter, in both investment and consumption. For example, in response to a deterioration in the terms of trade, the authorities might issue instructions to FTOs to import less and export more. With fixed domestic prices and unchanged wage payments, the diversion of output to improve the trade balance might well result in the build up of domestic excess demand pressures. In effect, balance in one segment of the economy would be sacrificed to achieve balance in another.

The "modified" CPE

Reform initiatives in CPEs have typically taken one of two forms: repeated attempts to improve or "perfect" the existing system of planning and management; and market oriented reforms, which recently have become the more popular approach. Countries undertaking these market-oriented reforms (the so-called modified planned economies, or MPEs) have emphasized greater price flexibility, fewer controls on inputs and foreign trade, greater financial discipline, and a generally deeper concern with avoiding market imbalances.

In practice, however, the reforms carried out by MPEs have frequently turned out to be less thorough and comprehensive than initially contemplated, mainly due to the bevy of constraints that reformers in these countries have faced. These include opposition by entrenched bureaucrats and managers to reforms that would adversely affect them, at least in the short run; ingrained attitudes resulting from decades of life under central planning; existing cumbersome institutional arrangements affecting trade with other planned economies; and the opposition of workers threatened with job loss and households faced with losing certain economic guarantees, such as subsidized prices for staple foods, housing, and services. As a result, MPEs have so far not managed to achieve degrees of financial discipline or price flexibility, or to develop generalized instruments of monetary and fiscal control, comparable to those prevailing in many market economies.

Sequencing and inflation

The disturbing lack of comprehensiveness and depth of many of these reform efforts has been combined, in most MPEs, with growing inflation and to some extent chronic external imbalances. This raises the question whether reform and greater disequilibrium must go hand-in-hand.

In principle, there is no reason why market-oriented reform need create an underlying inflationary bias and a serious threat to the balance of payments. After all, much of the increase in the price level in the MPE might be expected as the authorities seek to reduce or eliminate an already existing excess demand problem, by raising administered prices and freeing other prices. In this way, repressed inflation of the past is released. But this should largely be a once-and-for-all increase in the price level, provided financial policies are sufficiently tight. In the final analysis, aggregate demand management, the external balance, and the rate of inflation are issues of macroeconomic policy, not of economic reform *per se*.

The *sequencing* of reform measures, however, may have an important bearing on the tightness of macroeconomic policy in practice. In particular, inflationary pressures may increase if retail prices are allowed to rise at a faster pace – and wages are liberalized more rapidly – than important institutional changes that permit the strengthening of competition and financial discipline. These changes in turn, however, are likely to be possible only if there is a more fundamental shift in attitudes regarding the trade-off between economic efficiency on the one hand, and income equality and job security on the other.

This inflationary process may develop in the following way. Large retail price increases in economies with a history of largely repressed inflation may trigger demands for wage increases that – due to rising inflationary expectations following the price increases – may well outpace the current rate of open inflation and lead to an increase in the real wage. Egalitarian attitudes and formal or informal indexation arrangements, which have developed over decades of central planning, may also result in the productivity-related wage gains of some being effectively translated into broadly similar nominal wage increases for all. Consequently, the growth in the overall real wage may significantly outpace the rate of growth of labor productivity. Moreover, greater wage differentiation, typically one of the objectives of market-oriented reform for its supply-side effects, will not be enhanced.

Such excessive wage demands may well be realized despite the authorities' intention to indirectly control wage increases through fiscal mechanisms that subject enterprises paying "excessive" wages to highly progressive penalty taxes. In practice, in most of these countries, there has existed neither the political will nor the institutional safeguards to prevent the accommodation of such excessive wage increases through discretionary tax reliefs and credits to enterprises. In other words, the price increases indirectly lead, given the absence of financial discipline, to uncontrolled growth of net domestic credit to enterprises and the government.

This real wage growth is likely to result in an increase in domestic demand, which may be excessive in the sense that the growing demand pressures outstrip the domestic supply capacities of the economy. Part of this demand may be absorbed, of course, by a weakening of the trade balance, as exports are directed to domestic consumption and imports are stepped up. The potential for this type of response will be limited, however, in some cases quite considerably, by already existing heavy external debt burdens. To the extent that growing incomes outstrip the domestic supply and external borrowing capacities of the economy and the desire of households to add to their savings, excess demand pressures will accumulate that may lead the authorities to permit a further round of price increases. If these price and wage policies are accompanied by a structure of interest rates that is negative in real terms, households may not want to add to their savings, and enterprises will have the incentive to overinvest in stockbuilding and new investment projects, the aggregate effect of which will be to exacerbate the inflation problem. Currency substitution will likely also be encouraged by these policies. The proclivity of an MPE toward the acceleration of underlying inflationary pressures (and, in turn, accelerating open inflation) may well be greater, the larger the extent of excess demand prevailing at the time that a market-oriented reform program is launched. But regardless of the initial level of excess demand, the critical sequencing issue is whether institutional and attitudinal changes fostering the imposition of financial discipline have effectively preceded, or at least occurred simultaneously with, the liberalization of wages and the administrative revision of and liberalization of prices.

Financial discipline

Clearly, in an MPE, the achievement of tight financial policies at the macroeconomic level critically depends on whether financial discipline has been imposed at the microeconomic level. Essential institutional and policy changes promoting financial discipline would include those that (1) reduce the possibilities for bargaining over financial reliefs and preferential credits; (2) encourage the growth of private sector activities; (3) facilitate more flexible and rapid resource allocation; (4) establish the basis for nondiscretionary (i.e., stable and uniform) fiscal policies; and (5) pave the way for a truly independent banking system. Imposing financial discipline without eliminating, or at least significantly reducing, price distortions might give rise to increased efficiency losses. However, if price reform indeed follows relatively rapidly, efficiency losses should be insignificant.

The imposition of financial discipline should be visualized as a central requirement of market-oriented reform and, in the context of the sequencing problem, a precondition for the success of a number of other reform initiatives. This is just a specific example of the general need in a reform program to ensure that the appropriate institutional groundwork has been laid before substantive liberalization of markets is implemented. Giving an early and prominent position to financial discipline in the reform process requires the political will at the highest levels to ensure that fundamental institutional reform, and the economic restructuring that successful reform entails, will actually take place.

The establishment of many new institutions, including the retraining of managers and workers to operate them, obviously cannot occur overnight. Hence, the critical importance of initiating these institutional changes as early as possible in the overall reform program. Such an approach need not imply that market-oriented reform should proceed only gradually. Rather, it suggests that what is needed is a bolder vision of institutional change, and more ambitious measures designed to accelerate changes in the institutional environment favorable to tightening financial discipline, than have heretofore occurred in MPEs. In this way, planned economies undergoing market-oriented reform may be able to avoid the acceleration of inflationary pressures and the problems that ensue, including the threat eventually posed to the success of the reform program itself.

PART VII

PRIVATIZATION

The logic of Parts I and II of this book was that a system of market relations is necessarily a more efficient means of using resources to maximize the welfare of individuals than central planning. Only in a market arrangement will prices reflect relative scarcities of goods and factors of production, a condition generally known as allocative efficiency. Further, the articles by Popkova and Keren argued strongly that mixing the market with a high degree of state ownership is in itself flawed and doomed to failure. Therefore, a vital part of the process of transition must involve the transfer of ownership from the State to private individuals, cooperatives, partnerships, or corporations.

However, it has also become clear that privatization, although simple in concept, is one of the most difficult of reforms. Valuing corporations in an environment where accounting rules are imperfect, disclosure patchy and prices distorted is bound to be a problem. There are also distributional issues that are contentious since many new owners will enjoy windfall gains, and many of the individuals with resources to buy shares or companies got them by questionable means in the previous regimes. The role of foreign investment is also politically divisive, with nationalism colliding with a pragmatic need for capital and management skills. Finally the way to promote an efficient and competitive environment from a monopolistic state structure is not at all simple, and has been a problem in privatization programs in developed countries.

Our first reading addresses the most basic of the issues. It is "The Right to Property and Economic Activity," taken from the report of a committee appointed by President Gorbachev and Boris Yeltsin under the leadership of the leading Russian economist, Stanislas Shatalin. Grigory Yavlinsky (now well-known for the Harvard "Grand Bargain Plan" – see Philip Hanson's discussion of this plan in Article 33 of this book), who is the lead author. The argument of this section of their report is simple. All citizens have the right to own property and the right to engage in economic activity. This in itself is a sharp change from the previous order throughout Eastern Europe in which legal property was by and large limited to personal possessions and almost all private economic activity was illegal. The committee is clear that state assets must not be *given* away to the citizenry because, it is argued, anything free will not be valued. Little is said on the technique of privatization, and the ideas on valuation and disposal may be somewhat naive. On other points, especially the development of small and medium-sized private firms "to fight the dictatorship of monopoly" and to provide a favorable environment for technological innovation, the authors are closer to the mark.

A lot of literature on the economic prospects for the former Soviet Union has emphasized the absence of entrepreneurs and businesses in a society that has viewed market exchange and return to capital with hostility for more than 70 years. "Sub-Rosa Privatization and Marketization in the USSR" by Gregory Grossman gives us a glimpse at the second, or underground, economy that existed within the Soviet Union, and continues in the successor states today. Only about 70,000 people in the centrally planned Soviet Union were employed in plying the few legally permitted private occupations; however, Grossman estimates that, in the urban population, income derived from the underground private sector was about half as much as the "legally earned" official income. This underground economy has served as a "school of enterprise initiative, work habits, pecuniary calculus, risk taking." The skills imbued may not be the most appropriate for larger businesses; Grossman asserts that most of the income accruing to the entrepreneurs has been transferred rather than produced, with the State or the consumer as the loser.

"Proposals for Privatization in Eastern Europe" by Eduardo Borenzstein and Manmohan Kumar takes a broad and nonpartisan view of the options open for privatization in the Eastern European countries. Part I offers a commendably brief statement of the case for privatization in terms of the goal of promoting allocative efficiency. Part II starts by emphasizing the need for speed; a gently shrinking government sector would be composed only of the most inefficient firms as privatization removes the more profitable enterprises. Speed requires a large element of "give-away," or, at the least, sale at drastically reduced prices. Appropriate valuation would take too long. Moreover, demand for industrial securities would necessarily be low in countries where only the politically favored or the criminal have large resources and the lack of financial intermediation precludes borrowing. Since the State has, in theory, been holding the resources for the citizenry this has an equitable ring to it.

The central dispute, however, is whether the public should hold shares directly or collectively own some form of intermediary – mutual fund or holding company – that in turn holds the shares to the corporation. The disadvantage of all shares being held by the public is that the shareholders, in general, lack the know-how to oversee management or even to respond to financial results in the appropriate manner. Any emergent stock market is likely to be thin and subject to manipulation (see van Agtmael, Article 16), and, in such circumstances, the role of financial intermediaries who could research and oversee the newly create firms might be essential.

Part III considers some of the macroeconomic aspects of the privatization issue. Although speed and equity both favor give-aways to put shares into public hands this might have inflationary consequences. Citizens might choose to spend a sizable part of their new wealth on scarce consumer goods, threatening price stability. However, privatization itself might be a means of eliminating another inflationary threat, by absorbing the large monetary overhang that has resulted from government deficits that were financed by issuing new money, (see Nordhaus, Article 20). Though this would be welcome, if not monitored carefully, it might, in combination with sharp inflation, reduce the real money supply sufficiently to create a recession.

"Privatization in Eastern Europe" by David Lipton and Jeffrey Sachs provides a detailed proposal for the privatization of the larger elements of Polish industry, and draws a great deal on the authors' active roles in designing Polish economic policy.

The thrust of the paper is on creating conditions that will promote the good management of the newly privatized concerns in the medium- to long-term – the issue of *corporate governance*. Market logic requires that the owners should also have some control of the corporation, thus giving an incentive for long-run profit maximizing behavior. Supervision of management from a dispersed body of shareholders with little financial experience and little data is likely to be weak. The authors' solution is to structure the distribution of equity in slices, or *tranches*.

Through such a scheme, a wide holding of shares could be achieved. In allocating a substantial holding in all firms to financial intermediaries, such as pension and mutual funds, these organizations would have the incentive and the resources to develop the expertise to play a key role in oversight. Wherever possible a single "stable core" investor, whose interest in the business is long-term rather than speculative, would be allocated a large slice at fair market price.

The largest and in some ways the most successful privatization occurred under the Thatcher administration in the United Kingdom (1979-1990), and indeed the Thatcher program, and even Mrs Thatcher herself, proved inspirational to some of the East European leaders. Throughout much of that period Mrs Thatcher's chief economic advisor was Alan Walters. His paper, "Misapprehensions on Privatization," draws attention to the great differences, that are frequently overlooked, between the state sector in Britain and that in what he calls the Emerging Market Economies (EMEs). One of the main drawbacks in applying the Thatcher model is the very extent of the state sector in the EMEs; at the pace of the Thatcher program, which was considered at the time to be rapid, it would take 100 years to achieve a full divestment of state owned enterprises in Hungary. Despite this and other problems that he enumerates, however, Walters has no alternative to the Thatcher model, beyond speeding up the process.

22. The Right to Property and Economic Activity[*]

G.Yavlinsky et alia

The Right to Property

The right to property is realized through denationalization and privatization, giving over state property to citizens. By giving property back to the people the social orientation of the economy will manifest itself. This is not an act of revenge, but an act of social justice, a way to fix the right of man to his share of the present and future national wealth. Privatization, it should be emphasized, is also a way to distribute responsibility for the state and the level of development of the society to all citizens who choose to accept such responsibility. Privatization should be absolutely voluntary; it should in no way remind one of collectivization.

Property in the hands of everyone is a guarantee of stability in society and one of the important conditions to prevent social and national disasters. A person who has his own house and a plot of land, which he can at any time give over to his children, a person who owns shares or other securities, is objectively interested in the stability of society, in social and national peace and harmony. And, vice versa, our sad experience shows how dangerous for the society, for its normal functioning and development, is a person who has nothing to lose.

The program gives equal chances to everybody. But this equality of opportunity should not be seen as a mirror reflection of egalitarianism. To prevent privatization from becoming a means of legal and inordinate enrichment of the few, the procedure must ensure mass participation in ownership relations; practically everybody, even if he does not have any considerable initial capital, will have an opportunity to get his share of the national wealth. Equality of opportunity will be provided by a variety of forms of privatization which will give a chance either to lease property, buy

---

[*] Excerpted from "On the Program Developed by the Task Force Headed by Academician S. Shatalin" from *500 Days: Transition to the Market*. St. Martins Press: New York 1991. Reprinted by permission of the publisher.

217

it on credit, or acquire it on a shareholding basis.

Fundamentally important is the fact that the state cannot and should not give away its property without compensation. Property must be earned, because people do not believe in free property and do not value it sufficiently. But at the same time a part of state property should be considered already earned by people, and it can be given to them free or at a symbolic price; for example, small apartments in which people have lived for a long time, small weekend farms, etc.

Immediately after that we must start working to establish 50 to 60 stock companies out of big state enterprises by the end of the year, and also to give over or sell at a symbolic price certain (actually already earned) categories of housing and plots of land.

An inventory of the national riches of the country should be made, primarily of gold and currency reserves, strategic reserves, property of public organizations, unfinished construction, Armed Forces property and some other types of state property (cars, state dachas, etc.). Local soviets (district and city) will make inventories of uninhabited properties and freeze the major part of industrial construction projects upon inventory of the unfinished construction. The value of such property, of equipment not yet in place, of material resources in construction will be estimated. Having done all this work, it will be possible to start selling enterprises, cooperatives, and a part of material resources to the public.

Local soviets will estimate the price of trade enterprises, consumer services, local industries, small- and medium-sized enterprises of other industries. After the analysis of their financial position, the local press will publish lists of these enterprises with the dates and terms of their privatization. Then, under conditions of absolute glasnost regarding the course of privatization, they will start selling uninhabited space, small enterprises, workshops, stores, and stands. The program is aimed at giving people the opportunity to spend their money to buy property. Channeling a considerable amount of demand in this direction will help avoid rampant inflation as price controls are abolished by stages.

Local soviets will also make inventories of agricultural land, taking into consideration how it is being used. These actions will provide access to land to everybody who wants to farm. At the same time, there will be more land sold to people for weekend farming. Smaller plots will be sold at moderate prices; larger plots, at normal market prices. Special privatization bodies and land reform committees, along with regional and district soviets, will bear the main responsibility for realizing the citizenry's right to own property. The right of private economic activity is provided by the redistribution of property between the state and citizens in the course of denationalization, and also by the adoption of the law on entrepreneurship. The state will create an economic environment conducive to initiative and enterprise, will make the procedure of starting one's own business easier, and will support small businesses over big enterprises via reduced taxes and favorable credits. The program is built on the assumption that society needs small enterprises to orient production to the needs of every person, to fight the dictatorship of monopolies in consumer and production markets, and to create a favorable environment for quick introduction of new scientific and technological ideas (which are best accepted by small- and medium-sized enterprises).

The Right of Citizens to Economic Activity

But how will the people's right to property actually be realized? On the very first day of the program, equality of rights for any physical and juridical person to engage in economic activity will be declared. There will come an announcement of the privatization program changing big industrial enterprises into stock companies and selling off small trade, public catering, and consumer services enterprises. The same statement will announce property rights guarantees for any kind of property except property belonging exclusively to the state.

Amnesty for those convicted of entrepreneurship will be announced, and the entrepreneurship articles will be removed from the Criminal and Administrative Codes. Simultaneously, the struggle against encroachments on private property will be intensified.

The law will guarantee favorable conditions to denationalize enterprises on the initiative of work collectives. They are supposed to apply to the state property fund and the republics' state property management committees.

The state will stimulate the development of international economic contacts and trips abroad to work and study. Attempts to build a system screened from the outside world have resulted in the degradation and stagnation of most of our industries. Opening up the domestic market will force our entrepreneurs to compete with cheap imported goods. This will make our economy dynamic and flexible in catering to the market and, through the market, to the consumer.

S. Shatalin, N. Petrakov, G. Yavlinski, S. Aleksashenko, A. Vavilov, L. Grigoriev, M. Zadornov, V. Martynova, V. Machits, A. Mikhailov, B. Fyodorov, T. Yarygina, E. Yasin.

23. Sub-Rosa Privatization and Marketization in the USSR[*]

Gregory Grossman

An international committee of experts seeking to define the social conditions that maximize the scope and size of a country's underground economy would in effect rediscover Soviet-type socialism. Of course, the underground economy in some form or other – the aggregate of a country's ongoing illegal economic transactions and supporting activities is a universal and venerable phenomenon that spares no social system. One exists wherever there are taxes to be evaded, price or wage controls to be violated, a principal's property and prerogatives to be abused by the principal's agents and employees especially when the principal is the state – and other legal norms regulating economic behavior to be infringed – which is to say everywhere, and not the least in a Soviet-type society. The specific features of a particular underground economy are largely a reflection of the ambient socioeconomic, legal, and political institutions. Change the ambient system and the underground economy will adapt and change, but it will hardly disappear. Moreover, its vigor and vitality are probably not unrelated to the culture and prior history of the population, though, with time, cultural resistances to corruption and "economic crime" – to introduce a Soviet phrase – may be expected to recede before the force of economic self interest working within the given institutional setting and economic conditions, as seems to have happened in once relatively clean East European countries, such as East Germany – Prussia – and the Czech lands. In addition, it seems to be virtually impossible to extirpate an underground economy or its inevitable concomitant, corruption, by police methods alone, not even under a Mao or a Stalin.

Underground business is usually conducted on private account – though governments and their subdivisions have been known to trade in violation of

---

their own, not to say other countries' laws – and because it operates out of reach of all administrative authority, its prices and markets are necessarily free. It is also likely, except in the case of relatively small transactions, to employ money as the main medium of exchange, rather than to transact by barter. Hence, in capitalist market economies, the distinction between the underground and the aboveground economy is more legal than systemic. On the other hand, in the Soviet-type system, it is precisely the cited attributes, in addition to the legality criterion, that set the Soviet underground economy off from the ambient – that is, official, Stalinist – economy, which at least until very recently was almost entirely non-private and devoid of free markets and free prices and in which money has played largely a passive role.

An interesting question, therefore, implicit in this article's title, is whether the Soviet sub-rosa economy may not, in some manner or other, perform a significant constructive role in the course of the Gorbachevian economic reform, which reform, as we know, aims to introduce substantial – and, of course, legal – privatization of business activity; to marketize the economy, that is, to supplant the command system with a market mechanism of sorts; and to increase the overall use of money as the economy's primary exchange medium. We shall return to this question; but first a quick glance into history and a closer look at the Soviet sub-economy.

A Glance Back

One need hardly stress that the USSR's underground economy is as old as Soviet rule – indeed much older. Gogol's *Inspector General*(1836) and *Dead Souls*(1842) depict official corruption and elaborate schemes of bribe extraction that might as well be taken from contemporary Soviet reality. Writing about the first years of Soviet rule, Thomas Remington has vividly described the dependence of the young revolutionary regime, as well as of the population, upon black markets during the period of so-called war communism (1918-21), a time of extreme shortages and of severe repression of private economic activity. Moving on to the late 1920s, we find in I. and E. Petrov's *Twelve Chairs*(1928) and *Golden Calf*(1931) the fictional but almost believable images of the con man Ostap Bender, making the most of the partly capitalist era of New Economic Policy, and – presciently – of the reclusive Koreiko, already scheming to snatch riches from the emergent Stalinist economy by exploiting its weaknesses and rigidities from within. Turning from fiction to the Communist Party's own archives, we find, with Fainsod, conclusive evidence of official concern with illegal economic activity during the early 1930s.[1]

Nonetheless, historical information on the Soviet underground economy is scant and spotty. It would seem that its main growth occurred after World War II, when it swelled, ramified, and matured into the major and highly complex and potent social, political, and economic phenomenon that it came to be in more recent decades. Khrushchev's campaign against "economic crime" in the early 1960s, to the point of reintroducing the death penalty, appears to have produced only a brief setback, judging by private eyewitness information. The Brezhnev-Chernenko period was doubtless a great boon to underground economic activity, corruption, and various related phenomena and their consequences.

The Favorable Climate

Returning to the opening sentence of this article, we proceed to take a brief look at the extremely favorable conditions for underground economic activity and other types of illegal personal gain in the USSR as of, say, the eve of Mr. Gorbachev's accession to the general secretaryship of the Communist Party of the Soviet Union in March 1985. The developments since this event will be discussed later. The narrative in the next several paragraphs proceeds in the present tense inasmuch as the situation has changed little to date except in the direction of greater propitiousness.

The favorable circumstances include various systemic features: for example, money is in excess supply while nearly all prices and wages are administratively fixed or controlled; markets are more the exception than the rule; nearly all productive assets – including inventories, of courses – are officially owned; decision making is highly centralized and bureaucratically executed; shortages abound; quality and service in the official sector are miserable; nearly all producer goods and resources and some important consumer goods and services are bureaucratically allocated or rationed; and virtually all independent private gainful activity is forbidden, except in agriculture. Confronting this situation is a cynical population starved even for material necessities, educated above its economic reach, and with a modern existence mostly beyond its grasp. Confronting the population is an inert and heavily corrupted apparatus of rule and enforcement.

In the very few areas where individual private activity has been traditionally permitted, it has been hemmed in and discouraged by administrative and

---

[1] Merle Fainsod, *Smolensk under Soviet Rule*, (New York: Random House, 1958), pp. 200-206.

ideological hostility, high taxes, extortion by sundry officials, supply shortages, a bar on hiring labor, and so forth. It is small wonder that on the eve of the Gorbachev era only some 70,000 persons – about 1 per 4,000 population – were legally pursuing, as individuals, the permitted trades and professions and paying direct taxes and that only about 150,000 were legally renting out private space in a country with a fearsome housing shortage. But, *per contra*, millions were so engaged illegally, though often on sufferance and with palm greasing, paying no income taxes, and depending heavily on materials stolen and equipment borrowed from the socialist sector.

Overlooking the damage to the state and to the fisc and taking the overall system as is, much of this sub-rosa activity is, of course, most useful in that it supplies goods and services of great variety and often relatively superior quality, which the official sector cannot provide properly, if it provides them at all, or cannot provide as cheaply, because the goods are massively stolen from that same official sector, as happens with gasoline, or because taxes on them are avoided, as in the case of home brew. Incidentally, the underground economy supplies goods and service not only to households and to the private sub-rosa production sector but to the official production sector as well.

Furthermore, millions of individuals buy scarce and cheap and sell dear, a practice called "speculation," which is a criminal offense; millions steal and embezzle from the state or defraud it by overstating their production accomplishments; millions defraud the buying or selling public; millions abuse their official positions, take graft, tribute, bribes, kickbacks, outsize tips and gifts – all of which opportunities abound at every step. Much of this criminal – or at least gray – activity is taken for granted by the public, whether it approves of it on moral grounds or not.[2]

Some Technicalities

The crucial importance of theft from the state for the Soviet underground economy cannot be overstated. We note again that in the Soviet Union – and, with some exceptions and modifications, in all other Soviet type economies

---

[2] It should come as no surprise that defrauding the state can be particularly lucrative. The largest such scheme yet to surface is the cotton affair, in which, during the late 1970s and early 1980s, enormous quantities of nonexistent cotton were sold from Central Asia–mainly Uzbekistan–for a take of billions of rubles–the exact amount is still unclear–with the help of massive bribery extending up to Brezhnev's son-in-law Yurii Churbanov, deputy minister of internal affairs, that is, of the police. Nearly all the Party and government leadership of Uzbekistan was implicated.

as well – nearly all of the natural resources, capital equipment, and non-consumer inventories have been owned by the state or at least by entities under its closest control and that of the state's boss, the Communist Party. The formal custodians of these assets have too often been incompetent and/or negligent, venal, crooked, or, at any rate, ineffectual, while public respect for socialist property has been very low. Consequently, a considerable portion of socialist – mostly state-owned – assets has been routinely and widely misappropriated or misapplied for private benefit, often on a large scale and not least by the ostensible custodians themselves. If not turned directly to personal use, the goods and services pilfered from the socialist sector, as well as labor and equipment time stolen from the socialist employer, feed massively into underground production and black markets.

Indeed, a considerable, though unascertainable, part of black production on private account takes place within the very walls of socialist firms. In turn, a considerable proportion of that is what we call crypto-private, that is, private production concealed behind the socialist firm's facade and masked to the point that it is identical in physical appearance and price with the officially produced goods in the same facility at the same time. The privately produced portion is, of course, not reported to the competent authorities. The profit to the underground operators derives from the fact that all inputs, labor included, used in the production of the private portion as well as of the officially reported portion of the output belong to or are paid for by the state. In other words, the secret of success of this ingenious stratagem is that crypto-privately produced goods are absolutely indistinguishable from those produced for the plan, either to customers or to authorities – except the authorities who are in on the deal and abet it by channeling extra supplies and other inputs to the operation.

Several aspects of the crypto-private mode of illegal activity should be mentioned. First, because it can potentially draw on the very large resources of the state for private gain, it is able to generate very large underground profits, though it is not the only underground operation capable of doing so. Second, it does so not without a great deal of large-scale bribery in a variety of planning, administrative, supervisory, and other offices, thus strongly contributing to the overall corruption of the system, though in this regard the crypto-private technique is certainly not alone. Finally, the crypto-private segment of the underground economy is not a candidate for privatization through legalization precisely because it is nominally part of the official sector, that is, it is ostensibly already legal. It may be, however, under certain conditions, be a rather logical area for limited privatization through private leasing from the state. Nor is there much private – underground – capital sunk into production capital in crypto-private ventures; rather, it is sunk primarily, and often in large amounts, into the form of bribes and protection money, so that there is very little by way of tangible assets for which one's property rights can be formally legalized.

Effects and Consequences

A questionnaire survey conducted by the Berkeley-Duke study among emigrants from the USSR suggests that in the late 1970s the urban population alone, which constitutes 62 percent of the total population, derived on the average about half again as much income from all nonofficial sources, including some legal ones, as it did from official sources, such as wages, salaries, pensions, and stipends. Even more important is the contribution of informal sources to personal wealth. In interpreting ratios such as the just-cited 0.5:1.0, however, it should be borne in mind that the levels and distribution of legitimate income from official sources would be considerably different in the unlikely absence of substantial informal income. For instance, many jobs are officially paid very little precisely because they provide good opportunities for illicit supplementary earnings – for example, jobs in retail trade. Lucrative positions are not infrequently sold and purchased for money up front plus a periodic tribute. A Soviet specialist has estimated the annual value of illicit consumer goods and services for the mid-1980s at 80-90 billion rubles, which would add about a fourth to the value of the goods and services sold to the public by the state.

Except in the very common case of illegal activities that involve only one person and that are not very visible, the gain from underground operation does not generally stay with the direct, or initial, receiver, say, the retail sales clerk who short-weights his customers or collects under the counter or both. Rather, a large part of it is often passed upward through an elaborately organized money pyramid. The direct payees' take is shared with their superiors, and likewise all the way up, which may be a very high level indeed, judging by stories in the media and by private information. Simultaneously, at each level of the pyramid, part of the money flow is diverted toward various power holders – "necessary people," in Russian parlance – officials of the Party and the government, police, inspectors and auditors, crucial suppliers, and, these days, also increasingly to professional extortionists and blackmailers – illegally acquired wealth is a relatively safe target for the criminal. Many people, including many at the pyramid's base, are trapped in the system – in fact doubly trapped: they need their illegal take to make ends meet, and they dare not drop out of the system for fear of reprisal.

Spending and earning, surviving and succeeding in an underground economy that ranges through various shades of gray to black is a way of life for the Soviet people, as it is for the people of many other countries as well. But the underground economy is and does more than that. It incriminates and thus renders vulnerable a large part of the population. It is a crucible of moral values. It shapes the public perception of reality against which official versions are judged. It tests the regime's mettle and ultimately its legitimacy. It provides visions of social alternatives. Finally, and more concretely, it furnishes the material foundation for existing alternative social structures.

Indeed, at least two alternative social structures rest on the second economy. The first, better known abroad but much the smaller in size, is the world of political dissidents, ethnic and religious activists, refuseniks, opters-out, nonconformist writers and artists, and *samizdat*[3] publishers. To this counter-society and counterculture, the second economy – in itself a counter-phenomenon, an implicit indictment and rejection of the official system – has furnished much material support, especially in the pre-Gorbachev years.

The second, and very different, edifice is the all-permeating but shadowy structure of formal-informal alternative power, the world of political and social realities, of corruption, unofficial networks, patronage and clientelism, extortion, intimidation, large payoffs, organized crime, and purposive violence. It is a world of surviving or newly fostered "neotraditionalism" – as it were, satrapies in which near absolute power derives at once from formal hierarchical status and tacit official sanction from above, and from the informal realities – often mingled with ethnicity, territorial considerations, even religion. In this world of the "Mafia" as the Soviets now call it, there is no demarcation between underground and aboveground.[4]

The Underground and Perestroika

With its own sub-rosa private enterprise and free markets, the underground economy has probably been both a boon and a bane for Gorbachev's attempts

---

[3] [Editors' note: *samizdat* publications are unofficially and illegally published documents, frequently photocopies.]

[4] The problems of organized crime and the Soviet Mafia, and their links with the formal power structure, especially at very high levels, have been the objects of grave and rising concern in the Soviet media and from the public at large in the last few years. These problems were also addressed from the podium of the newly formed Congress of People's Deputies in May and June 1989.

to move the legal, aboveground Soviet economy along its rocky road of privatization and marketization. First let us examine the boon, where the most important effects have probably been intangible, perceptual, and even ideological, accumulating over decades. By its vigor and vitality, its flexibility and resourcefulness, the second economy has vividly underscored the negative lesson of the ineffectualness and wastefulness of the traditional, Stalinist "command economy," as it is now called in the USSR, too. The positive lesson – the potential superiority of a significantly privatized and marketized economy over the traditional version – may not have been learned as widely. The idea of market socialism with substantial privatization, not to say out-and-out capitalism, and of corresponding economic insecurities and inequalities holding sway in the USSR does not seem to have had in 1985, or four Gorbachevian years later, anything like overwhelming popular acceptance.

The underground economy has doubtless been a school of enterprise, initiative, better work habits, pecuniary calculus, risk taking, and other attributes of a market oriented economy. But the students in this school have been predominantly small, individual tradesmen and – less so – professionals. Its curriculum may not have been well suited to produce market-oriented managers for considerably larger business undertakings, sophisticated bankers, or effective vice-presidents for marketing. Moreover, much of the underground economy has been a zero-sum game: the state or the buyer loses, the individual wins – not a healthy outlook for marketization.

Yet, according to our informants who came out of that milieu, there is also a remarkable amount of integrity among and mutual trust between underground operators – indispensable qualities where business understandings cannot be committed to paper for security reasons. Our expressions of surprise were met by surprise: "After all, we were businessmen, not Party crooks!" More generally, we do not subscribe to the assumption that potential entrepreneurial and managerial abilities hardly exist in the Soviet population. We suspect they are there all right, albeit unschooled and underskilled, and if they do exist, the credit belongs to the second economy.

If the underground is a drag on the economic reform, this is largely for two reasons. First, it fosters a great deal of politico-economic conservatism in the anti-*perestroika* sense. Millions of people have cultivated their little illegal or gray niches and would rather keep the known risks than face the unknown brave new world. More significant, as we have seen, the big-time underground and the organized underworld that it has spawned have melded with a part of the official political – administrative and police – pyramid of power. Here the stakes are enormous – not just vast wealth and great power but also personal security and even one's head. The last several years' purges, prosecutions, convictions, executions, and suicides of the once mighty drive the lesson home. True, every economic system creates its countereconomy; so will *perestroika* if it succeeds. But the grandfathers will be new, as will their political partners. Hence a good part of the old establishment's resistance to economic reform, to the legitimization of privatization and marketization.

In any event, during the four-plus years since Gorbachev's coming to power, the underground seems to have prospered and swelled further, despite a major renewed campaign against it and the newly enacted opportunities to turn legitimate. Major reasons are to be found in the evolution − or lack of it − of the official economy, namely, the rapid expansion in the money supply with prices still largely, but not firmly, fixed, and therefore a rapid increase of excess demand by both consumers and producers, aggravated shortages, and other windfalls to black production and markets. The continuous confusion engendered by *perestroika* probably helped, too. The drastic anti-alcohol measures promulgated in May 1985 were followed by sharp increases in official prices of liquor and wine and inevitably by an explosion of bootlegging and home brewing and by a serious drop in tax revenue. The campaign against economic crime − "nonlabor income" − was announced in May 1986, in prophylactic anticipation of the widening of the scope of legitimate private activity, which was promulgated in November 1986, but the campaign quickly caused so much disruption in the economy, especially in informal food supply, that its enforcement was relaxed and has been tapering off since.

We cannot dwell here on the limited and ambivalent legitimation of private activity by individuals and producer cooperatives, legitimation that had embraced over 2 million people, including part-timers, by mid-1989. To some extent this new private sector must have brought underground producers and traders into the open, but many of the now lawful operations doubtless combine illegal activities behind the new facades and, in fact, seem to have stimulated additional underground activity around themselves. Any rumors of the economic underground's early indisposition, let alone demise, or of the wasting away of corruption and organized crime are definitely premature.

24. Proposals for Privatization in Eastern Europe*

Eduardo Borenzstein and Manmohan S. Kumar

I. The Case For Privatization

What is the basic case for privatization? The evident failure of the central planning system has created a near consensus that a move to a market economy is necessary to achieve standards of living comparable to those of industrial economies in the West. Many conditions may be regarded as necessary to support such a move, but it can be argued that the most important ones are a competitive environment in which market prices reflect relative scarcities, and enterprises and individuals make decisions mainly in response to undistorted market signals. Private ownership leads to the achievement of these conditions because of the incentives for the private owners to ensure that their costs of production are minimized and that their output mix is determined in response to market signals. The privatization process would also provide the means for owners to monitor, assess, and control the performance of the managers effectively running the enterprises.

There is, nevertheless, a question about whether the goal of efficiency can be achieved by leaving the enterprises in public hands as at present but requiring these enterprises to respond to market signals in their operations. Both the cumulative evidence from Eastern Europe and theoretical reasons suggest that the answer is in the negative. There have been a number of attempts – most notably in Hungary – in the 1970s and 1980s at "enterprise reforms" designed to give market incentives to state enterprises, the results of which have been disappointing. Moreover, there are several conceptual reasons to doubt that any such enterprise reforms could be successful. In the first place, the government has other objectives that may not coincide with profit maximization by enterprises. This would be the case, for example, for objectives such as price stability, maintenance of high employment, and

* From *IMF Staff Papers*, vol. 38, no. 2, June 1991. Reprinted by permission of the International Monetary Fund.

regional development. Second, even if enterprises enjoy full autonomy and markets are liberalized, how well could the state supervise the behavior of management? The problem here is that the most objective method to judge management performance is by the valuation of enterprises in a stock market – that is, by the number of interested investors that are ready to risk their own money when they perceive a mispricing. However, the operation of an efficient stock market requires that enterprises themselves be owned, and in fact controlled, by private agents rather than the state. Third, the minimal risk of bankruptcy for public enterprises would distort financial markets and the allocation of savings. Fourth, due in part to public pressure, it is unlikely that sufficient competition would be allowed in the industries in which public enterprises operate.

In addition to considerations of allocative efficiency, privatization can also be regarded as a key and indispensable process by which the very institution of private property in the productive sphere would be reintroduced in the socialist economies. Until very recently, enterprises in most of these economies were not structured as joint stock companies, and for many even now the legal status is unclear. Therefore, in this kind of environment, a full-scale privatization could help create the *ethos* in which other market reforms can be introduced and be successful.

The above considerations suggest that the privatization of productive enterprises is a necessary condition for the move to an efficient market economy. In this respect, for both economic and political reasons, the process of privatization should be speedy and comprehensive. The success of the adjustment measures undertaken in Eastern Europe will depend to a considerable extent, even in the short run, on the response of the enterprises. The objective of the market-oriented reforms is that enterprises orient their production and investment toward activities where they can perform in an efficient and competitive manner. If, because of the existing property structures and the associated lack of incentives, enterprises do not respond to market signals, the stabilization and adjustment measures are unlikely to produce fully the desired results.

Moreover, a number of Eastern European economies are in a transitional phase where, although the system of economic incentives associated with central planning is no longer operational, a market economy is still not in place. The unclear situation regarding property rights and the effective lack of management supervision may allow managers to dispose of enterprise assets for their private benefit, resulting in the decapitalization of enterprises and a breakdown of the production process. From a political perspective, a rapid transformation of the ownership of the means of production is considered to be necessary to ensure a complete break with the old regime.

While recognizing the need for a rapid and massive change in the ownership structure, several observers have expressed concern over possible adverse effects of the process. It has been suggested, for instance, that it could lead to a sharp increase in unemployment as the newly privatized enterprises shed excess labor and become more efficient. It is also thought that it could lead to a highly skewed redistribution of income, which, in turn, could lead to a political backlash. Although these concerns have some validity, they do not support the case for postponing privatization, but instead argue for taking steps to ameliorate the transition costs. The transition to a market economy is bound to be costly, in particular in those sectors where resources have been misallocated to a significant extent, but a halfway transformation of a centrally planned system can only produce an inferior outcome for the economy as a whole.

II. Privatization Proposals

Despite some early attempts, it is evident that standard privatization techniques, in the form of public or private offerings, are unlikely to serve as appropriate vehicles for transferring the ownership of thousands of enterprises in Eastern European countries. This is so mainly because of the virtual impossibility of making an adequate estimate of firms' market values, the lack of entrepreneurial skills in the private sector, and the lack of private sector savings to purchase the firms being privatized. Because of the severe distortions in prices, trade, and management structures, the past performance of a firm might be of little help in assessing its profitability potential. This factor creates an insurmountable problem for the direct sale of many enterprises. Furthermore, the lack of domestic savings and of enterprises capable of putting together a financing package means that many sales would have to be made to foreign investors, which is regarded in some countries as politically unacceptable.

But what would happen if an alternative, gradualist and piecemeal, approach were to be followed? This approach would entail privatizing, say, a handful of enterprises each year, so that it would take several years until a substantial proportion of enterprises were turned over to the private sector. During the process, the state would continue to control and manage large parts of the industrial sector. In this context, comparison is frequently made with the privatization process in several Western European industrial countries during the 1980s, where public sector enterprises continue to play some role

Table I - Comparison of Distributive Privatization Proposals

Proposal	Structure of Ownership	% Owner-ship	Management Supervision	Mechanism of Privatization
Vouchers (Proposed in Czechoslova-kia,Romania, etc.)	Private shareholders	100	Supervision by shareholders	Free distribution of vouchers exchangeable for enterprise equity
Citizens' shares (Feige)	Citizens Central government Republics Private and foreign	50 10 20 20	Mainly by private and foreign owners	Citizen shares sold at undervalued prices, private shares auctioned with right of first refusal to workers and managers
Financial intermediaries (Frydman/ Rapaczynski)	Citizen-owned mutual funds	100	By private intermediaries that bid for the enterprise they would like to acquire	Free distribution of vouchers to the public; intermediaries funds sell stock to the public in exchange for vouchers used to bid for enterprises in a series of auctions
Financial intermediaries (Lipton and Sachs)	Citizen-owned mutual funds Pension funds Banks Workers Managers Government for later privat'tion	20 20 10 10 5 35	By competing mutual funds that overlap in the same firms, by banks, and eventually by a "stable core" of private investors that will acquire shares from the government	Free distribution except for sale to private investors at a later stage
Privatization companies (Blanchard and others)	Citizen-owned holding co's	100	By holding companies themselves controlled by competition, government supervision, and the use of performance based compensation	Free distribution of shares in holding companies to all citizen
Self-management	Workers and managers	100	Current employees acquire rights to profits and assets of enterprises; ownership rights non-transferable	Legal structure in Hungary and Poland allowed some "spontaneous" privatizations by current management

in the industrial sectors. This comparison, however, overlooks the critical fact that the Western European countries have an established market economy environment with financial markets and ownership and control institutions in place. Therefore, in general, market signals lay a key role in these economies. In this setting, if a handful of enterprises are controlled by the state, their performance can be easily judged relative to private enterprises.

A second consequence of the gradualist and piecemeal approach would be that the least efficient enterprises would remain in the public sector domain the longest, and indeed might not be sold off at all. Given the potential number and large size of these enterprises, they would constitute a significant drain on the public sector finances and could easily jeopardize the whole reform process.

In light of the severe difficulties likely to confront the standard privatization procedures in Eastern Europe, several alternative proposals have been put forward. These proposals typically rely on some form of distributive scheme, by which at least some share of ownership in the state industrial enterprises would be transferred for free, or for a nominal charge, to the private citizenry. Such a transfer would avoid the problems of valuing enterprises arising in part from the absence of capital markets and solvent investors. However, any scheme of this kind would itself introduce a number of difficulties related to the allocation mechanism for ownership, to the exercise of control of the enterprises, and to the roles of government and workers in the new corporate structure. This article analyzes the key features of the various proposals, paying particular attention to these difficulties.

The more salient features of the different "comprehensive" privatization proposals discussed below are summarized in Table 1. While these proposals are not exhaustive, they do identify the essential features of any distributive privatization scheme. In some cases, they have been put forward by economists with an academic interest in the problem, and in other cases, by policymakers and consultants with a specific framework of action in mind.

Voucher Schemes

The centerpiece of distributive proposals is some scheme to distribute to every citizen a share of equity in the enterprises being privatized. Some of these schemes have been termed "voucher" schemes, referring to the vouchers, or certificates, that each citizen would receive giving an entitlement to some equity shares. The idea of a voucher system appears to have originated in proposals for privatization in Czechoslovakia. Although the detailed implementation of the scheme is still to be decided, it has already been included in one form or another in privatization laws approved or under consideration in both Czechoslovakia and Romania. It is also being emulated to some degree in Poland.

Most schemes envision a free voucher distribution that benefits all adult citizens of the country – partly for the reason that the state is not considered to be the owner of the enterprises, but only an administrator, while the community as a whole is the ultimate owner. In addition, a high value is placed on achieving an egalitarian wealth distribution, and the free distribution of equity in the privatized enterprises would help to redress, at least partially, existing inequalities. The voucher distribution would not, however, cover the whole sector of public enterprises, since some enterprises would remain in the state sphere and some would be privatized by other means. Furthermore, in most versions of this scheme, only a fraction of the capital of the enterprises being privatized would be distributed by the vouchers.

According to the particular details of the scheme, the vouchers may or may not have a monetary value or be tradable between individuals. In the Czechoslovak initiative, the vouchers were to be denominated in "points" and could only be used to bid for shares in state-supervised auctions of individual state enterprises. There might be several issues of vouchers that could be used in auctions of particular groups on enterprises; it is also possible that each particular issue would not be distributed to the whole population, but to smaller groups instead. In the privatization initiative in Romania, the vouchers may have a predetermined monetary value, and it appears the intention is to offer enterprise shares at a value close to book value.

 Although in most of the above variants of the voucher scheme, vouchers entitle the holder to acquire shares in a particular enterprise, in one of the first schemes for privatization in the USSR, put forward by Edgar Feige,[1] each citizen would receive shares in an aggregate of industrial enterprises, some 46,000 in all. According to this variant, a bundle of equity shares would comprise an equal fractional ownership share in each and every state enterprise. This bundle is termed a "citizen share." Of the citizen shares, 50 percent would be divided equally among all citizens, and the rest would be distributed among the central government, the individual republics, and private investors.

A "pure" voucher scheme would face two serious problems of implementation. First, the public at large is highly unlikely to be able to bid in a rational

---

[1] Edgar Feige, "A Message to Gorbachev: Redistribute the Wealth," *Challenge*, vol. 33 (May-June 1990), pp. 46-53.

manner in the auctions for individual enterprises. One reason is the shortage of expertise to assess the value of enterprises. More important, the past performance of firms would not necessarily reflect their underlying profit potential, because of the highly distorted price structure and prevalent subsidies under which the firms have been operating in the past. The second problem is posed by the enormous scale of the required auction process. Even if conducted in successive stages, the auction process would include bidding by literally millions of individuals, for each and every one of hundreds, if not thousands, of enterprises. The auction would necessitate some iteration process until a price for each of the enterprises were found such that all enterprises were sold, and all vouchers used up. If the auction process left some unsold enterprises or unused vouchers, it would mean that the enterprises being sold were not valued correctly, and the bidding would have to continue. In addition, if the vouchers had a monetary value and were tradable, they could also threaten macroeconomic stability, since their issue would constitute a large increase in monetary balances (or in close substitutes to money). The problem might be temporary, however, to the extent that privatization becomes operative and the second-stage sale of equity shares absorbs liquidity. Also, the liquidity value of vouchers would be considerably diminished if they were nontransferable (as in Romania).

The Case for Financial Intermediaries

Even if the distribution of shares through the voucher scheme could be successfully completed, questions as to whether the resulting ownership structure would provide an efficient system for management supervision would remain. Because of the substantial externalities involved in overseeing the actions of managers, a widely dispersed shareholding might imply that no individual shareholder would undertake significant supervision functions. While it is true that once the firms were under private ownership, the risk of bankruptcy would be present and would motivate managers to avoid losses, inefficient enterprises do not instantly go bankrupt and could continue to function for a long time before facing serious financial problems. Nevertheless, if bankruptcy were the only potential constraint on management, the system could inhibit managers and in fact lead to too little risk taking. More important, an essential mechanism of management discipline, namely takeovers, is not very effective with broadly dispersed shareholdings. This means that, in the limit, should ownership become equally distributed among all citizens, managers would have little effective scrutiny over their actions and not enough incentive for profit maximization. This suggests that a pure voucher scheme is unlikely to have general applicability. At best, it might have a limited application for the privatization of small enterprises, in which the likely bidders would have some idea of the productive potential of the assets and have a chance to acquire control of the enterprises through the public auction.

A response to the problem of monitoring is required. Under the Feige proposal, up to 20 percent of shares would be auctioned separately for each enterprise to the private sector and foreign investors, with special incentives being offered to workers and managers. Private shareholders would be the group entrusted with the main responsibility for monitoring management performance. In addition, the participation of workers and managers would be expected to provide additional work incentive and improve efficiency. There are, however, some problems with this private auctioning scheme. As noted above, market valuation of enterprises would be extremely hazardous even for managers and workers. Furthermore, the process might take a long time, during which the enterprises would still be public enterprises for all practical purposes. Eventually, it might also be the case that government would be able to sell only the most efficient enterprises, and be left effectively controlling a large number of loss-making firms, having to face worker resistance to liquidation of these enterprises.

A different solution to the enterprise control problem is contemplated by a number of proposals suggesting the creation of financial intermediaries that would hold shares in the individual enterprises, with the public in turn owning the equity of these intermediaries. For example, Frydman and Rapaczynski,[2] with reference to Poland, have proposed that citizens transfer their vouchers to intermediaries – mutual funds – in return for shares in those funds, and the mutual funds use the vouchers to bid for equity in different enterprises. The existence of the intermediaries would not necessarily exclude direct purchases of equity in the enterprises by households. In order to simplify the auction logistics, Frydman and Rapaczynski propose that a series of smaller auctions (comprising 150–200 companies) be conducted, each one of them using a designated issue of vouchers, with the unused ones becoming worthless after the auction.

A different proposal that would involve financial intermediaries has been

---

[2] Roman Frydman and Andrzej Rapaczynski, "Markets and Institutions in Large Scale Privatization," *Adjustment and Growth: Lessons for Eastern Europe*, ed. by Vittorio Corbo, Fabrizio Coricelli, and Jan Bossak (Washington: World Bank 1991).

put forward by David Lipton and Jeffrey Sachs,[3] also with reference to Poland. This scheme envisions free distribution of shares to several financial intermediaries (some of them newly created) and the creation of a system of institutional enterprise control. The system of enterprise control would be implemented by an active participation of the different financial intermediaries on the boards of directors of the enterprises. Some five mutual funds would be created and would collectively receive 20 percent of the shares; these mutual funds would be organized as joint stock companies, with all adult citizens receiving a share in one of the mutual funds. Other institutions receiving shares and expected to be active on boards of directors would be newly created private pension funds (which would eventually replace the government pension system) and commercial banks and insurance companies, which themselves are undergoing privatization. Workers, managers, and directors would also receive some shares and, over time, private investor groups would be sought.

Although the corporate structure envisioned in this scheme might eventually generate an efficient system of enterprise supervision, there would be a transition period during which the control of enterprises would rest mostly with the government. During an initial period – of uncertain duration – only the government and the financial intermediaries (whose managers would at the outset be appointed by the government) would participate in the corporate boards of directors. This has two implications. On the one hand, even though mutual funds would be private, their managers would effectively be subject to little shareholder control. On the other, state participation in the governing corporate boards might effectively lead to a controlling position for the government, or at least to a large influence on, and potential distortions of, business decisions. Thus, despite its minority voting power, the government would be able to exert considerable influence, and it is not hard to conceive of situations in which the government's policy objectives might differ from a strict profit maximization objective. This problem could be avoided to some extent, however, if government shares were of a nonvoting nature.

---

[3] David Lipton and Jeffrey Sachs, "Privatization in Eastern Europe: The Case of Poland," *Brookings Papers on Economic Activity*: 2 (Washington: The Brookings Institution), pp. 293-341.

A proposal by Blanchard and others[4] suggests the creation of a different type of financial intermediary. The financial intermediaries in this proposal would be holding companies with a prescribed temporary life span, which would act merely as privatization agencies. In contrast to some existing or proposed privatization agencies in several Eastern European countries, the holding companies in this proposal would be private companies. The sole purpose of these holding companies would be to restructure and later sell (or liquidate) each group of enterprises. These enterprises would have a predetermined dissolution date, say in about ten years, by which time they should have completed their functions and paid as dividends the revenues from privatization. Ownership of the holding companies would be equally distributed among all citizens, which would provide substantial financial resources to the private sector to support the eventual purchase of the enterprises as they came up for sale.

This scheme does not conceive of any predetermined framework for the eventual structure of ownership or control of the enterprises. Thus, the holding companies would be free to use any method they chose to sell or liquidate firms, and would be able to sell to any party, including foreigners or workers in the firm. Corporate structure would then be left basically to market forces, which is a positive feature, considering that neither economic theory nor evidence has yet produced a clear-cut answer to the problem of optimal enterprise governance. The proposal does, however, raise some questions about whether the appropriate conditions for privatization can be generated as the holding companies prepare the enterprises for divestment. In particular, the lack of financial institutions and expertise and of entrepreneurial culture and economic agents with the capacity to become major shareholders might be difficult to overcome, even after a number of years.

The creation of financial intermediaries, however, may only add another layer to the corporate governance structure without solving the problem created by the dispersion of the ultimate ownership. Frydman and Rapaczynski stress competition between intermediaries, both for vouchers pledged by citizens and in bidding for enterprises, as market mechanisms to avoid bureaucratization of the intermediaries. There is the danger, however, that by allowing bidding for the enterprises, the government would be able to dispose of only the more efficient enterprises. Lipton and Sachs, in contrast, believe

---

[4] Olivier Blanchard, Rudiger Dornbusch, Paul Krugman, Richard Layard, and Lawrence Summers, *Reform in Eastern Europe* (Cambridge, Massachusetts: MIT Press, 1991).

that the institutional structure they propose for corporate governance would generate the proper incentives through competition among the different financial intermediaries that would be created. Blanchard and others explain that, since shares in holding companies would be tradable, the evolution of their market value would put pressure on managers through public opinion, and the government would retain the right to remove managers of the holding companies in extreme situations. Despite all these safeguards, the complete lack of experience with the operation of private corporations and of financial markets probably means that in Eastern Europe the problem of corporate control may not be completely solved in a short period of time under any framework.

Public Finances and the Role of Government

Any privatization plan has at least two important implications concerning the government. First what are the public finance consequences of the transfer of property from the public to the private sector, and second, what would be the role of the government or government agencies in the control of the private enterprises? At present, public enterprises in Eastern Europe are an extremely important source of revenue for the central government budget. Part of this revenue comes in the form of "dividend taxes," which are a sort of direct remittance of profits, and part from other direct taxes on enterprises. Since public finances rely almost exclusively on enterprise taxes, the current level of direct taxation would be too high were it to be transferred to a private enterprise system. Therefore, it would be necessary to create new taxes or take some other measures to make up for the lost revenue. In addition, in the distributive privatization schemes discussed above, the government is giving up assets that might have positive market values under the appropriate circumstances; this also represent a loss of revenue in present value terms that must be considered when medium-term fiscal strategies are being designed. Regarding government's role in the control of the privatized enterprises, some degree of involvement is probably unavoidable, at least initially, but it is important to ensure that this role does not distort the profit-maximizing motivation of enterprises.

The proposals noted above suggest differing solutions to the above two problems. In Feige's proposal for the USSR, for instance, the central government would receive 10 percent of the citizen shares and the republics' governments would receive 20 percent. These shares would provide a source of revenue that would reduce reliance on other taxes. There is an appealing feature to this scheme, in that, from the point of view of fiscal theory, owning shares is probably the least distortionary way for the government to obtain revenue. In Lipton and Sachs' proposal, the government would retain some shares, but only on a temporary basis. Also, in their proposal the free distribution of property does not necessarily entail a commensurate loss of assets because it substitutes for other expenses the government would have had to face. In particular, this applies to social safety net expenditures and to the recapitalization of financial intermediaries in difficult financial situations.

Regarding the control of enterprises, even ignoring arguments based on economic theory, the track record of public management of enterprises should suffice to establish the case for minimizing government involvement. The government will, however, have to play an important role in the surveillance of regulations concerning fair practices in financial markets, antitrust laws, and so on, and probably also in the organization and launching of the financial intermediaries. The proposals of Blanchard and others and of Frydman and Rapaczynski stress the objective of ensuring a minimal role for government in the control of enterprises.

The Self-Management Movement

An alternative mode of privatization, which does not appear to be generally favored, is via the self-management movement. This form of privatization implies the transfer of ownership rights directly to the workers of each particular enterprise. Generally, a worker's claim on the firm's profits or assets is not transferable – that is, it is contingent on being an employee. In some cases, privatization via self-management is based on the fact that, after successive enterprise reforms, legal property rights have become poorly defined and worker councils may already have acquired some de facto control over management and profits, including disposal of part of the firm's assets. For example, some instances of "spontaneous privatization" under very favorable conditions for buyers have taken place in both Hungary and Poland.

There are two major problems with this form of employee privatization. The first is a question of equity and fairness, since this type of transference of assets would benefit only a limited segment of the population (which is already privileged by holding jobs in the largest companies). The second problem concerns the efficiency of a self-managed enterprise. Economic theory suggests that such enterprises will underinvest and have shorter planning horizons than is the case otherwise. In addition, it would be complicated to attract private investors to acquire a minority stake in a worker-controlled enterprise, because workers could curtail dividend payments by granting themselves salary increases. Further, if shares were not transferable, worker mobility would be seriously impaired.

Short of an outright sale to workers, it is likely that whatever specific proposal is adopted workers are likely to receive part of the shares in the enterprises where they work. For instance, in both Poland and Romania privatization laws have already established that workers will either receive for free, or under concessional terms, a fraction of the enterprises' shares. As long as workers do not acquire control of the board of directors, fractional employee ownership is very different both from an equity and an efficiency perspective and should not pose any serious obstacle to implementation.

Distributive and Wealth Effects of Privatization

All of the above proposals have important consequences for income and wealth distribution as well as for private savings. To the extent that consumers are not perfectly Ricardian in their view of public finances, share distributions would represent an increase in private wealth; furthermore, the distribution of this increase would be completely egalitarian. Such distribution would then also serve the purpose of providing a cushion against social costs incurred due to a rapid economic transformation accompanied by increases in unemployment. The distributive effect is also considered an important political objective of privatization, since it would overcome a major drawback of a sale of state assets: that is, it would likely benefit only two sections of society – the communist elite ("nomenklatura") and black market operators. In addition, depending on the details of the proposal, individuals would receive a well-diversified portfolio of assets, comprising almost the whole industrial sector. Such diversification may help to avoid excessive riskiness to the individuals that lack the expertise or financial advice to manage their portfolios.

In some proposals the vouchers would be given to citizens at a nominal cost. Although in this case the shares would be substantially undervalued, their sale would be a means of absorbing any excess liquidity in the system or the existing monetary overhand. From a fiscal point of view, the sale may appear desirable as partially offsetting the loss of state assets. But, ruling out a significant participation of foreign investors, the enterprises might have to be sold considerably below their true market value in order to find enough potential buyers for all the shares, because the amount of assets held by households would not be sufficient. In some Eastern European countries, even though monetary assets are high relative to Western economies (the monetary overhang), total private assets are not very high because of the lack of opportunity to hold assets other than broad money.

The provision of a well-diversified portfolio for consumers is also given consideration in some proposals, with a view to ensuring that the distributive aspect of privatization benefits all citizens. Of course, consumers would be able to readjust their portfolio after some time, but many may choose not to take any action. In most proposals enterprises would in fact be grouped in such a way as to constitute well-diversified portfolios. The possible exception is the proposal by Frydman and Rapaczynski that allows the different financial intermediaries to bid for enterprises and possibly end up with very unequal portfolios. A risky asset composition for consumers may generate frustration about the benefits of the privatization process and pressures for the bailout of less successful intermediaries.

III. Related Macroeconomic Issues

From the macroeconomic point of view, the loss of revenue (in present value terms) for the government may become a pressing problem. Apart from enterprise profits or dividends, the current tax system in centrally planned economies is almost exclusively based on direct enterprise taxes, and would need to be reformed in the context of a market economy open to international capital flows. In Hungary, for example, *average* direct taxes on enterprises amounted to 78 percent of enterprise gross profits during 1986-88. Such a level of taxation would probably cause massive capital outflows in an open economy. In Czechoslovakia taxes on enterprise profits were remitted to the state – that tax rate was 100 percent. (Current rates are graduated but still high). Therefore, privatization will create the need to make up for lost revenues elsewhere (a value-added tax, for example), or to drastically reduce government spending. An interesting alternative would be to let government retain partial ownership in the privatized enterprises so as to retain some source of revenue. This type of revenue would be nondistortionary, and would avoid the need for taxes that distort resource allocation. Given the overriding objective of creating an efficient productive structure, it would be prudent to keep the government out of enterprise management, but this could be easily accomplished by issuing nonvoting shares to the government.

Another important macroeconomic problem with any privatization proposal that involves free distribution of ownership is the risk of generating a sharp increase in private consumption. The transfer of property to consumers would actually represent an increase in private wealth. Therefore, a sizable increase in private consumption would most likely follow. For example, suppose that the distribution of enterprise ownership represents an increase in private wealth equivalent to three times current consumption.[5] Even if consumers decided to spend only 10 percent of this increase in wealth, private consumption would increase by 30 percent. Although part of the increase in consumer spending could actually substitute for government safety net spending, it might be necessary to curb private consumption at the risk of jeopardizing the stabilization effort. For this purpose, some form of consumption tax would be an appropriate instrument. Given the difficulties involved in the implementation of a consumption tax system, a workable alternative could be a tax on dividends and on the proceeds from sales of citizen shares, which would be refundable if the resources were reinvested in some other productive asset. If citizens' assets were held through a few financial intermediaries, this tax would be simple to implement and monitor.

In the area of monetary policy, it has been suggested that the sale of state assets could be used as a means to sterilize the monetary overhang that is present in centrally planned economies after years of price controls. The concept of monetary overhang is, however, somewhat elusive. On the basis of both theoretical and empirical reasons, some authors discount the importance of the monetary overhang problem, arguing that if real monetary balances were evaluated at the "real" prices – that is, prices that include the cost of waiting in line to purchase goods or that prevail in parallel markets – there would be no undesired holdings of real monetary balances. Also, if prices increase very rapidly following liberalization, the monetary overhang can be eliminated so quickly that monetary policy rapidly becomes overly restrictive. This appears to be one factor explaining the sharp fall in output following price liberalization in Poland. Furthermore, even accepting the existence of a monetary overhang and the need to take some measures, the use of privatization would not be very effective for this purpose, simply because of the problem of timing. It takes considerable time to set up any large-scale privatization scheme, while price increases would immediately follow a price liberalization.

Concluding Remarks

The privatization proposals discussed in this paper are all concerned with transferring the ownership of the bulk of Eastern European state enterprises into private hands within a very short period of time. While the proposals do

---

[5] Assume that enterprises accounting for 50 percent of gross national product (GNP) are given away; if the capital-output ratio is 3 percent and private consumption is 50 percent of GNP, then wealth increase is as noted.

not correspond exactly to specific initiatives, they do provide a spectrum of the building blocks from which these initiatives could be assembled. The paper has discussed the relative strengths and weaknesses of the different proposals and elaborated some general principles for privatization. It has also discussed the macroeconomic ramifications of the privatization process.

A number of important conclusions emerge from the above discussion. In the Eastern European context, large scale privatization cannot be accomplished by traditional methods, and some form of distributive scheme will be necessary. In the design of such a scheme, particular attention should be given to ensure market competition and an efficient method of management supervision. The latter point is a major shortcoming of pure voucher schemes and the main reason to adopt some form of financial intermediaries between the enterprises and private citizens. The form of this intermediation might have to be decided by the circumstances in each country. Finally, there are a number of important fiscal and monetary implications of any particular privatization process that must be taken into account in both its design and implementation.

Despite the perceived need to undertake large-scale privatization, actual initiatives adopted by most countries to date have been quite limited. With the possible exceptions of Poland and Romania, instead of a wholesale privatization, the initiatives seem to be following a piecemeal approach. Not only does this limited approach have serious feasibility and equity implications, but the whole move to a market economy, and even macroeconomic stabilization, is unlikely to be accomplished without a fundamental change in property rights and economic incentives.

What, then, accounts for this apparent piecemeal approach? Part of the explanation could be that the current initiatives are actually not complete. The schemes that are being implemented are preliminary and are concerned in some sense with testing the environment for the large-scale privatization that would follow. A stronger reason, however, appears to be concern about the likely economic costs of structural reforms and increasing political resistance from different sections of the community. Some of the economic costs were discussed in the paper, and relate mainly to a short-run increase in unemployment and inflation. Under these conditions, the resistance to a large-scale privatization from groups that could claim some stake in the current regime would be strengthened. It should be emphasized, however, that high as the adjustment costs may be in the short run, the costs of not undertaking significant privatization may be far greater in the medium and long run.

25. Privatization in Eastern Europe[*]

David Lipton and Jeffrey Sachs

Corporate Governance and Financial Intermediaries

A privatization program in Eastern Europe must do more than simply return enterprise ownership to private hands. The government should strive to create an ownership structure that will effectively oversee the management of the newly privatized assets. That is, the government should foster an effective structure of corporate governance. Moreover, the government should encourage the development of financial intermediaries that will be important both for monitoring enterprises and allowing the private sector to diversify the risks of property ownership.

We put enormous stress on creating adequate long-term oversight management for two main reasons. First, there can be little confidence in the current managerial class in Eastern Europe. Many managers owe their positions to their Communist party allegiances rather than to their technical competence. Also, many competent managers won their positions because of their engineering expertise, which was crucial in a planned economy, rather than their ability to navigate the enterprise in the uncharted waters of an open market economy. Thus, an enormous effort will have to be made to evaluate current managers and to train and promote new ones.

Second, Eastern Europe lacks many of the individual and institutional actors that are normally involved in corporate governance in the West. Therefore, special care must be taken to assure that at least some institutions capable of effective corporate governance are created. In particular, unlike in normal market economies, Eastern European countries cannot rely on corporate oversight by any of the following: the original families and entrepreneurs that established an enterprise; outside directors who have a long involvement with an enterprise and understanding its history and corporate

---

[*] From "Privatization in Eastern Europe: The Case of Poland," *Brookings Papers on Economic Activity*, No. 2, 1990. Reprinted by permission of the Brookings Institution. Some footnotes omitted.

culture; a vast financial press and investment analysis sector that investigates, reports, and evaluates management behavior; or experienced regulatory institutions, such as the Securities and Exchange Commission, which pursue investigations of malfeasance and which require various forms of disclosure that are widely analyzed by the investment community.

Our basic proposal described in the next section is that the ownership of most enterprises should be divided up in tranches among various groups and financial institutions that will each have an incentive to monitor the enterprise and promote sound management. In our proposal a portion of shares is sold or given to workers; another part is transferred to pension funds and commercial banks; another part is transferred mainly to mutual funds that in turn will be owned by individual households; and another part is sold to a "core investor" group that continues both to hold a substantial proportion of the shares for several years and to manage the firm.

A Strategy for Achieving Effective Corporate Governance

There are two essential tasks in establishing effective governance of the productive capital now in state hands. The first, more urgent, task is to introduce a provisional system of corporate governance that can monitor a firm's management and prevent both managers and workers from squandering its capital income and capital assets before full privatization takes place. The second, longer-term task is to foster a structure of ownership in which the new private owners will be in a strong position to manage their newly acquired assets.

A vital, first step to privatization is the conversion of state enterprises into corporate form, (their corporatization), in order to concentrate the property rights of the enterprise in a corporate board of directors appointed by the owners. Inevitably, given a realistic timetable for any privatization scheme, the initial boards of almost all enterprises will have to be appointed by the government, with the subsequent boards to be appointed by private owners as they emerge during the privatization process. To reduce the enormous administrative burden of creating a large number of corporate boards, the task should initially focus on the 500 largest firms.

The long-term challenge of the privatization program is to create structure of ownership in which the owners have effective control over the enterprises. For example, if ownership of the enterprises is too widely dispersed, the individual owners will have little incentive to monitor management. Moreover, it would be useful to match firms with appropriate owners in the privatization process itself, rather than relying on subsequent trading to establish the "right" owners for a firm. The market for corporate control through takeovers is highly flawed with significant externalities and asymmetries of information. Therefore, the market cannot be relied upon to do a good job in matching potential owners and firms: many efficient takeovers may never be achieved. and many inefficient takeovers may be consummated.

These concerns lead us to three principles for establishing effective long-term control over privatized firms. First, the privatization process should avoid creating an atomistic ownership structure for the larger enterprises, in which hundreds of thousands or millions of owners each retain a small number of shares. Most ownership of the large enterprises should be held by intermediary agents such as pension funds, mutual funds, or commercial banks, or by large owners with concentrated stakes. This principle also conforms to the idea that small investors should hold diversified portfolios, through mutual funds perhaps, rather than shares in a single enterprise.

Second, the privatization process should be designed to foster at least one significant non-financial investor in each major industrial enterprise. This investor would hold around 20 percent of the shares, and would create a "stable core" of ownership of the firm, to use a concept developed in the French privatization process. In their privatizations of the 1980s, the French believed that their capital markets were too thin to rely primarily on public placements as the dominant method of privatization. They also lacked the investment banks that had guided public placements in the United Kingdom. Most importantly, there was concern that no single owner or ownership group would emerge with a significant stake in each enterprise.

Therefore, the French devised a scheme known as the "stable core." This involved soliciting a bid from a single investor, or group of investors working together, to buy 20 percent or more of an enterprise. This group committed a sum of money, prepared a management proposal, and submitted its financial bid. It also committed to hold its shares for at least five years. After reviewing the bids, the French government designated a winner to serve as the stable core. The winning bid reflected not only on the share price offered, but also the financial strength of the bidder, its reputation and experience, and the quality of its management plan.

In Eastern European privatization plans, as in the French plan, governments would attempt to market a 20 percent block of shares of each enterprise to an investment group that could be domestic, foreign or mixed. This group would be vested with significant representation of the corporate board in return for a requirement that the group hold the enterprise for a specified period of time, perhaps three to five years.

Third, the Eastern European countries should create a legal institutional environment in which financial intermediaries play a more active oversight role than is typical in the United States and the United Kingdom. The need for oversight by financial intermediaries resulted from the lack of other institutions or individuals in Eastern Europe that can be relied upon to help oversee an enterprise's corporate management. Thus, a great effort will be needed to economize on information that will be vital in corporate governance. Since banks, pension funds, and mutual funds will have such information, these institutions should also be assigned a major role in the governance process.

As a first step toward strengthening the hand of the financial intermediaries, the Eastern European economies should aim to develop universal banking, as in Germany and Japan, where the commercial banks hold stakes in corporate assets and play active roles in the oversight of enterprises. The new banks should place representatives on the corporate boards of directors and strengthen their capacities to participate in the restructurings of troubled firms. Of course, qualified banks cannot be created at once, but it will be far easier to build up the operational capacity of a dozen large banks (perhaps through management contracts with foreign banks) than to rely on the decentralized oversight of thousands of individual enterprises.

As a second step toward strengthening the oversight by financial intermediaries, newly created mutual funds and pension funds should be encouraged to appoint representatives to the boards of directors of enterprises in which they hold shares, and to create the institutional capacity to monitor closely a large number of firms. When the mutual funds and pension funds are initially licensed, for example, they could be required to present plans detailing how they will appoint directors to corporate boards and how they will develop the expertise needed to monitor these companies. One possibility is that they might subcontract the management oversight to an international management consulting firm.

Role of the Stock Market in Privatization

We doubt that the stock exchange can or should play a major role in the privatization process or, more generally, in the development financial markets in Eastern Europe in the next few years. While each country will surely develop a stock exchange, the liquidity of the exchanges will be low, and their capacity to raise corporate capital or serve as a market for corporate control will be highly circumscribed. Moreover, information concerning the fundamental valuation of firms will continue to be limited for many years, since firms will be operating for the first time in a market environment. Thus, we can expect that the markets will be subject to extreme volatility and will tend toward insider trading, not only because asymmetries of information will be pronounced, but also because the policing of the exchanges will be imperfect in the first few years. Nor are there likely to be many firms with a capital value that is large enough to support many institutional investors and small shareholders.

In general, the continental European economies rely much less heavily on stock markets than do the United Kingdom and the United States for raising and trading corporate wealth, and for gaining corporate control. One sign of the smaller role of the stock market in Western Europe is the low number of listed companies in most European countries. Austria, for example, has only 81 listed Austrian firms; Finland, 78; Norway, 122; Sweden, 135; and Switzerland, 177. In addition, hostile takeovers in these countries scarcely occur. There is little evidence to suggest, although, that this relative dearth of stock market activity has hindered effective corporate governance; many observers feel that the opposite is true: that active stock market trading encourages a short-term bias in managerial decisions. Given the difficulties of establishing an active stock exchange for a large number of firms, it seems safe to recommend that Eastern Europe follow the Western European lead, at least initially, and downplay the institutional role of the stock exchange.

A Strategy for Privatization

We now return to the basic question: how can a very large number of enterprises be privatized quickly while at the same time establishing an effective structure of corporate governance? We have argued that a large role must be played by new institutional investors, and a relatively small role by the stock market. We now describe a strategy for privatization that might be used for transferring ownership and control to private owners.

One key point in our strategy is that much of the privatization should be accomplished through the free distribution of shares to various groups including workers, pension funds, and mutual funds, rather than through the sale of shares in an initial public offering (IPO), which was standard practice in the well-known British privatizations. In Eastern Europe the free distribution of shares would help sidestep the difficult, costly and time-consuming process of enterprise valuation, and recognizes the scarcity of financial capital in private hands.

There is good reason to expect that the problem posed by valuation will be far more severe in Eastern Europe than it has been in the West. The economic environment is shifting in fundamental ways as the transformation into market economies proceeds. Not only is the domestic environment undergoing a profound change, but in several countries, international trade is being liberalized and currency convertibility has been introduced. The COMECON system now governing trade and payments among the Eastern European countries will be revamped in January 1991. Furthermore, the legal and regulatory environment is changing. Indeed, the level of interest rates needed, discount future profits for the purpose of valuation could be greatly influenced by the strategy for privatization itself. As a result of all of these changes, many key relative prices have shifted and will continue to do so. Finally, in many enterprises there will be changes in the structure of management or in the management itself that will have profound effects on the value of the enterprise. These factors each pose fundamental conceptual problems for asset valuation and, taken together, cast grave doubt on the viability of privatization schemes that require careful valuation of assets as a prelude to the sale of most enterprises.

Another key point in our strategy is that most enterprises should be privatized in a common manner, to avoid debates between the government and individual enterprises. To the extent that a common procedure is followed, it will be harder for individual enterprises to bargain for special advantages in the course of the privatization process. At the same time, however, it should be possible for an enterprise to proceed outside of the common procedure (for example, if it receives an attractive bid), and yet remain subject to various due process standards and government oversight.

Before detailing a method of privatization that uses the direct distribution of shares, let us consider the four fundamental limitations of IPOs in the Eastern European context. First, public offerings require a careful valuation of each firm, and a great deal of financial preparation. They tend to be time consuming in normal circumstances, and would be far slower in Eastern Europe, where valuation of firms is nearly impossible and where the financial infrastructure for IPOs does not yet exist. Second, the financial capital currently in the hands of the public is a small fraction of the value of the enterprises to be privatized, assuming a reasonable market interest rate (and thus a reasonable price-earnings ratio for the firm). Thus, any attempt to sell a large proportion of the enterprises would create serious financial problems. Third, IPOs are typically used, as has been the case in Britain, to secure a widespread ownership of shares by small investors (in order to create "people's capitalism"). While this aim may be desirable, it does not generally produce an effective structure of corporate governance, and from a logistical point of view is surely inappropriate for all but the largest enterprises.

Fourth, reliance upon IPOs would lead to the privatization of only the most profitable enterprises, and leave the marginal or unhealthy enterprises – which are viewed as less marketable – in the hands of the government.

Interestingly, there is one case in which a country tried to sell a large number of enterprises very cheaply in the context of an enormous credit squeeze: Chile, during 1975-78, just after the coup that toppled Allende and brought Pinochet to power. There, 232 firms were rapidly sold to the public through leveraged buyouts. The outcome in Chile confirms the worst fears of such a process.

Not only did the Chilean experience produce weak firms and undue concentration of wealth, but the government was (rightly) attacked for selling the firms at very low prices to the few financial groups who had some access to cash. According to Rolf Luders, a former Chile finance minister (1979-81) and a strong advocate of privatization in general,

> The First Round [of privatizations] was carried-out in the midst of deep structural transformation process, during which there was little interest on the part of foreigners to invest in the country, and which was accompanied by considerable political, social, and economic uncertainty. ...... These debt privatizations carried-out in an economically unstable environment, contributed to generate a considerable degree of *financial asset concentration, financial instability, and some important macro-economic problems.*[1] (Emphasis ours.)

Ironically, because the newly privatized firms were undercapitalized and heavily indebted, many of them collapsed during the financial crisis of 1982-83, and had to be renationalized.

One novel approach might rescue IPOs from the problem of limited purchasing power. The government might transfer purchasing power to the public in direct grants, rather than loans. This is the basic idea behind *voucher schemes*. The government issues purchasing power in a kind of voucher (scrip) that can be used solely to purchase shares. The initial distribution of vouchers can be made on an equal basis for the entire

---

[1] Luders, Rolf, "Chile's Massive State Owned Enterprise Divestiture Program, 1975-1990: Failures and Successes." World Bank Conference on Privatization and Ownership Changes in East and Central Europe, (forthcoming), p 44.

population, or according to other criteria. Care would have to be taken to ensure that vouchers do not become money substitutes, otherwise the issue of vouchers could lead to a sudden expansion of the money supply that is not synchronized with the sale of shares. As we mention later, the voucher schemes are still likely to suffer from the other weaknesses of IPOs: their time-consuming nature and their inability create an effective ownership structure.

In particular, the use of a voucher scheme in connection with IPOs may involve prohibitive administrative costs. If individuals swap vouchers for shares, the pattern of share ownership will involve a dispersion of holdings in small lots. A company worth $10 million – medium-sized by Polish standards – might be in the position of distributing only $300,000 in dividends per year (with a 15 percent rate of return and a 20 percent dividend payout ratio). If a voucher system involved the sale of enterprises to 25 million adult Poles, it could well lead to 100,000 or more shareholders per enterprise. As a result, the administrative costs would leave few resources for profit distribution.

The discussion in Eastern Europe of privatization through IPOs has led to the notion that only profitable enterprises would be privatized accordingly, the marginal or unhealthy enterprises would be left to the government to restructure or liquidate. This proposition arises naturally an approach to privatization based on the case-by-case sale of enterprises, because of the apparent difficulties of valuing and marketing enterprises that may not be sustainable. It would be preferable, in our view, for all enterprises, regardless of their financial position, to be corporatized and quickly put into private hands. There are several reasons not to leave the marginal and unhealthy enterprises in the hands of the state. First, these enterprises could remain in state hands for a long period as the government tries to determine whether restructuring or liquidation is appropriate. During this time, the enterprises would be targets for further asset stripping by an unrestrained management. Second, a corporate board of directors will be more competent and less subject to political pressures than the government in guiding the process of restructuring and, if necessary, liquidation.

An Illustrative Plan for Large-Scale Privatization in Poland

We now show how the considerations of the previous sections can be integrated into a single, workable plan. The goal would be the complete privatization of the 500 largest state enterprises in Poland's industrial sector within a period of four years. While the privatization strategy of the Polish government is still evolving and is likely to change further after the presidential elections, we believe that it will share some – though certainly not all–of the features that we outline here. Indeed, we would like to stress once again that we have benefitted from extensive discussions with Polish officials in crystallizing our own ideas.

To achieve a rapid privatization, a common track would be followed by most of the large enterprises. This has two advantages: the minimimization of negotiation between the state and the individual enterprises and the routinization of the process. Most firms would be privatized in tranches with each "slice" of shares transferred or sold to a different kind of investor. A minority of firms would be sold outright in a standard kind of privatization (either a public offering or a private sale).

At the beginning of the process, each of the 500 largest enterprises would be corporatized–that is, converted into a joint-stock company with the shares initially issued to the state as 100 percent owner. An initial board of directors would be appointed according to the privatization law: two-thirds of the seats would be appointed by the government (most likely by a private investment group that would be hired to assist the government), and one-third of the seats would be elected by the workers. The initial board of directors would serve for one year.

A few enterprises would then proceed with a British-style privatization through IPOs, private sales, or auctions, though we do not discuss these enterprises in this paper. (The privatization law should leave room for individual firms to pursue these routes, especially when private bidders come forward.)

The bulk of the enterprises would begin the privatization in tranches. The first tranche would be the transfer, or possibly sale, of shares to an enterprise's workers. The government would most simply mandate that the workers receive 10 percent of the enterprise shares for free (the law provides for the sale to workers of up to 20 percent of the enterprise for half price). The allocation of shares among the work force would be determined by the manager with the approval of the new corporate board. On this particular issue, it may be wise to require that the worker representatives on the board of directors also approve the share distribution plan among the workers.

In addition to the 10 percent distributed to the workers, around 5 percent of the shares would he reserved for compensation for the managers and the corporate board. Managers could receive stock options or outright share ownership as part of an incentive compensation package. We expect that the distribution of shares to managers, as part of their compensation package, could provide an important early spur to increased efficiency within the firm.

The second tranche of shares, around 20 percent of the total, would be used to capitalize a new private pension system. The shares would be distributed to several new pension funds, which would in turn be distributed to enterprises and individuals in order to back retirement payments. Each pension fund would receive a portfolio of enterprises and would be responsible for the active oversight of the corporations in its portfolio.

During the following few years, enterprises would be "hooked-up" with the new pension funds according to the size of the enterprise and the age and wage distributions of the employees. The basic idea would be for the state to scale back its own social security payments that are now made directly from the budget, and to increase the payments being made from the capitalized pension fund. The actual transition from budgetary expenditures to payments from private pension funds could be phased in over a period of five to ten years. If the pension funds receive the income from 20 percent of the shares of the 500 largest enterprises, the annual earnings would equal about $900 million, or about 20 percent of the annual pension payments now made from the central budget.

The use of share distribution to capitalize the pension system is not without complexity, and numerous logistical problems will have to be resolved in order to distribute claims in a fair way and reduce social security payments from the government in line with growing benefits from the private plans.

The third tranche would consist of 10 percent of the shares and would be used to capitalize the existing state-owned commercial banks and the insurance sector. Commercial banks would receive 6 percent of the shares (60 percent of this tranche) and would be expected to develop into active investors along German lines. At the same time, the commercial banks themselves would be converted into joint-stock companies and prepared for privatization.

The process of capitalization and commercialization of commercial banks would have two main benefits. First, as active investors, the commercial banks would begin to play an important role in scrutinizing the management of enterprises. Second, the capitalization would also help the banks to improve their weak balance sheets, which need recapitalization in any case. We estimate that with 6 percent of the shares of the 500 largest enterprises, commercial banks would receive a transfer equivalent to about 10 percent of commercial bank assets.

Privatization schemes that rely in large part on the free distribution of shares are sometimes said to be disadvantaged in that the government forgoes a large, potential revenue source. While this may be true when shares are distributed freely to workers or households, the revenue loss may not be incurred when public or quasi-public institutions are capitalized, as in the case of the pension funds and the commercial banks. The capitalization of the pension system will reduce the requirement of budgetary funding of the social security system by an equal magnitude. The capitalization of the commercial banks will likewise reduce a future claim on budgetary resources of the banks, by anticipating the need for a commercial bank recapitalization.

The fourth tranche will consist of 20 percent of the shares of the enterprises that will be distributed generally to the adult population of Poland (roughly 25 million). This part of the share distribution *will* be a loss of wealth for the state sector, since the distribution to households will not be recouped by budgetary savings elsewhere. There are prevailing models of how to distribute these shares. In one model the shares of the enterprises would be distributed to several private investment trusts (which are closed-end mutual funds), whose shares in turn would be freely distributed to the adult citizens of Poland. After the initial distribution of the shares, the investment trusts would be free to actively manage their portfolios.

Each individual would receive one share in one of the investment trusts, so that if there were, say, ten trusts, each would have around 2.5 million subscribers. The investment trusts would pass through dividend and other income to the shareholding public, after deducting the fund-expenses and fees. Each trust would be managed by a Polish entity but would contract with a foreign advisory firm to assist in the establishment of the trust, in the active management of assets, and in the administration of dividend distribution.

An alternative model has suggested free distribution through vouchers. Individuals would receive vouchers with a fixed face value in the domestic currency. Shares would be tendered at a fixed price after a quick valuation. Households could either buy shares with their voucher or buy claims on investment trust companies, which in turn would use the vouchers to purchase the tendered shares. The government could encourage the households to deposit their shares with the investment trusts as a sound method of diversification.

This second approach has won widespread support in Poland and is viewed as politically superior to the direct distribution of investment trust certificates, since it offers more choice to households. On the negative side, however, it is vastly more complicated, and could, in fact, clearly slow down the privatization process. With the voucher plan, unlike the plan to directly distribute investment trust shares, there must be a valuation of individual companies as well as a time-consuming public offering. In addition, the vouchers could be complex to issue and process.

The free distribution of investment trust shares could be completed within about one year, while the system relying on vouchers would probably take a couple of years more. In either case, after this phase is completed, the government will retain roughly 35 percent ownership in the partially privatized companies. A second board of directors would have to be formed upon the expiration of the one-year term for the initial board appointed by the government. The second board would be elected by the shareholders for a three-year period. The shareholder groups created by the pension funds, the banks, and the investment trusts would presumably dominate this board of directors and, thereby, firmly establish control over management. The board of directors could be elected by cumulative voting (essentially, proportional representation) to make sure that each of the major holders of shares places representatives on the supervisory board.

Following the free distribution of shares, any number of methods might be used to dispose of the remaining government holdings, including public offerings, private placements of shares, and further free distributions. Of course, if share sales are the predominant means of disposing of the last tranche, the government will have to undertake a careful valuation of each enterprise and prepare the sale. In addition, the government may wish to encourage enterprises and investor groups to come forward with privatization proposals in a decentralized manner, provided that each deal receives an adequate degree of scrutiny. In certain cases, the government may wish to retain a minority holding, and can look to Western European experience for an appropriate pattern of government equity positions in the corporate sector.

We consider the French concept of selling a block of shares to a stable core of investors to be an attractive technique for disposing of the last tranche. In the case of Poland, the government would entertain bids from domestic, foreign, or mixed investor groups. It should be possible to establish a stable core for most of the 500 largest enterprises and complete the privatization of these enterprises within a three-year period. The stable core would eventually become the primary investor group and, because it would be entrepreneurial in nature, would take a dominant role in supervising corporate management. In time, the supervisory role of pension funds, investment trusts, and commercial banks, although important, would no longer be the main force monitoring and controlling management behavior.

Central Features of the Illustrative Plan

We conclude this section by stressing what we regard to be the central features of the plan, and what we regard as illustrative but not fundamental. In our view, there are several key steps: corporatization that will establish the legal basis of the new economic system; a partial distribution of shares to workers and managers for political and incentive reasons; and the distribution of some shares to financial intermediaries such as banks and mutual funds, which will have some early responsibility for appointing corporate boards. Once this process goes forward for the bulk of the largest few hundred enterprises, it is not vital what fraction of shares the government holds; it could range from 30 percent to 50 percent of the enterprise. In the latter case, however, we would expect the government to be a silent partner in the day-to-day management of the enterprise.

We accept the proposition that long-term management of the enterprises will be enhanced if the government can sell a significant block of each enterprise to a core buyer. This will take time. The risks of waiting, however, will be significantly reduced if a large part of the enterprise is already in private hands, and if the preliminary struggle over the form of ownership, corporate versus worker management, for example, is exclusively settled in favor of a corporate structure.

26. Misapprehensions on Privatization[*]

Alan Walters

A decade ago, when the first Thatcher government began privatization, it was widely thought to be ideologically driven and thus, like other elements of the Thatcher reforms, doomed to fail. The privatization program did indeed have its ups and downs, but overall it must be reckoned to be a great success. One modest measure of the achievement is the Labour party's reluctance to propose any substantial renationalization proposals.

Another measure of success is the emulation of other nations. Privatization – broadly on the Thatcher model – has been enthusiastically and successfully pursued by socialist governments in France and Spain and by labor governments in New Zealand. Even in the Third World, a start has been made in closing down, liquidating or selling off the many state-owned enterprises (SOEs) acquired when socialization of production was so fashionable. Now these enterprises, if that is the right name for them, are a great burden to the taxpayer; they produce many – albeit phoney – jobs, but few useable goods. Shortages, queues, black markets and corruption are characteristic of these socialized economies, and it is hoped that privatization will deliver them from these hardships.

In the Eastern socialized economies, the same system and the same conditions prevail. Some of these states, now called emerging market economies (EMEs), comprising Poland, Czechoslavakia, Yugoslavia, Hungary, and now the Soviet Union, have become convinced that privatization is the one hope for their salvation as efficient industrialized democracies. The leaders of the EMEs have looked at the great success of the Thatcher privatizations – British Airways, British Steel, housing, Jaguar, even British Telecom and the water companies – and they have liked what they have seen. Nationalized British Airways and British Steel began the decade of the 1980s among the worst performers, in terms of productivity and profits (i.e., losses),

---

* From *International Economic Insights*, January/February 1991, vol. II, no. 1, pp. 28-30. All rights reserved. Reprinted by permission.

in the OECD countries. In 1990, they are among the best performing corporations in the West. Privatization was clearly thought to be the essential ingredient that worked such miracles upon the large SOEs.

And so it was. But this is a misleading and dangerous simplification. The naive belief of the EMEs, encouraged on occasion by enthusiasts from the West, is that all that SOEs need is a change in ownership from the state to private persons. The motivation of the new owners would then engender those efficient systems of production so characteristic of the West and so lacking in the East.

There was thought to be no point in trying to reform the existing SOEs while they remained in state ownership. They were managed by the nomenklatura management. I doubt that any political leader will seriously attempt the Herculean task of sorting the sheep from the goats among the *nomenklatura*. Somehow they hoped that privatization would do the sorting for them.

The SOEs were also vastly overmanned by highly unionized labor. A distinguished Hungarian told me that the state would not dare carry out the appropriate demanning. The nomenklatura managers would protest and, if necessary, botch the job by retaining sinecures and disrupting production, blaming "the inhuman policy of restructuring." The Hungarian asserted that the only way to demand efficiency was to privatize – and, he assured me, the private companies could then rid themselves of the make-work jobs that had been so prevalent in the enterprise in its nationalized state.

This prognosis is dramatically different from the successful Thatcher reforms and privatizations. The main contrast is that, under Thatcher, the reform of the nationalized corporation was carried through while it was in the public sector. The reductions in work force, the elimination of unprofitable plant and equipment, and the sharp increases in productivity, quality and service were all achieved while the enterprises were owned by the state. Indeed, the government appointed new managers – Ian McGregor and John King in those days – with a mandate to turn them into profitable and sound undertakings that could hold their own in the competitive private sectors. The managers and workers had the privatization timetable and, more important, diminishing access to the public purse in order to encourage their efforts.

But privatization occurred only after all the hard work of reform had been completed. Privatization simply ensured that the corporation would not slip back into the bad habits of the public sector – such as recourse to subsidies, monopoly privileges, and cheap capital.

Somehow the EMEs expect that they can skip this phase of preparation and reform in the public sector. One can sympathize. In Poland, Hungary, Czechoslavakia and the Soviet Union, the distrust of government and the serried ranks of the bureaucracy is universal. How can one expect the institution that got them into this mess to be the agency that will now extract them from it? But, of course, there has been a change of government, and slowly even the bureaucracy is changing its habits, if not its personnel. A government that is committed to a market economy and private enterprise should be able to institute reforms on the Thatcher model. Poland, Hungary, Czechoslavakia and the Soviet Union all have their incipient McGregors and Kings. The government should appoint, motivate and back them in the ruthless reforms so needed in these arthritic economies.

Of course there are objections. One of those strangest and most poignant is that the Thatcher privatizations were too slow and too little. In economies where up to 90 percent of non-agricultural production is in the hands of the state, the stentorian process of Thatcher privatization would be far too slow politically. Marton Tardos, the distinguished leader of the Free Democratic Party in Hungary, worked out that, at the pace of Thatcher's program, Hungary would take 100 years to privatize its economy. They want a market economy now – or, at most, in four or five years.

There was, however, nothing inherent in the Thatcher approach that dictated the pace of privatization. It was determined by legal, political and administrative factors. No insuperable technical reason (even including so-called capital market saturation) prevented the program from being speeded up, as indeed occurred after 1984. But I do not think it feasible to carry out the wholesale privatization envisaged in less than ten years.

Another set of objections arises from the fact that there is no capital market in any EME, so there is no way of valuing the worth of SOEs. Prices, moreover, have been distorted for so long that they are very different from both world prices and true domestic costs. Who knows what the expected stream of profits will be from purchasing, for example, the Gdansk shipyard? It was reported that the shipyard workers thought the yard was worth $500 million, while Arthur Andersen has valued it at between zero and $30 million. This illustrates the enormous uncertainties, both economic and political, that bedevil any potential deal.

This, however, is an argument for taking the Thatcher road and for not attempting to privatize until at least many of these political and economic uncertainties are resolved. Then one can write an honest prospectus for each of them. But there is another reason for the EMEs thrust to privatize, which has, in principle, nothing to do with the improvement of efficiency and management. This is to assuage the thirst of the inhabitants for the transfer of the powers of ownership from the state and its bureaucrats to the people. The establishment of property rights is, perhaps, the essential element of a capitalist system. And the major form of property in EMEs is industrial capital, housing and land. What could be more natural than to give shares to this property away to the people?

There are ingenious proposals for vouchers that would enable ordinary citizens to buy shares in holding companies or mutual funds, which would themselves hold shares in the erst-while SOEs. The mutuals would be required to diversify their holdings in order to avoid the risks of particular enterprises. In the classic phrase of Thatcherism, it would amount to returning the assets of industry back to the people.

But what about management under this system? In effect the management would be controlled by the managers of the several mutual funds or holding companies that have a substantial holding in each enterprise. The experience of Britain and the United States suggests that such institutional shareholders tend to be active portfolio holders rather than active and interested managers. There is no working model of a system built on active and interested management. I think it would be a very risky experiment. And the mind does boggle at the prospect of launching vouchers and an active market in mutual fund shares among the whole populace, where such instruments have been quite unknown for nearly 50 years. I doubt very much that the market would be at all transparent, and the opportunities for misrepresentation, market rigging, etc. would be enormous. One fears that capitalism would soon be discredited.

I have no alternative save the Thatcher model – with perhaps a souped-up engine. We know that works. That is a lot.

PART VIII

INTERNATIONAL
ECONOMIC ISSUES

Many of the problems of the Eastern European economies stems from their isolation from the world economy, and hence from a regime of prices that better reflect relative production costs and world prices. This situation was fostered by the use of exchange control and unrealistic, and frequently multiple, exchange rates. Just as freely determined market prices promote allocative efficiency within the various national economies, so bringing domestic prices into line with world prices will promote more efficient resource use. The steps towards this include freeing the foreign trade sector from the pervasive influence of the monopoly trading enterprises, allowing individual firms to determine their markets, and establishing currency convertibility to bring domestic prices into line with world levels.

While these objectives are highly desirable and open competitiveness will convey allocative benefits, the path towards liberalization is not easy, given the pre-existing situation. Norman Fieleke's article "The Liberalization of International Trade and Payments in Eastern Europe," provides our starting point. It describes how central planners addressed the issue of international trade, and the development and functioning of the now defunct Council on Mutual Economic Assistance (CMEA), sometimes known as COMECON or the "Communist Common Market." Just as national central planners attempted to control the flows of domestic resources, the role of the CMEA was to supervise and manage the flow of goods between nations. Ideally, all the needs of the CMEA were to be met within that area, and each nation was de facto allocated certain industries in which to specialize. With secure product markets and protection from competition both from the world outside and, through the nature of the planned solution, competition from within the CMEA, inefficiency thrived and innovation in both products and manufacturing technique was hindered. Thus, the infrastructure of the CMEA did little to foster the pursuit of comparative advantage.

The legacies of the CMEA – notably featherbedded industry and a high degree of bilateral interdependence – is a formidable problem that can only be corrected by trade reform. However, trade reform brings with it its own set of problems. Inflationary tendencies are inherent in liberalization as the price of domestic goods rise to world levels. Unemployment will mount as export sectors artificially developed within the CMEA are unable to contend with open competition. All East European countries will continue to be constrained by a severe shortage of hard currency, since export earnings will decrease while the demand for western consumer goods, long suppressed, will rise.

The currency shortage faced by East European nations, is, Fieleke notes, in some ways very similar to that faced by the Western European nations in the aftermath of World War II. At that time, a serious dollar shortage led to a proliferation of bilateral trade and barter agreements. The West European nations took, in 1950, a step towards the restoration of multilateral trade by the establishment of the European Payments Union, which lasted until general convertibility was restored in 1958. While noting initial similarities, Fieleke is skeptical about the value of the EPU as a model for an Eastern European Payments Union (EEPU). He observes that the EPU, while ultimately successful, was slow in assisting in the restoration of general convertibility, and that pace might be unacceptable in Eastern Europe today. Further, the difference in the pace of liberalization and the unfortunate history of the CMEA provide further barriers to the foundation of an EEPU.

The second reading, written by P.B.W. Rayment of the United Nations Economic Commission for Europe, asks "Is a 'Marshall' Plan Needed for Eastern Europe?" The first Marshall plan was, of course, the aid provided by the United States to Western Europe (indeed it was offered to Eastern Europe, but refused by Stalin) to aid in the reconstruction following the post-war devastation. The answer to the UNECE is that aid must be radically different from that provided by the Marshall plan. Aid to post-war Western Europe was "long on grant-aid" and short on technical assistance. Western European institutions did not need to be radically transformed; the market mechanism was largely in place despite its circumvention by wartime planning systems and the volume of destruction. What was needed was to rebuild physical infrastructure and "refill the pipeline" with intermediate goods.

The problems of East Europe, Rayment argues, are that the institutions must be radically transformed before large amounts of grants-in-aid are sent in. Were the original Marshall plan adhered to, the aid would be largely wasted because of the inability of the East European economies to absorb such a large transfer of resources in a situation where the basic market infrastructure is absent. Therefore, technical assistance in the construction of institutional infrastructure is, therefore, emphasized, effectively setting the Marshall plan upon its head. There is little doubt that the international community could afford a new Marshall plan; the burdens on the OECD community (Europe, the United States, and Japan) would be small in proportion to GNP, although the political will might be lacking.

A Note on Eastern Europe and the European Community

Most of the transforming economies regard the resolution to their international economic relations as lying ultimately in membership of the European Community. This would be politically attractive to the EC, since the involvement of the East European nations in a "European ideology" would have a moderating effect on politics in those nations. A large impetus behind the original establishment of the EC was to provide an alternative to the unattractive poles of fascism and communism, and certainly the politics of Spain, Portugal, and Greece have taken a centrist turn since their accession to the EC.

However, an early entry into the EC by Eastern European nations is unlikely for several reasons. First, the EC itself has a tight agenda in moving toward closer economic and monetary integration. Any new members would inevitably slow this process, especially since the establishment of the European monetary union sets minimum standards from all members on issues of budgetary deficit and inflation rates; these standards are well beyond the current performance of Eastern Europe and will require the development of a much better functioning and controlled system of public finance. Second, there are already many members in line, either officially or in the positioning process (including Sweden, Norway, Finland, Austria, Turkey, Cyprus, and Malta), who cannot be displaced despite political expediency. Third, the rich nations of Western Europe are reluctant to admit relatively poor Eastern Europe into the EC's redistributive programs – the social fund, the regional fund and the common agricultural policy. While the accession of the rich members of the European Free Trade Association will actually reduce the budgetary burden on the existing members, letting the East Europeans in would make net payers of all the pre-1984 membership. Fourth, the new southern members of the EC (Greece, Portugal, and Spain) have prospered as recipients of investment from Northern Europe and are unwilling to admit potential competitors for investment resources. Finally, and perhaps most importantly, admitting the Eastern European nations would open Western

Europe's borders to unlimited immigration at a time when high unemployment has made immigration a difficult issue throughout the EC.

A more likely option at this stage is that East Europe will be allowed
relatively free access to Western European markets, while full membership
will be postponed until well into the next century. Despite Fieleke's
pessimism, this would argue for an East European free trade area, of which
a payments union might be an integral part.

27. The Liberalization of International Trade and Payments in Eastern Europe[*]

Norman S. Fieleke

Few events can match the opening of the Berlin Wall as an historic symbol. Among the many things promised by that opening was the liberalization of trade that had been closely controlled for many years by the communist governments of Eastern Europe. This promise has virtually been realized in East Germany as that nation has unified with its neighbor to the West. Progress in other East European countries, however, has been slow because of concern over the costs of adjusting to freer trade.

This article examines the nature, motivation, and consequences of state-directed trading as it has been practiced in the centrally planned economies of Eastern Europe. Attention is then given to the issues in liberalization. Some general considerations suggest that state direction of foreign commerce may prove to be a tenacious legacy in at least some of the countries under consideration.

Foreign Trade under Central Planning: The Tail of the Dog

In the typical centrally planned economy, foreign trade is the tail - not the proverbial tail that wags the dog, but a more ordinary tail without much influence on the rest of the dog. The means of production are owned almost solely by the state, and central planners decide not only what will be produced by the state enterprises, but from whom the enterprises will obtain their inputs and to whom they will sell their output-and at what prices. The planners thus must balance supplies and demands for thousands of commodities. Goals are specified in terms of output quantities and are commonly

---

[*] From "The Liberalization of International Trade and Payments in Eastern Europe," *New England Economic Review*, March/April 1991, published by the Federal Reserve Bank of Boston.

unrealistically high, and prices bear little relation to those that would be set by free markets.

In this system imports are viewed more or less as necessary evils to allow fulfillment of the plan at acceptable costs. One reason for this attitude is that central planning was adopted in the first place in order to exercise detailed control over the domestic economy, and such control is generally considered vulnerable insofar as the economy is dependent on goods from abroad. Thus, planners are loath to rely upon foreign goods unless the resource cost of domestic substitutes is substantially greater. Similarly, exports, far from being a source of pride, are perceived as a resource drain that must be endured in order to pay for imports needed to fulfill the plan.

So that it can be subjected to detailed control, the foreign trade of the centrally planned economy is carried out chiefly by state-managed foreign trade organizations. Each reports to the Ministry of Foreign Trade and has exclusive responsibility for trade in a specified range of products. The volume, commodity composition, and geographic pattern of trade to be undertaken by each foreign trade organization is specified in plans approved by the central authorities.

Because the foreign trade organization must acquire the imports indicated for it in the plan, it is not free to bargain with foreign suppliers over the aggregate amount to be purchased, although it may encourage competition among them over price. By contrast, in marketing its exports the foreign trade organization must meet a revenue rather than a quantity goal, and might restrict the total quantity sold below that contemplated by the plan if the result were to raise the price enough to compensate for the diminished quantity.

Unlike free marketeers, central planners need to prescribe what goods will be given up to the rest of the world and what will be obtained in return. In order to regulate closely the quantities of imports and exports, and in order to assure that exports yield a desired level of imports, planners often enter into barter-like agreements and attempt to balance their trade not only worldwide but also country by country. Such barter and bilateral balancing agreements are, of course, more common in trade among centrally planned economies than in trade between centrally planned and market economies, which rely much more heavily on free markets to allocate resources.

To enforce their controls over exports and imports, central planners rely in part on controls over the use of currency for transactions relating to foreign trade. Foreign residents holding balances of a centrally planned economy currency are allowed to use them only for specified purposes. Because such foreign-held balances may not be expended for the purchase of many commodities, these balances are cursed with what is called "commodity inconvertibility." It is even more difficult for a foreigner to convert the currency of the typical centrally planned economy into freely usable currencies; thus, its currency also suffers from "currency inconvertibility."

Residents of the centrally planned economy, too, are strictly regulated in their purchases of foreign currency. Were they allowed freely to acquire foreign-currency balances, they would use those balances in part to purchase and import foreign goods, and might well spend less on domestically produced goods than projected in the central plan. Thus, foreign-currency balances accruing to foreign trade organizations in exchange for their exports must be channeled to the foreign-exchange control authority, which then allocates those balances for approved uses.

In countries that have embraced this system, the adverse consequences are plain to see. Because of the central planners' desire to minimize imports, domestic producers in these economies encounter very little import competition. This protection from foreign competition, combined with a dearth of domestic competition, allows the typical domestic producer to concentrate on satisfying the quantity goals set for it with goods that are decidedly inferior to those available in world markets. Nor is there much incentive to innovate, or to specialize in product lines for which perceived domestic demand and quantity goals are relatively low, however great the demand in the rest of the world.

Lacking the goad of competition, the typical centrally planned economy also lacks the price structure that would be set by competitive markets reflecting the underlying preferences of consumers and the true costs of production. This is not to say that such underlying preferences and costs are perfectly reflected by prices in the ordinary market economy, but the distortion is much greater in the typical centrally planned economy. Nowhere is the distortion more obvious than in the long queues of customers seeking meat and other goods whose supply falls far short of the demand at the controlled price.

In sum, central planning seeks to manage the flow of goods and services, so planners strive to insulate their economies from foreign developments they cannot control. Thus, foreign trade and the use of currencies for foreign trade are closely regulated; prices diverge widely from those prevailing in world markets; and domestic producers experience neither the competitive pressures nor the profit incentives that exposure to foreign markets has to offer.

The Council for Mutual Economic Assistance

Imagine the centrally planned economy writ large, embracing a number of such countries, and you have something like the CMEA (Council for Mutual Economic Assistance, also known as COMECON). The CMEA was founded in 1949 by the Soviet Union, Bulgaria, Czechoslovakia, Hungary, Poland, and Romania; the German Democratic Republic joined in the following year. It is these countries on which this article focuses, although the CMEA was joined by Mongolia in 1962, Cuba in 1972, and Vietnam in 1978.

The CMEA functioned into early 1991, and oversaw trade among its members. The organization's aims, principles, functions, and powers were set forth in its charter, which is worth quoting both for its ambitious scope and its socialist vernacular:

> *Article 1. Aims and Principles*: The purpose of the Council is to promote, by uniting and co-ordinating the efforts of the member countries, the further extension and improvement of co-operation and the development of socialist economic integration, the planned development of their national economies, the acceleration of economic and technical progress in these countries, higher level of industrialization of the less industrialized countries, a continuous increase in labour productivity, a gradual approximation and equalization of economic development levels and a steady improvement in the wellbeing of the peoples. . . .

> *Article 3. Functions and Powers*: to (a) organize allround. . . co-operation of member countries in the most rational use of national resources and acceleration of the development of their productive forces; (b) foster the improvement of the international socialist division of labour by co-ordinating national economic development plans, and the specialization and co-operation of production in member countries; (c) assist in . . . carrying out joint measures for the development of industry and agriculture . . . transport . . . principal capital investments . . . [and] trade.

The supreme authority of the CMEA was the annual Council of prime ministers. Council decisions had to be unanimous.

Almost from its inception, the CMEA failed to pursue its professed goal of region-wide economic integration. Instead, the member countries sought a high degree of self-sufficiency, with national economic policies formulated under the supervision of the Soviet Union rather than the Council, and with trade among the members regulated by bilateral agreements. By the second half of the 1950s, it had become clear that the costs of the autarkic policies being followed were very high. Thus, CMEA members tried to breathe new life into the Council and formulate a more genuinely regional economic policy, especially by agreeing upon product lines in which each member country would specialize and by agreeing to promote the regional mobility of factors of production as well as goods. These agreements were not carried out, however, and the economic plans of the member countries were not coordinated in keeping with any formal assessment of underlying comparative advantage.

In 1971 CMEA members strengthened their avowed commitment to economic integration, agreeing to eliminate gradually the obstacles they had imposed against the free intra-regional flow of goods and services, and agreeing also to reduce barriers against the movement of productive factors. Two principal instruments were to be employed to foster integration. Foremost was to be the coordination of national economic plans while the plans were still in the draft stage. The second instrument was to be a larger role for market forces in determining prices, interest rates, exchange rates, and the allocation of resources. Again, the rhetoric far exceeded the results, and in February 1986, Mr. Gorbachev assailed the CMEA's "armchair administration" and "endless committee deliberations."[1] Despite the criticism, by 1988 the best that the CMEA members could do was a communique reaffirming (with Romania demurring) an "earlier decision regarding the stepwise establishment of the conditions for the mutual free movements of goods, services and other production factors with the goal of creating eventually a unified market, after the preconditions thereof have been examined."[2]

What the CMEA actually embraced bore little resemblance to a free and unified market. Instead, trade among the members was closely controlled. Each country negotiated with every other member country an agreement specifying the composition and the volume of trade. Because prices within CMEA countries failed to reflect true underlying costs, the prices at which goods were exchanged were usually negotiated around a moving average of prices observed in other, freer markets. The prices so negotiated by differing pairs of countries were not identical, however.

On occasion the negotiated prices were clearly more favorable to some CMEA countries than current world prices would have been. The outstanding example is the relatively low price reportedly charged by the Soviet Union for its exports of petroleum and other raw materials to other CMEA members for many years. Soviet subsidies in this form seem to have been extended in much larger amounts to some East European countries than to others, perhaps

---

[1] U.N. Department of International and Economic Affairs 1989, p. 123.
[2] *Ibid*, p. 128

as a reward for political allegiance to the Soviet Union. Had such rewards been paid openly as lump-sum transfers, they might have been resented by the populaces of both the Soviet Union and the East European nations.

It would be a grave mistake to take these subsidies as the measure of net economic benefit or cost of the CMEA to the members receiving or paying them. As already noted, centrally planned economies generally suffer from their insulation from foreign competition, and the CMEA provided such insulation. Indeed, it was a vehicle for sustaining production techniques and output decidedly inferior to those in other industrial countries.

The differences in prices – and real wages – between CMEA countries provided an incentive to shift both goods and labor from low-price or low-wage countries to the higher-price or higher-wage countries. Such shifts, which would tend to establish roughly the same price for a good throughout the CMEA, are a *sine qua non* for economic integration, but they would have disrupted the detailed economic plans promulgated by the authorities and, therefore, met with official resistance. Thus, controls were imposed over the very movements of goods and labor that were crucial for progress toward the professed goal of economic integration.

The shortcomings and contradictions of the CMEA were epitomized in its approach to making payments between nations and settling imbalances in international accounts. Even though central planners generally strive to avoid exporting more than is required to pay for planned imports, and thus incline to bilateral balancing, circumstances might lead a CMEA country to realize a trade surplus, even with another CMEA member. For example, one CMEA country might fail to deliver all the exports promised another during a year. CMEA procedure was for the country with the export surplus to be credited with a "transferable ruble" balance in the International Bank for Economic Cooperation (IBEC) in Moscow, while the deficit CMEA member incurred an equivalent indebtedness to the IBEC, or a reduction in its transferable ruble holdings.

The transferable ruble is considered an inferior means of payment, however. Rather than rubles, goods are what the authorities in the surplus country wanted; and the transferable ruble balance cannot be exchanged for goods without first negotiating the exchange in the form of another bilateral trade agreement, which again may go unfulfilled. Further undermining the value of the transferable ruble balance is its failure to yield interest that can be converted into merchandise any more readily than the principal.

The general failure to use a convertible currency in CMEA transactions reinforced the tendency toward bilateral barter and blocked progress in knitting together the economies of the member countries. A CMEA country that found itself accumulating a significant transferable ruble balance had good reason to intensify its controls over trade and payments, especially for exports, in order to forestall further trade surpluses within the CMEA, while CMEA debtor countries, which were receiving essentially interest-free loans, had little incentive to increase their exports so as to repay their debts. On these counts, the CMEA tended to shrink rather than expand trade within its area.

Moreover, because the prices at which goods were exchanged within the CMEA were not appropriate to equate supply and demand, chronic shortages developed for some goods and chronic surpluses for others. The goods in short supply could readily be sold in world markets for convertible currencies at no discount from their CMEA prices and were dubbed "hard" goods, but goods in excess supply could be sold for convertible currencies only at a discount, often sizable, and were dubbed "soft" goods. Of the goods produced within the CMEA, fuels, food, raw materials, and various semi-manufactures and finished manufactures commonly fell into the soft goods category. Not surprisingly, CMEA members generally preferred to obtain hard goods in exchange for any hard goods that they exported, so that a tendency developed to balance not only the total trade, but trade in hard goods, between pairs of CMEA countries. This "structural bilateralism," as it was called, nicely illustrates the proclivity for one government control to beget another. The net result of such practices was that "socialist economic integration" proceeded little further than the lips of CMEA officials.

Steps Toward Liberalization

The dubious value of the transferable ruble led some CMEA countries that were accumulating them to seek more nearly convertible payments for their exports to other CMEA countries and to channel more of their exports to non-CMEA countries in exchange for convertible currencies. This, however, was only the tip of the iceberg. As the 1980's drew to a close, dissatisfaction with the CMEA had become widespread and profound among the member-ship, as had the dissatisfaction with central planning more generally. Calls were heard for radical reform or abandonment of the organization, and in January 1991 its termination was announced. Its passing should not be mourned.

For years the subject of reform had been debated within the CMEA without significant results; 1990 witnessed a turning point. Failing to agree on the recommendations tabled by a special reform commission in January 1990, the members of the CMEA appointed still another reform commission, this time to prescribe "radical" reforms. This latter commission proposed that the CMEA be downgraded into something like a regional economic secretariat, carrying out research and disseminating data, and playing little or no role in trade and payments negotiations among the members.

Also, in June 1990 CMEA officials reportedly adopted the goals of valuing their trade flows at world market prices and of settling imbalances in convertible currencies rather than in transferable rubles, although no precise timetable was promulgated. The Soviet Union is reported to have entered into agreements to start conducting its bilateral trade on this basis with the former German Democratic Republic, with Czechoslovakia, and with Hungary as early as January 1, 1991, although it is likely that the transition will require some time, with many initial exceptions to the new valuation and settlement rules.

In addition, several CMEA countries have eased, in varying degrees, their centralized control over their international trade. Producing enterprises have been allowed more latitude in selecting the foreign trade organizations with which they deal, and in some cases have even been allowed to deal directly with foreign firms. The result has been a relaxation, sometimes significant, of the state monopolization of foreign trade.

Perhaps the most publicized of these decentralizations occurred [in 1990] in the Soviet Union, where enterprises were granted widespread autonomy to trade directly with foreign partners without intermediation of the foreign trade organizations. The international payments system employed by the country was not revamped accordingly, however, and partly because of this failing the Soviet Union soon fell deeply into arrears on its foreign debt. This incident affords but one illustration, among many that could be cited, of a much debated and very thorny problem: how to sequence the various liberalizing reforms that are required to convert a centrally planned economy into a market economy. Although the issue is too complex to be treated comprehensively in this article, we can at least explore some approaches to reform, continuing to concentrate on the realm of international trade and payments.

What Next? Some General Considerations

Many issues of economic policy are too complex to allow unambiguously correct diagnosis and prescriptions to be drawn from the corpus of economic theory and experience. And on the question of the sequencing – including the speed – of liberalizing reforms, would-be analysts and policymakers soon discover that the accumulated knowledge to which they can appeal is extremely limited. As was stated in a recent publication of the International Monetary Fund[3], "There is no theory of the transition from a centrally planned to a market economy. Nor are there yet examples of centrally planned economies that have successfully made such a transition."

With so little guidance from both theory and experience it seems appropriate to begin with the hypothesis that liberalization should be introduced quickly rather than being phased in gradually, sector by sector. If it is true, as widely believed, that centrally planned economies have suffered from the government controls that pervade their economies, the remedy would seem to relax those controls immediately, just as one would remove a straitjacket. The IMF makes the case as follows:

> For a number of reasons, a rapid implementation of market-oriented reforms may be preferable to a gradual approach. The more rapid the reforms, the less those who benefitted from the old system and other interest groups will be able to obstruct or slow the implementations of the reform program. In addition, public consensus in support of reform...can best be maintained by ensuring that the tangible benefits of reform become visible as soon as possible. There is no convincing argument that the transitional costs of structural reform would be reduced if the reform process were prolonged or delayed . . . .
>
> The transitional costs . . . will . . . depend on the expectations of market participants . . . and on the credibility of the policy itself. . . . The credibility of an economic reform package, and hence the probability of it succeeding, is likely to be greater if it is comprehensive. Given the linkages in the economy, comprehensive reform increases the likelihood that each element of the program will reinforce other elements. Moreover, comprehensive reform helps ensure that the costs and benefits of economic transformation are broadly shared rather than concentrated on specific segments of society. . . .
>
> In practice, of course, everything cannot be done at once, and even a rapid approach to reform will involve shortrun choices concerning the pace of implementation of specific measures. . . . It would seem to be particularly important . . . that the establishment of macroeconomic stability and institutional changes such as modifications to the legal system, the creation of social safety nets,

---

[3] IMF, 1990, May, p. 70

and the establishment of financial discipline on [government] enterprises be emphasized at an early stage.[4]

This is one of the most cogent and succinct statements of the case for rapid liberalization. From this and other arguments, it seems clear that strong public support will be a crucial condition for success. Such support must extend to tolerance of occasional errors committed by well-intentioned policymakers who have the courage to embark on these uncharted waters, and tolerance of at least temporary reductions in income for many who will become exposed to more intense competitions as government intervention is reduced.

To forestall harsh opposition from those disadvantages by the reforms, the beneficiaries may have to contribute heavily to unemployment benefits, retraining programs, and the like. Even in wealthy market economies, it is uncommon for significant income-redistributing liberalizations to be introduced precipitously and without compensation for those distressed. Tariff reductions, for example, are generally phased in over several years so as to allow the adversely affected to make an orderly adjustment, and – at least in the United States – have been accompanied by generous adjustment assistance.

While most liberalizing countries may well decide against the immediate adoption of free trade, an early and substantial relaxation of controls over international trade and payments is probably critical to the rapid development of competitive markets. It is likely to take some time for markets to flourish within these countries and to establish relative prices that channel resources with great efficiency. In particular, monopolistic government enterprises cannot be broken down into smaller units and converted to private ownership in the twinkling of an eye. In the meantime enhanced foreign competition can exert a salutary discipline on these enterprises.

The opening up of trade will introduce the competitive price structure – or set of relative prices – that predominates for goods traded throughout the rest of the world. The importance of this reform can hardly be exaggerated. A key impediment to economic progress within the CMEA was an inappropriate allocation of resources (including, of course, human effort), as central planners failed to perform this allocative function as well as competitive markets. It is world prices to which the liberalizing economies must adapt if they are to reap the benefits of integration with the international economy.

---

[4] *Ibid*, p. 71

The Issue of Convertibility: A Payments Union?

As already noted, it has been the practice within centrally planned economies to restrict the use of the domestic currency, both for the purchase of domestic goods and for the purchase of foreign currencies. Until these countries allow their currencies to be exchanged freely for goods and for foreign currencies, their domestic prices will fail to reflect world prices, and the inefficiencies associated with this failing will persist. In addition to the inefficiencies already mentioned, foreign investment in the centrally planned economies has been greatly discouraged by the obstacles that prevent investors from earning and repatriating profits in convertible currencies.

In the typical country whose currency is inconvertible, many domestic prices are lower than would be the case with convertibility and efficiency. Indeed, one of the purposes of inconvertibility is to assist the government in suppressing prices below their free market levels. By restricting the use of the domestic currency to purchase foreign exchange, the authorities limit any bidding up of the price of foreign exchange, and of the domestic currency price of foreign goods, by those who would like to enter the market. This practice, of course, contributes to the widespread shortages, queues, and black markets.

Suddenly to allow convertibility and the associated free-market determination of prices would be to risk a sharp depreciation of the country's currency in the foreign-exchange market (or rapid exhaustion of the foreign-exchange reserves that the government could supply to the market in an effort to prevent the depreciation), a quantum leap in the general price level, and a marked rise in unemployment as the changing prices rendered many lines of activity less viable. These consequences are not idle fears but have in fact materialized in more than one country undertaking liberalization.

Seeking ways to minimize such transitional costs, many analysts have stressed the importance of pursuing anti-inflationary policies and of reforming the laws on private property, taxation, and commerce to provide a seedbed for private enterprise prior to any substantial liberalization. Others, doubting the adequacy of such measures, have proposed that the East European countries should ease the transition to freer international trade and payments by following the example of West European countries after World War II: they should form a payments union designed not only to conserve their scarce foreign-exchange reserves but also to transform their system of predominantly bilateral balanced into one of multilateral balancing, with the transformation occurring gradually over a period of years and culminating in full currency convertibility. The balance of this paper examines this proposal and finds its wanting, in spite of its cosmetic appeal.

Eastern and Western Europe: Historical Analogies

The reference to postwar Western Europe is intriguing, because the situation of the East European countries today is in many respects similar to that of their West European neighbors shortly after World War II. At controlled prices and exchange rates, shortages were widespread in Western Europe. To insure that their limited supplies of convertible foreign exchange would be used to acquire goods deemed essential, governments in the area generally exercised tight control over international trade and payments. Trade carried on by government monopolies could, of course, be regulated directly, just as in the centrally planned economies. Trade by private parties was controlled through the issuance of licenses authorizing the exportation or importation of specified quantities or values of merchandise.

International payments were regulated by exchange controls administered through the banking system. Businessmen were to sell to their domestic banks the foreign exchange they earned from foreigners, and they might buy foreign exchange from the banks for authorized purposes. If a commercial bank ran low on foreign exchange demanded by customers for approved transactions, the bank could acquire more at the country's central bank, while a commercial bank that accumulated excess foreign exchange could sell it to the central bank.

In order to avoid incurring deficits on their international transactions that would have drained their foreign-exchange reserves and stifled their trade, the countries of Western Europe entered into bilateral trade and payments agreements with one another, just as the CMEA countries did. Such an agreement specified the trade to be permitted between the two signatories and the exchange rate between their currencies.

Of course, in the event, trade between the parties to these agreements was less than perfectly balanced, and as a practical matter could not have been balanced on a daily basis. To allow for such imbalances, each central bank maintained an account with overdraft privileges at the other country's central bank. A central bank that was exhausting its stock of the other country's money could draw overdraft on the other's central bank; the drawing bank would then credit an equivalent amount in its own currency to the foreign central bank These overdrafts provided a "swing" that accommodated temporary imbalances, just as additional governmentally owned foreign exchange would have done.

A central bank on which overdrafts were drawn was, of course, extending credit, accepting in return deposit balances in the other country's currency. As these balances mounted, negotiations would commence on how the imbalance in trade might be eliminated or reversed or on how much of the debtor country indebtedness (that is, of its currency held by creditor's central bank) would be paid off in gold or in some currency acceptable to the creditor. To avoid accumulating balances of inconvertible currencies, a West European country was inclined to discriminate in favor of imports from the countries with which it was running trade surpluses. Again the parallel with the CMEA is clear.

The European Payments Union

In an effort to reduce this incentive for bilateral balancing, the West European nations embarked on an historic international financial arrangement known as the European Payments Union (EPU). Established in September 1950, the EPU functioned through December 1958. Because it fostered the revival of multinationalism in trade and payments among the countries of Western Europe, it became a model for proposed regional payments arrangements among countries with inconvertible currencies – including, most recently, an arrangement for Eastern Europe.

The rules and procedures of the EPU were complex and were modified as time went by, and only some of the salient features are summarized here. The cornerstone of the EPU was multilateral rather than bilateral settlement of payments imbalances among the members. As before, each member's central bank stood ready to lend its own currency to other member central banks in order to satisfy the demand for that currency at the agreed exchange rates. Each month the net amount of such lending or borrowing by every member vis-a-vis all the other members as a group was tallied by the Bank for International Settlements and recorded as a claim on or debt to the Union, expressed in an agreed unit of account. This procedure economized on the use of scarce foreign-exchange reserves and diminished the proclivity for bilateral balancing, since each country could offset a deficit with another country or countries with any surpluses it might have with still other countries. Confidence was inspired by the fact that each country's net claims or net debt were now with the Union rather than with other individual countries, meaning that credit risks were assumed by the group as a whole. Interest was paid to creditors and collected from debtors at rates rising with the duration of the debt.

Once a country's net debt to or claims on the Union exceeded the limit calculated by an agreed formula, the country was to make or receive settlement in gold or dollars for at least part of the excess. As time passed the requirements for settlement in gold or dollars was stiffened, a modification that put greater pressure on chronic deficit countries to reduce their overall deficits and also reduced the incentive to discriminate against imports from non-Union countries settling payments in convertible currencies, primarily the United States.

It is noteworthy that the liberalizing intent of the West European countries was manifested in 1950 not only by the establishment of the EPU but also by the initiation of a program to reduce nonmonetary barriers to trade within Western Europe. In October of that year the West European countries agreed to eliminate quantitative restrictions in a nondiscriminatory fashion from at least three-fifths of their imports from one another. Import quotas were further relaxed in subsequent years.

Despite the good intentions, the transitions to convertibility was neither rapid nor uninterrupted. Early on, both the trade liberalization program and the credit facilities of the EPU were tested by large payments imbalances. The West European countries met the challenge largely by increasing the amounts to be loaned and borrowed under the aegis of the EPU, and by adapting the pace of trade liberalization (reversing it for deficit countries and accelerating it for surplus countries), thereby buying time for other balance-of-payments adjustment measures to take effect. Also, the claims on, and debts to, the Union of some countries were converted into claims on and debts to other individual members. Without such flexibility the EPU would surely have foundered.

Progress toward convertibility was facilitated not only by this flexibility but also by U.S. aid and large overall deficits in the U.S. balance of payments. The counterpart of much of these deficits was an increase in the gold and dollar reserves of West European central banks. As these reserve stocks mounted, their holders became more disposed to making sales from them in exchange for their native currencies.

Thus, some eight years after the founding of the EPU – on December 27, 1958 – the major step toward formal convertibility was at last taken. Belgium, Luxembourg, France, Italy, the Netherlands, the United Kingdom, and West Germany, soon followed by other West European nations, announced that their currencies would be convertible for foreign residents. A nonresident of any one of these countries who earned its currency in a current-account transaction (such as exporting) could thereafter freely sell that currency in exchange for any other currency, including dollars, at the officially supported rates of exchange. Having performed its function, the EPU was then terminated.

A Model for Eastern Europe?

From this capsule review, it is clear that the EPU was successful, albeit slow, in dealing with some of the same maladies that have afflicted the East European countries, although the dislocations within the EPU economies originated chiefly in a devastating way rather than in the failure of central planning. Maladies common to both sets of countries have included a perceived shortage of convertible foreign-exchange reserves, bilateral balancing of international trade, foreign exchange-rates and internal prices distorted by controls, and inconvertible domestic currencies. If, as widely believed, the EPU materially assisted its members in overcoming these ailments, should the East European countries establish a similar union?

Despite the similarities between some of the problems faced by the countries of the EPU and Eastern Europe, closer scrutiny reveals differences that raise serious doubts about the usefulness of a payments union for Eastern Europe. To begin with, the EPU embraced a much wider trading area, and accounted for a much greater share of the members' total trade, than is true of the East European countries likely to favor a payments union. Proposals for an East European Payments Union (EEPU) have generally contemplated including Bulgaria, Czechoslovakia, the German Democratic Republic, Hungary, Poland, Romania, and the Soviet Union. Now, of course, the German Democratic Republic is no more; and the Soviet Union might well remain outside an EEPU, largely because, as a member, it would likely encounter requests for substantial ongoing credit from other members, especially as they begin to pay for Soviet oil in convertible currency at something like world prices.

Moreover, as the record clearly shows, past actions and relationships within the CMEA would be a poor foundation on which to begin the construction of a liberal trade and payments regime. In particular, a multilateral payments system could have been developed within the CMEA around the modifications of the International Bank for Economic Cooperation (IBEC) and the transferable ruble, but the opportunity went unexploited. The IBEC could have played a role similar to that of the Bank for International Settlements in facilitating multilateral rather than bilateral settlements, and the transferable among CMEA members in exchange for goods. Now the erstwhile CMEA members are liberalizing at widely differing paces, and some have already introduced a high degree of currency convertibility. If history offers any guide, to combine them into a payments union would be to run a high risk of slowing the pace of overall liberalization to that of the most reluctant members.

Finally, during the years of the EPU, central banks generally strove to restrain exchange-rate movements within very narrow ranges, while today many exchange rates are allowed to move much more freely under the influence of market forces. Were the East European countries to tolerate relatively free movement of their currency exchange rates in open markets, they would both establish convertibility for their currencies and obviate the need for complex and dubious transitional mechanisms such as payment unions. Of course, for exchange rates to settle at levels that reflect domestic market equilibrium prices, prices within Eastern Europe must be substantially freed from controls – as some of the countries have recently done – and measures supporting the development of free markets must be promptly introduced. To ease this difficult transition, industries that are particularly vulnerable to newly encountered foreign competition might be granted temporary tariff protection, to be phased out according to a well-publicized schedule.

Conclusion

Current experience is demonstrating that the transition from a centrally planned to a relatively free market economy is far from costless. However, the cost represents an investment that should yield immense returns in the longer run. Crucial to a rapid transition is the adoption of relatively liberal foreign trade and payments arrangements, including a high degree of currency convertibility.

A clear and present danger is that the countries undertaking the transition will fail to follow through as the adjustment costs materialize. State enterprises and controls have proved a livelihood for many who will resist their demise. Nonetheless, market-oriented systems will probably be adopted eventually in view of their demonstrated superiority, and countries that falter in their reforms may therefore merely prolong their agony.

28. Is a "Marshall Plan" Needed for Eastern Europe?*

P.B.W. Rayment

The Marshall Aid programme, provided 16 west European countries with some $12.4 billion over four years or roughly $3.1 billion a year. In 1989 prices this is the equivalent to $65.4 billion, or $16.4 billion a year.

In order to provide some scale to the numbers involved, suppose that a western aid programme for the eastern countries were based on this figure of $42 per head. Then, on the basis of 1989 estimates of population, total aid for the six east European countries would be around $4.8 billion a year: if the Soviet Union were included the total would be nearly $16.7 billion a year. This last figure is thus only slightly higher than the original Marshall aid programme adjusted for price changes.

Recently the President of the European Commission of European Communities provided some idea of the scale of aid he thought might be provided to eastern Europe.[1] He suggested that if the six eastern European countries were given the same support as provided by the Community to its own depressed regions, then the Community's budget would require an additional ECU 14 billion per year for the next 5-10 years, depending on the pace of transformation in the eastern countries. In addition a further ECU 5 billion a year would be needed for the European Investment bank. Such a level of assistance would amount to roughly $23 billion a year, which is nearly 5 times larger than the Marshall Plan equivalent for the six countries quoted above. In fact the EC proposal would be more than one third larger than the Marshall Plan equivalent for all the eastern countries (i.e., including the Soviet Union). Since the programme suggested by the EC President could run 5-10 years, his proposal would be some 6-10 times larger than the original Marshall Plan adjusted for price changes.

---

* From the *Economic Survey of Europe, 1989-90*, a United Nations publication. Reprinted by permission of the United Nations, New York.

[1] Address given by Jacques Delors to the European Parliament, "Presenting the Commissions Programme for 1990," Strasbourg, 17 January 1990, (EC press release).

In terms of western GDP/GNP these are not very large numbers: $16.4 billion, the Marshall plan at US prices of 1989, is only about 0.3 percent of either US GNP or the European Community's GDP – for the United States, the EC and Japan combined it would be just over 0.1 percent of GDP. Mr Delors' proposal of $23 billion would amount to some 0.45 percent of the Community's GDP in 1989.

However, the important question is not so much whether the western countries can afford a "Marshall Plan" on this scale but whether the eastern countries can absorb it. Throughout the 1970s, the eastern countries borrowed heavily from the west, gross debt rising by some $64 billion in eastern Europe between 1970 and 1981 and in the Soviet Union by over $27 billion. This inflow of resources, which for eastern Europe on an annual basis is considerably less than the sum suggested by Mr. Delors, appears to have had little impact on structural change and productive efficiency in eastern economies.[2] One of the objectives of the radical changes now under way in the political and economic systems of the eastern countries is, of course, to obtain a marked improvement in economic performance. This will require, *inter alia*, a greatly increased capacity to adopt new technologies throughout their economies. However improving such absorptive capacities requires fundamental changes in economic structures and in the behaviour of economic agents. These changes take time and there is no reason to suppose that the capacity of the eastern economies to absorb western resources on the scale described above has radically improved in the last year or so.

A crucial and fundamental difference between the transformation facing east European countries in 1945 and those facing eastern countries today is that the former did not have to reconstruct market economies from first principles. Although the free workings of the market mechanism were overridden or suspended in many countries for part, or most of the war, it was generally quite clear that this was a temporary state of affairs based on pragmatic considerations about how to focus activity on achieving a number of well-defined and limited objectives. A clear system of property rights remained in place and after the war enterprises were free to seek access to

---

[2] For this reason, and despite the need to re-equip industry, a cautious approach to foreign borrowing in the future has been advocated in the Soviet Union. Eduard Gostev, Deputy Chairman of Vneshekonombank, noted early in 1989 that some of the equipment purchased years ago by the Soviet Union had not in fact ever been installed. He also stated that some 2.7 billion rubles ($4.4 billion) worth of goods purchased with convertible currency had been wasted in recent years. *International Herald Tribune*, 31 January 1989.

foreign markets. Although there was argument over the extent to which governments should intervene to correct deficiencies in the workings of the market mechanism, there was a general consensus that the wartime planning systems would not be able to cope with the multifarious demands of a decentralised system in which consumers are ultimately sovereign. It should also be noted that the basic incentive structure of the market system was constrained by wartime planning in market economies; entrepreneurs still had incentives to improve efficiency and this contributed to the savings overhang at the end of the war. It also helps to account for the rapid response of domestic investment to the bottlenecks and other shortages of the immediate post-war years.

The basic system of economic organization which had prevailed in the Soviet Union since the late 1920s and in eastern Europe from the early 1950 is very different. The main features of that system may be recalled briefly: the central plan is the main instrument of policy and basically decides what individual enterprises should produce. Prices are determined bureaucratically and are used very little as an instrument of planning: producer prices have little influence on resource allocation, and the level and pattern of investment is allocated according to the priorities of the plan rather than the perceptions of enterprises as to profitable opportunities: consumer prices pay some attention to demand insofar as turnover taxes are supposed to be set at rates which would adjust demand to available supplies, which are determined by the central plan. Prices are based on average rather than marginal costs and therefore are unreliable as indicators of true social costs. Moreover, in practice, prices have remained unchanged for long periods and this has contributed to severe shortages. In the traditional model trade policy was essentially autarkic and foreign trade, which was monopolized by the state, was seen as meeting the residual needs of the system. The whole system was enclosed in a state where party, state and economic hierarchies were intermeshed but where one-party supervision was predominant.

The incentive structure of this system is such that micro-inefficiency is widespread and responsible for the endemic shortage which characterizes the planned economies. More fundamentally, enterprises will not be active in adopting new technologies and raising efficiency simply because there is no incentive to do so. The incentive structure, which reflects the restricted, non-allocative role of prices, also means that new enterprises cannot be set up in response to profitable opportunities and the failures of the established concerns. Entry and exit of firms is controlled by the plan and industrial structures tend to be dominated by large and inefficient and inflexible enterprises. In general, the widespread failures on the supply side have provided enterprises with strong incentives to meet their own need for intermediate goods; this, in turn, has led to a lack of specialization, overstocking (hoarding materials, etc.), and a lowering of efficiency throughout the productive system.

Attempts to remedy the deficiencies of this model have been made more or less continuously since the late 1950s. At first – and in some countries always – reform was concentrated on improving the traditional model, especially in regard to improving enterprise incentives (for example, replacing gross output targets with various bonus-setting indicators or even some degree of profit), but the basic sovereignty of the planners over the price mechanism was not in question. More radical reforms have been introduced in some east European countries since the late 1960s, and especially in Hungary which in 1968 introduced a significant degree of decentralization into the economic system. However, all of these reforms failed to alter significantly the behavioural patterns of enterprise. Most of the reforms before 1989 still left the central authorities with considerable powers to control and influence the economic behaviour of individual enterprises. Because of the close relationship between the political and the economic structures, reforms were always checked at the point where any further change in the system of economic management would challenge the establish interests of the party hierarchy. This is why the events of 1989 represent a radical break with the past: the end of one-party rule opens up the possibility of establishing decentralized market economies were the principal (but not necessarily only) economic role of government is to pursue macro-economic goals using the indirect methods of fiscal and monetary policy. This is now a stated objective in Czechoslovakia, the German Democratic Republic, Hungary and Poland.

The transformation of a centrally planned economy into a decentralized market economy of the western (or more broadly, the OECD) variety is both a precise and a vague concept; it is precise in terms of the general direction which is to be pursued but vague as to the precise destination. Indeed, from both the policy and analytical points of view the whole transformation issue is largely uncharted territory. It is often overlooked even by many economic agents in the market economies, that the actual functioning of markets and market economies depends on a detailed infrastructure of property rights, corporate and non-corporate, an extensive array of specialized financial institutions, regulations and regulatory bodies, labour law and procedures for settling disputes, and so on. Much of this infrastructure is embodied in institutions, but important elements are embodied in the conventions of business practice. Although all the leading market economies today share a number of basic characteristics, especially concerning the role of the price mechanism and decentralized decision-making the ways in which they arrange the details of the market infrastructure vary both as to style and to the relative importance attached to the different elements. Moreover, most of the market economies have shown considerable capacity to adapt their institutions and behavioural conventions to changing circumstances. Beyond a number of core elements, there is no single, homogenous model of a market economy. Thus, as a policy objective, the transformation of a centrally planned economy into a market economy is more a statement of general principle, than a detailed programme of action. The latter requires a detailed specification of how institutions should be changed or constructed, and how the behavior of individuals and enterprises should be adapted.

This discussion suggests that if policy makers are considering the Marshall Plan as a model for western assistance the appropriate thing to do is to turn it upside down. The entire structure of institutions and economic incentives in the eastern countries today is radically different from those in western Europe in 1948 and the capacity of the east to absorb new capital and technology has recently shown to be very limited. Whereas the Marshall Plan was long on aid and short on technical assistance, western aid to eastern Europe, at least initially, should reverse their relative importance.

Detailed proposals for technical assistance could be drawn up by the eastern countries themselves in the light of the particular arrangements that they consider will best suit their own preferences and traditions. In this the western countries should perhaps follow the wisdom of the Marshall Plan in leaving it to the recipient country to draw up its own programme for its transition to a market economy and to indicate the types of technical assistance required. In practice, assistance from western experts or international institutions may be desirable in preparing these programmes; not only can they help in identifying worthwhile projects but they can also advise on the appropriate presentation of submissions to western governments and international bodies. (ECA staff played a similar role in the formulation of requests for Marshall aid). Such programmes could also indicate needs for financial assistance, although it would be necessary to show that it could be effectually absorbed. By establishing some links between absorptive capacity, technical assistance and financial aid it might be possible to avoid one of the weaknesses of the Marshall aid programme, namely, that it did not do enough to strengthen incentives to better performance. Such links would also mean that the need for financial assistance would be derived from a coherent programme for solving specific problems rather than the sort of contingent arithmetic presented earlier.

Many suggestions have already been made as to the type of technical assistance that need to be provided to the east; management training and expertise in specific technologies are most often mentioned. However, what is less frequently referred to – but which the discussion above suggests should be given priority – is the infrastructure of market behaviour. The transformation of a planned economy into a market economy requires a major change in the rules according to which a society conducts its economic activity. The people who are expert in analysing such rules and assessing their impact on economic behaviour are not businessmen[3] or technologists, but economists, political theorists, anti-trust lawyers and some central bankers. The market economies and the international economic organizations are relatively well-endowed with such people and their advice and assistance in the early stages of the transformation process could be invaluable. Western specialists who are also familiar with the systemic problems of the eastern economies could make an especially valuable contribution. The assistance and advice of such western experts is important because they are the people who are also most familiar with the nature and causes of market failure[4] in the market economies.

In the public discussions of the possibilities of market economies in eastern Europe it is not always emphasized enough that the efficiency gains of a decentralized market system depend on the degree of competition in capital and labour markets. In the traditional neo-classical theory the superiority of market solutions rests on perfect competition and Pareto optimality. Since real-world markets are usually far from satisfying the optimality conditions of perfect competition, it follows that government intervention to improve the efficiency of markets can never be excluded on *a priori* grounds. In practice western governments have adopted numerous policies to deal with market failure, ranging from nationalization to competition policy. Since the early 1970s, however, the emphasis has been on making markets more competitive.

These are not academic points which can be brushed aside in the urgency of "getting things done." The east European economies at the present time, and irrespective of their location on the path towards a market economy, are

---

[3] A businessman qua businessman is no more an expert on the rules of a market economy than is a chauffeur on the physics of the internal combustion engine.

[4] Market failure principally arises from the presence of monopolies, externalities or public goods.

characterized by numerous distortions: markets are segmented and inefficient; markets structures tend to be monopolistic or, at best, oligopolistic; market and economic information is sparse and/or inaccurate. Given the large suppressed demand for consumer goods, these are ideal conditions for domestic (and foreign) enterprises to make super-normal profits once the price system is freed from control. These might be tolerated as a short-run phenomenon while a competitive market structure was being constructed, but there will always be a risk of strong social reaction to "profiteering" which could harm the process of reform. Such reactions were evident [in 1990] in the Soviet Union where there was considerable popular criticism of the prices charged and profits made by some co-operatives.

Similar caution is in order when rapid rates of privatization are proposed. The analysis of western experience in this area stresses the crucial importance of competition in order for the potential gains in efficiency to be realized. A change in ownership may simply transform a public monopoly into a private one, although the private managers will probably be better paid than when they were in the public sector. In the eastern countries there are major problems in establishing correct estimates of net worth when there are no efficient capital markets and when accounting rules bear little relation to those in a functioning market economy. In such circumstances there is a consider-able risk that social assets will be sold off at prices which would imply large transfers of wealth, either to the old managers and to former members of the *nomenklatura* or to newcomers from the west.

Foreign enterprises can play an important role in increasing the level of competition in the sectors in which they operate, in transferring technology, modern management techniques and so on. Many eastern governments recognize the advantages of opening their economies to foreign companies and are seeking to attract them by changing joint-venture and other relevant legislation. However, the rush to attract foreign investment into eastern Europe could be premature if a competitive market framework is still far from completion. It is a mistake to believe that all market economy enterprises require a competitive market economy in which to operate. As long as they have security of title to their assets and guarantees of profit repatriation, foreign enterprises like sportsmen, will be happy to play according to whatever rules are in place. If markets are not competitive, there can be no presumption that the activities of foreign companies will automatically contribute to a more efficient use of resources.

Many of the supply-side policies adopted by market economies in the 1970s were focused on deregulation and increasing competition. There is considerable expertise on these matters, both in official (national and international) institutions and in the law and economics faculties of the universities, on which the eastern countries can easily draw. There is also a variety of experience among the market economies which increases the chance of individual eastern countries finding policies and techniques which are in line with their own particular preferences and situation. A technical assistance programme could easily set up ways for the east to obtain expert advice in this area. It will not be expensive and in the long-run returns could be very high. Following OECD experience in this area, it can be very useful to discuss, compare and monitor the structural adjustment policies in individual countries in an international forum which can bring together all the donors and all the recipients of assistance.

Technical assistance will also be needed to set up a variety of financial institutions (clearing and investment banks, insurance and investment funds) which are vital for the efficient working of a market economy. There is an abundance of specialized technical expertise in all of these areas in the west, upon which the east may easily draw. However, because the possibilities are numerous, it might be wise to use first the more general advisers mentioned in the previous paragraphs to obtain guidance as to the types of institutions and financial expertise which are likely to be best suited to the particular needs and circumstances of individual eastern countries.

Another area which should be given high priority because of its importance to the efficient functioning of a market economy is statistics. The state of eastern statistics has been the subject of much comment, both in eastern and western publications. Much of this comment has focused on the poor coverage or inaccuracy of the published figures. The extent to which the latter is due to bias in the reporting systems, to defective methodology or to deliberate falsifications is difficult to determine. The fact is that there are major deficiencies in the existing set of official statistics; these shortcomings have recently been officially acknowledged in many of the eastern countries. However, an efficient market economy needs not only accurate statistics but different types of statistics from a centrally planned economy. In the first place, macro economic policy in a market economy relies in the main on various instruments of fiscal and monetary policy, rather than direct controls, and, as such, requires a different data set to that used by the central planner; some of the statistics, particularly in the monetary field, will only be generated, of course, after the relevant institutional changes have occurred. Second, reliable statistics (as well as other economic and commercial information) becomes essential to individual enterprises as they move from a command system to one where they must take their own decisions on output and investment in response to market signals. In the west, private enterprises often invest in collecting their own data based on sample surveys but a considerable amount of market information is culled from official statistics.

The reforming economies of eastern Europe will also require statistics to monitor their progress toward a market economy and to track the adjustment of economic behaviour to the new systems of incentives. Such data will be necessary for the effective adjustment of particular policies, but they may also be required by foreign donors of financial aid and technical assistance. In this context the institution of business surveys, as conducted by business organizations or research institutions in the west, could make a useful contribution.

It should be emphasized that the provision of comprehensive and reliable economic statistics is not simply a service to the business sector but a public good which makes a crucial contribution to the working of a market economy.[5] Moreover the provision of such statistics is essential for the closer integration of the eastern countries into the world economy; not only are they required for conducting international business at the enterprise level, but they are also a condition of membership of the Bretton Woods institutions.[6]

Statistics (including market research and related activities for enterprises) is thus another priority area where technical assistance could be speedily effective in helping to meet the requirements of the eastern countries. Once the needs for technical assistance are clear, a well-defined programme of financial assistance could easily follow (perhaps to provide PCs, computer software, etc.).

To summarize, it has been argued that despite a number of close similarities between the problems facing the western countries in 1945-1948 and those confronting the reforming eastern economies in 1990, the differences in the infrastructure of the two economic systems and in the capacity to absorb foreign financial aid are so large that it would be a mistake to assume that a repeat of the 1948 Marshall Plan would be a suitable western response

---

[5] "Perfect information," it will be recalled, is one of the optimality conditions of the neo-classical argument for the market economy. A respectable "free market" case can therefore be made for subsidizing the price at which official statistics are sold.

[6] [Editor's note: The Bretton Woods institutions are the World Bank Group and the International Monetary Fund, established as a result of the 1944 conference of World War II allies held at Bretton Woods, New Hampshire.]

to current eastern problems. For present purposes the structure of the original Marshall Plan should be turned upside down so that technical rather than direct financial assistance becomes the major component. The Marshall Plan could be imitated by encouraging recipient countries to draw up their own assistance needs in a coherent programme, but it is suggested that high priority should be given to technical assistance for (a) constructing the legal, financial, and institutional infrastructure essential for a competitive market system and (b) providing a comprehensive and reliable statistical service for both government and enterprises in their new roles in a decentralized market economy. It is not suggested that these two priority areas should "crowd out" or delay other innovations. Institutional reform must clearly proceed on a fairly broad front; for example, the decentralization of investment decisions from the central plan to individual enterprises will obviously require the creation of capital markets and stock exchanges. Similarly it will not be difficult to draw up long lists of candidates for technical assistance, from training and education in subjects such as economics, accountancy and statistics to the essentials of marketing and selling. But it is because the list of desirable projects is long that choices will have to be made, if for no other reason than not everything can be done at once. The top priorities mentioned here were selected because not only are they necessary conditions for *efficient* market systems but in the market economies they are so often taken for granted that they are frequently overlooked.

PART IX

THE POLITICS OF ECONOMIC REFORM

In the transformation of an entire economic system, political and economic issues are necessarily closely linked and the five readings in this section address some of the political dimensions.

One important question is why all previous attempts at reform in the Soviet-type economies (STEs) have failed, although the current centrally planned system is so manifestly inefficient. Jan Winiecki's "Why Economic Reforms Fail in Soviet-Type Systems," addresses this issue.

Winiecki's argument is that in a Soviet type economy (STE) there is a fundamental conflict between the development of property rights that lower transactions costs, and therefore contribute efficiently to economic growth and the general welfare, and the existing set of rights that maximize the earnings of the party *apparatchiks* and the ruling bureaucracy. This group is highly resistant to change towards a market system, or indeed any hardening of the budget constraint, because the avenues for extracting wealth through corruption would be severely constrained.

Consequently, although a small ruling group at the very peak of society might conceive of appropriate reforms to restore incentives, and therefore to maximize the output of the whole system, these very reforms threaten the interests of *apparatchiks* throughout the system, who then act in order to derail the reforms.

Winiecki's argument was, of course, developed in the context of a one-party system and indeed it is the Communist Party that proved the biggest enemy of reform. The open question, unanswered in this article, is whether or not the former party bosses still have the power to derail reform in a situation where the party has ceased to exist. There is a great deal of evidence that although stripped of their party standing, power in industry and in the countryside remains in the hands of the same individuals, who retain incentives to destroy reforms that will threaten their own unofficial incomes.

In "Perestroika from Below," Philip Hanson addresses some of these issues. Writing before the "counter-revolution" of August 1991, and the subsequent

292

demise of the Soviet Union, he sees more favorable evidence of a reform from below than above. At a time when the Gorbachev administration was dithering about drastic reform, Hanson identified important change in city and local government (where one official wanted to replace Lenin's portrait with that of Milton Friedman), in the growth of small-scale private enterprise, and the establishment of an independent business press.

The residents of Russia and the other republics that now comprise the Commonwealth of Independent States have not experienced market institutions in their lifetime. A natural question, therefore, is whether these people have enough knowledge of how markets work, and perhaps more importantly, enough understanding of the resultant inequality to tolerate the transformation. Looking at a series of opinion polls, Hanson sees a great tolerance for markets and market institutions, including the privatization of land.

Hanson also finds signs that the old *nomenklatura* is at least in part transforming itself with some success into a new bureaucracy. This has important implications for Winiecki's somewhat pessimistic views on the ability of the old bureaucracy to block reform. If the members of the old party machinery see a chance to succeed as bankers or industrialists they may well favor the new property rights that result from reform and abandon their old claims to income from kickback and corruption.

In "Popular Attitudes Toward Free Markets: The Soviet Union and the United States Compared," Robert Shiller, a Yale economist, collaborated with Maxim Boycko, a Russian economist, and Vladimir Korobov, a Russian sociologist, to devise and administer a questionnaire to assess the similarities and differences in economic attitudes between the populations of Moscow and New York. The results are somewhat surprising and indicate that probably too much prominence has been given to the differences of attitude between Russians and residents of market economies. However, that does not mean that the Russian population as a whole is inclined to be tolerant of the large price changes that are necessarily occurring in the transformation. What the data show rather is that New Yorkers would be prone to resist *perestroika* if they faced the same set of problems as the Russians.

A visitor to Eastern Europe today is immediately struck by the low esteem in which the Communist regime is held. Viewed in hindsight the revolutions that swept the then Communist Bloc in 1989 seem entirely inevitable. Why then is it that few predicted them, or at least few foresaw the speed with which it happened? In "Is It Surprising that We Were Surprised?" Timur Kuran offers an explanation in terms of *preference falsification*. Under the Communist regimes it paid to appear to support the government; any form of dissent could bring punishment or at least the loss of privileges. Faking behavior in this way, however, produced internal costs; militant dissidents found the internal price of living "outside the truth" too great. However, for many the cost of being less than true to one's own ideals was smaller than the gain of privileges.

Kuran shows that relatively small shifts in some individual's preferences can have far reaching effects. A few more people honestly declare their preferences, which increases the internal cost of lying for some and also reduces the expected value of benefits of loyalty to the old regime. That in turn prompts more people to declare their true preferences – and so on, until the popular pressure is enough to dislodge the old regime.

Now of course preference falsification works in reverse. No one will now own up to having supported the old regime out of anything more than expediency. It pays everyone to pretend that they were overt or closet democrats, because advancement in the new order will be a function of opposition to the old. Thus, Kuran's somewhat disturbing conclusion is that just as everyone appeared to be a Communist in the old regime, everyone appears to be a democrat now, and neither represents the truth. Preference falsification continues to exist and the road back to an accepted totalitarian regime is not as long as it now appears.

Now that the Soviet Union is no more, even the title of Philip Hanson's second piece in this section, "Soviet Economic Futures," seems anachronistic. However, the issues that he addresses are still current – what will the shape of the former Soviet Union be in a few years, and into the next century? Despairing of precise predictions, Hanson chooses to draw scenarios, broad outlines of the future that differ from each other in terms of fundamental assumptions. These scenarios are *Severe Fragmentation, Benign Fragmentation, Back To the Future* (a restoration of the old centrally planned system), *The Pinochet Version* (a market system under a totalitarian government), and *The Pollyanna, or Harvard, Version* (in which the Soviet Union successfully mutates into a balanced, democratic federal state). Although the Union is no more, none of these outcomes is necessarily ruled out, although both a restoration of the old union under hard-line communist leadership (the aim of the August 1991 coup) and the establishment of a market-oriented society under an all-union military dictatorship look less likely.

29. Why Economic Reforms Fail in Soviet-Type Systems[*]

Jan Winiecki

[This paper identifies] the membership and motives of groups having strong incentives to keep the STEs [Soviet-type economies] inefficient and prevent successful (i.e., market-oriented) reforms. We show how those groups operate, and analyze their effects on the economic performance of their countries. First the incentives for these groups to prevent decentralized management in the state sector are spelled out. Then, their incentives to prevent the expansion of the more efficient private sector are outlined. Third, having identified who benefits from the status quo and why, the paper discusses when and how market-oriented reforms are aborted, limited, or reversed by those who stand to gain from the reforms' failure.

Who Gains from the Status Quo and Why

Disincentives to Decentralized Management in the State Sector

Most analyses of Soviet-style systems focus excessively upon the distribution of power and neglect the distribution of wealth across the ruling stratum. By contrast, in an incentives-oriented analysis the distribution of wealth becomes the focus of attention. Power and privilege are viewed as means to acquiring wealth, and the desire to acquire wealth motivates the actions of the ruling stratum.

This shift of analytical emphasis does not mean that power and its distribution do not matter. On the contrary, the rulers of a STE may regard control over the working population as satisfying their need for power, either as an end in itself or as a means to attaining some long-run goal, such as the creation of "true communism." It is important, however, to realize that the

[*] From "Why Economic Reforms the Soviet System: A Property Rights-Based Approach." *Economic Inquiry*, vol XXVIII, no. 2, (April 1990), p. 195. Published by Western Economic Association International. Reprinted by permission of publisher and author. Some footnotes omitted.

means by which wealth is distributed is crucially important in determining the attitudes of elements in the ruling stratum toward decentralizing, market-oriented reforms. Without considering this issue, it is difficult to explain why economic reforms–badly needed by the rulers themselves to correct flagging economic performance–did not materialize or, if they did, why they failed or at best brought about very little improvement in economic circumstances.

At this point, Douglass North's explanatory framework for the structure and enforcement of property rights, as well as their changes over time, should be brought into the picture. Applying what North[1] calls a predatory theory of the state to the Soviet-type state, two, sometimes conflicting, objectives of such a state are identified:

(1)   to provide a set of public goods and services designed to lower transaction costs and increase the efficiency upon which the growth of wealth is predicated... and

(2)   to specify the fundamental rules of the property rights structure, i.e., the ownership structure in factor and product markets, in a way that maximizes the rent[2] flowing to the ruler and the ruling stratum. The fact that this structure is extremely muddled in STEs is irrelevant, since such a muddle, i.e., the dominance of non-exclusively owned resources in the state sector, actually facilitates the expropriation of rent.

The following hypotheses now arise from these considerations:

(i)   In STEs the fundamental conflict described by North, i.e., the conflict between efficient property rights designed to lower transaction costs and increase wealth and inefficient property rights designed to maximize rent to the ruling stratum, is strongly in evidence; and

(ii)   in such states the nominal ruler will avoid offending powerful groups in the ruling stratum, i.e., the *apparatchiks* and economic bureaucrats, who benefit most from the institutional and economic status quo.

---

[1] Douglas C. North, "A Framework for Analyzing the State in Economic History," in *Explorations in Economic History* , New York, NY: Academic Press Inc., July 1979, 249-259.

[2] [Editor's note: "rent" in this article means "economic rent," i.e., benefits that accrue to individuals because of their power over others or control over scarce resources, and not because of what they actually produce for society.]

In STEs the rulers agree to maintain a property rights structure favorable to those groups, regardless of the effect upon efficiency. In fact, modes of wealth distribution resulting from the STE structure of property rights differ so much from those in other pre-representative government states (i.e., traditional and "modern" autocracies), that institutional change leading to lower transaction costs and increased wealth is much more difficult to achieve. No STE, for example, has replicated the successful, efficiency-enhancing institutional changes of "authoritarian" South Korea or Taiwan.

In "old" autocracies the ruling stratum consists of either the traditional hierarchies or elites based on the military and the police. These appropriate to themselves a larger share of created wealth than they would obtain under a representative government. They get higher salaries and more "perks," while their status symbols (articles of conspicuous consumption or modern professional equipment) have a priority claim upon the state budget... [H]owever, the rulers of an STE preside over a ruling stratum consisting of these four pillars of the system: communist party *apparatchiks*, economic bureaucrats, the police, and the military. All may (and do) receive a larger share of the created wealth than is true in representative states. Their salaries may be relatively higher and their "perks" relatively more important in the STE shortage economy.[3] So far, the mode of wealth distribution appears to be the same as in "ordinary" autocracies.

In the STE, however, another mode of wealth distribution exists that maximizes the rent of two particular segments of the ruling stratum: party *apparatchiks* and members of the economic bureaucracy. This mode, unknown in other systems, enables these groups to benefit from their protracted interference in the process of wealth creation itself. There are two interconnected ways in which this is done.

The first is through the principle of *nomenklatura*, i.e., the right of the communist party apparatus, from the central party committee down to the enterprise committee, to "recommend" and "approve" appointments for all managerial positions in the economic (and public) administration and all managerial positions in enterprises. These appointments are made primarily on the basis of loyalty rather than managerial competence, and *apparatchiks* usually appoint themselves and their friends in the party to those well-paid jobs. *Nomenklatura* has adverse effects for at least two reasons:

---

[3] Salaries and costs of various subsidized services for the ruling strata are usually kept secret in communist regimes.

(i)   it signifies a severe limitation on the pool of talent from which managers are drawn; and

(ii)   given the well-known negative selection process under totalitarianism, the pool of *nomenklatura*-included talents is not only smaller but also of lower competence relative to any other pool in the society with similar occupational, age, sex, and other characteristics.[4]

Bureaucrats and *apparatchiks* learned long ago that their wealth does not depend primarily upon ideology or upon creating social wealth but upon the rents they extract through their control of the wealth creation process. Thus, loyalty to superiors is important in struggles between various coteries within the ruling stratum who position themselves to extract more benefits from the inefficient economic system. Power or ideology considerations alone, i.e., the attempts of any one group to set an ideologically different course for the party, rarely dominate.

A major mode of rent extraction involves the system of side payments or kickbacks from managers of (primarily industrial) enterprises. In a shortage economy, these kickbacks are mostly of a non-pecuniary nature. Enterprise managers offer to those who appointed them, and to other superiors and colleagues who may advance their careers, a variety of goods and services, and have the opportunity to benefit in the same way. More often than not these side payments involve goods in short supply which have a high black market price. These goods are, however, sold to favored people at list prices or even at reduced prices because of allegedly "lower" quality. (Actual lower quality goods do, indeed, reach the market en masse, but kickback-related goods are carefully selected for high quality!) These offers may include delegating workers from auxiliary factory divisions to build country houses at sharply reduced prices, to build one-of-a-kind furniture for the apartment of a superior on the same basis, etc. The relative unimportance of efficiency allows managers to absorb, without being held accountable, the costs of these

---

[4] In analyzing aspects of negative selection involving character traits, a Polish organizational psychologist – without pointing his finger in the too obvious direction – offers the following version of what may be called the *Copernicus-Gresham* law: "In bureaucratized, technocratic, punitive and pathological organizations, where fundamental laws of human behavior and human development are ignored, egoists, conformists, cowards and people without moral scruples begin to play more important roles than individuals concerned with everybody's welfare, people who are brave, honest and responsible. Under such conditions – in plain words – bad character drives out good character." (Jozef Kozielecki in *Zycie Gospondarcze* Nos. 51/52, 1986.)

kickback activities. Leakage of wealth thus takes place not only through the losses incurred and gains foregone by incompetent managers but also because of the time and effort spent on rent-seeking activities.

Both types of rent extraction exist because of the muddled structure of STE property rights. Since the means of production are in theory, but not in fact, socialized, since workers are "the hegemonic class" in a socialist society and the communist party is "the leading force of the working class," and appointment through the *nomenklatura*, or any other decision process for that matter, can be justified. It does not matter whether or not STE property rights were originally devised to achieve a socialist purpose or to maximize rents for the ruling stratum. What matters is that muddled property rights allowing protracted interference in wealth creation serve the latter purpose very well.

Under the *nomenklatura* system personnel shifts from the ranks of *apparatchiks* to those of the economic bureaucracy are by far the most frequent. The reverse flow also occurs, however, since young economic bureaucrats perceive that their professional career is advanced by a spell in the party apparatus. On the other hand, such interaction with the party and the *nomenklatura* is much less common for the police and the military.

The different methods of rent maximization used by groups in the ruling stratum are of primary importance for the prospects of reform in the Soviet system. All segments of the ruling stratum prefer the *status quo* to the alternative of representative government. But two segments only–party *apparatchiks* and economic bureaucrats–have, in addition, a strong incentive to maintain the undemocratic, centralized institutional *status quo* in the economic sphere. To see why this is so, consider that decentralization assumes, as a first step, the substitution of parameters for commands. Since parameters (in contrast to plan targets), such as the interest rate, need not be input- or output-specific, intermediate levels of economic bureaucracy become superfluous. A look at Figure 1 shows clearly that the liquidation of the intermediate levels of economic bureaucracy (the dashed-line rectangular area) makes redundant not only the bureaucrats employed in industrial ministries and unions, but also reduces the pool of well-paid jobs to which *apparatchiks* may be appointed through the *nomenklatura*. It is only to be expected that such changes will be strongly resisted by the powerful groups most strongly affected.

Similar resistance appears at the enterprise level. For example, strengthening enterprises' budget constraints by holding them financially accountable for the effects of management decisions will be resisted, since the costs of kickback-related activities would begin to affect the enterprises' balance

FIGURE 1

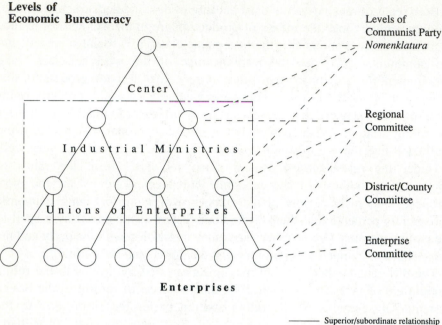

The rectangle displays the levels of economic bureaucracy rendered superfluous by real decentralizing, market-type economic reforms. Dotted lines show also which levels of party apparatus lose the chance to get themselves appointed to the well paid jobs covered by the *nomenklatura* in industrial ministries and unions of enterprises.

sheets as well as rewards and penalties for managers and workers. The effects would also be felt by every actual and potential receiver of kickbacks who would spread resistance even wider. Financial accountability could, in fact, affect the whole system of dependence based on loyalty. Conflict resulting from a divergence between the requirements of loyalty and those of financially sound performance is an everyday occurrence in modified STEs, like Poland and Hungary, where financial indicators matter to some extent. That conflict's outcome, however, is predetermined in favor of loyalty because of the operation of the *nomenklatura*. Simply put, managers caught between whether to follow the "suggestions" of their superiors or pursue other, more financially appropriate goals for their firm choose the former and ask for subsidies afterwards. Otherwise they might lose their jobs. That is why even in Hungary, the most reformed STE, the budget constraint continues to be "soft," to use Janos Kornai's well-known phrase.[5]

Predictably, *apparatchiks* and economic bureaucrats would most strongly resist attempts to replace *nomenklatura* by selections based on merit. As a result, *nomenklatura* has never been abolished for managerial posts in the economic sphere, the sphere where efficiency gains are most important for the rulers. While it is true that *apparatchik* and bureaucratic resistance is found throughout the STE, its intensity differs among sectors of the economy. Since the best paying managerial jobs under the *nomenklatura* (i.e., those enjoying best opportunities for kickbacks) are in industry, it is in industry that reform faces the strongest resistance and, correspondingly, the highest probability of failure. The economic history of STEs shows some partly successful reforms of state agriculture, a sector in which opportunities for rent extraction are less frequent and the benefits smaller. To date, no reforms of state industry, based on general parameters, accountability, or merit, have been successful.

The wealth-maximizing interests of *apparatchiks* and bureaucrats in maintaining the inefficient economic status quo is in sharp contrast with that of the current ruling groups in the Soviet-type states. On the other hand, while a "small but powerful group at the top," to employ Thalheim's phrase, does not necessarily need central planning in its system of rule and wealth-maximization, those upon whom it depends for maintaining that rule–those who control the STE–draw considerable benefits from the existing economic arrangements.

Before proceeding with the argument, the term "control of economic activity" by the economic bureaucracy and party apparatus requires some further definition. In an STE, this function has little in common with guidance toward efficient achievement of desired economic outcomes, at least those desired by the public or even by the ruler. Rather, the goal most often is to maximize rent for the ruling stratum. Control is process-oriented, rather than outcome-oriented, and is based on detailed prescriptions of how, when, and with what means to produce what outputs. The obedience of subordinates is

---

[5] J. Kornai, "Resource-Constrained Versus Demand-Constrained System." *Econometrica* 47 (4), 1979; J. Kornai, *Economics of Shortage*, Amsterdam: North Holland, 1980. [Editor's note: "soft budget constraints" are also defined by Kornai in Article 2 of this book.]

all-important, since this gives superiors a sense of control and of an ability to protect their rents. Ironically, control of the process does not confer control of the outcome because the consequences of following such detailed prescriptions are far from the expected ones: part of output exists only on paper; products are shoddy and obsolescent; deliveries are late; efficiency indicators miss plan targets and the managers are obviously unable to do anything to correct the situation. Another irony is that this style of control may impede realization of the ruler's own objectives, yet the ruler is also powerless because the *apparatchiks* and economic bureaucrats are essential for *his* (their) political control of the whole system. Controlling economic activity means simply that the *apparatchiks* and economic bureaucrats are able to issue commands ("suggestions" at the very least) affecting process or product. These commands are superficially in form, but not in substance, obeyed by enterprises.

The ruler-ruling stratum relationship clearly is crucial to understanding reform failure in the Soviet system. The juxtaposition of these two groups in this article should not be confused, however, with the oft-encountered "good czar, bad officials" approach to Russian politics. The rulers (or "ruling group") is actually representative of all the ruling stratum and reflects all the moral, intellectual and professional consequences of decades of system-specific negative selection. Thus, the czar is not any better than his officials. Nonetheless a great difference exists between the rulers and other groups in the ruling stratum. The ruler, alone within the ruling stratum, is interested not only in seeing reports that commands are fulfilled, but also, and more importantly, in seeing that the commands were actually fulfilled! No other group bears that ultimate responsibility. He will be blamed for any failure of the system by competing groups within the ruling stratum, and his interest in real performance makes the ruler more sensitive to falling efficiency and consequently more ready to reform the economy than is the average representative of the ruling stratum.

As a result, if rulers try to change the economic system significantly, they may face a revolt by functionaries who have the strongest incentives to maintain the *status quo*, placing their political dominance in jeopardy. Thus, rulers face both the rent-maximizing and the transaction cost constraints stressed by North. In periods of declining performance, the ruler feels the transaction cost constraint. Inefficient property rights do not generate the increased wealth needed, for example, to sustain the superpower status of the Soviet Union, or to avert consumer dissatisfaction in all Soviet-type states. On the other hand, if the ruler attempts a significant revision of the existing property rights structure, he risks loss of support from important members of the ruling stratum who will turn to competitors for political power. It is, moreover, a special feature of STEs that even if competitive constraints on the ruler diminish and reforms begin, their implementation is in the hands of party *apparatchiks* and economic bureaucrats. Reforms, if not aborted or weakened from the start, may then be sabotaged, distorted or finally reversed.

Clearly and unequivocally it is the *apparatchiks* and bureaucrats of STEs who gain most from maintaining the institutional *status quo*, and they are the groups which resist change most strongly. Given the key positions of these groups in the STE system, we may predict a very high probability of failure of decentralizing, market-oriented, efficiency-increasing reforms.

Disincentives to Expanding the Private Sector

Expanding the role of the private sector in an STE usually has the same objectives as decentralizing, market-oriented, efficiency-enhancing reforms in the state sector. Theoretically, private sector expansion could serve as a substitute for state sector reforms, and could provide the means to circumvent strong resistance to market-oriented change in the state sector. In actuality, attempts to reform the state sector have complemented simultaneous private sector expansion. Changes in policy toward the private sector have been numerous, however, since often the private sector has had to contend with various forced concentration drives in the state sector. In the course of these drives, large state enterprises often gobbled up small state and private enterprises alike.[6]

Analysts invariably cite ideology as the cause for the limited role of the private sector (except in agriculture) in Soviet type economies. The same ideological argument comes to the fore in two other circumstances: (i) when Western experts and journalists seek the sources of vilification campaigns and other obstacles to change that follow each official policy shift favoring the private sector, and (ii) when rulers must explain the unsatisfactory results of pro-private sector policy changes. In the latter case, the rulers usually produce some type of circular memorandum aimed at the economic bureaucracy or party committees and lecturing them on the need to overcome the "old-style," "dogmatic" approach with respect to the role of the private sector under socialism. These memoranda are usually ineffectual.

An ideological explanation for the failure to harness private enterprise to improve performance in a persistently disequilibrated and structurally

---

[6] The concentration drive in East Germany (GDR) in the mid-1970s is relevant here.

distorted STE fails for two reasons. First, ideological fervor has generally subsided, although admittedly to differing degrees, since the imposition of the STE system. This subsidence has occurred in all spheres of the society and suggests that ideology is not a good explanation for unabated hostility towards the private sector. Second, and more important, any ideological reservations have had to be overcome first and foremost at the top. When a policy to promote the private sector is announced, it is actually the ruler who has to "eat the toad", i.e., to confess directly or indirectly, that the state sector cannot do what the private sector is expected to do. Even policy changes announcing the most limited expansion of the private sector amounts to precisely such a confession. It would seem, then, that few lower level bureaucrats or party apparatchiks, whose position depends not on performance but on loyalty, will dare to sabotage the latest twist of the party line and remain ideologically hostile to privatization.

On the other hand, the ancient principle of *cui prodest* suggests that there must be strong disincentives for certain groups to follow the rulers' privatization lines. The two avenues of rent distribution, i.e., *nomenklatura* and kickbacks, operate simultaneously in a STE. However, in interactions between segments of the ruling stratum and the private sector, both are conspicuously absent, or extremely rare. There are no well-paid posts to be filled by *nomenklatura* appointment in small private enterprises, nor is there a "soft" budget constraint, so permissive to a variety of rent-maximizing kickbacks even under reform. A shift of activity from the state to the private sector reduces, therefore, the possibilities for party *apparatchiks* and economic bureaucrats to extract rent. Hostility towards the private sector is, therefore, based not on ideology or even actual rent losses, but on gains foregone when expansion of the state sector is curbed in favor of the private sector.

The story does not end here. A bureaucrat, or even an *apparatchik* who can indirectly influence each decision, *may* extract rent by taking a bribe for a concession to set up a private industrial firm, or to open a restaurant or a repair shop. But this way of extracting benefits violates private sector property rights, where resources are clearly exclusive, and is consequently much more dangerous. In plain words, taking bribes is a criminal act. By contrast, in a STE rent extraction from the state sector is either fully legitimized, i.e., through the *nomenklatura* and the rationing of goods at the center's order, or, as with system-specific kickbacks, belongs to the "grey area" between the improper and the criminal. Therefore, since negative selection assures that moral scruples are rare among ruling stratum rent-takers in a STE, something akin to a political earthquake, like the "Solidarity" period in Poland, is needed to threaten all who predatorially extract rent from a STE system. Otherwise, only a few luckless individuals whose punishment was decided upon by higher-ups will be the show pieces in trumpeted, but deceptive, anti-corruption campaigns.

It should be stressed that only so-called "secondary" corruption–that not legitimized within the ruling stratum–is the type usually punished in an unreformed STE. Such secondary corruption arises from conflicts between the utility function of the ruler and that of his agents. This is readily understandable in light of North's property rights approach. The inability of the ruler to constrain his agents perfectly would result in the diffusion of some of the ruler's monopoly rent and would, therefore, call down sanctions on the head of the offenders. Barzel[7] and Cheung[8] note the ruler's problem is rendered more difficult, and the rent diffusion is greater, when the measurement of output is more difficult and more costly. Since in STEs this measurement is most difficult in industry, one would expect diffusion is greatest precisely in that sector; Winiecki[9] has confirmed this. Diffusion is so great in fact that it trickles down to some of the ruled as well, through widespread falsification of performance reports by enterprises. *Nomenklatura*-covered managers and, to a smaller extent, but in larger numbers, all employees of affected enterprises may all benefit from these falsifications.[10]

When and How Reforms Fail: The Strategies and Tactics of "Counter-reformation"

Because decentralizing market-type reforms of the state sector and expansions of the private sector adversely affect rent extraction possibilities, the *apparatchiks* and bureaucrats who benefit from the existing STE arrangements embrace what may be termed a multifaceted "counter-reform-

---

[7] Y. Barzel, "A Theory of Rationing by Waiting." *Journal of Law and Economics*, 1974.

[8] S.N.S. Cheung, "A Theory of Price Control." *Journal of Law and Economics*, April 1974, pp. 53-71.

[9] J. Winiecki, "Investment Cycles and an Excess-Demand Inflation in Command Economies: Sources and Processes." *Acta Oeconomica* 28 (1-2), 1982; and "Distorted Macroeconomics of Central Planning." *Banca Nazionale del Lavora Quarterly Review*, 1986.

[10] According to A. Shitov, the vice-chairman of the Peoples Control Commission of the USSR, every third enterprise out of those checked was found guilty of such irregularities (*Planovoye Khozyaistvo*, No. 11, 1981). It is assumed by the author that those caught doctoring their reports make up only part of those who paint a rosy (or only rosier) picture to obtain plan fulfillment-related rewards.

ation" course. To understand how reforms may thus be reversed or aborted one must consider again the relations between the rulers (or ruling group) and key elements in the ruling stratum, especially the *apparatchiks* and economic bureaucrats.

In analyzing those relationships and the "counter-reformation," however, it is necessary to consider the ability of the members of large groups to act in concert. Olson[11] stresses that large groups are not always able to act as if guided by their collective interest, yet for STEs this generally valid point does not apply so fully to actions by the *apparatchiks* and economic bureaucrats. A large difference exists between, on the one hand, a large, perhaps opposition, group struggling to bring organized pressure on a government or a ruling party to effect certain outcomes and, on the other hand, a large group that consists for all practical purposes of the government and/or its ruling political party. "Counter-reformers" in STEs, indeed, usually are in the party and often coalesce around members of the ruling group itself. There are always one or few top party figures who think that cracking the whip, tightening discipline and increasing control are enough to solve the problem of falling efficiency. The hostile group's capability to act collectively is much greater in such situations for the simple reason that theirs is a very unusual, often majority, interest faction with access to mechanisms of political and economic control. If such a group sets itself to thwarting reforms outlined by the rulers and their advisers, the organizational and descriptive capacity of the "counter-reformers" may turn out to be markedly greater than that of politically powerful elements who are outside the mainstream of economic control.

Even if they do not act collectively but only individually, the "counter-reformers" unusual position in the party and the bureaucracy will help them throw sand into the machinery of reforms... For example, they can twist and distort decentralizing reforms pertaining to all state enterprises in a given industry or region, or they may forbid establishment of private enterprises in a given industry or region. These actions symbolize an Olsonian "free rider" situation in reverse: everyone outside the informally organized group of "counter-reformers" brings his valuable individual contribution to the common cause of resisting reform.

The preceding considerations suggest that (1) aborting reforms costs less effort by the interested parties than reversing reforms later, and (2) reversing

---

[11] Mancur Olson, *The Logic of Collective Action.* Cambridge, Mass.: Harvard University Press, 1965; and *The Rise and Decline of Nations.* New Haven: Yale University Press, 1982.

less consistent reforms (with inconsistency deliberately built into the systemic modifications) costs less effort than reversing more consistent reforms.

Although the counter-reformers are very effective in adjusting their obstructive actions to different circumstances, they probably cannot always implement their first-best (i.e., completely reform-suppressing) solutions and may try to abort reforms, at least in part.

Aborting reforms neither means that no changes whatsoever are introduced nor that all changes are repudiated. It means, rather, that the reforms actually introduced do not threaten the property rights structure in the state sector through which *apparatchiks* and economic bureaucrats maximize their rent. Abortive reforms also do not alter either the institutions or the procedures of central planning. Examples of such abortive or sham reforms abounded in the 1980s in such STEs as Bulgaria, Czechoslovakia, and the German Democratic Republic. The 1980s Soviet reforms likewise belong to the category of abortive reforms.

The second-best solution for the *apparatchiks*/bureaucrats is to introduce internally inconsistent quasi-reforms, which modify the system so inconsistently that they are doomed to fail. To the category of quasi-reforms belong the Polish reforms of 1956-1958 and 1973, and most of the East European reforms of the 1960s. Quasi-reforms may increase the effort *apparatchiks* and economic bureaucrats must expend in controlling economic activity, but that increase is only temporary, since reversal of the quasi-reforms is assured because of problems created by the inevitable reform and system contradictions. In any case, the structure of property rights remains intact.

With inconsistencies often obvious from the start, beneficiaries of the traditional STE model need only to wait until the first problems appear to begin their campaign for reform reversal. Usually they do not need to wait for long, since STEs always enter reform periods in a state of larger or smaller disequilibrium, and reforms can thus be blamed for the persistence of disequilibrium even if no other reform-related adverse consequences have appeared. Actually, major adverse consequences will, in any event, likely arise because of quasi-reform and system inconsistencies. To be sure, small efficiency gains may be registered, but they are temporary and disappear over time under the impact of the process of reform reversals.

...Counter-reform measures designed to maintain an unchanged degree of control over economic activities can be supplemented or reinforced by other measures. These may include expressions of various policy preferences or *ad hoc* regulations that contravene the thrust of reforms and, if implemented, reduce the ability of enterprises to react to profitable opportunities. These measures also raise costs, reduce quality, increase obsolescence of outputs, and otherwise make firms less efficient. Ironically, counter-reformers use the adverse results arising from their interference as evidence of the failure of the reforms themselves during the next campaign for reversal.

Propaganda against reforms supplements these other measures. It often includes two types of arguments: "reforms increase inflation," although reforms usually only bring hidden inflation into the open; and "reforms increase inequality," although reforms usually, at least at the beginning, reward more efficient smaller enterprises and reduce existing, unjustified wage and salary differentials favoring employees of large enterprises. Also, isolated critical anecdotes by individuals or by employees in large enterprises are often overblown in the press and mass media, strengthening the campaign against reforms by conferring upon it a quasi-legitimacy.

Conclusions

Despite the pessimistic analyses offered in this article, one should not conclude that economic reforms in STEs will inevitably fail. ...[U]nder certain conditions of long-term economic decline, such as apparently affected all East European STEs in the 1980s, political changes may positively affect the chances for the success of economic changes.

Winiecki[12] suggests two scenarios which could lead to real economic reform. The first involves the breakdown of consensus within the ruling stratum and the defeat of those interested not only in maintaining political power but also in maintaining the existing structure of property rights in the economic sphere, i.e., the party *apparatchiks* and economic bureaucracy. The other scenario assumes a gradual self-limitation by the communist party as the economic decline drags on and as the costs of maintaining the existing system increase as a result of falling absolute wealth and the augmented efforts needed to control economic and non-economic activities. Since the decline of STEs is multifaceted, combining falling living standards, rapidly increasing pollution, and increasing mortality, many hard questions will be asked within the ruling groups and the ruling strata. Accordingly, the probability of the occurrence of one of these scenarios may increase. Either scenario would enhance the prospects of successful economic and political reform in STEs as they approach the last decade of the 20th century.

---

[12] Jan Winiecki, "Soviet-Type Economies: Considerations for the Future." *Soviet Studies*, October 1986, 543-61.

30. Perestroika from Below*

Philip Hanson

In Soviet society today, there are already more signs of a readiness to adapt to the market than most Western Sovietologists ever expected to see. These include not just passive popular acceptance of the idea of change, but also the growth of "*perestroika* from below"–small-scale private enterprise and spontaneous institutional innovations at the grass roots as well as initiatives by regional and local authorities.

One encouraging sign for the future is the economic radicalism of several of the new republican leaderships. Republican elections have brought in governments whose members are often young and free of past associations with the old party-state apparatus; Boris Yeltsin's Russian republic policy-makers are only the most visible example...

There is a similar development in the new liberal city and district governments–most conspicuously in Moscow and Leningrad[1], but not only there. Like many of their counterparts in the new republican leaderships, the new leaders in the democratic city governments tend to be young and, in Western terms, of a radical right persuasion. Typical of this new breed of leader is Anatoli Chubais, Leningrad's deputy mayor for economic policy. In a recent interview he was asked about his office decor. How, the interviewer inquired, would he cover the bare patch on his office wall where previously there had been a portrait of "the latest (Soviet) leader"? Whose portrait would he want to hang there? "Mm..." Chubais said, "Let me think about it. No doubt some economist. Well, let's say Friedman or Hayek."[2]

The new republican and city governments have already begun to act on their liberal convictions. The Russian republic is moving to allow the privatization of land. The Estonian government has a joint-stock company law in place seven months or so before the central government in Moscow. City

---

* From "Soviet Reform: Perestroika or 'Catastroika'?" from *World Policy Journal*, Spring 1991, vol. VIII: #2. Reprinted by permission of the World Policy Institute.

[1] [Editor's note: Leningrad was renamed *St. Petersburg* after a popular referendum in June, 1991.]

[2] Chubais interview about the Leningrad free economic zone, "Ekonomika stoit no golove. Kak vyzhit?" *Leningradskii rabochii*, October 26, 1990, p. 6

governments have developed plans for free economic zones, started selling off shops and small service concerns to private owners, and begun to privatize housing. New policies are even being launched by authorities below the municipal level, such as the councils of the Leningradskii and Oktyabrskii districts of Moscow, which moved to license new small private firms in their areas as soon as national legislation permitted.

The rapid evolution of views among policymakers in Moscow, curiously enough, can also be considered a reflection of the widespread readiness for change, since it shows an elite whose interests and origins lie with the old order succumbing to the prevailing atmosphere. Despite verbal fudges and legislative loopholes, the Soviet government's approach came in 1990 to be, in a Polish phrase, "West of center." The Soviet legislation on joint-stock companies, small enterprises, foreign direct investment, and banking clearly shows the growing acceptance of the market among policymakers. The change in name of one 1990 law as it passed through the committees of the Supreme Soviet is symbolic: what started out as the Law on the Socialist Enterprise ended up as the Law on Enterprise.

Another sign of change from below is the growth of private enterprise. The eruption of petty trade onto the streets and squares of Moscow has already been mentioned. True, "the market is not a bazaar," as the reform economist Evgenii Yasin has said. He was pointing out that a modern market economy is a very complicated mechanism indeed. Still, a bazaar *is* a market, and an expansion of petty street trade is a natural element of the early stages of marketization.

The signs of entrepreneurship go far beyond petty trade, however. They include the new independent business press, exemplified by the magazine *Kommersant*; the small private firms and cooperatives springing up throughout the country; the moves to set up commodity markets in Ryazan and Samara and stock exchanges in Moscow and Leningrad; and even the commercials on the in-house video channel at the Hotel Vladivostock for Yurii Luzan's used Japanese car business.

Finally, indications that the Soviet public is ready for real economic reform can be found in the results of recent public opinion surveys. While Soviet sampling methods and survey design do not always conform to Western standards, some Soviet polling groups have cooperated with reputable Western organizations, and there is evidence that the methods in at least some of these surveys have been sound. These studies have shown a remarkable degree of popular acceptance of the idea of competitive markets.

A survey conducted in May 1990 in both urban and rural areas found 56 percent of respondents, faced with a choice between "the market patch of development" and "strengthening planning," choosing the former, and less than half as many the latter. (The balance consisted of "don't know" responses. A high proportion of "don't knows" is characteristic of these surveys, which is hardly surprising).[3] Asked where they thought their society was heading, 37 percent of the respondents in the same survey opted for "a renewal of socialism or a society combining the best of socialism and capitalism"; 9 percent chose capitalism as the likely outcome; 15 percent selected "a society with the worst features of capitalism and socialism combined"; and a wise 36 percent found it "hard to say."

A poll of 800 Muscovites conducted in April and May 1990 found nearly three in five favoring a transition to the market, although a majority, when asked how they themselves expected to fare in a market economy, said they expected to be worse off. In the same survey, when invited to describe unemployment as "good for society," "normal," "abnormal," or "tragic," 39 percent chose "normal"–the most popular of the four answers, though outvoted by "abnormal" and "tragic" taken together.

Asked where they would most like to work, the same respondents opted two to one for a joint stock venture, private firm, cooperative, or their own business, instead of a state enterprise. Asked to say yes or no to the establishment of private ownership of enterprises, 57 percent were in favor, while 31 percent were opposed. A remarkable 79 to 13 percent approved of private ownership of land, and 70 percent were in favor of allowing Western investment in the Soviet Union, with only 23 percent against.[4]

A somewhat later opinion poll on the sensitive issue of private ownership of land suggested that the results from Moscow were not far out of line with attitudes elsewhere in the country. That survey found majorities not only in Moscow and Leningrad, but also in provincial centers and smaller towns favoring the sale of land to individuals. In the countryside itself there was not an absolute majority in favor, but at any rate a plurality: 46 percent were for, 42 percent were against, and 12 percent didn't know.[5]

---

[3] V. Rutgaizer, S. Shpilke, "Reforma ekonomiki: za i protiv," *Izvestiya*, May 24, 1990. [Editor's note: For a more recent survey, see the article by Shiller, Boycko, and Korobov, Article 30 in this book.]

[4] *Moskovskie novosti*, no. 20 (May, 1990), p. 10.

[5] V. Gavrichkin, "Zelmya na prodazhu?" *Izvestia*, November 12, 1990.

Particularly encouraging to reformers is the evidence that favorable attitudes toward the free market are stronger among younger than among older people and among better-educated that among less well-educated people. For example, several surveys have found that specialists, managers, individuals with higher education, and young people tend to look favorably on cooperatives, while opposition to cooperatives is concentrated in the older, less skilled groups in the population. The change in public opinion over time has also been encouraging. Curiously, while the economic situation has deteriorated and the gap between state and free-market prices has widened, opinion has, if anything, become more favorable to the market and private enterprise. It seems that the new privations of the past year or so are seen as a legacy of the past rather than as a consequence of reform.

What is one to make of these opinion poll results? I would suggest two things. First, ideology has little influence on what most Soviet people regard as desirable economic institutions. Second, many Soviets believe that the West is prosperous because it has something called markets, and that it produces plenty of food because it has private farming. What cannot be deduced from these surveys is that people necessarily have a clear idea of what a market economy is like. Nor can it be inferred that, whatever they think a market economy is, they are ready to go through a period of reduced consumption and increased insecurity in order to get to it.

If experience in other countries is any guide, the depth of the Soviet people's desire for systemic change must be doubted. In Poland, socialism and planning were widely regarded, by the mid-1980s, as barbaric devices imposed on a long-suffering nation by foreigners who were either stupid or malevolent or both. Yet less than a year's experience with a determined and painful effort to escape from that system led the Polish public to turn on the leader who presided over this effort.

If this could happen in Poland, there is little doubt that it could happen in the Soviet Union. Nobody, said H. L. Mencken, ever lost money by underestimating the intelligence of the American public. Well, nobody will ever lose votes in a Soviet election by underestimating the farsightedness of the Soviet people. This is not because they are Soviet but because they are people.

A successful transformation process would be painful, at least temporarily, for two main categories of people in the Soviet Union. First, there are the various groups that were privileged under the old system and probably will not remain so. In the unlikely event that the transition as a whole were to go smoothly, these people might not lose in absolute terms, but most of them would lose at least in the sense that they would see their position near the top of the income league taken over by others.

One of these privileged groups is the party-state apparatus of regional party secretaries, senior officials in central planning offices, and managers of big enterprises. Some of these members of the old *nomenklatura* are already trying to turn themselves into a new bourgeoisie, and some will undoubtedly succeed. Regional party officials have been active in setting up banks and other commercial organizations and putting party property into these new ventures; there is even one that calls itself the *Kompartbank*, signaling its Communist Party connections. But many will not make the change successfully.

Other groups were privileged under the old system, but in less obvious ways. For example, it was for many years a privilege to have a Moscow or Leningrad residence permit or, to a lesser extent, a residence permit for any leading Soviet city. Beginning in the late 1970s there was considerable deterioration in the infrastructure and services in Moscow, but even so it had seemed to be one of the eternal verities that the shops were better stocked in the leading cities than in smaller provincial towns. The distance out-of-towners would travel to shop for everyday items in Moscow was one measure of these advantages. Moscow's privileged status has already been undermined as a result of local trade wars, and it would be eliminated completely in a market economy.

The privileged groups identified above are substantial, but the second category of potential losers is probably larger. This consists of people who will lose their jobs, at least temporarily, or have to take real wage cuts if they stay in their present place of work. There will inevitably be such people because a successful transformation into a market economy will entail improvements in both allocative and internal enterprise efficiency.

The rise in allocative efficiency will show up in a major change in the composition of output. Loosely speaking, many workers will have to stop making things that nobody wants. More precisely, there will be reduced labor demand in those lines of production whose output level at some future market equilibrium will be below the present level of production. Civilian engineering is likely to be particularly vulnerable insofar as the old system created what Peter Wiles once called a "solipsistic enclave" of machines to make machines to make machines... ad infinitum.[6] Another vulnerable sector is that part of the construction industry that specializes in the building of factories,

---

[6] Peter Wiles, *The Political Economy of Communism* (Oxford: Basil Blackwell, 1962).

since the old system was biased toward the construction of additional factory space as opposed to the re-equipping of existing plants.

The increase in enterprise efficiency will show up in reduced labor demand per unit of output in many–probably most–lines of production as production units become better motivated to economize and keep costs down. For example, the growth of family farming will tend to undercut the enormously costly production of the giant state and collective farms. There will also be an indirect effect of the same kind, as increasingly cost-conscious producers will cut their usage of fuel and raw materials as well as labor per unit of output. This will feed back to the demand for labor in the extractive industries and in the transport and processing of primary products.

In the long run, of course, a mixed, market economy should be capable of providing much higher levels of average prosperity than the old system, that is the point of the whole exercise. But the creation of a market economy that functions successfully in the modern world could take a while. The message that could subvert the whole enterprise is one that comes not from Marx, but from Keynes: in the long run we are all dead.

Perhaps, then, those who advocate an authoritarian regime to push through a market transformation have a point. My own view, and it may be merely sentimental, is that they do have a point, but not a very convincing one. It is true that the liberalization of Soviet politics has not uniformly helped the process of economic transformation. Above all, it has released centrifugal forces–both secessionist movements and less ambitious strivings to assert regional interests–that cut across and complicate the attempts to change the economic system.

Yet even if the return to authoritarian rule now being attempted can be sustained–a point on which I am more skeptical than Jerry Hough was in the Fall 1990 issue of this journal[7] – it is hard to believe that the Soviet leaders will do all the right things needed to marketize the economy. They could perhaps achieve some macroeconomic stabilization and promote a program of limited reform (the parallel suggested by British economist Stanislaw Gomulka is the regime of Gen. Wojciech Jaruzelski in Poland after martial law was declared in 1981). But the view that an authoritarian central leadership could preside over a transformation into a mixed economy, with decontrolled prices and substantial privatization, is in my opinion misguided. There are four reasons for taking this view.

---

[7] Jerry Hough, "Gorbachev's Endgame: Positioning for Radical Reform," *World Policy Journal*, vol. 7, no.4 (Fall 1990), pp. 639-672.

First, the Soviet leaders' track record suggests they lack the wisdom and technical know-how that are needed. Second, by reimposing authoritarian controls they stand to forfeit Western technical assistance. Third, since quite early in the post-Stalin period Soviet rulers have lacked confidence in their ability to initiate tough economic policies. They were consistently unwilling to risk worker unrest even when the KGB, the labor camps, and censorship were in full flower, and seem even less likely to do so now. Fourth, the Soviet rulers' background and personal interests bias them against transformation into a market economy. They owe their positions to the party-state apparatus, which in turn derives its power to control the economy from the near-absence of a private sector. In this respect, the South Korean example of so-called "authoritarian modernization" is not as relevant to the Soviet Union as some Soviet writers have suggested.

31. Popular Attitudes to Free Markets[*]

Robert J. Shiller, Maxim Boycko and Vladimir Korobov

What are the important barriers to the success of free markets? At this time of transition in the Soviet Union and other Eastern economies, the answer to this question is of the utmost importance. One view is that major obstacles are the attitudes, morals, and understandings of the people themselves, not just the institutions or politics they live with. Leonid Abalkin, former Deputy Prime Minister of the Soviet Union and prominent economist, complained that

> ...it is not easy to develop a stratum of talented people, with a good understanding of the market. For that, it is necessary to put aside fixed patterns of thinking, inherited from the past, to consider afresh our morals, and our system of values in general.[1]

This has been a recurring theme, appearing quite often in the Soviet Parliament and government bodies, in the mass media, and in academic journals: it is argued that the general public in the Soviet Union is not prepared to accept and fully use markets.

We have undertaken surveys of randomly selected individuals in the Soviet Union and in the United States with questions ... that are aimed at providing evidence on *fundamental* parameters of human behavior related to the success of free markets. Sometimes our questions are about aspects of everyday life that are not directly affected by government economic policies. Other questions are about basic economic intuition. Sociologists have notes that popular answers to such questions often differ substantially from the answers that would be suggested by the dominant ideology that is expressed by

---

[*] From "Popular Attitudes to Free Markets: The Soviet Union and the United States Compared," *American Economic Review*, August 1991, vol. 81, no. 3. Reprinted by permission of the American Economic Asssociation and the authors. Some questions and some footnotes omitted.

[1] Leonid Abalkin, "Too High a Price," *Literaturnaya Gazeta*, 6 June 1990, no. 23, p. 9.

opinion leaders.

Questionnaire Design and Survey Methods

Our questionnaires included 36 questions,[2] addressing various aspects of human behavior related to free markets.[3] Some of our questions probed public opinion on certain issues, but mostly the respondents were asked to consider some imaginary situation that they might experience and to describe their behavior in, or judgment of, that situation.

When designing the questions, we tried to do our best to make them equally comprehensible to the Soviet and the American respondents. For that, first of all, we took great care in selecting our scenarios of imaginary situations that would possibly make the same sense for both audiences, despite the very different institutional environments that they generally face.

Second, we put a lot of effort into selecting suitable wordings, so that the questions would sound as much alike as possible in the two languages. Originally the questionnaire was developed in English, but then we made several rounds of translating it into Russian and back, each time adjusting the wordings where appropriate. We also usually said something like "5 percent" rather than "a little" to reduce further ambiguities in translation.[4]

The survey was conducted by means of telephone interviews with randomly selected individuals of 18 years of age or older. We documented responses from 391 residents of Moscow and 361 residents of the greater New York City consolidated metropolitan statistical area. The 36 questions were subdivided into three parts (designated A, B, and C in the question numbers), and each respondent was asked to answer only one part consisting of 12 questions. We were able to document about 120 - 130 responses per question in each country. The two samples were generally representative of their underlying populations, and also rather close to each other in terms of basic characteristics: average age was 45 in the Soviet Union and 42 in the United States; 60 percent of U.S.S.R. respondents and 58 percent of U.S. respondents were female; 50 percent of U.S.S.R. respondents and 66 percent of U.S.

---

[2] [Editor's note: Not all of the questions are included here.]

[3] Original questionnaires in both English and Russian, as well as further information about the samples and statistical methods, are available from the Cowles Foundation, Yale University, as part of Discussion Paper No. 952, August 1990.

[4] In an independent evaluation of our translation, William Mahota, Professor of Slavic Languages and Literature, Yale University, wrote, "I have closely compared the Russian and English versions of Shiller, Boycko, and Korobov's survey of attitudes toward economic problems, and found that the language of the two versions corresponds virtually exactly."

respondents had attended some college. In both countries, those who agreed to participate in the survey were perhaps a little more articulate and informed than average for their respective populations, but it is our impression that as a result, they generally had no difficulty understanding the questions.

The closeness of characteristics of the samples makes it generally possible to attribute any differences that we find to genuine differences between Soviets and Americans and not to differences in the composition of our samples.[5]

There are somewhat fewer telephones per household in Moscow. At the end of 1988, there were 2.70 million telephones in private apartments in Moscow; at the same time, there were 3.05 million private apartments, implying 89 telephones per 100 apartments. In 1990, an estimated 93 percent of all household in the New York consolidated metropolitan statistical area had telephones. Only 61 percent of New York households had listed phones, but with random-digit dialing, nonlisting does not affect results.

An obvious criticism of our samples is that Moscow is probably not representative of the Soviet Union at large; the people there may be a little more educated or aware of economic issues. However, New York City, sometimes referred to as the business and financial "capital" of the United States, may also be populated by those who are more "advanced" in their attitudes toward markets than the rest of the country, so that the intracountry bias is possibly in the same direction. Even if this argument is not entirely convincing, we feel that a comparison between the two cities is quite meaningful by itself. The respondents in our two samples may represent the more economically active and influential people in the two countries. Thus, our results may be more relevant to understanding economic events in the two countries that if we had taken a representative sample of everyone in the two countries.

Fairness of Price Changes

One important potential obstacle to the clearing of free markets is a popular feeling that price increases may be unfair. If sellers feel that they cannot

---

[5] With sample sizes of a little over 100, the standard error of an estimated proportion is just under 5 percent if the estimated proportion is 50 percent; it is 4 percent if the estimated proportion is 25 percent or 75 percent; and it is 3 percent if the sample estimated proportion is 10 percent or 90 percent. Thus, for example, an estimated sample proportion of 25 percent has a 95 percent confidence interval of 17 - 33 percent.

raise their prices, then they will be forced to use nonprice rationing to distribute their goods, contrary to market principles.

It is widely believed in the Soviet Union (and possibly elsewhere) that the Soviet people, being for a long time accustomed to stable, government-sanctioned prices, will be characteristically reluctant to accept market prices. Consider the following statement of V. O. Rukavishnikov, a prominent Soviet sociologist:

> ...[T]he public attitude toward possible increases of prices of consumer goods that are in short supply is extremely negative, because this solution to the problem of the queues is likely to lead to a situation with lots of goods on the counters, with no queues, but with few people being able to buy the goods; 83.7 percent of the people surveyed are against this solution [4.4 percent support it, and 11.9 percent did not answer].[6]

Such a result may reflect general human behavior, not just Soviet behavior.

For a meaningful evaluation of the attitudes toward free prices in the Soviet Union, it is useful to compare Soviets and Americans responding to identical questions in identical contexts. We report several similar scenarios...designed to address this issue:

B2. *On a holiday, when there is a great demand for flowers, their prices usually go up. Is it fair for flower sellers to raise their prices like this?*

Response	USSR	USA
Yes	34%	32%
No	66%	68%
N:	131	119

B11. *A small factory produces kitchen tables and sells them at $200 each. There is so much demand for the tables that it cannot meet it fully. The factory decides to raise the price of its tables by $20, when there was no change in the costs of producing tables. Is this fair?*

---

[6] V.O. Rukavishnikov, "Ochered" [The Queue], *Sotsiologicheskieye Issledovaniya [Sociological Studies]*, 1989 (4), 2-12.

Response	USSR	USA
Yes	34%	30%
No	66%	70%
N:	131	120

A9. *A new railway line makes travel between city and summer homes positioned along this rail line substantially easier. Accordingly, summer homes along this railway become more desirable. Is it fair if rents are raised on summer homes there?*

Response	USSR	USA
Yes	57%	61%
No	43%	39%
N:	98	115

The critical point here is that there is virtually no difference between U.S.S.R. and U.S. answers. In the first two scenarios, we discover a tendency in *both* countries to report that price increases are unfair. In the third scenario, in *both* countries most people think that price increases are fair. Here, our comparison-group methodology displays its full power. Notions of fairness are very situation-specific: flower sellers are unfair if they raise their prices, while landlords who do so in the circumstance described are usually not. Notions of fairness are *not* country-specific. The bottom line from all of this is that there is little foundation to the aforementioned claims that Soviets are *characteristically* resistant to unfair price increases.

We were able to expand our understanding of fairness by asking about the policy implications of the fairness judgments. After the question about flower sellers we asked:

B3. *Should the government introduce limits on the increase in prices of flowers, even if it might produce a shortage of flowers?*

Response	USSR	USA
Yes	54%	28%
No	46%	72%
N:	123	115

After the question about the manufacturer of tables we asked:

*B12. Apart from fairness, should the factory have the **right** to raise the price in this situation?*

Response	USSR	USA
Yes	57%	59%
No	43%	41%
N:	118	118

In only one of these two questions, the first (B3), was there a significant difference between Soviet and American responses. Soviets *are* more likely to want to restrict the flower seller from raising prices, but both Soviets and Americans tend to agree that the manufacturer of tables has, in effect, the right to be "unfair." (The answers to the second question (B12) show that, in both countries, beliefs that something is unfair need not translate into an opinion that something should be illegal.)

Another perspective on the fairness issue can be gained by posing a question without the word "fair," but asking whether an action is "moral." Here, we have changed the context of the question to a price increase between sale and resale, raising the issue of profiteering:

C10. A small merchant company buys vegetables from some rural people, brings the vegetables to the city, and sells them, making from this a large profit. The company honestly and openly tells the rural people what it is doing, and these people freely sell the company the vegetables at the agreed price. Is this behavior of the company, making large profits using the rural people, acceptable from a moral point of view?

Response	USSR	USA
Yes	49%	59%
No	51%	41%
N:	120	116

Again, the Soviets are not dramatically more concerned with profiteering, and this difference is not statistically significant.

We wanted to learn whether people would impose on themselves the hardships caused by rationing of quantities, and so we asked:

C4. Suppose that the government wishes to reduce consumption of gasoline. They propose two methods of attaining this goal. First, the government could prohibit gas stations from selling, for example, more than five gallons to one person. Second, the government could put a tax on gasoline, and prices of gasoline would go up. From your point of view, which of these methods is better?

Response	USSR	USA
First	43%	36%
Second	57%	64%
N:	104	109

Now, neither the Soviets nor the Americans tend to think that it is a good idea to force people to buy gasoline in small quantities. The Americans were only slightly less likely to favor the rationing solution.

Overall, the reported evidence suggests that there is actually little ground to believe that the Soviets are characteristically more hostile toward free-market prices. The strong opposition to price reform (implying price increases) that undoubtedly exists in the Soviet Union should not be attributed to peculiarities of national character; rather, the economic and political interests should be given more weight. Obviously, by setting prices free, central planners will lose an important instrument of control over enterprises as well as some arbitrage opportunities that result from disequilibrium pricing.

Attitudes Toward Income Inequality

Popular notions of fairness are essentially related to attitudes toward inequality. Given the history of Communist ideology, it would seem that Soviet citizens might be more intolerant of inequalities of income and wealth. Of course, "from each according to his abilities, to each according to his needs" has long been a Communist slogan. With the reputation of the United States as the most capitalist country, it would seem that American citizens might be much more tolerant of inequalities of income and wealth. However, we found no evidence to support such a notion.

One question, designed to see whether people would object to pro-market reforms because of envy of those people who would succeed under such reforms, found that the *Americans* were the most resistant.

A4. Suppose the government wants to undertake a reform to improve the productivity of the economy. As a result, everyone will be better off, but the improvement in life will not affect people equally. A million people (people who respond energetically to the incentives in the plan and people with certain skills) will see their incomes triple while everyone else will see only a tiny income increase, about 1 percent. Would you support the plan?

Response	USSR	USA
Yes	55%	38%
No	45%	64%
N:	114	99

The plan described makes everyone better off, so any objections would have to be motivated by the relative inequality created by the plan. Only about half of the Soviet respondents supported the plan, but even fewer of the U.S. respondents responded that way.

Popular Theories about the Importance of Incentives

One theory to explain the slowness of the Soviet Union to implement a market system is that people there do not believe in one of its alleged principal advantages: the incentives that the system creates for hard work. The Soviets are reputed not to think that most people are basically motivated for personal gain and to believe instead that people work better if they are in a social context that makes their work personally meaningful to them.

When our respondents were asked directly about this, it turned out that there was very little difference between the Soviet and American responses.

A1. *Do you think that people work better if their pay is directly tied to the quantity and quality of their work?*

Response	USSR	USA
Yes	90%	86%
No	10%	14%
N:	121	119

We also asked out respondents if they had heard about the capitalist theory that because of the importance of incentives, income inequality is a necessary evil:

A2. *Some have expressed the following: "It's too bad that some people are poor while others are rich. But we can't fix that: if the government were to make sure that everyone had the same income, we would all be poor, since no one would have any material incentive to work hard." Have you heard such a theory or not? If yes, then how often?*

Response	USSR	USA
Often	38%	7%
Once or twice	39%	38%
Never heard it	23%	55%
N:	125	120

Surprisingly, the Soviet respondents were more familiar with this theory than their U.S. counterparts, perhaps due to current extensive discussions of this and related subjects in the Soviet mass media.

A3. *Do you yourself personally agree with this theory?*

Response	USSR	USA
Yes	41%	38%
No	59%	62%
N:	110	116

Neither country seems to like this theory a lot, but the opposition to the theory is weaker among our respondents in the Soviet Union. It is the American responses that are more surprising here. Agreement with this theory is not actually contrary to Communist theory of the past 20 or so years. Alistair McAuley,[7] in a survey of Soviet academic economists and lawyers, concludes that "most Soviet economists appear to advocate what one might call a meritocratic structure of wages."

Negative Attitudes Toward Business

Many scholars have claimed that the Russian people have a long-standing aversion to business and dislike of businessmen. Alexander Gerschenkron[8] wrote that "There is no doubt that throughout most of the nineteenth century

---

[7] Alistair McAuley, "Social Welfare Under Socialism: A Study of Soviet Attitudes Towards Redistribution" in David Collard, Richard Lecomber, and Martin Slater, eds., *Income Distribution: The Limits to Redistribution*, Bristol, U.K.: Scientechnica, 1980, pp. 238-257. (Citation from p. 242.)

[8] Alexander Gerschenkron, "Social Attitudes, Entrepreneurship, and Economic Development," in Alexander Gerschenkron, ed., *Economic Backwardness in Historical Perspective*, Cambridge, MA: Belknap, 1962, pp. 52-71. (Citation from page 60.)

a grave opprobrium attached to the entrepreneurial activities in Russia... Divorced from the peasantry, the entrepreneurs remained despised by the intelligentsia." The idea is commonplace that the Communist revolution may have had its roots partly in such feelings. We sought to find whether there is evidence that such feelings today really set Soviet citizens apart from their U.S. counterparts.

We sought first to find whether people in the two countries feel that they would be esteemed by their relatives and friends if they were successful in business:

C1. *Suppose that as a result of successful business dealings you unexpectedly became rich. How do you imagine it would be received by your relatives at a holiday family gathering? Would they congratulate you and show great interest, or would they be judgmental and contemptuous?* Response choices: 1) They would show interest, would congratulate; 2) They would be judgmental and contemptuous; 3) They would be quiet, indifferent.

Response	USSR	USA
1	72%	92%
2	12%	6%
3	16%	3%
N:	113	117

The Americans get greater support from their relatives and friends, though most of the Soviets expect congratulations.

C9. *Do you think that, if you worked independently today as a businessman and received profit, your friends and acquaintances would respect you less and not treat you as you deserve?*

Response	USSR	USA
Yes	19%	4%
No	81%	96%
N:	115	120

This evidence suggests that on the whole nether country lacks respect for businessmen, but there is less respect for them in the Soviet Union.

A way of getting at attitudes toward success in business without mentioning specific purchases is to make people choose between a general notion of success in business or in some other arena of life:

B4. *Which of the following achievements would please you more?* Response choices: 1) *You win fortune without fame: you make enough money through successful business dealings so that you can live very comfortably for the rest of your life;* 2) *You win fame without fortune: for example you win a medal at the Olympics or you become a respected journalist or scholar.*

Response	USSR	USA
1	65%	54%
2	35%	46%
N:	92	117

Although the U.S. respondents answered the question much more freely (response rates: USSR = 67 percent; USA = 98 percent), of those who did answer the Soviets were relatively more attracted by wealth.

A5. *Is it important to you that your work benefits the country, and is not just to make money? Is it very important, somewhat important, or not important?* Response choices: 1) Very important; 2) Somewhat important; 3) Not important.

Response	USSR	USA
1	69%	40%
2	25%	45%
3	6%	15%
N:	130	119

The U.S. respondents are more for the money here, though of course we could also interpret the results as indicating that they feel freer to *admit* this.

Yet another way to get at attitudes toward business success is to try to elicit from respondents their prejudices against businessmen:

C11. *Do you think that it is likely to be difficult to make friends with people who have their own business (individual or small corporation) and are trying to make a profit?*

Response	USSR	USA
Yes	51%	20%
No	50%	80%
N:	111	121

On this question, Soviets are much less sanguine about businessmen than are the Americans.

C5. *Do you think that those who try to make a lot of money will often turn out to be not very honest people?*

Response	USSR	USA
Yes	59%	39%
No	41%	62%
N:	114	117

Indeed, relatively more Soviets do tend to expect businessmen to be less honest.

These last two questions show that U.S.S.R. respondents attach negative prejudices toward businessmen; but a caveat is in order. When evaluating these prejudices, it is important to keep in mind that many Soviets have never met a businessman in an informal situation, to say nothing of knowing one well. Their answers may be determined by what they read or hear, not by personal experience.

Still, the prejudices that Soviets have today are probably obstacles toward development of business enterprises. The questions in this section, which have various interpretations individually, tend generally to support the notion that Soviets indeed display a somewhat less warm attitude toward business and may be less interested in business careers.

It should of course be borne in mind that the differences we found were often value differences, differences in what each person wants in his or her own life. Perhaps economists should not argue over them or be concerned about them.

Perceptions of Speculation

Many barriers to free market activity are supported in the Soviet Union on the ground that these activities represent "speculation." Unfortunately, the term "speculation" has a wide range of meanings. Sometimes the term "speculation" in the Soviet Union refers to activities that consist of taking (in effect stealing) goods intended by the government for some people and selling these at a profit to others. To what extent such activities are immoral when they are already illegal is not our concern here. We are concerned instead with the ultimate harm that is thought to follow from allowing forms of "speculation" that are legal in capitalist countries.

Soviet opposition to such speculation might come about as a result of opinions that speculative price increases are unfair, or as a result of opposition to income inequalities that might result from allowing people to speculate, or from the anti-business sentiments that we discussed in the preceding section. However, we have yet to explore a separate issue: whether speculation is viewed as disruptive in that it creates excess price volatility or shortages. Such a view would further justify laws against speculation.

B6. *If the price of coffee on the world market suddenly increased by 30 percent, what do you think is likely to be that blame?* Response choices: 1) *Interventions of some government;* 2) *Such things as bad harvest in Brazil or unexpected changes in demand;* 3) *Speculators' efforts to raise prices.*

Response	USSR	USA
1	17%	13%
2	51%	36%
3	32%	51%
N:	109	111

Surprisingly, the Americans were more likely to hold speculators responsible. To put this result into proper perspective, it is worthwhile to note that currently in the Soviet Union the "speculators" are vehemently blamed by the government and certain populist movements for "aggravating shortages" and bringing about price increases. The general public seems to be more skeptical about speculators' capabilities.

This finding was further confirmed by responses to another question that addressed the issue of speculation more directly:

C8. *Grain traders in capitalist countries sometimes hold grain without selling it, putting it in temporary storage in anticipation of higher prices later. Do you think this "speculation" will cause more frequent shortages of flour, bread, and other grain products? Or will it cause such shortages to become rarer?* Response choices: 1) *Shortages more common;* 2) *Shortages less common;* 3) *No effect of shortages.*

Response	USSR	USA
1	45%	66%
2	31%	26%
3	24%	8%
N:	110	112

Thus, it is true that Soviets tend to blame speculators for shortages, but the Americans do so even more.

Overall, the present survey did not provide evidence that Americans were any more enlightened in their understanding of the functioning of free markets.

Understanding of Compensated Price Changes

At the time this paper was being written (June 1990), there was a heated debate going on in the Soviet Union about whether the public would tolerate the compensated increase in the price of bread and other grain products suggested by the Ryzhkov government. While the opinions expressed undoubtedly were heavily motivated by political issues at stake, it was rather discomforting to hear repeated assertions that a fully compensated price increase was unacceptable because it would adversely affect the standard of living.

Our survey, completed just before the Ryzhkov government put forward its proposal, directly addressed the issue of a compensated price increase:

C6. *Suppose the price of electricity rises fourfold, from 10 cents per kilowatt hour to 40 cents per kilowatt hour. No other prices change. Suppose also that at the same time your monthly income increases by exactly enough to pay for the extra cost of electricity without cutting back on any of your other expenditures. Please evaluate how your overall material well-being has changed. Would you consider your situation: 1) Somewhat better off; 2) Exactly the same; 3) Somewhat worse off?*

Response	USSR	USA
1	9%	3%
2	77%	63%
3	14%	34%
N:	120	121

Expectations of Possible Future Government Interference

Much recent economic theorizing has emphasized that economic agents respond not only to current government policy but also to anticipated future government policy. Unless the government can commit itself to a new policy, economic agents may, in making long-term decisions, assume that an older policy regime is still relevant. Thus, another impediment to the development of markets in the Soviet Union may be the lingering effect of a memory of the old regime and a feeling that some of its features may be back in the future.

We did find a substantial difference that relates to expectations that the government might usurp the investments people make in private business:

C7. *How likely do you think it is that in the next few years the government will, in some way, nationalize (that is, take over) most private businesses with little or no compensation to the owners? Is such nationalization quite likely, possible, unlikely, or impossible?* Response choices: 1) *Quite likely*; 2) *Possible*; 3) *Unlikely*; 4) *Impossible*.

Response	USSR	USA
1	20%	5%
2	40%	11%
3	29%	53%
4	11%	31%
N:	114	118

From the Soviet answers here, it would appear that there should be substantial reservations about investing too many resources in cooperatives.

We thought also that Soviets would have a rather weak incentive to save, because of a feeling of insecurity of their savings. After our survey, the Pavlov government actually imposed restrictions on the amount one can withdraw from bank accounts, but our Soviet respondents did not show strong anticipation of such government interference with savings.

B8. *How likely is it, from your point of view, that the government in the next few years will take measures, in one way or another, to prevent those who have saved a great deal from making use of their savings? Is it quite likely, possible, unlikely, or impossible that the government will do this?* Response choices: 1) *Quite likely*; 2) *Possible*; 3) *Unlikely*; 4) *Impossible*.

Response	USSR	USA
1	17%	15%
2	44%	37%
3	21%	39%
4	19%	9%
N:	112	117

There is some evidence of less confidence of the Soviets, best visible in the "(1+2)/(3+4)" proportion: 61/39 for the Soviet Union; 52/48 for the United States. This difference is not statistically significant, however, and it is well below our prior expectations. Perhaps Americans were thinking of pressures on the federal government from the deficit and of actions the government might take, such as reneging on their savings-and-loan obligations, or changing the social-security system or medicare system.

Interpretation and Conclusion

...Because the differences between the Soviet Union and the United States we found were often small or nonexistent, we feel that perhaps too much prominence has been given in discussions of the transition to a market system in the Soviet Union today to the differences between Soviets and people in market economies. The pressing and immediate problems faced in the Soviet Union today may be instead political and institutional in nature. When a country inherits an institutional and political framework that has been anti-market, it serves certain entrenched interests in that country to resist change. Thus, individuals who benefit from the present system may make public appeals to fairness, abhorrence of income inequality, and other attitudes to try to stop change. Alternatively, well-meaning Soviet government planners may feel constrained by their incorrect belief that the Soviet public is much more concerned with fairness or income inequality than are the publics in capitalist countries.

Indeed, we have found here that Soviets are concerned with fair prices and with income inequality, so that these concerns might help prevent change to a market economy. However, at the same time, these concerns appear to be little different among Americans. Perhaps Americans would resist perestroika with as much vigor if they inherited the Soviet political and institutional system.

32. Is It Surprising That We Were Surprised?*

Timur Kuran

Many aspects of the East European Revolution are controversial but on one point everyone agrees: it caught the world by surprise. Even local dissidents were stunned by the sudden turn of events.

We will never know how many East Europeans did foresee the explosion of 1989, but at each step, accounts painted a picture of nations united in amazement. To my knowledge, only one study addresses the issue systematically. Four months after the breaching of the Berlin Wall, the Allensbalch Institute asked a broad sample of East Germans: "A year ago did you expect such a peaceful revolution?" Only 5 percent answered "yes," though 18 percent responded "yes, but not that fast." Fully 76 percent admitted to being totally surprised. These figures are all the more remarkable given the "I-knew-it-would-happen" fallacy – the human tendency to exaggerate foreknowledge.

Yet in hindsight the revolution appears as inevitable. In each of the six countries the leadership was despised, economic promises remained unfulfilled, and basic freedoms existed only on paper. More importantly, winds of change in the Soviet Union were making Soviet intervention increasingly unlikely. But if the revolution was indeed inevitable, why was it not foreseen? What kept us from noting signs that now, after the fact, are so plainly visible?

1. Preference Falsification and Revolutionary Bandwagons

Consider a country featuring two camps competing for political power: government and opposition. Members of society, indexed by *i*, all place themselves publicly in one camp or the other, although a person may privately feel torn between the two camps. I am thus distinguishing between an individual's *private preference* and *public preference*. The former is

* From "The East European Revolution of 1989: Is It Surprising That We Were Surprised?", *American Economic Review*, May 1991, vol. 81, no.2. Reprinted by permission of the author and The American Economic Association. Some footnotes omitted.

effectively fixed at any instant, the latter a variable under his or her control. When his two preferences differ the individual is engaged in *preference falsification*.

Let S represent the size of the public opposition, expressed as a percentage of the population. Initially it is near 0, implying that the government commands almost unanimous public support. As a mass-supported seizure of political power, a revolution, may be treated as an enormous jump in S.

Now take a citizen who wants the government overthrown. The likely impact of his own public preference on the government's fate is negligible, so his private preference plays no direct role in his choice of whether to side publicly with the opposition. His public preference depends on a tradeoff between two payoffs, one external and the other internal.

The external payoff to siding with the opposition varies positively with S. The larger S, the smaller the individual opponent's risk of being persecuted for his outspokenness, and the fewer hostile supporters of the government he has to face. The latter feature reflects the fact that government supporters, even those privately sympathetic to the opposition, participate in the persecution of dissidents, as part of their personal efforts to establish convincing pro-government credentials.

The internal payoff is rooted in the psychological cost of preference falsification: the suppression of one's wants generates lasting discomfort, the more so the greater the lie. Specifically, person i's internal payoff to supporting the opposition varies positively with his private preference, x^i.

The higher x^i, the costlier he finds it to suppress his anti-government feelings. An individual's private preference thus plays an indirect role in his choice of a public preference, as a determinant of his internal payoff to supporting the opposition.

Thus i's public preference depends on S and x^i. As S grows, with x^i constant, there comes a point where the external cost of joining the opposition is outweighed by the internal cost of self-suppression. This switching point is i's revolutionary threshold, T^i. Note that if x^i should rise, T^i will fall.

People with different private preferences and psychological constitutions may differ in their revolutionary thresholds. Imagine a ten-person society featuring the threshold sequence

$$A = \{0, 20, 20, 30, 40, 50, 60, 70, 80, 100\}.$$

Person *1* ($T^1 = 0$) supports the opposition regardless of its size, just as person *10* ($T^{10} = 100$) always supports the government. The remaining eight people's public preferences are sensitive to S. Initially, the opposition consists of a single person, or 10 percent of the population, so $S = 10$. Because the nine others have thresholds above 10, this S is self-sustaining.

This equilibrium happens to be vulnerable to a minor change in A. Suppose that person *2* has an unpleasant experience with the government, which exacerbates her alienation from the regime. The consequent rise in x^2 lowers T^2 from 20 to 10. Since $S=10$, person *2* joins the opposition, moving S to 20. This new S is self-augmenting, as it drives person *3* into the opposition. The S of 30 then triggers a fourth defection and in this manner S feeds on itself until it reaches 90 – a new equilibrium. A slight shift in one individual's threshold has thus generated a revolutionary bandwagon, an explosive growth in public opposition. Now consider the sequence

$$B=\{0, 20, 30, 30, 40, 50, 60, 70, 89, 100\},$$

which differs from A only in its third element is 30 as opposed to 20. As in the previous illustration, let T^2 fall from 20 to 10. Once again, the preexisting equilibrium becomes unsustainable, and S rises to 20. But the opposition's growth stops there, for the new S is self-sustaining. We see that a minute variation in thresholds may alter drastically the effect of a given perturbation.

Neither private preferences nor the corresponding thresholds are common knowledge. So a society can come to the brink of revolution without anyone knowing this not even those with the power to unleash it like person *2* in A. For any number of reasons the threshold sequence may shift dramatically in favor of the opposition. But this will not necessarily trigger a revolution. In the sequence

$$C= \{0, 20, 20, 20, 20, 20, 20, 20, 60, 100\},$$

the average threshold is as low as 30, possibly because in private most people sympathize with the opposition. Yet $S=10$ remains an equilibrium.

When a revolutionary bandwagon does take off, long-repressed grievances burst the surface. In addition, people who were relatively content embrace the new regime attributing their former public preferences to fear of persecution. Reconsider A, recalling that a 10-unit fall in T^2 drives S from 10 to 90. The last person to jump on the bandwagon has a threshold of $T^9= 80$, a reflection of her great sympathy for the government. Accordingly, she does not switch until the opposition's victory is guaranteed. Having made the switch, she has every reason to feign a longstanding antipathy to the old regime. In doing so, she makes it seem as though the old regime enjoyed even less genuine support than it actually did. This illusion is rooted in the very factor responsible for making the revolution a surprise: preference falsification. Its effect is to make it even less comprehensible why the revolution was unforeseen.

The outlined theory unites social evolution and revolution, continuous and discontinuous change, in a single model. Private political preferences and the corresponding thresholds may shift gradually over a long period during which public opposition is stable. When the cumulative change has established a latent bandwagon, a minor event may precipitate a sharp jump in public opposition.

2. The Revolution of 1989

Given communism's failures, the existence of East European dissent is easily understood. Less comprehensible is the rarity of dissent—prior, that is, to 1989. For decades, East Europeans displayed a remarkable capacity to put up with tyranny and inefficiency. This subservience is attributable partly to punishments the communist establishment imposed on nonconformists. Yet official repression is only one factor in the durability of communism. It met with the approval of disillusioned citizens and relied crucially on their complicity. People with every reason to despise the *status quo* applauded politicians they mistrusted, joined organizations whose mission they opposed, and signed defamatory letters against dissidents they admired, among other manifestations of consent and accommodation.

In a famous essay[1], Vaclav Havel speaks of a greengrocer who places in his window the slogan "Workers of the World, Unite!" Why does he do this, Havel wonders, "Is he genuinely enthusiastic about the idea of unity among the workers of the world? Is his enthusiasm so great that he feels an irrepressible impulse to acquaint the public with his ideals? Has he really given more than a moment's thought to how such a unification might occur and what it would mean?" No, the greengrocer does not mean to express his real opinion about anything. He displays the slogan simply for the right to be left alone. The greengrocer's prudence has an unintended consequence; it reinforces the perception of a society united behind the Party. It thus becomes a factor in other people's willingness to continue doing and saying the things expected of them.

Later in the same essay, "something in our greengrocer snaps" and he makes "an attempt to live *within the truth*." As a consequence, he is transferred to the warehouse at reduced pay, and his hopes for a holiday in Bulgaria evaporate. Also, his peers take to harassing him—not out of inner conviction but to avoid being persecuted themselves.

This brilliant vignette suggests that the regimes of Eastern Europe were

---

[1] "The Power of the Powerless", in his et al. *The Power of the Powerless: Citizens Against the State in Central-East Europe*, Paul Wilson, trans., Armonk: M.E. Sharpe, 1985.

substantially more vulnerable then the quiescence of their populations made them seem. Millions were prepared to turn against communist rule if ever this became safe to do.

What lowered the level of fear sufficiently to get the revolution underway? With the benefit of hindsight it appears that Gorbachev's reforms in the Soviet Union played a key role. In Eastern Europe these kindled hopes of greater independence and meaningful social change. But why did we not foresee where they would lead?

An examination of the news media before the revolution shows that arguments in the air pointed to the unlikelihood of fundamental change. Even if Gorbachev wanted to liberate Eastern Europe, it was not clear that he could. Surely, Soviet conservatives would insist on retaining their country's security belt. Moreover, tensions within the Soviet Union were sowing the seeds of a conservative coup. Some observers expected Gorbachev to survive, but only by reversing course and becoming increasingly repressive.

For all this pessimism, Gorbachev's policies did fuel expectations of a freer Eastern Europe, reducing the perceived risk of dissent. In terms of our model, they shifted the thresholds of East Europeans increasingly in favor of revolt, making it ever easier to spark an explosion. But obvious as this was, no one could see that public sentiment would shift so soon and so massively.

Pinpointing the specific event that pushed the bandwagon over the hill is akin to identifying the cough responsible for a flu epidemic. There were several turning points, any one of which might have altered history. One came when East German officials canceled Party leader Honecker's order to fire on demonstrators in Leipzig. The demonstration's peacefulness made many more East Germans sense that change was imminent. Another turning point came with Gorbachev's remark that his country had no right to interfere in the affairs of its neighbors. At the time, some East European leaders were contemplating the use of force, and this statement may well have been a major factor in their exercising restraint.

When the greengrocers decide that they have had enough, Havel had predicted, East European communism will collapse like a house of cards. So it turned out: when the masses took to the street, support for the *status quo* just vanished. In one country after another a few thousand people stood up in defiance, joining long-persecuted activists. In so doing they encouraged additional citizens to drop their masks, which then impelled more onlookers to jump in. Before long, fear changed sides; where people had been afraid to oppose the regime, they came to fear being caught defending it. Party members rushed to burn their cards, claiming they were always reformists at heart. Top officials began sensing that they might face retribution for resistance. They hastened to accept the opposition's demands, only to be confronted with bolder ones.[2]

The East European Revolution has been billed as the triumph of truth over lying. This designation conveys the end of feigned support for communism, but it conceals the continuation of preference falsification. Lying has not ceased but changed character. Now it provides cover to East Europeans afraid to admit their yearnings for the old order.

It is tempting to attribute our amazement at the events of 1989 to the inadequacy of our theories concerning political stability. Our most popular theories of revolution certainly left us ill-prepared for the suddenness with which public sentiment turned. For instance, Theda Skocpol's "structuralist" theory,[3] which shows how changes in international relations can produce social uprisings, does not explain the involved discontinuities. A solid understanding of the interdependencies among individual public preferences (whose significance Skocpol explicitly rejects) would doubtless have prepared us better for an East European explosion.

Yet, once again, these interdependencies are largely hidden from view. And for reasons explained above, the knowledge that preference falsification is pervasive does suffice to establish that a revolution is imminent. We can sense that multitudes are seething with unarticulated discontent without knowing what it would take to turn the possibility of revolt into reality. In principle of course, we can develop techniques for uncovering the relevant interdependencies. But for all practical purposes we lack the means to find and process all the requisite information. Also, there are irremovable political obstacles to the correct interpretation of whatever information is produced. In view of all this, it is safe to say that no theorizing could have prepared us adequately for 1989.

I ought to point out that this is not the first time a major uprising has come as a surprise. The French Revolution of 1789, the Russian Revolution of February 1917 and the Iranian Revolution of 1979-80 are among the successful revolutions that stunned their leaders, participants, victims and observers. The failed ones include the Hungarian uprising of 1956 and the Prague Spring of 1968. In all these cases, preference falsification was a prime

---

[2] For a chronicle of events, see Ash, Timothy Garton, *The Magic Lantern: The Revolution of 1989 Witnessed in Warsaw, Budapest, Berlin and Prague,* New York:Random House, 1990.

[3] Theda Skocpol, *States and Social Revolutions: A Comparative Analysis of France, Russia and China*, Cambridge: Cambridge University Press, 1979.

factor in the suddenness with which public sometimes shifted – and in the cases of failure, shifted back.

Because preference falsification afflicts politics in every society, though in varying forms and degrees, we are likely to be surprised again and again. But obstacles predicting particular revolutions do not rule out the production of useful general insights into the process of revolution. Even if we cannot predict the time and place of the next big uprising, we can prepare ourselves mentally for the mass mobilization that bring it about. Equally important, we can understand why it may surprise us. There are many spheres of knowledge where useful general theories foreclose reliable predictions of specific outcomes. The Darwinian theory of biological evolution illuminates the process whereby species evolve, but without enabling us to specify the future evolution of the swordfish.

The theory of biological evolution and the present argument have a common virtue: each reveals the source of its predictive limitations. In the case at hand, the source is *imperfectly observable nonlinearity*. In ways that we cannot hope to grasp fully, public preferences depend on their determinants nonlinearly. This is why an intrinsically insignificant event may generate a massive rise in public dissent.

The notion that small events may unleash huge forces goes against much of twentieth-century social thought, with its emphasis on linearity and thus continuity and gradualism. So does my suggestion of inescapable unpredictability. Lest this be considered offensive to the scientific spirit, I should note that establishing the limits of knowledge is itself a contribution to the pool of useful knowledge. As Friedrich von Hayek[4] reminds us, it is also necessary for charting a realistic scientific agenda.

-----

[4] Friedrich August von Hayek, "The Pretence of Knowledge" (1974), *American Economic Review*, December 1989, 79, 3-7.

33. Soviet Economic Futures[*]

Philip Hanson

1. The Extreme Uncertainty of the Soviet Economic Future

Forecasting what will happen in the Soviet economy used to be less difficult than forecasting developments in Western economics. Now it is a mug's game. It is no longer clear that there will still be a single Soviet economy on the present territory of the USSR in two or three years time. Even if there is, it is not at all clear what sort of economy it will be. In this situation the Russia-watching economist naturally wonders whether the time has come to take up stamp-collecting.

Oil-industry economists had a similar experience in the 1970s. It became obvious that nobody had a clue where the oil price was going to be in a month or one year's or two year's time. One response to this was to give up forecasting or projecting the future price, or a narrow range of future prices, and to deal instead in "scenarios" that could differ from one another, not just in one or two assumptions or the odd co-efficient, but radically. Those who think that scenarios have some value, say that working them out can at least show that some developments are impossible; can provide you with sign-posts; a check-list of possible future events to look out for, in order to see which road you are on; and can prepare the observer for possibilities that they might not otherwise have envisaged. In the hope that there is some truth in this, I offer the following scenarios for *perestroika*, first up to the mid-90s and then up to the end of the century:

> Severe Fragmentation
> Benign Fragmentation
> Back To the Future
> The Pinochet Version
> The Pollyanna, or Harvard, Version.

---

[*] From "Soviet Economic Futures," *Russia and The World*, Issue 20, 1991. Copyright (c) Russia and the World Publications, University of Leeds. Reprinted by permission. Footnotes omitted.

2. Up To 1995

Severe fragmentation would mean the break-up of the Soviet Union into separate, geographical areas (not just Union republics, but regions and cities) which did nor acknowledge a common authority or an agreed system of rules for economic cooperation. This would be incompatible with the maintenance of the highly-developed division of labor on which Soviet production has been based. The flows of raw materials, components, spare parts, machinery and other current material production inputs between production units in different regions may be relatively inefficient, but they are extensive and they have been the basis of a functioning economy. If the Soviet economy were a "cellular" economy, like China, with regions that were substantially self-sufficient in production, the effects on total output would not be drastic.

But this is not the case. What I have in mind is more than a failure to negotiate a viable Union Treaty or an Economic Union among all or most republics. Severe fragmentation would entail continuing local trade wars, such as the food trade war that broke out in 1990 between Moscow and the surrounding agricultural regions; or Yakutia's insistence that its diamonds are a Yakut's best friend (and nobody else's). It would be almost impossible in this situation to avoid hyperinflation: nominally, at least, there would still be a single currency, but there would be no cooperation in controlling the budget expenditure of various regional authorities or managing the money supply. Barter transactions between regions would continue, but the numerous local commodity exchanges that have sprung up would be unable to develop properly. Local attempts at market reform would be nullified by the further rise of inter-regional trade barriers that they would provoke. If one city de-controls prices while areas around it do not, would-be sellers will seek to sell in that city, and be prevented by their own authorities from doing so because they will be reducing supplies to their "home" region. A lot of this is already happening.

Officially, total output in the first half of 1991 was ten percent down on the first half of 1990. Fragmentation is not the only reason for this, but it is probably the main one. There are various guesses about the outcome for 1991 as a whole; perhaps a 15 percent decline from last year. If severe fragmentation continues, output would flatten out at some stage; at what level and when, is impossible to say, but there would be no reason to expect an upturn by the mid-1990s. The existing production capacities and the existing distribution of skills are based on elaborate - even though distorted - patterns of specialisation; they cannot be reshaped quickly to fit the needs of a suddenly-cellularised economy. It is hard to believe that in this situation there would not be very severe food shortages in some regions.

Benign fragmentation seems a reasonable label for the following situation: there is no Union Treaty, or at any rate no Union Treaty that maintains a single market with a single currency that has been stabilised by fiscal and monetary discipline exercised over the USSR as a whole; but at the same time centrifugal tendencies within large republics are contained, and cooperation between them does not disintegrate. (A Union Treaty covering the "core" nine republics, with the Baltic states, Moldova, Georgia and Armenia seceding, would cover 93 percent of the present Soviet population, and what I have in mind is a failure to reach such a "9+1" agreement; the secession of the six may be a tricky matter, but it is not fundamental to the future of the core). This limited fragmentation would have much less drastic results than the severe kind if the fragments concerned were prepared to do business with one another and to stabilise separate currencies of their own. Each of these republics' governments would be confronted with the fact that they could no longer leave it to somebody else–the Union authorities or other republics to exercise self-discipline in state spending and the printing of money. They would have no escape from incipient hyperinflation except by their own efforts. Each would therefore have to stabilise its own currency and balance its own budget.

One approach would be to peg the currency in question, whether Ukrainian or Russian or Estonian, to a strong Western currency such as the Deutsche-mark. Some republics might succeed in stabilization and others might not, but spill-over effects between successful and unsuccessful areas would be contained; the adjustment to a small "economic space" would be much less drastic for the big republics than under severe fragmentation, and if the failure to reach a Union Treaty was not messy and rancorous, it might be possible to maintain something close to a single market, and perhaps eventually to move back to a single currency. The fall in output over the next three-to-four years would be less drastic than in the first scenario, though it would probably continue through the period of unsuccessful negotiating over a new Union Treaty. It is reasonable to argue that the shift from several currencies to a single currency shared by a group of countries, as in the plans for European Monetary Union, should bring economic gains. The reason for treating benign fragmentation as one of the more attractive scenarios is not that it is ideal, but that the conflicts between republics may be so intractable that it may be the best outcome that is attainable.

The third and fourth scenarios both rest on a resumption of central, authoritarian control from Moscow. In a *back to the future* scenario, the restored authoritarian control would be used to restore centralised resource allocation. In the *Pinochet version* it would be used to push through a market reform. Even the back to the future scenario need not involve a resurgence of Marxist ideology. Indeed it probably would not: the ideology has been too dead for too long in the USSR to resurge. It would require simply that traditionalists in the military, military industry, the KGB, and the Party apparatus, sensing the need for order by means of central control, manage to secure that control. They then use that political control to administer the economy from the top. They might claim the support of workers. For that matter, they might at first have the support. But in both these scenarios they would not allow political competition from then on. Having restored central control of resource allocation they would have to run the economy in much the same way as it was run under Brezhnev, because resources can only be allocated by a hierarchy if they are not allocated through the market. The speeches might refer, not to Marx or Lenin or the radiant future, but to social justice, Judaeo-Masonic conspiracies or Russia's special destiny; there would still have to be material balances, output targets, success indicators and something bearing an uncanny resemblance to Gosplan. In the long-run results would be much the same as those of the old system: an average level of prosperity stuck well below that of Western Europe; a regime of job security, and inequalities based on access, not money income. This scenario might be one in which the level of output was quite rapidly restored. It has been pointed out that there is no shortage of people able to run the traditional planning system, whereas the know-how to operate a market economy is in short supply; therefore an operating administrative economy could be up and running—or at least doing a slow march—much sooner than a market economy. And the existing structure (number and size of enterprises, product-mix, etc.) is more appropriate to a Brezhnevian economic order.

The fourth scenario is the *Pinochet version*: authoritarian control combined with marketisation a la Pinochet or Lee Kuan Yew. This would almost certainly bc combined with nomenklatura privatisation. In other words, some members of the traditionally powerful groups in Soviet society would re-assert political control and others would parlay their political assets into commercial assets. This would be slightly reminiscent of the way the samurai, or warrior class, set about industrialising Japan after the Meiji Restoration of 1868.

Is the Pinochet version possible? It might be argued that it isn't, for three reasons. First, the element of social discipline that would have to be involved would no doubt include campaigns against "corruption," and these would shade into attacks on private business, or at least would make for a degree of uncertainty in the expectations of a new business class, inimical to any rapid growth and development of business. Second, the new authoritarianism would alienate Western governments and deprive the country of Western financial assistance. Third, the nomenklatura is hardly a nursery for entrepreneurs.

On these points, as in much of the elaboration of possible futures, there is no hard evidence. It does seem to me, however, that the counter-arguments to these three propositions are quite strong. To the first, it might be objected that the nomenklatura is not going to prosecute and persecute itself. To the second it is plausible to suppose that the stability brought about by coercion might alienate Western governments and divert Western taxpayers' money elsewhere, but might also be much more attractive to Western private investment than a morally worthy but precarious state of Soviet society. On the third point, it is wise, I believe, not to tack too seriously the relentless insistence of Russian intellectuals on the stupidity of the old Party state apparatus. This prejudice (*apparatism?*) is understandable but rather childish - while many members of the old apparatus may be very limited people, the sweeping dismissal of the whole class rests on two things: a failure to make Julian Critchley's distinction between being *able* and being *clever*; and a desire for revenge.

Western businessmen with experience of the USSR often express, even off the record, the highest regard for particular senior Soviet officials. They are also apt to deplore both the system in general and a perceived weakness of "middle management, but they know a dynamic captain of industry when they see one, and they commonly believe that they have seen some in the Soviet Union. Judged, at least from afar, someone like Arkady Vol'sky, the chairman of the new Scientific-Industrial League (which aims to represent "employers") seems a good example. He has in the past been an aid of Andropov's, a senior official in the Party's Central committee apparatus and the government's trouble-shooter in Nagorno-Karabakh.

Compared with the back to the future scenario, this Pinochet scenario would probably mean a later and less certain halt to the fall in output. Too many new rules of the game have to be devised and too many new skills have to be learnt. But in both these scenarios the central authorities can end the process of regional fragmentation, and they ought to be able to re-impose financial discipline. By about 1995 the economy would certainly be in better shape than under the severe fragmentation scenario, and possibly in better shape than under benign fragmentation, if the latter had taken a further year or more to emerge as the outcome of the present inter-regional strife.

The last scenario I have called the *Pollyanna or Harvard version*. In it the central authorities and the republics swiftly agree on a viable Union Treaty, with democratisation of the Union authorities following soon after; and the inter-republic sharing of assets, liabilities, budget revenue and budget expenditure is not just an agreed solution but one that enables budgets to be balanced and the money supply brought under control. The reference to Harvard is to the Sachs-Allison-Yavlinsky Grand Bargain proposals; since Harvard colleagues of Sachs and Allison have been among their harshest critics, the Harvard label is a little unfair.

The objection to this is simply that it is too good to be true. The republics, or at least the core nine republics, reach a mutually acceptable deal over who gets what. A consistent and feasible transition process is rapidly implemented. The Union government acquires a democratic basis. The military go quietly. It is not impossible, but I suspect it is the least likely of the five scenarios. So far as output levels over the next three or four years are concerned, it ought to be rather better than benign fragmentation, because the benefits of a single market and currency area would be restored, and perhaps rather similar to the Pinochet version.

3. The Longer Term: To the Next Millenium

In the longer term, the benefits and disadvantages of the different scenarios play out rather differently.

The first scenario, of severe fragmentation, would be followed by continuing chaos and stagnation of output at a low level. This reduced productivity and material prosperity would not necessarily go on falling beyond some minimum level compatible with regional self-sufficiency. On the other hand, the technological lag behind the West would be widening. There could well be some improvements, however, in particular regions, probably on the periphery: examples might be the Baltic states, the Leningrad/St. Petersburg region, and some or all of the Soviet Far East. These regions could, in the absence of either help or hindrance from Moscow, begin gradually to integrate into the international economy under local leadership who would welcome in foreign capital and make the most of their potential as entrepot locations for a distressed but resource-rich hinterland.

The second scenario, of benign fragmentation, would be happier, with the establishment of a market environment in all or most of the former USSR facilitating a rapid growth of output possibly starting before the end of the century. But fragmentation is fragmentation and this development could share with the previous one the possibility of highly uneven development geographically, amongst the various successor states. The average level of prosperity, nonetheless, would be higher.

The third scenario, of authoritarian recentralisation could be expected to lead to a resumption of stagnation after a rapid recovery of lost output levels. After all, a return to the old system, even with the accompaniment of political rhetoric that was more Peronist than Leninist, would be a return to the old systemic disincentives to efficiency and technological change that led to the whole Gorbachevian project of Perestroika in the first place. If it was not associated with a return to militarism and xenophobia, however, it could produce substantial improvement in the oil, gas and other extractive industries; here Western commercial investment bringing in more effective technologies and management, could go ahead even in the absence of a general market reform. All that energy and mining companies need is a host government that welcomes them in and a sufficiently stable situation to give them confidence that they can get the crude oil, gas and ores out of the USSR. For Western investment in manufacturing, services and agri-business to be substantial, a market environment is needed; but this is not the case for the natural-resource sector.

The fourth scenario was authoritarian marketisation with the nomenklatura emerging as the new business class. That would be compatible with rather better performance in the late 1990s than the previous scenario. But the new business elite will be strongly tempted and able - to hold onto monopoly positions inherited from central planning and to restrict import competition severely.

In these respects a liberal, reforming leadership that has come in as an anticommunist movement with popular support, is likely to do better. This sort of leadership starts without a large element of insiders with vested interests in keeping the monopoly power they start with. The new governments in Poland, Hungary and Czechoslovakia, though differing in many ways over economic strategy, all seek to avoid charges of presiding over a shift "from plan to clan." Hence the voucher privatisation schemes and other devices for diffusing economic power.

For this reason the Pinochet version would probably turn out to be rather undynamic in the longer run. It would be capitalism of a sort, but with less freedom of market entry and exit, at any rate for potential domestic competitors, than in the Far Eastern newly industrialising countries.

Finally the Pollyanna scenario would have advantages over any other, in the longer run as well as in the near future. The problem remains that it also wins the implausibility stakes.

Some Conclusions

All of these scenarios are, by definition, speculative. Some are more plausible than others; none is impossible. There could be developments that combine elements of two or more of them, and there could bc crossovers from one to the other. For example, there might be a recovery from severe to benign fragmentation when all concerned faced up to the acute deprivation that the former would bring; equally, there could be a shift from severe fragmentation to one of the authoritarian outcomes.

Two of the scenarios would leave what is now the USSR in a state of economic stagnation at the end of the century: severe fragmentation would have this result at a low, even disastrously low level; the back to the future scenario would probably play out at levels of production and consumption that were well above those of the poorer Third World countries, but the situation would be a sad one nonetheless, in the light of the hopes that were entertained by many Soviet people for much of the past few years. The Pinochet scenario of authoritarian market reform would be capable of producing growth in the long run, but it might well be only the relatively sluggish growth of a protectionist and highly monopolised capitalist economy. The remaining two scenarios look likely to be more successful in the longer run than the others. But if I am right in thinking that the sweetness and light scenario with a unified, stabilised and marketised economy is a bit too good to be true, then the scenario of benign fragmentation may be the most attractive practical possibility, at least for those republics that have the stronger qualifications for a move to the market.

If the present decade does see a more or less successful transition to the market, either for the present USSR as a single, federal state, or for a slightly slimmed down federation or, more plausibly, for a collection of successor states, we are not at all well-placed to judge how rapidly productivity and prosperity would rise. Even after market institutions were in place, it would take time for all concerned to learn how to work effectively within those institutions; meanwhile, what the IMF and World Bank refer to rather blandly as "structural adjustment" would be under way, with widespread job losses and job hunting and gradual absorption of displaced workers into new occupations and new workplaces. Economic theory suggests that a country with a large technological backlog to catch up but a well-educated labor force, once it gets onto a growth track, should grow faster than the average for those highly-developed countries that are already at or close to the world technology frontier. Simple models of growth can show a reformed Soviet Union raising its total output at 4 per cent or so a year, as a long-term trend rate. But we have no way of knowing how long it should take to get launched on that trajectory, or whether the complicated inheritance from the Soviet past may actually prevent the economy, even under favourable circumstances, leaving the launch-pad at all.

Afterword

This article was completed on 9 August, 1991, ten days before the attempted coup in Moscow. That attempt, and its outcome, do not rule out any of the economic scenarios completely. But the two authoritarian scenarios now look a lot less likely–at any rate as scenarios for the whole of the USSR.

Of the two remaining scenarios, my guess is that the two involving fragmentation are now on balance the more likely, while Pollyanna is a shade less implausible than she was before the coup.

On the one hand, the Nine plus Gorbachev are free to go ahead and sign a soft-centered union treaty; and the gang of eight, though they were at sixes and sevens about how to go back to the future, were right about one thing; that the Union treaty as drafted does nothing to solve the inter-republic fiscal and monetary chaos.

On the other hand, it is possible that the core republics will now be more prepared to work constructively with a weak but purged centre to create a single market and single currency area.

By and large, fragmentation looks a lot more likely, and one can only hope for the benign version. Different economic scenarios in different successor states or regions have an even greater probability than before.

Finally amidst the euphoria we should not underestimate the economic difficulties. The events of August, 1991, have shown that Russians would take to the streets to defend their new political liberties, despite the fact the patchy, halting economic liberalization has made most of them poorer. Will they still do this in 1993 or 1994, if the attempt at economic liberalization has still not delivered at least the expectation of new prosperity?

PART X

THE STRATEGY OF REFORM

The four broad elements of any comprehensive reform package are (1) macroeconomic stabilization; (2) price decontrol; (3) privatization; and (4) integration with the world economy. But this list is deceptively simple. Each of these elements has its own set of prerequisites, and each is linked to the others in a complex web of logical and practical interconnections. Designing a sensible sequence of moves sometimes seems impossible. Grigory Yavlinsky − one of the authors of the radical 500-day plan for the Soviet economy − has said that transforming from market to plan is easy, like making fish soup from an aquarium. But the reverse transformation − from plan to market − is like trying to build an aquarium out of fish soup.

In this section, we consider the reform process as a whole. We ill see that designing a comprehensive reform package is much more difficult than designing each of its components.

Our first look at this problem is "The Strategy of Transition," where David Lipton and Jeffrey Sachs argue for what has been called the "big-bang" approach: a comprehensive reform process pushed through at a rapid pace, while the new regime still has the political capital to do it. In terms of sequence, they make two major points. First, macroeconomic stabilization − a tightening of monetary and fiscal policy − should be done first. Otherwise, continuing excess demand will perpetuate the conditions of the "shortage economy," in which no other aspect of the market can take hold. Second, since privatization will take many years, it is important not to wait for it, but to push on with other reforms even while the bulk of the economy remains in state hands.

Philip Hanson, in "Elements of Economic Reform," looks specifically at the Soviet Union, and, like Lipton and Sachs, argues the need to initiate as many aspects of reform as possible right from the beginning. But after examining the complex interdependencies between individual elements, he is more pessimistic about the duration of the process in the Soviet Union.

For example, Lipton and Sachs seem optimistic that a tight macroeconomic policy can rapidly stabilize the economy and thus set the stage for further reforms. Hanson, however, points out that fiscal and monetary restraint are

348

probably not feasible without some prior privatization, because the state, as long as it remains responsible for enterprises, will simply print up rubles to keep them afloat. But privatization requires potential buyers to forecast the future earnings of assets, which in turn requires knowing something about future prices for inputs and outputs, i.e., price decontrol. Finally, price decontrol without prior stabilization will be inflationary. Thus, we are caught in a seemingly insoluble situation: macro stabilization requires prior privatization, and privatization requires prior price decontrol, and price decontrol requires prior macro stabilization. Hanson, like most writers on this subject, offers no easy solutions to this problem.

The remaining two articles suggest, in more detail, the scope and complexity of the reform process. In practical terms, reform cannot proceed with a sequence of distinct actions, but rather requires simultaneous movements on several fronts. In "From Central Plan to Market," the World Bank gives one idea of how this simultaneous process might unfold in a generic Eastern European economy; and in "Recommendations for Reform," David Kennett summarizes the details as seen by the staff of four international organizations that will play a crucial role in helping the process along. Seeing all of these recommendations in one place helps us fathom the enormity of the task facing the region. After reading the other articles in this volume, you should be able to explain why each element is important to the reform process as a whole.

34. The Strategy of Transition[*]

David Lipton and Jeffrey Sachs

Both the economic logic and the political situation argue for a rapid and comprehensive process of transition. History in Eastern Europe has taught the profound shortcomings of a piecemeal approach, and economic logic suggests the feasibility of a rapid transition. Moreover, the macroeconomic situation is deteriorating in many countries, and therefore requires urgent attention.

The transition process is a seamless web. Structural reforms cannot work without a working price system; a working price system cannot be put in place without ending excess demand and creating a convertible currency; and a credit squeeze and tight macroeconomic policy cannot be sustained unless prices are realistic, so that there is a rational basis for deciding which firms should be allowed to close. At the same time, for real structural adjustment to take place under the pressures of tight demand, the macroeconomic shock must be accompanied by other measures, including selling off state assets, freeing up the private sector, establishing procedures for bankruptcy, preparing a social safety net, and undertaking tax reform. Clearly, the reform process must be comprehensive.

Politically, as well, there are powerful arguments for moving rapidly. Fragile governments facing a deep economic crisis are best able to carry out strong measures at the beginning of their tenure. For this reason, Machiavelli's famous advice is that a government should bring all of the bad news forward.[1] Indeed, barring a political disaster emanating from the Soviet Union, probably the greatest political risk facing Eastern Europe is not a resurgence of communism, but the Argentine trap of political and social paralysis, in which coalitions of workers, managers, and bureaucrats in the declining sectors succeed in frustrating the needed adjustments.

For a government committed to a rapid and comprehensive program of

---

* From "Creating a Market Economy in Eastern Europe: The Case of Poland," *Brookings Papers on Economic Activity*, vol. 1, 1990. Reprinted by permission of the Brookings Institution.

[1] And the former Bolivian Planning Minister, Gonzalo Sanchez de Losada, who brilliantly achieved his country's stabilization and reform process in 1986-89, used to put it even more succinctly: "If you are going to chop off a cat's tail, do it in one stroke, not bit by bit."

adjustment, the first step must be to end excess demand. The shortage economy leads to rampant rent-seeking, queuing, hoarding, an anti-export bias, and an anti-private sector bias. Thus, excess demand must be eliminated first. Fiscal and monetary austerity in turn (and in conjunction with a currency devaluation) will permit the establishment of a stable convertible currency and thereby an end to the bureaucratic allocation of trade.

The second step of reform, which can be undertaken in parallel with the macroeconomic austerity program, should be to create market competition, based on the deregulation of prices, free trade, the full liberalization of the private sector, and the demonopolization of the state sector. Prices should be deregulated quickly, in parallel with the macroeconomic austerity program, because the proper relative prices are crucial for all the necessary resource reallocations. Price deregulation might lead to a one-time jump in prices, but not to an ongoing inflation, as long as macroeconomic policies remain tightly constrained.

Some economists have argued that price deregulation is too dangerous in the monopolistic conditions of the Eastern European economies. But such a view does not withstand closer scrutiny. Most sectors in most countries already have numerous firms and an even larger number of separate production plants that could become separate firms. Far more important, for most industrial sectors, free trade policies (based on currency convertibility, combined with a cut in trade quotas and tariffs can provide an enormously effective mechanism for generating competition. Free trade instantly brings to bear on domestic firms the competition of the rest of the world. Even if the domestic production structure is highly concentrated when viewed internally, markets may be highly competitive if foreign producers are allowed to import without restriction.

For some nontradables industries, such as food processing in Poland, the private sector will be able to compete effectively with the state sector in a matter of weeks. But the private sector will emerge only if the proper price signals exist. Thus, a transitory period of monopolistic prices might well occur in some areas, but attempts to avoid this transitory period could lead to the failure to develop private sector competition in the longer term. In a small subset of industries, such as public utilities, telephones, and intercity rail transport prices will inevitably continue to be set by the state, as in almost any Western European economy.

The third step of the reform process should be privatization, and it is likely to take many years. In the meantime, state enterprises will have to be run on a tight leash – with wage controls and curbs on investment – to check their financially wasteful tendencies.

In addition to these tasks, several specific challenges must also be addressed. First, as unemployment will surely rise under the reform program, the governments will have to introduce a variety of labor market policies, including unemployment insurance, job retraining, and a credit allocation to individuals who start small businesses. It should be remembered, however, that the unemployment starts from negligible levels, so that even steep rises in unemployment will tend to raise the unemployment rates to levels now existing in Western Europe. Second, Poland and Hungary, and possibly others, will have to renegotiate the terms on sovereign debt. Third, since the state sector will remain significant for several years, further efforts – in terms of rules for wage setting, investment, and restructuring – must be undertaken so that the economy does not fall back into financial crisis after an initial stabilization.

Skeptics often ask whether the austerity and liberalization program outlined here can produce stable prices and economic growth. They observe that in Latin America such programs have indeed ended inflation, but at the expense of hampered growth. In the case of Eastern Europe however, one can identify the primary engine of growth in the coming years: economic integration with Western Europe.[2] If convertibility, free trade, macroeconomic stability, and liberalization of the private sector are all achieved, the power of natural market forces will reduce the gap between Poland's $1,100 per capita income and Western Europe's per capita income more than 10 times that level.

With skilled workers in Eastern Europe now earning about $1 an hour, the region will provide an enormous opportunity as a production site for European, Japanese, and U.S. firms selling mainly in the West European market. By April [1989] there were 1,200 applications for joint ventures pending with the Polish Foreign Investment Agency. Hundreds, if not thousands, of firms are already examining factory sites in Eastern Europe as potential locations for parts of their production process. They are finding a highly skilled labor force, with engineers, machine tool operators, foundry workers, and so forth, that will – under stable economic and political conditions – be able to integrate effectively into European-wide production

---

[2] In Latin America, macroeconomic stability with outward orientation has in fact produced favorable growth results, especially compared with countries still mired in high inflation and protectionist policies. But many Latin American countries, unlike those in Eastern Europe, are predominantly dependent on volatile natural resource exports, and these countries have suffered serious terms of trade declines in the past decade.

operations. To achieve the full fruits of trade liberalization, existing trade barriers (in both directions between East and West Europe) should be removed. The Eastern European countries must negotiate a new association status with the European Community to give them guaranteed future access to Western European markets.[3] Existing restrictions of the Coordinating Committee for Multilateral Export Controls (COCOM), banning the export of high-technology goods to Eastern Europe, will have to be removed. Investment treaties, guaranteeing repatriation rights on foreign investment, must also be negotiated.

Much of the pessimism about growth in Eastern Europe results from the focus on the necessary decline of the region's heavy industrial sectors. More attention should be paid to the obvious and crucial sectors, particularly in services, house construction, and light industry, that will grow considerably. Intense shortages exist in these areas, and, even under the arduous business conditions of reform communism, the private sector has been staking out a foothold in these areas. Ample opportunities exist for rapid expansion in these areas.

---

[3] In the longer term the EC should be expanded to allow for the actual membership of the East European countries.

35. Elements of Economic Reform[*]

Philip Hanson

It is of course an easy sport to pick holes in Soviet transition plans. There is no evidence that anybody could design a transition program for the Soviet Union that would win the support of most economists and also look likely, if put into practice, to pass a political survival tests. Still, the weaknesses in Soviet understanding of economics and the unrealistic aim of painless transformation have handicapped Soviet policy-making so far. Both Hungary and Poland, in different ways, have shown that a better start can be made. It might be useful, therefore, to identify the elements of a successful economic transformation, analyze the links among these elements, and draw some conclusions about the ways in which such a transformation might come about.

The main elements in a transition to a market economy are financial stabilization; the decontrol of prices and quantities, accompanied by demonopolization where necessary; the transfer of assets from state ownership to a variety of identifiable proprietors; and the opening up of the economy to competition from imports in the product market and to foreign investors in the capital market.

Financial stabilization is needed at some stage in the transformation because a market economy cannot be established without a currency that enjoys a certain minimum acceptability in transactions and as a store of value. If rapid open inflation is either under way or widely expected, market institutions will have trouble taking hold. Decontrol of prices and quantities of products is by definition a prerequisite for the existence of a product market. Demonopolization, where possible, together with public regulation of natural monopolies, is needed to make the market reasonably efficient.

Privatization of a high proportion of productive assets is a more contentious matter. It is widely agreed, however, by Soviet reformers as well as Western economists, that privatization is needed in order to create a capital market,

---

[*] From "Soviet Reform: Perestroika or 'Catastroika'?" from *World Policy Journal*, Spring 1991, vol. VIII: #2. Reprinted by permission of the World Policy Institute.

and that a capital market is needed for three main reasons. First, it will generate meaningful valuations of capital, without which product prices would not reflect the opportunity costs of all the resources used in making products. Second, it will encourage firms to increase internal efficiency by providing an incentive to increase the value of assets and by subjecting firms to market discipline through the threat of bankruptcy or takeover. Third, it will allow the market to decide on the allocation of capital among branches of the economy and among technologies within branches, which seems to work less badly for most sectors of an economy than leaving that decision to central planners. Certainly the historical evidence is clear: state ownership of all of a nation's assets is worse for internal and allocative efficiency and for technological dynamism than arrangements under which identifiable proprietors and potential proprietors compete for ownership and control of a large proportion of the nation's capital.

As for the requirement of internationalization, a pedant might argue that it would be possible to marketize an economy without opening up its product and capital markets to international competition. This is true in the sense that a closed, market economy is conceivable. But both traditional gains from trade and productivity gains from international technology transfer exist, and it would make little sense to operate a protectionist, inward-looking regime when the institutions and rules of the game in the domestic economy were such as to facilitate integration into the world economy. It is a large part of the Western world's economic strength that the barriers to trade and investment among Western countries have been relatively low since the early 1950s.

The need for all the elements I have identified is now conventional wisdom among Soviet reformers. What is more contentious and unclear is how the different elements in the transformation process fit together. To begin with, there is no simple or obvious sequence in which they should be implemented, such as: first stabilize, then decontrol, then privatize, then internationalize. One reason for this is that each of these processes takes time, and the length of time needed is hard to predict. The Polish and Hungarian experiences show, for example, that there is no quick way to sell or even give away big blocks of state assets in the form of large enterprises – least of all when the institutional infrastructure of modern accounting, commercial law, and capital markets is absent. Another reason is that the linkages among the different elements are numerous and run in all directions. Let me describe just a few of them.

First, an attempt at financial stabilization ahead of any other measures –

especially privatization – may well be ineffective. In other words, cutting the state budget deficit, establishing a two-tier banking system with a central bank and separate commercial banks, and putting in place arrangements for controlling the money supply may not be enough to squeeze out inflationary pressures. As long as the great bulk of production units remain state-owned, they will have every reason to keep bidding for more resources and no incentive to economize on inputs; in the words of Hungarian economist Janos Kornai, they will continue to have soft budget constraints. Thus the managers and workers of state enterprises will continue to act in ways that generate excess demand, and a state-owned banking system will probably continue to respond passively by making more credit available, even if a formal apparatus of reserve ratios and other constraints on lending is put in place.

Privatization should also ideally accompany stabilization because the sale of state assets will contribute to budget revenue and will thus be a useful, if not necessary, part of the process of achieving budgetary balance. For large state enterprises, an interim stage of what a recent International Monetary Fund (IMF) report on the Soviet economy calls "commercialization" (conversion into joint-stock companies owned by competing, conglomerate state holding companies) may be needed. With this more diluted form of state ownership in place, the authorities may be able to effect some hardening of enterprise budget constraints by means of tough fiscal and monetary policies.

Second, privatization ahead of the decontrol of product prices and quantities will be highly problematic, if not unworkable. The valuation of assets depends on their expected future earnings. Expected earnings, in turn, depend on the prices of the inputs these businesses will use and of the products they will produce.

This is one reason for starting with petty privatization of activities like retail trade, consumer services, and small-scale building concerns. It is not just that they are small units that can be bought or leased by families. Equally important is that they sell their output to households, which have hard budget constraints and to that extent "real" demand; free-market prices already exist for many of the items sold. In general, therefore, existing controls on product prices do not prevent some reasonable estimate being made of the likely future earnings of small-scale businesses, at least in the near term. For much of the economy, however, asset valuation remains mysterious as long as product prices are controlled and convey little information about relative scarcities. In a classic catch-22, the reverse is also true; it is difficult to predict the future earnings of enterprises without knowing the free-market prices of the items produced. For this reason, it is hard to see privatization proceeding very far without the decontrol of product markets.

Third, there is a link between product-market decontrol and international integration. The decontrol of product markets may not accomplish much in the way of creating competition in the domestic economy as long as those markets are protected from import competition. Purely domestic liberalization would leave markets with the high degree of concentration characteristic of centrally administered economies.

Fourth, import competition is also relevant to privatization. The value of assets will usually be much lower if the products they make are expected to be competing with imports than if this is not the case. A factory producing Trabant automobiles in what used to be East Germany is a different proposition in this respect from a factory producing Skodas in Czechoslovakia, where there is still no competition from automobile imports.

Fifth, the success of attempts to open up the economy is dependent in both obvious and subtle ways on the success of domestic marketization. It is obvious that a currency cannot be made convertible in the sense that people outside the country could freely exchange it against other currencies and would wish to hold it, until it is also convertible into goods – in other words, until there is a market in which command over the currency reliably conveys command over resources.

It is perhaps less obvious that there are severe problems with opening up an economy merely by decontrolling product markets, removing import controls, and setting an exchange rate that undervalues the currency and thus encourages exports and discourages imports. Outside the natural-resource extraction sector (which is admittedly a major Soviet strength), success in exporting depends heavily on factors other than price: product quality, technical level, service, marketing, and so on. After all, Soviet manufactures have for years been sold abroad at whatever price in foreign currency would undercut the competition, yet the Soviet share of Western manufactured-goods imports is not only tiny but has been declining since the 1960s. It follows that privatization, because it fundamentally alters the behavior of producers, is probably a necessary precondition of any growth in export market share.

There are many other links among the different elements in the transformation process that could be explored, but the five described above are enough to make the point. A transformation process that consisted of each element introduced sequentially would run into enormous problems. At the same time, it is clear that doing everything at once is impossible, if only because the various policy measures take different – and somewhat unpredictable – lengths of time to implement. It is also clear that some of the sequencing of reforms attempted so far has been damaging.

For instance, extending rights to engage in foreign trade and encouraging investment from abroad before getting very far with domestic marketization have probably done more harm than good. And devolving product-mix decisions to enterprises while prices and supply allocation were still centrally controlled has contributed to inflationary pressure by facilitating shifts toward producing higher-cost and higher-price items, regardless of demand.

I am not suggesting, however, that the sequencing issue is so complicated that the only thing to do is forget about it. A few conclusions do seem tenable. The first is that a very strong case can be made for at least initiating all of the sets of policy measures within the same short period of time, since large time lags separating the launching of the various measures will generally be damaging.

The second is that the initial announcement of a complete package of measures has a lot to be said for it. Expectations are crucial, and it is hard to see how the population's reactions to one measure can be very constructive if there is confusion about what else is coming.

The third is that it does make sense to introduce two things at the outset: a package of legislation that will provide the framework for a mixed economy (laws on commercial contracts and liability, on companies, on foreign direct investment, and so on) and a financial squeeze aimed at minimizing the open inflationary effects of price decontrol. At the same time, it may be realistic to anticipate that there will in any case be a period of rapid inflation, and to accept that general indexation of incomes will only prolong it.

The final point that can safely be made about sequencing is that it must of necessity be cardinal, and not just ordinal. In other words, thought has to be given to the specific time intervals between the launch of one measure and the launch of the next. Merely to say that measure A should precede measure B is not to say anything very useful. Should it precede it by a day? A month? A year?

These reflections suggest that the approach of the Shatalin plan[1] had a lot to be said for it. The rigorous-looking timetable may have seemed arbitrary and implausible, but at least it acknowledged the internal linkages among the

---

[1] [Editor's note: What Hanson calls the "Shatalin" plan was the radical 500-day plan commissioned and then rejected by Gorbachev in late 1990, authored by Stanislaw Shatalin, Grigory Yavlinsky, and others. Articles 10 and 22 in this book are excerpted from that plan.]

elements of the program and gave some means of monitoring progress and harmonizing expectations.

The success of an attempt at transforming the economy depends of course on a good deal more than the technical issue of sequencing. Another key prerequisite is the existence of a suitable infrastructure of skills and institutions. The operation of a Western market economy requires many institutions and skills whose existence Westerners take for granted. These include a viable framework of commercial law, plus the commercial lawyers who go with it; accounting methods that enable the balance sheets and income and expenditure flows of firms to be monitored, plus skilled accountants; a system for collecting taxes from people and privately owned firms, plus a tax service capable of running it with some minimum amount of honesty and reliability; local and central state authorities for licensing, regulation, monitoring of safety standards, and so on, staffed by civil servants who are not all in the pockets of the commercial firms they deal with; a telecommunications system that does more than provide voice telephony on a radial pattern between the center and other places; and banks and capital markets with the skills required to run them.

A slightly less obvious requirement is a housing market. If there is to be an effective labor market, it must be possible for people to move geographically. For the great majority of Soviet citizens this is immensely difficult, since moving to a new area usually means finding someone to swap one's state housing with. The alternative is putting one's name on a housing list that may have a waiting time of 10 years or more. Selling off state housing would help, but there is no good reason for most occupants of public housing to buy when they can go on renting for less than the cost of maintaining their apartments. So a precondition for creating a labor market is creating a housing market, and a precondition for that is raising housing rents substantially.

All these examples provide reasons for expecting the transformation to be slow. Neither the institutions nor the skills of a market economy can be put in place quickly. Yet the linkages among different elements in the transformation process make a slow process of change very hard to sustain unless somehow the populations acceptance of that change can be maintained through reversals and delays. This raises what is probably the most fundamental question facing reformers in the Soviet Union: whether a consensus supporting marketization can be created and sustained...

36. From Central Plan to Market*

The World Bank

Transforming a centrally planned economy into a market economy requires complex and unprecedented reforms. There is no experience to guide transitions of the current magnitude. And most countries in transition are simultaneously creating a new political order. There is relatively little disagreement that the transitions have to be made, but there is much controversy about the theory, timing, scope, speed, and sequencing of reforms.

Three sets of issues arise. One concerns the economic implications of a policy sequence: will one kind of reform achieve its objectives while other economic distortions remain? Another question is political: will mounting opposition derail reforms scheduled near the end of the sequence? Finally, there is technical feasibility. New legal, accounting, and financial systems will require greater technical expertise and longer gestation periods than reforms that include only price deregulation.

One school of reform proposals puts change in ownership at the head of the sequence before or alongside changes that address macroeconomic stability and markets. The rationale is partly political. With early privatization, there is less risk that the economy will remain state-controlled and greater pressure for complementary market-oriented reforms. But another school of thought begins with macroeconomic and market-building reforms: it leaves privatization – at least for large state enterprises – to a second stage. (Under both proposals some agricultural, retail, and residential assets would be privatized early.) The rationale is that private ownership requires financial institutions, experience, and expertise that do not yet exist in the transitional economies. Without this infrastructure, rapid privatization could lead to widespread corruption and economic and political chaos. Within each school there are further differences on the proper order for addressing particular distortions.

No single reform sequence will fit all the transitional economies. Reform histories vary; unlike others, Hungary has had more than two decades of experience with decentralized economic decisions. Macroeconomic conditions range from great instability (the Soviet Union) to relative stability (Czechoslovakia). Private sector activity has been relatively higher in predominantly agricultural countries such as China and Viet Nam but negligible in more industrialized nations.

A preferred sequencing (see Figure 1) would include early steps to stabilize the macroeconomy and deregulate domestic- and external-sector prices to give clear, accurate signals for economic activity and for the valuation of enterprises. These steps would be accompanied and followed by intense efforts to rationalize enterprises, improve economic decision making, reform trade policy, and build managerial skills and a strong financial sector. Privatization of large state enterprises would become the next priority. Protection would be cut and the economy would be opened to foreign competition on a firm, preannounced schedule – first in goods and later in capital markets. Institution building would be a basic theme from the start at all levels: the legal contractual system, the structure of ownership, and the roles of key organizations in the economy would require reform and restructuring.

Large-scale privatization would not be at the head of the sequence, but to address the risk in delaying it, there would be early legal commitments (the distribution of shares) that would guarantee private ownership within a reasonable time. The program would be fast in that each type of reform would move at the maximum rate consistent with developing institutional capacities. Indeed, a three-to-five year time span seems optimistic in light of the progress achieved so far in the transitional economies.

Reforms will surely involve painful adjustments. Inflation and unemployment will worsen as price controls are removed and the real economic losses of some activities are revealed. Political opposition may mount with these developments and the rise in income inequality that comes after radical change in the incentive structure. But progress in exports and the availability of consumer goods could soon follow. And, given the relatively strong human resource endowments in Eastern Europe, prospects for growth could be excellent.

Area of Reform	Year of Reform

	0	1	2	3	4	5	6	7	8	9	10

Macroeconomy — Stabilize | Maintain Stability

Markets
Goods and services

Prices — Liberalize most prices | Liberalize prices of some necessities (including housing)

Trade — Remove QRs | Adjust tariffs to modest level

Distribution — Privatize demonopolize | Develop

Labor Market — Deregulate hiring and firing | Liberalize wage bargaining

Financial Market — Restructure and develop | Liberalize and privatize

Ownership structure

Small enterprises — Develop and privatize

Large enterprises — Evaluate | Restructure and privatize

Foreign investment — Revise regulations

Government
Legal framework — Reform property law commercial law, taxes | Extended reform to other areas

Institutional framework — Reform legal and regulatory institutions and fiscal administration

Social safety net — Meet emergencies | Institutionalize

Note: Shading indicates intensive action. QRs quantative restrictions

37. The IMF/IBRD/OECD/EBRD Recommendations for Reform: A Summary

David Kennett

At the Houston Summit held in July 1990, the heads of state of the Group of Seven (G7) countries asked the leading multi-lateral economic agencies – the International Monetary Fund (IMF), the World Bank (IBRD), the Organization for Economic Co-Operation and Development (OECD), and the European Bank for Reconstruction and Development (EBRD) – to prepare a detailed study of the then Soviet Union, make recommendations for its reform and establish the criteria under which Western economic assistance could effectively support such reforms. After an intensive, but rapid, study the multilateral agencies reported back in December of 1990. Their summary report ran to about 50 pages, and it was supported by some 1400 pages of detailed background papers.[1]

To illustrate the complexity of the reform process, here is an outline of their summary – a listing of the primary areas of reform that must at least be initiated, before large-scale western aid can be implemented[2].

Fiscal Policy
* Get rid of the turnover tax, the USSR's current form of indirect taxation and institute instead a value added tax; this tax would be less distortionary to the economy and is more capable of harmonization with the tax regimes in the European Community.
* Introduce a realistic and simple income tax with non-punitive marginal rates; at present the top rate of 60% is too high to preserve economic incentives, and the current complexity of the rate schedule

---

[1][Reading 19 in this volume, "Statistical Issues" is excerpted from the background papers.

[2]The $24 billion in US aid to Russia, which was announced in late March, 1992 was conditioned on movement along the avenue of reform laid out by the multi-lateral agencies and summarized here.

adds substantially to administration costs.

* Phase out subsidies for food, energy, intermediate goods and other services; despite the commitment to reform such subsidies were actually rising under the Gorbachev administration.

* Curb social expenditure – although this will be difficult in the face of an estimated 6 million unemployed, and a half million persons displaced by ethnic tensions.

* Introduce bonds with attractive real interest rates, in excess of inflation, to finance state debt and soak up the "ruble overhang" – the money held in bank accounts and cash, which comprises savings forced by the absence of consumer goods.

* Retain most of the taxing power at the center, and share revenue downward. (This recommendation effectively ended with the collapse of the U.S.S.R. in December, 1991.)

External Economic Policy

* Dispense with multiple exchange rates, and establish a realistic single rate.

* Agree on division of the responsibility of external debt and foreign exchange reserves between union and the republics.

Incomes Policy

* Index wages to only 50%-70% of inflation, allowing real wages to fall.

Prices

* Announce timetable for conversion to world prices. (This was partly achieved by the price liberalization of January 2, 1992, although that reform fell short of full liberalization.)

* Introduce an export tax on energy and mineral products until domestic prices have been raised equal world prices. (At present they are perhaps only 20% of world market prices, and therefore encourage enterprises to export rather than supply the domestic market.)

* Use a rationing device, probably stamps, to ameliorate shortage problems in the consumer sector during the transition.

Ownership

* Auction off small enterprise in retail trade, wholesale trade, and transportation. It is essential to provide effective finance and a

delayed payment schedule to assist buyers.
* Put large enterprises in state holding companies with equity shares (held by state initially). Prepare to ready to sell off the shares to the public.
* End any preference in access to materials for publicly-owned companies.
* End production monopolies, except where they are "natural" - e.g., electricity supply.

International Trade
* The establishment of single exchange rate is priority.
* Initially introduce a new single 30% universal tariff, and recognize the need to liberalize further to match the lower tariff levels in other nations.

Direct Foreign Investment
* Reform of the legal and fiscal structure is vital; it is essential to give foreign-owned corporations a non-discriminatory status compared to domestic firms, providing neither an advantage nor a disadvantage.
* Any screening of foreign investors must be transparent and non-obstructive.
* Explicit protection for foreign capital against confiscation and expropriation is required.
* The establishment of a credit market essential.

Banking
* Convert state banks to joint stock banks and commercialize them under prudent banking standards.

Social Security
* Requires urgent reform; the burden of a social safety net will increase with rising unemployment and refugees. The use of an effective means test is too difficult to implement at the moment, but some of targeting is essential given limited fiscal resources.

Labor
* The first step in labor market reform must be to abandon tariff wages (wage rates determined by the central planning authorities, bearing little relation to supply and demand.) It is essential to get govern-

ment out of the process of wage determination in the long run but the transition problems require an incomes policy in the short- to medium-term.

Legal Reform
*   Priority must be on the creation of a system of property rights.
*   End all union and republic laws that criminalize behavior that is both rational and economically beneficial (e.g. "speculation").

Accountancy
*   Introduce a standardized western system; this is a priority for technical assistance, since the valuation of industry prior to privatization requires standardized accounting.

Environment
*   The environment is in a state of crisis and must not be put on back burner because of the budget.

Distribution of goods
*   Priority for immediate privatization of distribution network.

Transportation
*   Raise rail rates and mass transit fares to provide funds for modernization.

Telecommunications
*   Create regional monopolies and reform tariffs in the central network.
*   Access to modern telecommunications is a high priority in creating a favorable business environment.

Agriculture
*   Liberalize all prices.
*   Reform land tenure arrangements with guarantees of permanency.
*   Defer any new investment in collective agriculture until all reforms in place.
*   Food processing should be a priority to reduce waste of agricultural output.

Energy
*   Take steps to restore output of oil, gas and electricity all of which fell sharply during 1990.
*   New investment is required to augment electrical generation capacity.
*   Reform energy prices to bring them in line with world levels. (They are now about 20% of world prices, and this differential has worsened in recent years due to rouble depreciation.)

Mining and Extraction
*   This industry has been over-capitalized in the past in order to earn hard currency, but this distortion must stop.
*   Prices at which output is sold to domestic enterprises must be raised.
*   Price increases will give incentive for recycling and hence help the environment.

Manufacturing
*   End monopolies.
*   Privatize through the intermediary stage of holding companies.
*   Harden budget constraints.
*   Improve accounting.

Housing
*   Reform of property rights is vital.
*   Facilitate sale of property and leases.
*   Create financing opportunities for purchase by individuals.
*   Foster competition in housing supply.

The Role of Western Assistance
*   Primary focus must be technical assistance for legal reform, creating markets and fiscal and monetary policy.
*   Food aid will be required in the transition.
*   Project assistance should be a priority to retailing and small-scale wholesaling, transportation and distribution networks, telecommunications and food processing.